The Amazing Lives
of Africa's Royal Women

African Princess

Joyce Hansen

Illustrated by Laurie McGaw

A JUMP AT THE SUN / HYPERION /
MADISON PRESS BOOK

First published in the United States by
Hyperion Books for Children
114 Fifth Avenue
New York, New York 10011-5630

First U.S. edition, 2004

Library of Congress Cataloging-in-Publication Data on file.

ISBN 0-7868-5116-3

Visit www.jumpatthesun.com

Printed in Singapore

Africa's Royal Women

What do we imagine when we think of Africa? Is it a great wilderness teeming with elephants and lions? A place where children starve and people die of dreadful diseases? Often these are the images of Africa that we see on television or in the movies, but they do not tell the whole story.

Africa is not a country, but many countries. It is the second-largest continent on Earth. Africa is snowcapped mountains, blue seas and rivers, powerful waterfalls, steamy rain forests, tawny desert plains, green valleys, and modern cities.

The peoples of Africa are as varied as its landscape, with their own languages, music, art, religion, stories, and ways of life. The six African princesses and queens whose stories are told in this book give us views of Africa we do not often see. They represent Africa's rich and diverse cultural heritage.

As young girls, some of them were looked upon as outsiders. Others were good students. Some knew at a very young age that they wanted to be leaders, and even took on the role of warriors. And one princess was a tall tomboy who liked to play basketball!

Thousands of years and as many traditions separate these royal women, yet there are striking similarities among them. They were all courageous risk takers who knew exactly what they wanted. From Hatshepsut of ancient Egypt, who boldly declared herself pharaoh, to the modern-day Elizabeth of Toro, who has withstood the tyranny of two Ugandan dictators, each one accepted her responsibilities and at some point in her life sacrificed her own happiness and well-being for others.

All of the women in this book became successful and effective leaders. They were businesswomen, warriors, administrators, and builders during times when most women had little real power. Their dramatic stories contain lessons for our own lives.

The Princess Who Became a King

On a hot day in 1922, there was great excitement at a dig site in what had once been the Egyptian city of Thebes. The archaeologists had stumbled upon a pit containing hundreds of pieces of ancient granite statues. Some of the pieces were as small as fine gravel; others were so huge that a crane was needed to lift them. (The head archaeologist, Herbert E. Winlock, said later that putting the fragments together was like working on one hundred jigsaw puzzles, each one with pieces missing.) The statues were of a pharaoh wearing the traditional kilt and crown — as well as the beard — of an Egyptian ruler. But the pharaoh's face was that of a woman!

On some of the broken columns, the dig team found the name *Hatshepsut* written in hieroglyphs. Was this the same Hatshepsut who had reigned over Egypt around 1479–1457 B.C.? Herbert Winlock knew that her empty burial tomb had been found a few years earlier at Deir el-Bahri but that her mummy had yet to be discovered. If this was the same Hatshepsut, he wondered, why had so many statues of her been destroyed? As the archaeologists studied and pondered, the story of an extraordinary woman began to emerge after thousands of years of silence.

(Left) This limestone bust of Hatshepsut wearing a pharaoh's beard was once part of an eighteen-foot statue that stood in the temple at Deir el-Bahri, where her tomb was housed. (Opposite) Hatshepsut attired in the ceremonial garb of a pharaoh.

This gold model of an Egyptian barge was found in an ancient tomb. Wheels were added by the craftsman to speed the soul's journey into the afterlife.

The crowds on the banks of the river cheered wildly as the gilded royal barge came into view. Standing next to the pharaoh was a lovely young girl in white linen robes — his eldest daughter, the Royal Princess Hatshepsut. For Pharaoh Thutmose I, these trips along the Nile from Thebes to Memphis gave him an opportunity to inspect his kingdom and see his people. We can imagine him pointing out to his daughter the great monuments and temples, teaching her about the world they lived in. With Hatshepsut's mother, the Royal Wife Ahmose, and other members of the royal family, they would stay in temporary palaces called the "Mooring Places of Pharaoh."

Throughout her childhood, Hatshepsut had a very close relationship with her father. She was the only surviving child of Ahmose. Sadly, with the exception of Hatshepsut's half brother, Thutmose II, all of the pharaoh's other children had died. Hatshepsut and Thutmose II, who would someday marry and rule Egypt together, must have been a great comfort to the pharaoh. Egyptian royalty married close family members in order to keep the royal blood "pure" and to keep wealth and power within the ruling family.

Hatshepsut's carefree days and nights spent in the palace at Thebes ended when she became a teenager. Her beloved father died, and her life changed completely. Historians are not certain whether Hatshepsut was older or younger than Thutmose II, but either way she could not become the new pharaoh because she was a woman. Pharaohs were not only supreme rulers; they were also divine. Their right to rule came directly from the gods. The pharaoh was the head of all of the priests (a very powerful group of men) and was the only person who was allowed to communicate directly with the gods. Next in line to be the new pharaoh was Hatshepsut's half brother, Thutmose II. Princess Hatshepsut became his Royal Wife.

Hatshepsut probably accepted her marriage to Thutmose II as her duty. If she refused to marry him, the Theban royal family would be weakened, and other people would try to claim the throne. She was only fourteen or fifteen years old when she married, but like her father, Hatshepsut had a deep sense of responsibility. Childhood things were put aside, and she gracefully stepped into her role as the "King's Great Wife," although she preferred the title "God's Wife of Amun." The title of God's Wife of

Amun was politically important, as it gave Hatshepsut influence over the powerful priests and allowed the royal family to control the vast wealth and property of the Amun temples.

In the years that followed her marriage, the young queen had a daughter, Neferure, whom she loved very much. As well as being a mother, Hatshepsut seems to have been a supportive queen and wife. She might even have shared power with her husband.

Unfortunately, after a short reign of three years, Thutmose II died, and his son by a lesser wife, Thutmose III, became the new pharaoh. There was one serious problem — he was a small child. Hatshepsut was appointed Queen Regent. This was not an unusual situation. In the past, Egyptian queens had acted as regents, governing for their young sons or other male relatives.

But Hatshepsut was different. She had learned how to rule from her father and had taken on some of her husband's royal duties. For her, it must have seemed as though the gods had intervened in her life. She was finally going to be given a chance to rule on her own, at least until the young pharaoh was old enough to govern.

Although she was only seventeen or eighteen years old when her husband died, Hatshepsut was a successful ruler. She knew from her years at court how to deal with the important priests and nobles who helped run the country. Maybe it was a sign of things to come, but she had two obelisks built while she was Queen Regent. When these massive columns were completed seven years later, she did something that had never been done before. Hatshepsut had herself crowned as pharaoh!

Hatshepsut's Obelisks

Towering almost a hundred feet into the sky, one of two massive granite obelisks that Hatshepsut erected at the temple of Amun in Karnak still stands (at left, in photo) beside one built by her father. They were carved without any iron tools, and no one knows for certain how the Egyptians managed to raise them. Egyptian obelisks have been the model for many other structures, including the Washington Monument, which is almost six times taller than Hatshepsut's obelisk.

The Expedition to Punt

Hatshepsut understood the importance of building strong trade relationships with other countries. She sent a mission to the fabled land of Punt, thought to be located in present-day Ethiopia or Somalia. The expedition returned from Punt with valuable goods such as gold, ebony, ivory, and myrrh trees (used for making incense). Hatshepsut was so proud of the successful mission that she had the entire story of the voyage carved on the walls of her mortuary temple (left).

Hatshepsut became one of only a few female pharaohs to rule Egypt in three thousand years of history. She must have been confident, smart, and fearless to take such a bold step. She also must have had supporters among the powerful nobles and priests at court. Hatshepsut had obviously earned their respect and confidence. This would not have been an easy thing to do. She would have had to convince them that a female pharaoh would not anger the gods and bring terrible hardship to the Egyptian people.

Hatshepsut's reign did not bring down the fury of the gods. Historians believe she ruled for fifteen years, bringing peace and prosperity to her people. As a pharaoh, she is best known for her monuments at Karnak and Deir el-Bahri.

Hatshepsut was a builder. From the time she sat at her father's side gazing at the pyramids of Giza or visiting the temple complex at Karnak, she understood the importance of building monuments and temples to the gods. For the ancient Egyptians, life was a preparation for death, leading to eternal life in heaven. However, the Egyptians did not want to be forgotten on earth. They left grand monuments behind so that they would be remembered forever.

Hatshepsut asked her loyal and trusted adviser, Senenmut, to plan and build her mortuary temple at Deir el-Bahri. She named it Djeser-Djeseru, meaning "Holy of Holies." Nestled near her father's burial tomb, it was an elegant building. It was also very different from other styles of architecture at that time, just as Hatshepsut was so different from other women.

Fifteen years into her reign, Hatshepsut once again broke with tradition. She celebrated her jubilee. Normally, a jubilee was held thirty years into a successful reign. After the celebration Hatshepsut followed in her father's footsteps and had two more obelisks built and placed in front of the temple at Karnak. One still stands there today.

Hatshepsut may have been in her forties when she died — an old woman in those days. For years, scholars believed that Thutmose III was so angry at his aunt for crowning herself pharaoh that he knocked down her statues. But the time Hatshepsut spent training her nephew to become a successful ruler suggests that she was a loving woman, not a power-hungry one. And Hatshepsut's monuments were destroyed twenty years after her death. If Thutmose III had been angry with Hatshepsut, why did he wait so long to erase her memory? And why didn't he destroy the images and statues that showed her as a princess and a queen?

Perhaps Thutmose III was having political problems and his throne was threatened. Maybe he destroyed anything that depicted Hatshepsut as pharaoh in order to show that there was a direct line of kings from Thutmose I and II to himself, with no Hatshepsut in between.

We will probably never know who destroyed her statues or why. What we do know is that Pharaoh Hatshepsut can now take her place among the great kings and builders of Egypt.

(Above) This scarab beetle pendant from the time of Hatshepsut was probably worn by the owner as a protective charm. (Below) Hatshepsut's splendid mortuary temple at Deir el-Bahri.

Chapter Two # Born to Rule

❊

Amina of Zaria

(c. 1533–1610)

It had always been hard for Amina to sit quietly. Even as a toddler she had been a restless child who seemed to know exactly what she wanted. One day as she played with some other children, she spotted her grandfather across a reception room. He was the king of Zazzau (located in present-day Nigeria), one of the seven Hausa city-states, and he was talking to the chiefs of the towns under his rule. Quickly crawling past servants, bodyguards, and other people connected with the court, Amina made her way toward her grandfather. Before anyone could stop her, she sat down right in front of him. Everyone gasped. Her mother must have worried that her child was interrupting important state business. Amina's grandfather wouldn't have time for a baby — especially a little girl. But he picked her up, sat her on his lap, and continued to talk to his chiefs and counselors.

From that day on, whenever the king held court, Amina would be there, sitting on his knee or nearby. He never turned her away. After her grandfather died in 1535 and his brother became the new ruler, Amina continued to go to the king's court whenever it was in session. No one stopped her, even though she was only about two or three years old.

12

(Left) Islam had been introduced to the Hausa by the year 1500. This decorated Hausa version of the Koran is only three inches across and three inches high. The words have been translated from Arabic to Hausa, but the letters are still Arabic. This type of writing is called ajami. *(Opposite) Amina of Zaria sits proudly on her horse.*

Her great-uncle ruled for only a year before he, too, died. This was a sad and unsettling time for Amina's family. Because there were no male heirs to the throne, the family's royal dynasty would end. Finally, Amina's mother, Bakwa Turunku, realized that if she did not act decisively and quickly, her family would no longer rule. In earlier centuries, queens had governed parts of what is today northern Nigeria. Bakwa Turunku, perhaps inspired by the queens who had gone before her, seized the throne.

One of the first things the new *sarauniya* did was change the name of the city-state of Zazzau to

Zaria, after her youngest daughter. It is unlikely that Amina resented this honor given to her younger sister. After all, as the queen's eldest child, Princess Amina would one day rule the state named after her sister. This was an ideal situation for Amina because, while she was growing up, she never lost interest in attending the meetings of the court.

But on her sixteenth birthday, Princess Amina faced a turning point in her life. This was the age when Hausa girls, even royal ones, were expected to marry and become mothers. It was taken for granted that they would learn how to run a household — whether it was a royal compound with servants and slaves or the small house of a simple farm family. Amina, however, had other ideas.

We do not know how this strong-willed young woman felt at this time in her life because few of her thoughts have been recorded. We can understand, though, how it feels to be pressured to follow the wishes of your family and your traditions when in your heart you have your own desires and aims.

This was a girl who wanted to be queen and who must have realized that she could be an accomplished one. She was the daughter and granddaughter of rulers. She came from a tradition that had nurtured strong, politically active women. Her attachment to her grandfather and her early years watching him rule had had a profound influence on her. So while other young women were learning how to be wives and mothers, Amina decided to continue learning how to be a ruler.

As the eldest daughter of Zaria's ruler, Amina had many young men who wanted to marry her. One of her suitors is said to have spent all his wealth trying to win her hand in marriage. The king of Kano, another Hausa city-state, sent her a gift of more than one hundred slaves. Other would-be bridegrooms sent expensive robes and valuable gifts, but Amina wouldn't change her mind. She absolutely refused to marry and is quoted as saying, "[I will] never be subject to the control of a man."

*(Above) Finely dressed Hausa horsemen parade along a street in the city-state of Kano,
Nigeria, during the popular Durbar Festival. The annual festival honors the emir, or king, of Kano.
(Opposite) A home in a Hausa village with a granary out front.*

Instead of marrying at sixteen, Amina became an official of the court. Her mother died in 1566, and although Amina was the heir apparent, her mother's younger brother ruled for about ten years. During her uncle's reign, Princess Amina apparently became a superb warrior. Amina may have taken part in military campaigns not because she was warlike, but because she was determined to be the next ruler and to prove that she could protect her state and its people. It was important to keep Zaria strong and independent and to maintain its position as the center of the Saharan and Sudanese trade routes.

Around 1576 — when Amina was in her mid-forties — her uncle died and Amina became queen. She proved herself to be one of the great Hausa rulers and warriors, reigning for thirty-four years and building a prosperous empire.

As far as we know, Amina never married or had children. Like many women, especially in past centuries, she had to make a choice. If she wanted to be a leader, she had to sacrifice marriage and motherhood.

It is believed that Amina died in the town of Altagara in 1610. But her spirit lives on in the songs and legends of this ancient land. People believe that during the five months of drought, she and her warriors race on horseback across the bone-dry ground like the dust devils that come with the unbearable heat. When July brings the miraculous rains that turn the landscape a lush green, Amina rides among the date palms and the silk-cotton trees. And in November when the days and nights turn cool, she leads her swift Arabian steed along the shallow rivers and up into the red hills of Hausaland.

Chapter Three # The Warrior Queen

✤

Njinga of Matamba

(c. 1582–1663)

In 1483, Portuguese explorers sailed three small ships into the mouth of the Congo River. They were surprised by the large number of people they met. The people of the Kongo kingdom were as surprised as the Portuguese. They looked at the sails on the Portuguese ships and called the strangers *ndele*, "masters of the white birds."

At first, the king of Kongo thought the strangers would help open new trade routes overseas. Trade was important to the people of West Central Africa. They were farmers, artists, and craftspeople who wove fine cloth out of palm bark and created jewelry of silver, copper, and other metals.

By the beginning of the sixteenth century, Portuguese missionaries, settlers, and traders had followed the explorers to Kongo. While the missionaries tried to spread Christianity, the traders found a business that could make them even more money than silver and copper — the slave trade. Slavery already existed in Africa. It was often used as a punishment for crimes or for paying off a debt. Sometimes people were captured during wars and enslaved by the enemy.

The Portuguese and other Europeans took advantage of this system of slavery. They needed a large number of slaves for their South American colonies and for their plantations and settlements along the African coast. Buying and selling humans became a growing and profitable business in this part of Africa. Kings and chiefs started wars

✤

(Above) A French artist painted this fanciful depiction of Queen Njinga in 1780. A more accurate portrait (opposite) shows her in leopard skin, with a headband made of cowrie shells and copper earrings and armband.

17

Slavery in Africa

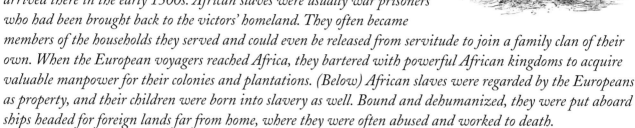

❄

Africa already had a long history of domestic slavery by the time Europeans arrived there in the early 1500s. African slaves were usually war prisoners who had been brought back to the victors' homeland. They often became members of the households they served and could even be released from servitude to join a family clan of their own. When the European voyagers reached Africa, they bartered with powerful African kingdoms to acquire valuable manpower for their colonies and plantations. (Below) African slaves were regarded by the Europeans as property, and their children were born into slavery as well. Bound and dehumanized, they were put aboard ships headed for foreign lands far from home, where they were often abused and worked to death.

simply to capture people to sell to the Portuguese. In return, they were given guns. These weapons gave them superior military power, and they were able to expand their kingdoms.

The Portuguese built the port city of Luanda on the Atlantic coast. Here they traded with the Africans who supplied them with slaves. By the 1530s, slave catchers began to gather like storm clouds over the country to the south of Kongo — the kingdom of Ndongo. (The Portuguese called the country Angola, mistaking the title of the king — *Ngola* — for the name of the country.) In fact, as early as 1520, slave catchers were capturing and enslaving people living in northern Ndongo.

When Princess Njinga was born in Ndongo around 1582, her people, the Mbundu, had been at war with the Portuguese for many years and had been able to keep them from moving into the interior of their kingdom. However, the Mbundu and the Portuguese had not always been enemies. At one time, Ngola Kiluanji, Njinga's father, had traded with Portuguese slavers, selling them criminals and captives of war in exchange for weapons that helped him enlarge his kingdom. But soon, the Portuguese wanted to take over the trade routes and slave markets controlled by the Mbundu. The ngola wouldn't allow this to happen.

When Princess Njinga was growing up, she must have heard about her people's successful battles against the Portuguese armies made up of enslaved Africans and tribes who were enemies of the Mbundu. She likely often saw the worry on her mother's face when the warriors were away too long. Njinga's father was not only the ngola, but a warrior, too. She would have heard the cries of the women when their men didn't return.

During her childhood, Princess Njinga had her own battle to fight. Although her father was Ngola Kiluanji, her mother had been a slave in the royal household. As a young woman, Njinga's mother had caught Prince Kiluanji's eye, and soon he wanted to marry her. His family objected. They did not think a slave, and especially one who was not Mbundu, would be an appropriate first wife. Instead, the prince was forced to marry a woman who

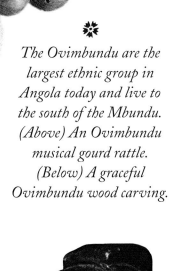

The Ovimbundu are the largest ethnic group in Angola today and live to the south of the Mbundu. (Above) An Ovimbundu musical gourd rattle. (Below) A graceful Ovimbundu wood carving.

19

The Portuguese established a presence in a number of African countries. This bronze figure of a Portuguese man is from Nigeria.

came from a high-ranking Mbundu family. She became his first wife, but his great love was still Njinga's mother. Soon afterward, Njinga's mother became the prince's second wife.

Njinga and her two sisters, Mukambu and Kifunji, were looked upon as outsiders at court because they were not fully Mbundu. As a child, Njinga may have deeply resented her position in the family. Her younger half brother, Mbandi, was the only true heir to the throne. Maybe she and her sisters were teased by the other royal children. These experiences probably helped make Njinga strong-willed and gave her the determination to fight for her rights and, later, for those of her people.

Njinga's teenage years, however, were normal for a young royal woman of her time and place. She was close to her father and he was very fond of his clever daughter, making sure that she was educated in military, political, and religious matters. Between the years 1596 and 1617, Njinga married and gave birth to a son. For a while Njinga, her husband Azeze, and their child lived peacefully away from the endless wars and conflicts around them. Then, in 1617, her father died.

With his death, the royal court became a dangerous place. Mbandi became the new ngola. He tried to kill everyone who could challenge his claim to the throne. His brother died under mysterious circumstances. And when Njinga's young son died, rumors flew that Mbandi had had him killed as well. Sadly, Njinga never had any other children.

There is no record of Njinga's words or feelings during this horrible time. The record is written in her actions. With her husband and two sisters, she fled the Ndongo capital. But she left with a plan in mind.

Her brother was not the soldier and warrior their father had been. The Portuguese, with the help of Imbangala warriors — old enemies of the Mbundu — were finally making their way into the interior of the kingdom. The Europeans were beginning to take control of Mbundu affairs, especially the lucrative slave trade.

In one attack, Portuguese troops captured Mbandi's mother and wives while he escaped to the islands on the Kwanza River. Mbandi's kingdom was about to collapse. Yet, in spite of their recent military victories, Portuguese officials in Luanda realized that they could not successfully carry on the slave trade without the ngola and his chiefs. A new governor in Luanda, Joao Correia de Souza, wanted to end the war.

Most of the books about this time in Princess Njinga's life say that Mbandi asked her to be his ambassador and meet with the Portuguese. But why would he ask Njinga to negotiate on his behalf? Was it a way of making peace with her? Did he realize that his wise sister would be a good ambassador for the Mbundu people?

A recent theory suggests another reason for Njinga's visit to Luanda. Perhaps she saw a way to seize the throne from her brother. With the old kingdom in a weakened state, Njinga could align herself with the Portuguese and hope that they would help her become leader of the Mbundu kingdom. She had few allies among the Mbundu because under their law a woman could not become the ngola. (By this time, her husband had also died.) Perhaps the time had come, too, for her to avenge the death of her son.

In 1622, Njinga traveled to Luanda with a group of her followers and servants to meet with the governor. One of the most famous stories about Njinga occurred during this visit. When she was presented to the governor, who was sitting in a large chair, she noticed that there was no chair for her. Refusing to be treated as a servant or a slave, and to show that she

Njinga sits upon the back of a servant during an audience with the governor of Luanda.

✺

was the governor's equal, she ordered one of her servants to get down on her hands and knees. Njinga proudly sat on the servant's back and looked straight into Governor de Souza's eyes. She began the meeting by telling him that her brother wanted peace but that her people had certain demands.

Early in the talks, Njinga agreed to Christian baptism — something her father had never done.

Slaves, including young children, had to endure a torturous journey to the coast. There, they were put on boats and sent to the Americas or plantations elsewhere in Africa.

This was probably a political move rather than a true conversion. Njinga knew that the Portuguese often refused to negotiate with Africans who had not been baptized.

Njinga and the governor discussed peace terms and, after much negotiating, a compromise was reached. The Portuguese would withdraw from Mbundu territory and restore Ngola Mbandi to his throne. In return, the Mbundu would help the Portuguese with the slave trade by reopening slave markets and trade routes.

In 1624, Ngola Mbandi died. Once again, rumors of murder filled the air. Some people said that Njinga had had him killed. Despite these suspicions and the Mbundu laws forbidding a woman from becoming the ngola, the forty-two-year-old Njinga took over the throne.

That same year, a new governor arrived in Luanda. He ignored the agreements between Njinga and Governor de Souza. Queen Njinga soon realized that she no longer had Portuguese support. Because she was a woman, she didn't have the loyalty of all of the Mbundu people, either. So she came up with another way to keep the throne. She took in slaves who had fled the coastal plantations of the Portuguese settlers, as well as Imbangala war slaves from the Portuguese army. Soon she had built up her own army.

When Njinga refused to return these slaves to the Portuguese, the governor in Luanda put a puppet ngola on the throne in Ndongo. Njinga fled into exile on the islands of the Kwanza River. From there, she attacked Portuguese slave traders and their African allies who were bringing slaves through what was left of the Mbundu kingdom.

In 1626, Portuguese leaders in Luanda declared war on Njinga. Her two devoted sisters, Kifunji and Mukambu, fought by her side. A year later, they were captured and held prisoner in Luanda. Mukambu escaped, but Kifunji remained a prisoner for a long time.

After three years of war, the Portuguese were determined to put a stop once and for all to Njinga and her warriors. They pursued her relentlessly. Njinga had to find somewhere to rebuild her forces and continue her fight for the independence of her people. She retreated to a region at the very outskirts of the former Ndongo kingdom, the lowlands of Matamba. The recent death of its old king had left Matamba without a ruler. In earlier times women had ruled that kingdom, so Njinga followed in their footsteps and became Queen of Matamba.

Njinga expanded her army, and by the 1640s Matamba was the largest state in the region. She controlled the number of slaves coming through the territory and sold prisoners of war to buy firearms and ammunition. In 1641, when Dutch traders forced the Portuguese out of Luanda, Njinga became allied with the Dutch. She also gained the support of several Mbundu chiefs. But by the mid-1640s tragedy struck once more. The Portuguese captured Mukambu for a second time and killed her sister Kifunji. Njinga must have been devastated by these events.

In 1648, the Portuguese army recaptured Luanda, and the Dutch left Angola two years later. Njinga made peace with the Portuguese in 1656. She was also rebaptized in the Christian faith. It is possible that she negotiated a peace settlement and was rebaptized in order to gain her sister Mukambu's release from prison. It is also possible that after many years of war she was tired of fighting, and found comfort in the Christian faith.

Queen Njinga died in 1663 at the age of eighty-one. She was a complicated, extraordinary woman who kept her people free and independent for over thirty years. Perhaps by the end of her life, she had also won the battle in her heart. She was no longer an outsider, but finally belonged to her people.

Christianity was brought to Angola by the Portuguese in the early sixteenth century. This Angolan brass staff (right) features an African figure representing Jesus Christ.

Chapter Four

The Amazon

Tata Ajaché of Dahomey

(C. 1848– *)

The predawn sky was fiery red and filled with smoke. Cannons roared, muskets crackled, and screams pierced the air.

The ten-year-old girl stared in fright and wonder at the female warriors attacking her town. As one of the soldiers grabbed her arm and led her away, she was too shocked to cry out. On that day in 1858, the famous women soldiers of the West African kingdom of Dahomey took about 1,500 people captive. Tata Ajaché was among them.

Tata was taken away from the only home and family she had ever known. She joined other young slave girls and boys carrying the soldiers' supplies. Tata was frightened and missed her family. She might even have witnessed their deaths. But all she could do now was follow her captors as they made their way to the Dahomean capital city of Abomey.

Every slave captured in war belonged to King Glele. Once the soldiers reached Abomey, Tata was held with the other slaves until the annual celebration that the Europeans called "Customs" took place. At this important event, the king would decide what would be done with captive slaves. Tata no doubt cried on the inside, but showed the world a brave face as she waited to find out what would happen to her.

❈

(Left) The blade of a ceremonial weapon that once belonged to the king of Dahomey is etched with the now-faded figures of gods and animals. (Opposite) Tata Ajaché in her Amazon uniform.

* The date of Tata Ajaché's death is unrecorded.

(Above) The king of Dahomey leads his army of women into battle in this eighteenth-century illustration. As the king and his warriors pass by, the ruler's subjects throw themselves to the ground as a sign of respect.

She didn't have to wait long. Shortly after Tata's arrival, almost the entire nation gathered in the capital to take part in the weeklong Customs ceremonies. It was a time for asking the ancestors for the continued strength and well-being of the nation. Thousands of people gathered in Singboji, a large square in front of the palace. The sound of a gunshot from behind the high mud walls of the palace compound startled Tata as she stood in a special area of the square with the other slaves.

Suddenly a large group of female warriors emerged from the palace. (Europeans who had first seen the Dahomean female soldiers called them Amazons, after the women warriors in Greek myths.) The Amazons danced and sang as they led King Glele out of the palace:

Arise Amazons, arise soldiers of Glele,
The powerful king of Abomey.
The cold and dry north wind
Has reached into the palace of Glele,
The powerful king of Abomey.

Some of the Amazons held a giant umbrella over his head as King Glele walked, followed by his wives and children, through the joyous crowd in the square. People danced and sang praises to the tall, handsome king. Drums, bells, and flutes drowned out the bird cries. Music and cheering filled the air.

When the first of many parades ended, the high-ranking men and women of the court, along with male and female army officers, gave speeches praising King Glele. They then received promotions and titles from the king. As the week wore on and the ceremonies continued, important visitors arrived on horseback. The Great Council met with the king to discuss military matters, trade, and relations with Europe and with other African states.

A large part of the Customs was the tradition of gift-giving. All of the chiefs and leaders of the towns in Dahomey had to pay tribute or taxes to the king. The king, in turn, gave them gifts. He also threw cowrie shells (valued as money) to the crowd and gave them to soldiers and loyal followers along with gifts of cloth and jewelry.

Finally, it was time for King Glele to decide what would happen to the captive slaves. Tata waited anxiously. Some of the slaves were given as gifts to those who had shown loyalty to him. Others were given to the soldiers who had captured them, and some, especially young strong males, were sold to European slave traders and sent to work on plantations in faraway countries.

There must have been something special about Tata. Maybe it was the proud way she held her head high and the courageous look in her eyes. Her captors recognized her inner strength and bravery and decided she would be trained with other enslaved boys and girls to be a warrior. These young captives were called *soudofi*.

By the beginning of the nineteenth century the Amazons had reached a force of about three to five thousand strong. Being a slave in the royal household among the elite female fighting force meant that Tata could rise in rank and power. She was an *ahosi*, a term used for

Cowrie Shells

Tata was rewarded for her loyalty partly with cowrie shells. Cowries have been used as currency by societies around the world for thousands of years. Europeans were amazed that Africans preferred the small white shells to gold coins. Cowries were traded for goods, and were displayed in furniture, clothing, and jewelry to show the owner's wealth. They are still used as decorative items today. (Below) A Dahomean necklace with cowrie shells.

According to one European visitor to Dahomey, Amazons *"fully understand the use of the musket, and load and fire with remarkable rapidity."* In addition to guns (shown in the illustrations, left and right), Amazons also fought with spears, bows and arrows, clubs, and swords.

everyone involved with the palace — whether a slave like Tata or the king's closest adviser from one of the most important families in the kingdom.

At first Tata was a servant in one of the Amazon units. She carried whatever she could — bed mats, clothes, rations of toasted grain and bean cakes, bullets, and gunpowder. As she grew older and stronger, she began military training along with the other girls. Tata learned how to use various weapons such as muskets and swords. She was taught how to take care of her own injuries. In the forest, she learned how to survive thirst and hunger and how to imitate birdcalls so that she could secretly communicate with other soldiers. She was soon in top physical form.

Many large West African cities and towns were protected by walls. The young soldiers practiced climbing walls and forcing their way through barricades of thorn bushes — barefoot. This tough training no doubt helped Tata survive one of the deadliest battles the Amazons ever fought.

When Tata was about sixteen or seventeen years old, she most likely took part in the battle at Abeokuta. In 1864 King Glele marched on this Yoruba city to avenge his father's death in a previous war. The Dahomean army, including about three thousand Amazons, began the 120-mile trek from Abomey to Abeokuta. They arrived nearly a month later. As a girl, Tata had been captured from a village near Abeokuta. But she could barely remember that life and that time. She was now an Amazon warrior who owed allegiance only to her king and her sister soldiers.

The next day, at a signal from their commanders, the Amazons raced to the walls surrounding Abeokuta. The cannon and musket fire drove them back, but they kept up their attack. Only four soldiers were able to break through the enemy's defenses before being killed. All were Amazons.

In the end, the king and his army failed to capture the city and returned to Abomey. It was during this time that King Glele might have first noticed Tata Ajaché. The king gave the beautiful young warrior cloth and cowrie shells as a reward for her loyalty and bravery in battle. Although the Amazons were not supposed to marry and have children, the king and Tata fell in love.

Their relationship remained secret until Tata became pregnant. King Glele knew the Amazons' strict rules about celibacy and asked Tata not to tell anyone that he was the father of her child. Tata's commanding officer tried to get her to reveal who the father was, but the young soldier refused. Even when she was threatened with severe punishment, Tata remained loyal to the king. And although she must have been as miserable and frightened as she had been when she was a young captive, she stayed strong and kept her word.

For her loyalty to King Glele, Tata later received a house and other gifts from him. One of the most important gifts she received was the title of *Djedokkpo*, which gave her the status of a queen. Even so, Tata continued to fight in military campaigns and did not retire from the army until 1889 when King Glele died.

Tata Ajaché remains a symbol of loyalty and bravery. Once a slave, she became a queen.

Amazon Dress

King Glele's father outfitted his army in uniforms, which was unusual among African armies of the time. When Tata became an Amazon, the uniform (shown below) consisted of striped tunics of silk, velvet, or cotton, and headbands or caps emblazoned with the regiment's insignia. Colored sashes were fastened around the waist. If the Amazons were carrying muskets, they would wear cartridge belts as well. Uniforms in muted colors were reserved for battle; brightly colored ones were worn on parade or for festivals.

Chapter Five

Sister of the Country

❋

Taytu Betul of Ethiopia

(1851–1918)

The large eyes of the young Ethiopian princess were fixed on the seer's face as he spoke: "Taytu Betul Hayle Maryam, someday you will be crowned."

Taytu must have carried these words in her very soul. Despite many hardships and dangers throughout her life, Taytu's spirit remained unbroken and, in the end, the prophecy came true.

Princess Taytu was born about 1851, surrounded by the splendor of the Ethiopian nobility — a world of servants, glittering jewelry, richly decorated houses, and beautiful artwork. Her family traced its roots to Menelik I, the first emperor of Ethiopia. Traditionally, the rulers of this ancient nation have come from the northern highlands, where a great civilization flourished from 800 to 300 B.C. According to legend, Menelik I was the son of Israel's King Solomon and Ethiopia's Queen of Sheba. His descendants were considered the only rightful heirs to the throne, the only ones who could call themselves "The Lion of Judah." No wonder Taytu believed the prophecy. Her background placed her family at the pinnacle of Ethiopian society.

Taytu's father, Prince Betul Hayle Maryam, was often away at war. During this period in Ethiopian history called the "Era of the Princes," the lords and princes of the various provinces fought, each trying to hold on to or expand his territory. Some of them supported the emperor, and others fought against him. Prince Betul died in battle on June 29, 1853, when Taytu was three years old. Her mother, Yewub-dar, later remarried and moved with Taytu and her younger sister, Desta, into a monastery where her new husband worked. Taytu's two older brothers had become soldiers and were away fighting.

❋

(Opposite) Taytu appears here in her Empress's crown and robes, with one of her palaces in the background. As a devout member of the Ethiopian Orthodox Church, Taytu often wore an ornate cross similar to the one shown at left. Ethiopian silver crosses were made from melted-down European coins.

The Queen of Sheba

❋

Both the Bible and the Koran describe how the Queen of Sheba traveled from Ethiopia to Jerusalem to meet the famed King Solomon (left). The same story is told in the Kebra Nagast *(Glory of Kings), an Ethiopian national saga that was written in medieval times. But the* Kebra Nagast *also says that after the queen returned from Jerusalem she gave birth to the future King Menelik I — an ancestor of Menelik II and of Taytu.*

While their stepfather worked for the monks, helping them with their business affairs, the two sisters and their mother led a quiet life away from the battles being fought in other parts of the country. It was a good place to be. Because she lived in a monastery, Taytu learned how to read and write Amharic, the official language of Ethiopia, and Ge'ez, the ancient language of religious books. She played chess, wrote poetry, and practiced playing the lyre. As she grew older, she also studied religion and law. She was very well educated, more so than most girls and young women. It appears that Taytu continued her studies wherever she lived, as if she were preparing herself for events to come.

At the age of ten, Taytu's life changed again. All women, whether rich or poor, royal or common, were expected to marry and have children, and preparation for marriage began at a young age. Taytu could no longer play in the monastery grounds with her sister and friends. Instead, she spent time with her mother, learning about the duties of a wife and the running of a household.

Marriage among the nobility in Ethiopia was a very serious matter. It sometimes brought together families who had fought each other in the past, or it helped them acquire land and property. Often the marriages were arranged by the bride's and groom's families, and the young couple had no choice in the matter.

In 1866, at the age of sixteen, Princess Taytu married. By this time Tewodros II had seized power. Taytu's family thought it would be wise to ally themselves with this powerful ruler by arranging the marriage of their eldest daughter to a general in the emperor's army. We have no record of Taytu's thoughts on her marriage. She simply did what was expected of her.

Sadly, whatever joy her marriage brought Taytu was short-lived. A few days after her wedding, her husband was arrested. Although she was a princess, Taytu was also taken and forced to serve soldiers during a military campaign. She cooked, carried gear, slept on the ground, and took care of the sick and dying soldiers. Perhaps Taytu was being punished for something her husband had done, or perhaps the emperor still resented her brothers, who had fought against him in his battle to take the throne of Ethiopia.

Forcing a young woman of Taytu's background to be a servant was cruel. Yet her pride in her heritage and her faith in God must have given her strength. She survived, but her husband was executed. Taytu was now alone and penniless. Fortunately, a relative was a nobleman at the emperor's court and helped the young princess during this difficult time.

In 1883, twenty years after the death of her first husband and after several other unhappy marriages, the prophecy Taytu had heard as a child came true. The thirty-eight-year-old Taytu married Menelik II, king of the Ethiopian province of Shewa. A marriage to a woman such as Taytu, from an important northern family, gave Menelik ties to the northern provinces. Taytu also brought to the relationship a good education, a love for her country, and her faith. Like her husband, Taytu was a devout member of the Ethiopian Orthodox Church. One of the first things she did as queen was to have a new church built at Entotto in Shewa.

From the beginning of their marriage, Menelik II spent most of his time helping the new emperor, Yohannes IV, put down rebellions and uprisings. At this time, in addition to problems in the provinces, Ethiopia was trying hard to remain independent. Africa was being carved up into European colonies. In 1885, Italy, with the help of Great Britain, occupied an island on the northern coast and began pushing inland. Menelik supported the emperor in his struggles to unify the country and to keep the Europeans from seizing control of Ethiopia.

While Menelik was away on a military campaign in 1886, Taytu devised a clever plan to deal with several hundred army deserters

(Above) An 1892 Ethiopian silver coin shows Taytu's husband and the inscription "Emperor Menelik II, King of Kings of Ethiopia." Menelik was the first ruler of the country to issue a modern national currency. (Below) This large golden crown studded with precious gems was worn by the emperor on state occasions.

33

A New Capital

In 1886, Taytu chose a site in the foothills of the Entotto mountains for a new Ethiopian capital city and called it Addis Ababa, meaning "new flower." It is still the capital of Ethiopia today. The founding of the city marked the beginning of the country's modernization, and brought many benefits to Ethiopian families of the time (middle, right). The new capital boasted the country's first hospital, modern schools, paved roads, buildings for government ministries and an impressive palace for Menelik and Taytu. The city's magnificent St. George's Cathedral (top and middle, left) was built in 1896 to commemorate Ethiopia's victory at the Battle of Adwa (see page 36). The faithful (top) and priests (bottom) gather at the cathedral for Timkat, the annual celebration of the baptism of Jesus.

camped nearby. She lured them with the promise of food, and split them up by giving some of them passes to show the district governors. Then, at a prearranged signal, Taytu and the governors arrested all the deserters simultaneously. One impressed witness wrote, "The whole country was amazed at what Weyzero [Madam] Taytu had done!"

After Emperor Yohannes was killed in a battle to put down an uprising near the Sudanese border, Menelik declared himself emperor. The king and queen of Shewa were crowned emperor and empress of Ethiopia in 1889 in coronation ceremonies of magnificent splendor — jewels and a golden crown for Taytu, and a golden sword, scepter, and crown for Menelik. Taytu received the title of *Itege*, meaning "sister of the country," in another spectacular ceremony held two days after her coronation. Thousands of people holding lamps and torches lifted their arms to the heavens, lighting up the night sky to honor the new empress.

The couple formed a strong bond. Their work together would eventually lead to the creation of the modern Ethiopian nation. But leading the country out of its ancient feudal past would not occur without much pain and hardship. The empress stayed by her husband's side, offering support and advice during the long, difficult years ahead.

After being crowned, their first challenge was the famine that had spread throughout the country. Imported cattle had infected farm animals with a fatal disease. When their animals died, the farmers could not plow their fields or plant their crops. Without crops and cattle, the people starved. Some of their subjects asked the royal couple for help. Menelik and Taytu set up an area outside the church in Entotto where bread was passed out to those in need.

The empress also helped her husband in Ethiopia's diplomatic relations with other countries. She discovered that a treaty signed between Italy and Ethiopia was a trick to fool the Ethiopians. The wording of the agreement in Italian was different from the wording in Amharic. In Italian, the agreement gave Italy control over Ethiopia. Taytu warned her husband, and a quarrel with Italy over the treaty soon led to war.

Menelik (above) depended on Taytu's diplomatic skills in his absence. The new empress (below) once prevented a rebellion by coordinating a small show of force and eloquently reminding citizens of the area of their patriotic duty. Afterward, according to one historian, "a great calm settled from one end of the empire to the other."

The Battle at Adwa

The power struggle between the Italians and the Ethiopians under Emperor Menelik erupted at the Battle of Adwa in 1896 (above). The Ethiopian army was larger and better equipped than the Italians had expected. The emperor spent more than one million dollars — the equivalent of twenty million dollars today —

to equip his troops with modern rifles and artillery. Menelik (left) led over 100,000 men into battle and achieved a stunning victory over the Italians. Word of this triumph spread around the world, garnering respect and admiration for the emperor and empress and sparking international interest in their country. (Right) A French magazine featured these two members of the emperor's guard on its cover when one of its journalists traveled to Ethiopia in 1903.

Taytu was by her husband's side as he left the palace in the capital city of Addis Ababa in 1895 to march on the Italians at Adwa. Five hundred soldiers guarded the empress and her entourage of about one hundred women as they traveled with the troops. Taytu and her servants took care of preparing the food for the soldiers. This trip was entirely different from her forced march with the troops many years ago. The royal couple and their nobles enjoyed all the comforts of home — or as many as were possible. Yet, Adwa was not "home," and Taytu had not been forced to come along. She chose to be on the battlefield to give her husband and the soldiers her support.

Italian soldiers who were captured at the Battle of Adwa celebrate their release after the signing of the Peace Treaty of Addis Ababa.

The Ethiopians defeated the Italians at Adwa. Emperor Menelik was honored at home and abroad for his victory over a European army. On October 26, 1896, Ethiopia and Italy signed the Peace Treaty of Addis Ababa, recognizing the independence of Ethiopia. A relatively peaceful period followed. Menelik was considered a great emperor, and both he and his empress commanded the respect of the people. He unified much of the country and began to modernize Ethiopia by introducing the telegraph, the printing press, a national currency, a railway, and a postal system. The emperor himself drove the first car in the country.

By 1907, the emperor's health had begun to fail. He organized a cabinet of nine noblemen, close and trusted friends, to help him run the country. But Taytu was actually in charge. "It is the forehead of Taytu that is holding up the empire," someone close to the court wrote.

Menelik's young grandson from an earlier marriage was named his heir. When the emperor died on December 12, 1913, Taytu immediately left Addis Ababa. She spent her last years in a house in the hills overlooking the capital, and died there in 1918 at the age of sixty-seven.

At a time when most women had little power, Taytu used her intelligence to become a leader of her people and the true power behind the throne.

The Princess of the Mountains of the Moon

On a February afternoon in 1975, a friend gave Princess Elizabeth of Toro a book containing the Psalms. "You will go through peacefully," the friend said, trying to comfort Elizabeth. The princess then stepped into a car and fled the lush green valleys and snowcapped mountains of Toro in western Uganda. But would she be able to escape? Her stunning looks and regal bearing were known throughout the country. The government was offering a reward to anyone who could tell them where she was hiding.

As a child, Elizabeth would never have believed that one day she would have to be smuggled out of the land of her birth. Elizabeth Bagaaya's roots went deep into the ancient culture of the Kingdom of Toro. She understood, even as a young girl, the duties and responsibilities she would one day take on as the daughter of a king and as the Royal Sister, the *Batebe*, when her younger brother Patrick succeeded their father to the throne.

Princess Elizabeth was born in 1940, the daughter of King George Rukiidi III and Lady Kezia Rukiidi. Toro, Buganda, Ankole, and Bunyoro were once independent kingdoms but had become the British colony of Uganda in 1891. While the kings no longer ruled their subjects as they had in the old days, they were still loved and respected by their people. Like the British and European royal families, the Ugandan royal families preserved the rituals and traditions of their former kingdoms.

(Opposite) The moon rises above Uganda's majestic Mountains of the Moon in Princess Elizabeth's homeland, the kingdom of Toro.

After Elizabeth finished grade school, her parents decided to send her to boarding school in Buganda. The *Kabaka*, king of Buganda, was Elizabeth's uncle and would be her guardian while she was in his kingdom. In her autobiography, the Princess remembers the day her father left her at the royal palace in Buganda: "I wanted to burst into tears, but princesses never, never cry. He went off with his entourage — and I was on my own."

No more waking up to the glorious sight of the Mountains of the Moon or the sound of the drums, signaling morning wake-up. No more walking to school with the other royal children and their friends. No more going to Girl Scouts.

Elizabeth especially missed the late afternoons back at the royal compound when school was over. At four o'clock the Toro flag was lowered and a special ceremony, called the Procession of the Royal Spear, began. Elizabeth and the other royal children watched in awe as a man carrying the Royal Spear, a symbol of the power of the king, entered the courtyard. Followed by three other men, he carried the spear to the Throne Room, telling stories about the history of Toro as he walked. After the ceremony, the children played games — tennis, hide-and-seek, and board games.

In the evenings, Elizabeth spent time with her mother. Lady Kezia recited traditional poetry, taught her how to play the harp, or simply chatted with her daughter and the other royal children. Before bedtime the children's nannies took them to say good night to the king in the two-story Court House. In its front room, the king sat on a carved wooden throne surrounded by members of the royal family, clan and district chiefs, servants, and ordinary people. The adults would talk, tell stories, and recall events in Toro's history. "We always seemed to be laughing and happy," remembers Princess Elizabeth of this time in her life.

When Elizabeth went away to boarding school she became a foreigner, an outsider, the "new girl." She had to get used to a different way of life shared with other girls who weren't always friendly or kind to her. Eventually, though, she adjusted to the strict routine of her new school —

England's prestigious Sherborne School for Girls was Elizabeth's home for over a year. She shared her heritage with the other students by organizing a choir to sing a song in the Rutoro language at a school music festival.

waking up early to the sound of a drumroll, carrying water in a bucket for washing, and cultivating a patch of land on the school's banana plantation. She sang and acted in school plays and turned out to be a good basketball player because she was so tall. And then, just when she had made friends and settled into her new school, Elizabeth became a "new girl" again.

This time Elizabeth was sent even farther away, to an English boarding school, to complete her high school education. The move from Uganda to the Sherborne School for Girls in England was particularly difficult. She wrote that she was shocked when she first arrived because she was the only black student: "I felt that I was on trial and that my failure to excel would reflect badly on the entire black race."

Under a lot of stress but determined to succeed, the princess learned how to handle yet another strict routine. The girls had to be out of bed at 7:10 in the morning when the first bell rang. Twenty minutes later they had to be washed, dressed, and ready for breakfast. "During my early terms at Sherborne, I would be reduced to tears every morning as I ran in all directions, appealing to someone to help me knot my school tie."

Prayers were said before classes. The prayers had a calming effect on Elizabeth after the early-morning rush. But then she had to face learning two new languages, Latin and French. (Elizabeth's native language was Rutoro, although she spoke English, too.) Her classmates were far ahead of her because some of them had been studying these subjects for six years. As if that were not enough, Princess Elizabeth had only one year to prepare for the entrance examination to Cambridge, one of England's most prestigious universities.

But Elizabeth was not about to crumble. She came from a proud, strong, and determined people. Only two other African women had ever been accepted into Cambridge. Elizabeth became the third. Her parents were very proud of her and wanted her to be prepared to take on the role of Batebe when her brother became king. Although the monarchy was largely ceremonial, education and knowledge of the law were important to the royal family.

The Batebe of Toro

Elizabeth's role as the Batebe of Toro was an important one. The Batebe, the "first lady of the kingdom," is the most powerful woman in Toro — even more powerful than the king's wife. The Batebe is the eldest full sister of the king, meaning that the succession requires not only a male heir, but a female one as well, in order to be complete. Like her Aunt Ruth before her, Elizabeth had the important duty of being the trusted adviser to her brother, the king. Because she was, in essence, her aunt's successor, Elizabeth and her aunt formed a strong bond. Even after Elizabeth's brother Patrick became king and Elizabeth became Batebe, Elizabeth continued to rely on her aunt's wisdom and strength.

At Cambridge Elizabeth studied history, English literature, law, and political science. As a "symbol of her country and her culture," Elizabeth couldn't afford to get behind in her schoolwork, but she found time for fun, too. The popular princess went to parties with European royalty, traveled to Italy and France, and no longer dressed like a prim missionary's daughter (her English guardian had been a missionary). Instead, she wore beautiful designer dresses.

In 1962, Elizabeth proudly accompanied her beloved father King George when he was knighted by the Queen of England.

The year 1962 proved to be a momentous year for both Elizabeth and her country. She graduated from Cambridge with a degree in law, and Uganda became an independent nation after many years as a British colony. Three years later, after further training, Elizabeth became a lawyer. To celebrate, the princess gave a wonderful party for hundreds of friends and relatives in an old mansion in London. After a night of dancing, Princess Elizabeth awoke in her apartment to the telephone ringing. Her father had died. The responsibilities the king had been preparing her for were at hand. As she got ready to fly home to Uganda, her sister said through her tears, "Elizabeth, *you* have to be strong."

It was good advice. Elizabeth's brother Patrick was only seventeen years old and still in school in England. His twenty-five-year-old sister, his Batebe, would have to give him help and guidance. Their uncle, the Kabaka, was the president of the new nation, and he and Prime Minister Milton Obote were in a power struggle. Upon Patrick's arrival in Uganda, each man had sent a car to the airport to pick up the young king. Elizabeth had to try and keep her brother out of the quarrel between the two men. Independence had opened up old wounds among the various regions and ethnic groups in Uganda, and a difficult time lay ahead.

Princess Elizabeth, along with the other people of Toro, mourned the king for nine days. After the mourning period, Patrick was crowned King of Toro. Shortly afterward, they learned that Milton Obote had abolished the position of prime minister and declared himself president. After making sure that their uncle was not hurt, Elizabeth and Patrick continued the coronation celebrations. Although they were worried and upset about the Kabaka, they knew that the celebrations were important to the people of Toro.

Right after the coronation, Princess Elizabeth went to Kampala, the Ugandan capital, and completed a six-month internship with a law firm. She became Uganda's first woman lawyer. Again, Elizabeth's happiness was short-lived. On May 23, 1966, Milton Obote ordered his troops to attack the Bugandan king's palace. All of the chiefs were arrested. Elizabeth was afraid that her uncle might have been killed, but was told that he had escaped to London.

The following year Obote abolished all of the Ugandan kingdoms. The Toro royal family was forced to leave their palace, Lady Kezia's home for more than thirty years. Relatives and friends began to warn Elizabeth that, like her brother, she should leave Uganda and go into exile. As a well-educated former princess who was loved by the Toro people, she, too, was in danger.

Elizabeth continued to work at the law firm until another princess came to her rescue. Princess Margaret of England invited Elizabeth to take part in a charity fashion show to raise money for sick children in the British Commonwealth. Elizabeth was not surprised when the government refused her request to go to England. The monarchy had been abolished, and Uganda was a republic. The government wanted to send someone else to represent Uganda, but Princess Margaret said that the invitation had been sent to Elizabeth, not the government. Finally, Obote backed down.

Princess Elizabeth of Toro was the star of the glamorous fashion show in London. She was tall and slender, with beautiful large eyes that shone against her rich dark skin. Black models were rare in the 1960s. After the show, Elizabeth received offers from some of the best British modeling agencies and was asked to pose for fashion magazines.

Some of Elizabeth's friends advised her not to become a professional model. After all, she was a lawyer and a princess. Elizabeth had another idea. "Beauty," she wrote, "is not one's own but rather a reflection of one's people, one's country." Perhaps modeling would be a way for her to bring the problems of her people and the dangers of Obote's government to the attention of the world. Once she became well-known, people might listen to her.

The princess's graceful beauty and innate sense of style made her a favorite with photographers.

43

Renowned British photographer Patrick Lichfield took this stunning photo of Elizabeth for Vogue *magazine.*

Elizabeth became a supermodel. She was photographed throughout Europe and appeared in many prestigious magazines. The former first lady of the United States, Jacqueline Kennedy, had met Elizabeth in London and encouraged her to move to New York City. There, her career soared as she was photographed for *Vogue*, *Harper's Bazaar*, and *Ebony*. She spent weekends in Harlem, where she had found a small Ugandan community.

On January 25, 1971, Elizabeth was in Paris. A friend called to tell her that Obote's police state had just been overthrown by General Idi Amin. At first Elizabeth was frightened for her family but soon learned that they were fine and that the whole country was celebrating Obote's overthrow. It seemed like a great new day for all Ugandans as General Amin freed political prisoners and changed laws that had prevented journalists from writing about the government.

Amin welcomed all the royal families back to Uganda. Although he was reluctant to allow the former kings to rule again, even in a ceremonial way, he gave some royals positions in the government. Elizabeth accepted the position of roving ambassador for Uganda. She began her duties by traveling to other African nations. She met with government officials and tried to gain their support for the new government in Uganda. What better representative than a beautiful, intelligent, well-educated woman — and a princess as well?

Elizabeth could easily have gone back to New York or London or Paris and continued her successful modeling career. But she was her father's daughter. "My name was a daily reminder of my responsibility," she wrote.

After two years as President Amin's roving ambassador, Elizabeth watched sadly as her country began to fall apart once more. During his first year in office, Amin executed as many as 6,000 of the army's 9,000 soldiers because he believed them to be loyal to Obote. Amin then expelled all Asians (mostly Ugandan-born descendants of Indian and Pakistani immigrants) from the country and turned over their businesses to corrupt army officers who didn't know how to run them. The economy began to decline. High-ranking Ugandan politicians and intellectuals began to leave the country, often out of fear for their lives. But Elizabeth wanted to continue working for her people and decided to stay.

In 1974, Amin appointed Elizabeth minister of foreign affairs. This was an important position and the first time a woman in Uganda had ever been given this kind of honor. Amin knew the treasure he had in Elizabeth. She took her responsibilities as foreign minister seriously and worked to repair Uganda's damaged reputation. She only hoped that Amin would not do anything to destroy what she had accomplished.

Elizabeth successfully settled a dispute between Kenya and Uganda, but while she was in Kenya, she heard the shocking news that the former foreign minister had been murdered. Elizabeth had to face the fact that Idi Amin was turning out to be as bad as Obote, and that Ugandans, through no choice of their own, had exchanged one tyrant for another.

The princess returned to Uganda and tried to continue her work. In March of 1974, she heard gunfire near her home in Kampala. Amin's forces had put down an attempted coup. Afterward, the president trusted no one and set up a network of spies. Now, more than ever, people lived in fear. Amin murdered thousands of ordinary citizens, politicians, intellectuals, clergy, journalists, and anyone else whom he suspected might not be loyal to him. Entire villages were wiped out. Often, he simply had his victims' dead bodies thrown into the Nile.

As minister of foreign affairs, the princess headed a delegation to the 29th Session of the United Nations General Assembly in New York City. She realized how important it was for her to bring some pride and dignity to the image of her country during this difficult time in its history. She gave a moving speech before the General Assembly about her hope for cooperation and understanding among all nations. Her speech received a lot of attention — some of it unwanted.

Idi Amin began taking a personal interest in her. She ignored him as best she could. After the United Nations meeting in New York, the Uganda delegation toured several other countries, including France and Germany. The president constantly telephoned her while she was on tour, making sure she was where she was supposed to be. Someone jealous of Elizabeth's success had been feeding lies about her to Amin. He angrily ordered her back to Kampala.

A friend warned Elizabeth that it was not safe for her to return. But Elizabeth decided to go back. "I had not been raised to run from danger," she wrote in her autobiography. Not long after her return, she was dismissed from her position. One night there was a knock on her door. It was the police. They arrested her on a false charge of stealing government funds and she was put in jail. When word spread of her arrest, Ugandans were outraged and hundreds came to sit in protest around the police station. People around the world complained about her arrest as well. Not wanting to look bad before the world, Amin let her go.

Still determined to remain in Uganda and dreading another exile, Elizabeth left Kampala and went to Toro. She worked for a church and lived quietly in a small house in the church compound. But her troubles with Amin were not over. One of his friends warned her that if the president asked her to marry him, it would be dangerous for her to refuse. After it became known that she would not marry Amin, her life was truly in danger. She escaped to Kenya in February of 1975 and made her way to Vienna and finally to London.

Four years later, Princess Elizabeth returned home. This time she hoped she would never have to leave again. Amin had been overthrown, although not before murdering an estimated 300,000 people during his reign. Election campaigns were being held and Patrick was running for office. This was an historic occasion because a king had never before run for election.

Unfortunately, the election was not a fair one, and Elizabeth's old enemy, Milton Obote, won. Soon afterward, he began to kill his opponents. Thousands of people died, and Elizabeth and Patrick were once again in danger. In 1980, a miserable Elizabeth made her way to Britain. The one bright spot in her life was Wilbur Nyabongo.

While she was campaigning for her brother, Elizabeth had met Wilbur, a handsome young engineer. The two were not exactly strangers. Their families were distantly related. Wilbur's grandparents had been honored chiefs and he shared Elizabeth's pride in their heritage. In 1981, the attractive pair married in London. They were both committed to freeing their country from Obote's grip and worked for the National Resistance Movement. Because she knew important people around the world, Elizabeth was able to raise money and find support for the movement. She also wrote her autobiography at this time to help inform more people of the tragic events in her country.

Finally, Obote was overthrown. The new president, Yoweri Museveni, had been the leader of the resistance movement. President Museveni appointed Princess Elizabeth ambassador to the United States in 1986.

Although she was very successful as an ambassador, Elizabeth missed Wilbur. She was working in Washington, D.C., and he was working in Nigeria. When news came that Patrick was getting married in Uganda, it seemed the perfect opportunity to celebrate with her family and to spend time with her husband. But once again in Elizabeth's life, joy turned to pain. When she reached Entebbe Airport in Uganda, she was told that Wilbur had died in a plane crash. Instead of attending her brother's wedding, she buried her husband in the shadows of the Mountains of the Moon, alongside his ancestors.

As Uganda's foreign minister, Elizabeth represented her country at the 29th Session of the United Nations in 1974.

As she had done so many times in her life, Princess Elizabeth weathered this terrible loss and continued to work. She held her ambassador's post until 1988, then retired from politics.

Today Princess Elizabeth is involved with health and education projects in Uganda through her organization, The Batebe of Toro Foundation. Political life in Uganda has improved under Museveni; however, it is still not a true democracy. Political parties are not allowed — only individuals may run for office. In 1993, the traditional Ugandan monarchies were reinstated. Elizabeth is now the guardian, along with Museveni, of the current king of Toro. He was crowned in 1995, when he was only three years old.

Princess Elizabeth of Toro exemplifies what royalty actually means — not crowns and jewels and palaces, but strength, sacrifice, loyalty, tradition, and love. Today she is a living symbol of what the royal women of Africa have meant to their peoples for thousands of years.

Index

Picture Credits

All original illustrations and maps are by
Laurie McGaw unless otherwise indicated.

BAL — Bridgeman Art Library
C/M — Corbis/MAGMA
EL — Erich Lessing/Art Resource, NY
MEPL — Mary Evans Picture Library
SC — Schomburg Center/Art Resource, NY
WF — Werner Forman/Art Resource, NY

2: SC.
6: Jürgen Liepe.
8: Jürgen Liepe.
9: R. Sheridan/Ancient Art and Architecture
    Collection Ltd.
10: EL.
11: (Top) The Metropolitan Museum of Art,
    Rogers Fund, 1936 (36.3.2). Photograph
    © 1992 The Metropolitan Museum of
    Art. (Bottom) EL.
12: WF.
14: WF.
15: Jane Sweeney/Lonely Planet Images.
17: Private Collection/The Stapleton
    Collection/ BAL.
18: (Top) MEPL. (Bottom) The Stapleton
    Collection/C/M.
19: (Top) The Field Museum, A113853c.
    (Bottom) The Field Museum,
    A105153c_F8530.
20: The Metropolitan Museum of Art, Gift of
    Mr. and Mrs. Klaus G. Perls, 1991
    (1991.17.31). Photograph © 1991 The
    Metropolitan Museum of Art.
22: North Wind Picture Archives.
23: WF.
24: The Art Archive/Private Collection/Dagli
    Orti (A).
26: Historical Picture Archive/C/M.
27: SC.
28: (Right) MEPL.
30: National Museum of African Art/
    Smithsonian Institution.
32: Private Collection/BAL.
33: (Top) Goldberg Coins. (Bottom) WF.
34: (Top) John Hicks/C/M. (Middle) Photos
    by Vincenzo Chimisso courtesy of
    Columba Chimisso Fuller. (Bottom)
    Michael S. Lewis/C/M.
35: MEPL.
36: (Top) Private Collection/Archives
    Charmet/BAL. (Bottom left and
    right) MEPL.
37: MEPL.
40: Sherborne School for Girls.
42: Hulton-Deutsch Collection/C/M.
43: Hulton-Deutsch Collection/C/M.
44: Photograph by Patrick Lichfield, Camera
    Press London.
47: Time Life Pictures/Getty Images.

Selected Bibliography

For young readers:
Carter, Dorothy Sharp. *His Majesty, Queen Hatshepsut*. New York: J. B. Lippincott, 1987.
Koslow, Philip. *Hausaland: The Fortress Kingdoms*. New York: Chelsea House, 1995.
———. *Dahomey: The Warrior Kings*. New York: Chelsea House, 1997.
McKissack, Patricia. *Nzinga: Warrior Queen of Matamba*. New York: Scholastic, 2000.
For older readers:
Bay, Edna G. *Wives of the Leopard: Gender, Politics, and Culture in the Kingdom of Dahomey*.
    Charlottesville, VA: University of Virginia Press, 1998.
Nyabongo, Elizabeth. *Elizabeth of Toro: The Odyssey of an African Princess*. New York: Simon
    & Schuster, 1989.
Prouty, Chris. *Empress Taytu and Menelik II: Ethiopia 1883–1910*. Trenton, NJ: The Red Sea Press, 1986.
Schwarz-Bart, Simone and André Schwarz-Bart. *In Praise of Black Women 1: Ancient African Queens*.
    Madison, WI: University of Wisconsin Press, 2001.

Acknowledgments

The author, illustrator, and Madison Press Books would like to thank the following people who so
generously lent their time and expertise to us on this project: Edna G. Bay; Peter Brand; Elizabeth
Giorgis; Linda Heywood; Charles Kanyarusoke; Colleen Kriger; Beverly Mack; and Stephen
Rockel. Laurie McGaw would also like to extend warm thanks to the women who modeled for
three of the princesses: Rhoda Ewukuba Andrews, Tianna Makhurane-Clunis, and Tiahara
Thompson. And for their enthusiasm and help with the project, many thanks to Kerry
Carpenter, Judith Andrade, and Gertrude King.

Chairman and Founder: Albert E. Cummings
President and CEO: Brian Soye
Editorial Director: Hugh M. Brewster
Associate Editorial Director: Wanda Nowakowska
Project Editor: Imoinda Romain
Editorial Assistance: Shima Aoki

Art Director: Gordon Sibley
Graphic Designer: Jennifer Lum
Production Director: Susan Barrable
Production Manager: Donna Chong
Printing and Binding: Tien Wah Press

Madison Press Books 1000 Yonge Street, Suite 200, Toronto, Ontario, Canada, M4W 2K2

Complete Guide to Creative Needlepoint

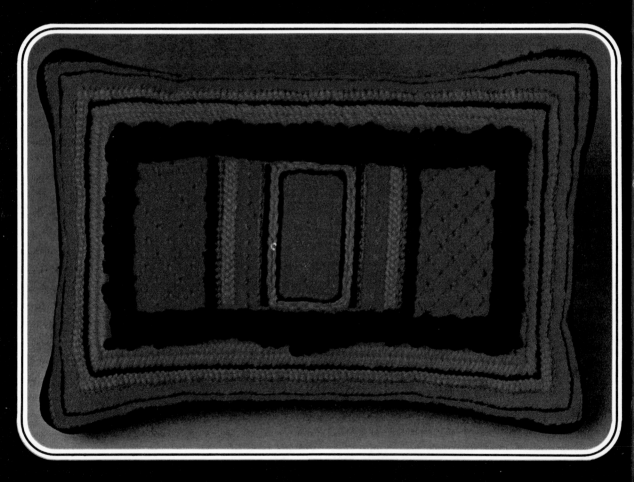

1 This pillow is worked on #5 rug canvas using two
full strands of Persian yarn. The design centers on
a rectangle of No. 179 Scotch Stitch, and works out
symmetrically on both sides with areas of No. 36 Continental Stitch, No. 151 Outline Stitch, No. 30 Chain
Stitch, No. 96 Fishbone Stitch, No. 9 Back Stitch, No.
106 Gobelin Stitch, No. 51 Cross Stitch, No. 207
Turkey Stitch, No. 47 Cross Stitch, No. 111 Gobelin
Stitch, No. 66 Cross Stitch, No. 26 Cashmere Stitch.

Complete Guide to Creative Needlepoint

Jo Bucher

CHL CREATIVE HOME LIBRARY
In Association with Better Homes and Gardens
Meredith Corporation

iv

Library of Congress Cataloging in Publication Data
Bucher, Jo.
    Complete guide to creative needlepoint.
    1. Canvas embroidery.   I. Title.   II. Title:
Creative needlepoint.
TT778.C3B8   746.4'4   72-6674
ISBN 0-696-34300-2

Registered trademarks that appear in this book are:
    Velcro, "Pop-in Pillows," and *Mylar.*

CHL CREATIVE HOME LIBRARY

© 1973 by Meredith Corporation, Des Moines, Iowa
Printed in the United States of America

Contents

Acknowledgements

I AM AGAIN INDEBTED to Peg Campbell for the use of her library of unusual, out-of-print needlework books. My thanks to the following people who either loaned their needlework or contributed in some way to making this book possible: Ruth Bohls, Bill Bucher, Sandy Bucher, Dr. John L. Gleave, Arthur Kuns, Diane Norton, Doris Paulinson, Nancy Rickert, and Jean Shelly.

J.B.

Credits

Ruth Bahls:
> work for color wheel sampler, *p. 270* (design by Jo Bucher).

Jo Bucher:
> design and work for everything pictured in this book that is not credited here.

Sandy Bucher:
> work for blue and white pillow, *p. 303,*which was adapted from a transfer design.

K. A. Kuns:
> design and work for man's vest, *p. 279.*

Diane Norton:
> design and work for watermelon and fish pillows, *p. 256;* work for picture of birds which was taken from a chart.

Nancy Rickert:
> design and work for lamp bases, wastepaper basket, toilet paper holder, *p. 302;* sampler belt, *p. x;* fly swatter,*p. 260;* tissue box holder, *p. 297;* orange and black pillow, *title page;* bedrest, *p. 2;* luggage rack straps (work by Jo Bucher), *p. 243.*

Jean Shelly:
> design and work for hat band, *p. 260.*

2 This charming needlepoint doll, shown dressed in doll clothes, is done on #14 mono canvas using Persian yarn. The stitches (mostly No. 11 Basketweave) are described on pages 37 through 40. The director's chair on which she sits is done on #5 rug canvas using rug yarn. It is worked entirely in No. 119 Herringbone Stitch with the color sequence reversed so that the seat is predominantly dark while the back is light.

About the Author

Jo BUCHER has been involved with needlework for many years as a designer and as a teacher, lecturer and author. After receiving her certificate from the Embroiderers' Guild in New York City, she went on to teach needlework to adult evening courses, women's groups and seminars. An exhibitor in national and international needlework shows, Mrs. Bucher is also part-owner of a needlecraft shop, Stitch Witchery, in Denville, New Jersey, and of a mail order company supplying needlework materials, American Crewel Studio. She has written one other book, *The Complete Guide to Embroidery Stitches and Crewel.*

The cummerbund at the left is done on #24 mono canvas with silk floss and metallic thread. It is worked from the center out in No. 10 Bargello Stitch; the edges are worked in crewel yarn using the No. 17 Brick Stitch. The other belts are done on #14 mono canvas with Persian yarn. Two are worked entirely in No. 10 Bargello Stitch and one is a sampler of 30 different stitches.

Complete Guide to Creative Needlepoint

Introduction to Needlepoint

I have tried to make this the most complete needlepoint book possible—the kind of book I wish I had had when I started my needlework career.

And so I have assembled what I believe to be the most comprehensive collection of needlepoint stitches ever published in one book—218 in all, including three exclusive new stitches from England never before published in this country.

But this isn't all. I want to show you how to make the most wonderful variety of objects with these stitches—everything from important decorative accents for your home to charming small items (coasters, eyeglass cases, luggage tags, watchbands, and so on) that you can carry in your handbag to work on wherever you go, and that make the most personal, and therefore treasured, gifts. There is almost no end to the things you can make. You will find many in this book and inspiration for many others in good needlework shops—in fact, new ideas are all around you.

To help you realize them, I have included instructions for special needlepoint techniques and special effects, as well as for the small decorative touches—cordings, tassels, pompoms—that enhance them.

And almost the most satisfying of all, to me, are the clear, detailed instructions for finishing and mounting all your needlework.

This, then, is needlepointing from start to finish. I hope the book will inspire you to create beautiful things that will become your family heirlooms of the future.

4 The bedrest, done on #5 rug canvas with rug yarn, features No. 11 Basketweave and No. 36 Continental Stitches. The small black and white pillow and the pillow in the foreground are actually the same design. Both are done on #5 rug canvas with rug yarn; stitches are No. 190 Spider Web, No. 103 French Knot, No. 23 Buttonhole, No. 32 Chain, No. 95 Fishbone, and No. 36 Continental. The pillow at the left, done on #5 rug canvas using Persian yarn, is worked entirely in No. 10 Bargello Stitch. The patterned pillow on the right is done on #5 rug canvas with rug yarn and is worked entirely in No. 119 Herringbone Stitch. Assembling needlepoint pillows is discussed on page 306.

A Brief History

The craft we call needlepoint today has been known by a number of names during its long history. Most often it has been called canvas embroidery (or canvas work), for that is what it is: embroidering with any variety of materials on a mesh canvas. The origin of the term needlepoint is a little hazy. It is strictly an American term, as is the more recent Quickpoint.

While there are over 200 known needlepoint stitches all of which are illustrated and taught in this book, there are relatively few basic stitches from which all the others have derived. Of these, the Tent Stitches have perhaps the earliest origin. The name comes from the fact that the ancient Egyptians used these slanted stitches when sewing up their tents. As often happens, a technique that starts as utilitarian eventually becomes transformed into a decorative art. Today these same slanted stitches are worked in needlepoint in a number of different ways and have several different names, but the surface effect is still the same; which one you use depends on your design and its purpose. Another very old stitch is the Cross Stitch, which by now has come to have many attractive variations.

The term tapestry work has long been used in Europe, since needlepoint designs were often imitations of the woven tapestries that were made in the 14th to 16th centuries. The designs, usually of pictorial scenes, were often worked in the Gobelin Stitch (named after the great tapestry weaver of that name) and thus resembled woven tapestries.

During the 17th century, Florentine, Hungarian and Eyelet Stitches were also much in evidence, worked in silk and metallic threads as well as wool. By the 19th century most canvas embroidery was used for upholstery. Needlepointed chairs and other furnishings can still be seen in museums, their perfect state attesting to the beauty and longevity of this art form.

Today needlepointing has become an important craft with many applications. In addition to the original Tent Stitches, we have a whole range of decorative and useful stitches—to give textured or looped or raised effects, or to serve as background or filling for every sort of design.

Basic Equipment

For all needlepointing, whether your project is a small coaster, an important chair cover or a rug, there are only three essential items: canvas, yarn or other thread, and needle.

Canvas

Canvas is available in a large range of sizes from the most delicate (40 threads to the inch) to heavy rug canvas (three threads to the inch). The thing to look for, whatever the size, is a uniform weave with no knots. All canvas contains sizing which adds strength and stiffness and gives a smooth finish that allows the working yarn to pass through with ease.

The canvas number indicates the number of threads per inch. For example, a #10 canvas has ten threads to the inch, both horizontally and vertically, which gives 100 intersections per square inch. Thus, if you are doing one of the Tent Stitches, you would be taking 100 stitches per square inch.

Art needlework shops, needlework departments in stores, and mail-order houses carry canvases in polished cotton thread in both mono (single) and penelope (double) mesh. Mono canvas is easier on the eyes when working, particularly in fine sizes. Penelope is useful for combinations of Petit Point and Gros Point and for certain other stitches that need the extra mesh for anchoring. (Where penelope canvas is needed, this is indicated in the directions for the individual stitches.)

Canvas is usually sold by the yard, and

you can buy as little as one-quarter or one-third of a yard. Canvas widths vary according to canvas sizes—generally, the finer the mesh, the narrower the canvas. For an average-size project—a pillow, say—you may not need the entire width, but the extra piece will be useful for practice. In fact, it's a good idea to keep your extra pieces in various sizes to experiment and try out the effect of new stitches in different sizes.

Needlepointing can also be done on evenweave fabrics, such as the traditional linen, cotton, jute and woolen evenweave, particularly if some of the background cloth is to be left exposed. In addition, there are the new plastic meshes, as well as wire mesh such as hardware cloth and chicken wire.

The photographs of some of these canvases and evenweaves (on pages 5, 6 and 7) will give an idea of their variety and appearance. A good needlework shop will have a wide selection and usually good advice as to which type best suits your needs. In general, the more detail you want, the finer the canvas should be.

Yarn or Other Thread

The canvas you select, as well as the type of project and the stitches you plan to use, will determine the kind of yarn or thread you use. For wall hangings, where there is no problem of wear involved, you can use any thread that gives the desired effect. If you plan to use couching or "over embroidery"—that is, embroidering small details over your stitches already worked, usually over basic Tent Stitches, a variety of threads or even fabric strips can be incorporated to give unusual effects.

Traditional yarns and threads have not changed a great deal over the years, but new dyes and mothproofing now give reasonable assurance that with proper care your needlepoint will survive for years to come.

Wool is my favorite for needlepointing. It is easy to work with and gives a rich appearance to the finished work. It is also extremely durable.

The most versatile of the wool yarns available today is Persian. I prefer the Paternayan yarns, which come in over 300 colors and are generally sold in four-ounce hanks, although many needlework shops will cut up the hanks and sell individual strands or small quantities for small areas of color.

Each strand is made up of three two-ply threads which separate easily. This means that Persian yarn can be used on a wide range of canvas sizes, using two or three threads on the finest canvas, while the full strand will cover #12 mono or #10 penelope canvas completely.

However, covering the canvas also depends on your stitch tension and this varies with each individual. If you pull too tightly, the background canvas may be exposed and you will have to add a thread to cover it. Or, if you have difficulty placing stitches next to each other and have to tug the yarn through, the yarn is too heavy and one or more threads should be removed from the strand.

There are also a few other Persian yarns on the market now. Their color ranges are less extensive and their thickness varies, so you will have to test to estimate the quantity required for your project. *In this book all yarn requirements are based on the Paternayan Persian wool yarns.*

Regular knitting wools are not recommended for needlepointing. They don't wear well and are very elastic, which makes them difficult to handle. I wouldn't advise using them on anything but, perhaps, a wall hanging, although sometimes they can give just the right color or texture to a small area.

Crewel wool is still used a great deal, particularly on the finer canvases. Crewel yarn is composed of a single thread, but as with Persian yarn, several threads can be used together. As the textures are similar, Persian and crewel yarns can be used on the same project.

MONO CANVASES
(All are reproduced in actual size.)

A: #24 canvas
B: #18 canvas
C: #16 canvas
D: #14 canvas
E: #12 canvas
F: #10 canvas

PENELOPE (DOUBLEWEAVE) AND RUG CANVASES
(All are reproduced in actual size.)

A: #10 penelope canvas
B: #7 penelope canvas
C: #5 ½ penelope canvas
D: #5 rug canvas
E: #4 ½ rug canvas
F: #3 ½ rug canvas

OTHER CANVASES AND EVENWEAVES
(All are reproduced in actual size.)

A

D

B

E

C

F

A: #14 doubleweave disposable canvas
B: #28 evenweave linen
C: #17 doubleweave cotton
D: #8 woven patterned canvas
E: #8 openweave linen
F: #8 doubleweave jute

Crewel yarn is thinner, so you will need more threads of crewel than of Persian yarn to cover a specific piece of canvas. Appleton crewel yarns are excellent. Although they come in fewer colors, there is a wider range in each color so they give especially good results for Bargello work and any other kind of shading.

Appleton crewel yarns come in small skeins, but both Appleton and Paternayan can also be bought by weight in some shops. Check this before starting a large piece as it will affect the cost considerably.

Rug wools are very satisfactory to work with; the canvas size will determine the type you need. Rya wool is the finest of the rug wools. It is two-ply and is generally worked on a specially woven backing, using three threads at once, which gives the unusual shading effects seen in Rya rugs. The threads can also be used individually; their luster puts them in a class by themselves.

Paternayan makes two weights of rug yarn—the lighter is four-ply, the heavier yarn is three-ply. Both have a lovely sheen. Double strands of regular Persian yarn can also be used on some rug canvas, and its tough fiber will wear as well as rug wool.

Most of the thicker rug yarns don't separate so they must be tested for size on your particular canvas.

One manufacturer, DMC, has recently introduced a wool yarn that works up well on larger canvas (single, it works up well on #7; double, on #3½ rug canvas), but it doesn't wear as well as real rug wool and should be limited to projects that won't have to withstand much wear.

The variety of other threads for needlepointing is constantly increasing. One of the old standbys is *cotton embroidery floss* which works well on finer canvas; because it is mercerized, it gives the appearance of silk. Embroidery floss has six threads to the strand and is put up in small skeins in a wide range of colors. *Soft cotton* is also packaged

in small skeins in a good color selection. Because soft cotton is not mercerized, it has a matt surface and looks like string as it comes out of the skein. It works up nicely on #14 canvas in a Tent Stitch.

There are also *crochet cottons*, mercerized and soft, in a variety of colors and sizes. Crochet threads are usually twisted and can't be used on larger canvases as they don't fluff up enough to cover, but they sometimes add just the effect desired. *Rug cotton* works up very nicely on the larger canvases. Read the labels carefully, and avoid the type that contains rayon; this fuzzes up when worked and it doesn't wear well.

Cotton threads are reasonably easy to use, but care must be taken with the floss; the six threads that compose it are not twisted so you have to be careful to keep a uniform tension on all of them as you work. Most other cotton threads are twisted, so this is no problem.

Silk threads really need a bit of practice before working with them on a project. Smooth hands are the greatest asset when working with any silk thread, as even the slightest roughness of skin or nails will tend to snag the silk. (Some ladies like to use surgical gloves, available at drugstores, for working with silk; they take getting used to but they solve the problem.) Running silk thread *lightly* over a cake of beeswax helps, but be careful not to coat the silk too heavily.

Twisted silk (similar in appearance to cotton pearl) and stout silk are not quite as fussy to work with.

Synthetics of all sizes and textures provide an unlimited field for experiment. The many synthetics (and new ones appear every day) will have to be checked out when you intend to use them. Some fuzz up, some have short fibers that thin out, and so far, on the whole, they are not very good for canvas work.

Metal threads need special handling. Many cannot actually be worked in the various stitches, but can enrich a project when couched down onto the canvas surface. One of the metallic threads that will take stitching is manufactured in Germany by Schurer. It comes in small skeins in gold and silver, and a good needlework shop or mail-order house will have a selection.

Note that metal thread is often woven and tends to ravel. A touch of white glue applied at the end after threading prevents this. Press between fingers to remove excess glue. Prepare several needles so the glue will be dry when you are ready for a new thread.

A fine book that covers the subject completely is *Metal Thread Embroidery* by Barbara Dawson, published by the Charles T. Branford Company, Newton Center, Massachusetts, in 1968.

Swiss straw, strips of fabric, and *linen* threads can also be used on the proper background. There is really no end to what can be used, but do try out the effect of both your thread and your stitch on the background you are planning to use. It saves time in the long run since picking out takes longer than needlepointing and isn't nearly as much fun.

Needle

Needles are manufactured in a number of sizes to accommodate almost any thread you are likely to use. The best needles for needlepointing are called *tapestry needles:* they have a large eye and a blunt tip. The blunt tip is important as it prevents splitting the canvas thread and the working yarn.

The important things to remember when selecting a needle are that the needle should be able to slide through the canvas openings without stretching them, and that the eye of the needle should be large enough for the working yarn. If the eye is so small that the yarn pops out around the eye, it will wear thin as you work. This will affect both the tension and the appearance of the finished piece. It's advisable to try out your needle and thread on a small sample of canvas before beginning your actual work.

Needles are sold by size in packages of all one size or assorted sizes. The smallest generally used is size 24 and the largest is size 13. For very fine canvas work, size 22 or 20 is best. The most common is size 18, which can be used on #10, #12 or #14 canvas. On rug canvases you would need size 16 or 14 to take the heavier strands of yarn, while size 13 is for the largest mesh rug canvas and the thickest rug yarn or fabric strips. Photographs 5 and 6 (on pages 5 and 6) show a range of needle sizes together with the suitable canvas and yarn or other thread. (Instructions for threading the needle are on page 13.)

Additional Useful Equipment

There are some other useful items that will make your needlework easier.

Sharp scissors are a must, and several sizes are desirable. Most important is a pair of small pointed embroidery scissors (about three-and-a-half inches long) which you can keep in your workbasket. (I attach a little brightly colored cord to mine so they are instantly visible wherever I may put them down.) The traditional stork scissors first made in Victorian times are now being copied again, but good ones may be fairly expensive. Good scissors are important—it is most frustrating to try to cut yarn with dull scissors.

Large heavy scissors are necessary for cutting canvas. Don't use your embroidery scissors or any fabric-cutting scissors on canvas, or their cutting edges will be ruined.

I find a properly fitting *thimble* a help, although this isn't considered as necessary as it used to be. Thimbles are made out of anything from plastic to gold. Be sure to get the size that fits your thimble finger—too large or too small a thimble is only a bother. People fortunate enough to have nice long nails can

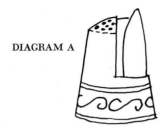

DIAGRAM A

have a small section cut out of the top of the thimble, as shown in DIAGRAM A.

A *small crochet hook* is another useful item to have handy in your workbasket. There will be times when you end up with a bit of yarn too short to finish off with a needle. It isn't desirable but it can happen. Leave the thread hanging loose on the back, and use a crochet hook to catch it under several already-worked stitches.

A crochet hook will also come in handy if you have to pick out stitches in any area. If you're left with short ends just use the crochet hook to draw them back under adjoining stitches (on the wrong side, of course).

A *seam ripper* and *tweezers* are also useful for the times when you will be forced to rip out stitches—either because of a mistake in working or because the color or type of stitch may not please you when you see it actually in place.

It's a good idea to slip a small crochet hook or tapestry needle under a few stitches at a time to raise them off the canvas while you cut them with your embroidery scissors, or better yet, with the seam ripper. After all stitches have been cut, the easiest way to remove them is to pick them out with the tweezer. I find those with handles most comfortable to use.

A heavy *carpet and buttonhole thread* will also be useful for mending—for sooner or later you may have to mend one or more of your canvas threads if you accidentally cut them while ripping out a bit of yarn. You can repair the damaged canvas by weaving in another thread—either carpet and buttonhole thread in the canvas color, or an unraveled thread from another piece of canvas of the same size. Starting a few holes away from the damage, weave in and out following the over and under pattern of the canvas. Do this back and forth, and be sure the loose ends of the repair threads end up on the back of the work.

A *yardstick* and *12-inch ruler* are needed to measure your project on the canvas. A flexible *tape measure* is needed to check sizes when you don't have a flat surface, as with pillows and lamp bases.

Any canvas will tend to ravel if the edges aren't finished off in some manner. You can hem back some edges, using a zigzag machine stitch, but some sort of *binding* is preferable if you're going to do work with an embroidery frame and/or do your own blocking. You can use masking tape, but be sure it's at least an inch or more wide so the edges are well covered. Surgical adhesive tape is even better as it will not come off when the canvas is wet during blocking. Fabric bias binding, machine-stitched in place, is strongest and most durable.

Long T-pins come in handy for pinning at various stages of construction (as shown in photograph 41, page 294, for instance), and are much better than ordinary straight pins.

Long-pointed push pins are essential if you are doing your own blocking.

White glue is another essential that you will need to keep canvas edges from raveling wherever you trim them, as well as for finishing off many projects. Use a white glue such as Sobo or Soft Grip, which are waterproof, transparent when dry, and do not penetrate or stain yarn or canvas. (Do *not* use Elmer's or other water-soluble glues.)

Needlepoint Designs

Creating or adapting designs for your needlepoint can be very rewarding. It gives you the greatest possible freedom either to coordinate furnishings (by borrowing a motif from your wallpaper, for example) or to accent them with totally different designs. Many people, unless they have studied art, are timid about designing and selecting colors for their needlepoint, although this is no more difficult than selecting home furnishings, accessories and clothing, which they've been doing for years.

Making your own design will also greatly reduce the cost of your needlepoint. If you compare the prices of blank canvas and pre-designed canvas, it will be obvious where the cost lies (though this is as it should be since you are paying for creative work).

Finding Designs

You can find suitable designs for needlepoint anywhere—in your own home, in magazines and books, in fabrics and gift wrapping papers, in post cards and greeting cards. Children's coloring books and children's original drawings provide great projects for beginners.

What you want, especially at the start, are designs with simple outlines and not too much detail, set in a fairly large background area. The large background will enable each motif and the various textured stitches to show up properly.

Remember that the needlepoint stitches themselves will create details of texture and shading so your design should be kept as free of detail as possible.

Stitching effects may also be created with color. A color wheel from an art supply store can be useful, but for most projects you will want colors that blend with your decor or add a bit of accent color. The most important thing to remember is that combining too many colors and kinds of stitches will give a "busy" effect. Simplicity is best, especially at the start. Later, experience will enable you to judge your effects.

You can create abstract designs by cutting or tearing pieces of paper and spreading them out on a piece of graph paper the size of your overall project. Move the pieces around until you like the way they look, then trace around them. You can try out various color combinations by cutting shapes out of color pages of old magazines.

Found objects, such as shells, stones, gemstones and metal objects, as well as leather and fabric appliqués, can be used in combination with stitches to achieve modern designs.

You will also find many interesting design ideas in books on interior decorating.

Transferring Designs to Canvas

Once you have selected your design, there are several methods of transferring it to your canvas.

In order to center your design, you must first find the center of your canvas. Fold it in half lengthwise and then across the width; the point at which the fold lines cross is your center. Mark this with an *indelible* neutral color. It's a good idea also to mark the outer edges of the whole pillow, chair seat, or whatever. (You should have a straight border of extra canvas at least several inches wide on all sides, as described on page264.)

If the design is the correct size, it can quickly be transferred to the canvas.

First place a piece of tracing paper over the design. Hold it in place with masking tape, then trace the complete design.

Now you will need a piece of graph paper, which is ruled off into squares like your canvas. Graph paper comes in many sizes—#10, or 100 squares to the square inch, is most common. Choose the size of paper that best matches your canvas. Note that you can eliminate the graph paper and transfer the design directly from the tracing paper to the canvas. But the graph paper squares approximate the canvas squares, and thus are better to work from.

Place the tracing paper with its design

outline on top of the graph paper. Slip a piece of carbon paper between the tracing and graph paper, with carbon side facing the graph paper. (I prefer dressmaker's carbon because it doesn't smudge.) Trace over the design outline again. It will now be transferred to the graph paper.

You will have to make slight changes in curved and slanted lines to adjust them to the squares. This can be done on the canvas as you work, but it's a good idea to figure it out beforehand on the graph paper. You can also fill in colored areas to see how the completed work will appear.

When the graph paper outline looks perfect to you, go over it with a heavy black line so it will show up well through the canvas mesh.

If, at this point, your design needs to be enlarged or reduced in size, there are several ways of doing this.

The quickest, and also the most expensive, is to have a *photostat* made to the correct size. Be sure to ask for a positive print (black lines on white) as this is easiest to see. Use carbon paper to transfer the design to graph paper, as above.

Another method of enlarging or reducing is by *squaring*. First mark off your design into squares. (Use the original, or make a tracing of it.) Draw a grid of squares over the complete design. On another sheet of paper the size of your finished design, mark off an identical number of squares—if your paper is larger, each square will be larger; if your paper is smaller, each square will be smaller. Then, square by square, copy the drawing outline from the original grid to the larger (or smaller) one. Use carbon paper to transfer the design to graph paper, as above.

Or you can invest in a *pantograph* which really speeds up enlarging and reducing designs. A wooden pantograph costs about $5.00 at art supply stores. Directions come with it, but essentially it works so that as you trace the original design, another pencil

is set in motion simultaneously, copying the design in a larger or smaller proportion. Use carbon paper to transfer the design to graph paper, as above.

For all of these methods you may want to invest in a clear plastic sheet, called Mylar, instead of tracing paper. Sold by the sheet at art and engineering supply stores, Mylar is transparent and will not tear. The same sheet is also available overprinted with squares in various sizes.

Now you are ready to transfer the design to your canvas.

Place graph paper (or original tracing paper) under the canvas on a flat surface and hold them in position with masking tape.

Follow the graph outlines and copy them onto the canvas with *permanent* ink; this is most important because your ink must never run and stain your yarn. There are some permanent felt-tip marking pens on the market, but be sure to test the ink to make sure it won't run in water or silicone spray. Use a light or neutral color of ink so the outline won't show through the finished work. (Do not use lead pencil, as it smears the yarn.)

You can also paint on your design outline with acrylic. Use the smallest nylon brush for this (other types are too soft to work well on canvas), and be sure to thin the acrylic paint with water so it goes on easily and does not clog the canvas mesh.

You may wish to paint the various areas of color onto your canvas, but this isn't necessary if the outlines are clear and you have colored your graph to guide you. In any case, the acrylic colors will only give a general idea as the wool colors will not exactly match them.

Measuring for Later Blocking

Later, when your needlepointing is completed, you can do your own blocking and thus save a great deal of money. Blocking methods are described on pages 264 to 265, but in order to use them you must measure your canvas now before it has been worked.

The reason for blocking is that the pull of the yarn in stitching distorts the canvas—that is, pulls it off the center so the sides end up slanted instead of squared off.

Some stitches distort the canvas more than others, but unless your canvas is laced onto a frame (as described on pages 15 to 17) all stitches will cause some distortion.

Blocking will restore the canvas to its original shape, but if your design is irregular in shape—anything that does not have squared outer edges—you must make an outline of that original shape to guide you later. (This is not needed for square or rectangular designs, as their outer edges can be lined up with the guidelines on your blocking board.)

After you have outlined your design on the canvas, mark center guidelines from side to side and from top to bottom of the entire canvas. An easy way is to fold the canvas in half in both directions and then mark along the fold lines, either with an indelible marker or with a colored basting thread. The marking should extend beyond the edges of your project, clear out to the border of your canvas.

Next, place your marked canvas on a larger square of heavy wrapping paper (or other sturdy paper) and draw on it the outline of your *entire* canvas. Then extend those horizontal and vertical registry lines on your canvas clear out to the edges of the wrapping paper. Put the paper aside for later use when the needlepointing is complete and ready for blocking.

Working Tips

When you are ready to start needlepointing, these small working tips will help make the stitching go smoothly.

1. Figure the length of your yarn. The determining factor is the fineness of the canvas: the finer the canvas, the shorter the thread should be. This is because the yarn will be passing through many more canvas meshes per square inch, and a long thread will become frayed. For very fine canvas 12 inches of yarn may be enough. For medium size canvases (#10, #12 or #14) your working yarn should not be longer than 30 to 36 inches. There are a few stitches that cover extended areas quickly and do not pass through every hole. With these, a somewhat longer yarn may be used, but it should not be long enough to tangle. I find that cutting a hank of Paternayan Persian yarn at both ends gives a good length of working yarn; this is the length I refer to in giving yarn requirements for individual stitches.

2. Wool yarns, especially Persian, have a rough and smooth direction. Always thread the needle so the yarn pulls through in the smooth direction. To feel the smooth direction of your yarn before threading the needle, run your thumb and forefinger down the yarn in both directions. Never fold yarn in half to use because then half would run in the rough direction.

3. To thread a needle with yarn, fold the yarn end over the pointed end of the needle; then pinch the yarn tightly between thumb and forefinger and withdraw the needle. Still holding the folded yarn tightly pinched, ease the needle eye down over it. When the tip of the fold is threaded you can easily pull the rest of the yarn through.

4. Start work with a fairly long fold-over and slide the needle toward the loose end of the yarn every few stitches. This is important to keep your steel needle from wearing the yarn thin from constant pulling in any one spot.

5. Most stitches tend to twist the working yarn, which can be a nuisance. To untwist it, give your needle a quarter- or half-turn away from you (in the opposite direction of the twist) every four or five stitches or so. (This rapidly becomes automatic.) Or you

can untwist your yarn from time to time by letting it hang straight down, needle and all, and unwind itself.

6. When working for a long period of time, particularly in warm weather, your needle seems to slow down and not pass through the work so quickly. This isn't imagination—it really does happen because the moisture on your fingers causes oxidation. This can be corrected by passing the needle through one of those little strawberries attached to many pincushions; these are filled with a polishing material that will restore your needle's smoothness.

7. When starting work on an empty canvas, leave a short tail end of yarn (one or two inches) hanging underneath as you pull your yarn up to take the first stitch. Then with your free hand hold the tail end down flat, and in the path of your work, so your first stitches will anchor it in place.

Or you can start with the waste knot method. Here you knot the tail end and insert the needle from the right side to the underside of the canvas so the knot remains on the surface. Start your stitching about an inch away and in the same path as the starting stitch. As you work your first stitches will anchor the long tail. When you reach the knot cut it off and continue stitching.

To start a new length of yarn next to some previous work, simply run the needle under four or five adjacent stitches on the underside before your needle emerges to start stitching.

8. Finish off in the same way—by running your needle under a few adjacent stitches on the underside or back under the last few stitches you have taken. Don't start and finish off in the identical place, or lumps on the right side will result that will remain even after blocking. Stagger the starting and finishing off so they are as evenly spaced as possible. Clip off any dangling ends as you go so they won't tangle.

It is best to finish off your yarn and start again in a new place rather than to carry the working yarn under the back of the canvas. Threads carried under can cause lumps as well as puckering.

9. Try to keep your yarn tension firm and even—not so slack that the stitches sag, or pulled so tight that the bare canvas shows through. With practice you will fall into an easy rhythm with just the right tension.

10. When working with several colors, keep separate needles threaded with your various colors—ready to pick up and work.

11. Always check to make sure that your slanted stitches all slant in the same direction wherever they appear on your canvas (unless, of course, you are varying directions for a special effect).

12. When working on a large canvas, roll up the canvas to the point you're working on, and pin the rolled section with large safety pins through the meshes at the sides. Roll from the underside up: this will help keep the surface clean, as you will then be holding the underside as you work.

13. Usually it's best to needlepoint the design areas and then fill in the background around them. Backgrounds should be started at the outer edges of the canvas and worked in toward the design areas.

However, you needn't work the background to completion, which can be a bore. I like to start background work around one completed design area and work as long as it's enjoyable. Then I go on to work another part of the design.

14. When your work is finished, it's a good idea to hold your canvas up to the light to reveal any canvas spots that may have been skipped. This easily happens when working on very fine canvas, or in a combination of Petit Point and Gros Point, and it can easily be corrected at this stage by filling in any bare places.

15. Where the finished size will be important—as with pieces meant for upholstery or for clothing—be sure to allow an extra

half-inch in both directions for the pulling-in of the canvas when the stitches are worked. Check measurements carefully after blocking. At this time you may have to add an extra row to the edge if necessary. If you need an extra row or two in one direction only, you can generally achieve this in the blocking, by pulling a bit. (The piece will become a bit narrower in the other direction, but this may not matter.) For very large pieces, allow proportionately more for pulling-in.

Working with a Frame

While needlepointing is generally done in the hand, and a frame is not needed for the actual stitching, a frame can be very useful if you are working on a large project like a wall hanging, a rug or even a chair seat. Such projects are too large to carry around conveniently, so it's better to have your canvas set up on its frame ready to work on whenever you choose.

Photograph 8 shows a piece of evenweave laced onto a simple four-sided Slate Frame, as these are called. There are a number of these on the market all of basically the same construction. As you see, the top and bottom cross pieces are round, enabling the canvas to be rolled up at either end as you finish needlepointing and move to an unworked canvas area. The canvas is tautly laced to the side pieces, which are squared off.

As photograph 8 shows, all canvas edges are reinforced with twill tape to take the strain off the lacing.

At the top and bottom of the frame the rollers have a piece of tape attached. Your canvas binding is sewn onto this to hold it firm. Match the center points of the roller tape and your canvas and pin together, using long T-pins (described on page 10) which are strong enough to go through tape and canvas. Start at the center and work out to the sides. Then with a strong thread like carpet and buttonhole thread sew the canvas and roller tapes together. Start with a small

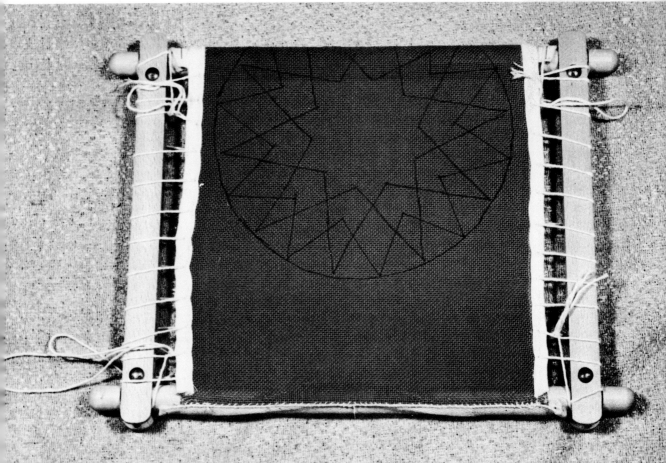

8

knot at the center and work out to the sides, overcasting closely and stretching the canvas slightly as you go.

When top and bottom are firmly sewn onto the rollers, you are ready to lace up the sides. Roll up the end you will not be working on (shown at the top of photograph 8) and attach the side pieces to the rollers as directed for your particular frame. (Usually this is a screw or peg arrangement.)

A strong string is best for lacing the canvas sides to the frame. Do not detach from the ball. Thread a curved upholstery needle,

as shown in photograph 9, and pull through just enough string to start working. Insert the needle into the canvas binding from the top down, bringing the needle back over the wooden side frame. Continue down the side at one-inch intervals, pulling free a little extra string as you go. Leave about two feet of string at each end, and cut away from the ball. Complete both sides in the same way.

Give a final tightening to the frame screws (or pegs) so the canvas is held very firm. Now pull up the strings, making sure they run straight around the frame sides.

9

Photograph 10 shows how to fasten off the string at the ends. Anchor the string around the corner crossbars, then use a crochet hook and make a slip knot through the *underside* of the second lacing string.

Photograph 10 shows the two loops of the slip knot being made. A third long loop is taken and remains hanging free, as shown in photograph 11. This knot is easily untied by pulling at the free end. When all four ends are tied the canvas is ready for work.

Whenever you expect not to be working for a time, untie the corner knots and loosen the frame screws a bit to release tension on the canvas. Tighten again when you're ready to work.

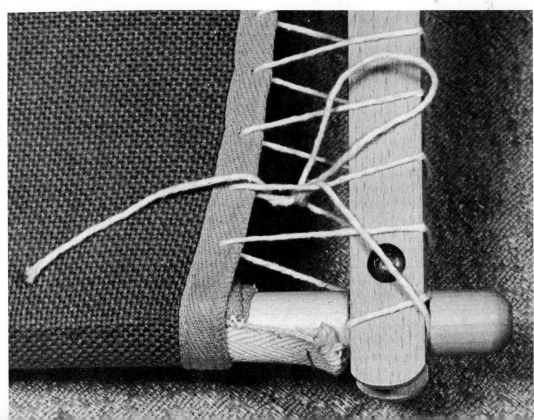

12

A small folding frame support has come on the market as this book is being written. This great invention is called the "Needle Easel," and is available in needlework shops and through mail order houses.

As photograph 12 shows, the canvas is mounted onto a frame which is firmly held by the easel. The easel is adjustable in height and angle for any sitting position, and can be used in a chair or sofa, or in bed. As it folds flat for easy carrying, it can also be used while traveling.

How to Use This Book

In the book's second section—"Dictionary of Stitches"—you will find complete directions, in text and working diagrams, for over 200 needlepoint stitches. The stitches are arranged in alphabetical order and numbered in sequence.

Throughout the book all the stitches are

referred to by number as well as name—No. 9 Back Stitch, for instance, or No. 161 Plaited Edge Stitch—to make it easy for you to refer back to their original instructions.

Read the stitch instructions as well as studying the diagrams, as helpful hints are included in the text to make work easier.

Most stitch directions call for #12 mono canvas, since this is a good size for the beginner to work on, and a full strand of Persian yarn which will cover the canvas nicely. Where a stitch calls for penelope canvas, this is noted, along with the yarn requirement to cover one square inch so you can judge the amount of yarn you will need for your project.

The effect of a stitch will vary on different sizes of canvas and according to individual working tension, so be sure to do a test swatch before embarking on a project. If you don't like the effect on #12 canvas, try it on another size.

It's also a good idea to practice a new stitch and master it before applying it to your project. Mistakes are sometimes hard to pick out when the entire background is worked, and it's better to be letter-perfect. You can keep a looseleaf notebook of your practice and test canvases. Make notes on the side tape, or staple the canvas onto thin cardboard. An ordinary hole puncher will go through both tape and canvas so they fit onto the notebook rings.

Do try all the stitches. Some of the results will be surprising, since diagrams can't show the beauty of the finished effect. Eventually you will find that you prefer certain stitches, but the real needleworker is always on the lookout for new and special stitches to give a particular textural or decorative effect to a project.

The basic stitches are identified in the index by an asterisk. If you are new to needlepoint, start with these. Another help is Appendix A, in which all the stitches are categorized according to their best usage—that is, for a background, border, shading, and so forth.

Left-handers will find special directions for all stitches needing them. (Stitches worked in two directions—both left and right—need no special instructions for left-handers.) There are two basic changes in directions for left-handers:

When working a line, place a mirror next to the diagrams and work according to the mirror image, reversing the words right and left in the text. Another method is to place tracing paper over the diagrams and copy them, then turn over the tracing paper and work according to the reversed directions shown.

When working a stitch that moves from top to bottom of the canvas, turn the diagrams upside down and reverse the words right and left in the text.

Now, on to the stitches. I hope you will have fun with them.

2

Dictionary of Stitches

1 · ALGERIAN EYE STITCH NO. 1 (*Star Stitch, Eye Stitch*)

CANVAS: #12 mono   NEEDLE: Size 18

TO COVER ONE SQUARE INCH: 1 length Persian yarn (when worked over
2 canvas threads, not including
Back Stitches)

NUMBER OF THREADS: 1 full strand

This stitch is very simple and can be worked over one, two or three canvas threads. The two-thread eye is probably easiest to practice on.

The starting point doesn't matter too much, except for working over an area. The main thing to remember is that the needle always emerges on the outside and is inserted in the center to complete all stitches. This is for neatness and ease of work, since a needle emerging in the center would split threads already there and give an untidy appearance. Thus, all even numbers are in the center (as indicated by the letter E when there isn't enough room for the numbers).

To start: hold a short end of yarn underneath the canvas and towards the upper left (the direction the work will take). Left-handed people working in reverse direction hold the short end from middle right to lower left, where they start work.

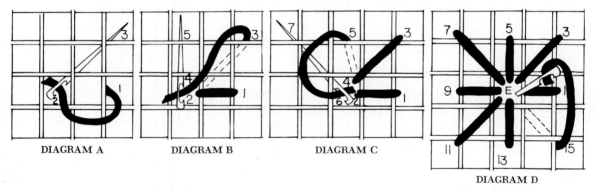

DIAGRAM A   DIAGRAM B   DIAGRAM C

DIAGRAM D

DIAGRAM A shows the work begun, with the yarn emerging at 1, inserted at 2, then emerging at 3. DIAGRAM B shows the second stitch in progress, with the yarn emerging at 3, inserted in what will be the center at 4, and emerging at 5. DIAGRAM C shows the needle inserted in the center again at 6, and emerging at 7. DIAGRAM D shows the final stitch that completes a single Algerian Eye.

This makes a nice little isolated stitch that gives a slight raised effect when surrounded by flat stitches. When covering an entire area, it may be worked horizontally or diagonally, whichever is most comfortable.

To work horizontally: complete only the first four stitches, through number 8, in the center on DIAGRAM D. From there, start a new eye to the left and work the top from 1 through 8, as before. Keep working to the left, leaving bottom half incomplete, until the required amount of canvas is covered. The return journey starts on the last eye at the end of the row, with the needle finishing the bottom of the eye from 9 to 16. The needle then moves right to fill in the bottom of the next eye, and so on to the end of the row.

To work diagonally, see DIAGRAM E. Here the first eye is completely worked, through number 16, in the center. Then the needle passes underneath (following the dotted line) and emerges at 17, directly below 1, to start the next eye. This is worked halfway up, through number 26 in the center. Then the needle moves up to work half the next eye, numbers 27 to 35, as shown in upper left in DIAGRAM E, and so on to the top of the row.

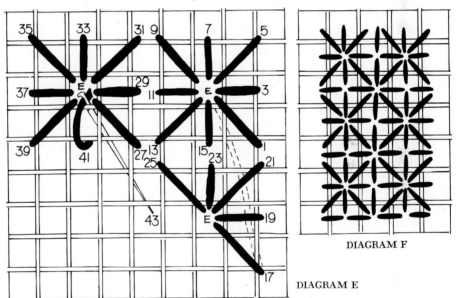

DIAGRAM F

DIAGRAM E

DIAGRAM E also shows the process of the down journey, as the eye is completed from 37 through 42 in the center. The needle then passes down to 43, to work the bottom of the eye below it, and so on down the row.

DIAGRAM F shows an area of Eye Stitches worked with No. 9 Back Stitches between them. This can be done just for the effect; it is also a way of covering the canvas threads exposed when the Eye Stitches are pulled too tightly. The Back Stitches may be worked in contrasting color.

2 · ALGERIAN EYE STITCH NO. 2

CANVAS: #12 mono   NEEDLE: Size 18
TO COVER ONE SQUARE INCH: 1½ lengths Persian yarn
NUMBER OF THREADS: 1 full strand

This is almost the same as No. 1 Algerian Eye Stitch, the difference being the number of stitches in each pattern. The needle goes into every opening around the outside edge rather than into every other one, as the diagram shows.

This makes a nice isolated stitch which is effective for filling as well. By giving a little yank each time the yarn is inserted in the center, a little opening is formed to produce an unusual and interesting look.

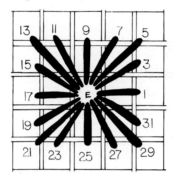

3 · ALGERIAN EYE DAISY STITCH NO. 1

CANVAS: #12 mono   NEEDLE: Size 18
TO COVER ONE SQUARE INCH: 1 length Persian yarn
NUMBER OF THREADS: 2

This is a combination of two modified Eye Stitches; the difference is that they do not make square patterns.

It can be worked quickly on the diagonal, but is probably easiest to work horizontally from right to left. Left-handers should reverse the pattern and work from left to right, beginning at the upper left and working half around one daisy before starting the adjacent one.

Begin at the upper right and work as in DIAGRAM A, which shows the first stitch completed and the second one in progress, with the needle inserted at 4 and emerging at 5 to start the next stitch in the circle. DIAGRAM B shows the first half of the daisy being completed. (E stands for all even numbers inserted at the center.)

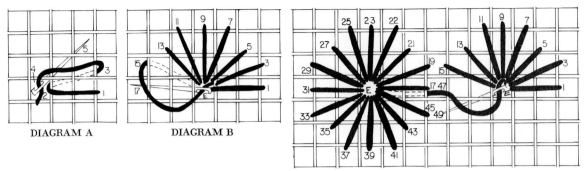

DIAGRAM A   DIAGRAM B

DIAGRAM C

In DIAGRAM C, moving from the right, we see that the top halves of two daisies have been completed. And on the return journey the bottom halves are done. The numbers show the sequence. After the second daisy is completed, the needle emerges where it originally started (at 17 in this case), in position to work the bottom half of the first daisy.

As the stitches are not square, it is often necessary to work smaller daisy patterns to fill empty spaces between the large ones. One method of doing this is shown in DIAGRAM D: the small daisies are worked just like the large ones and spaced so their outside edges fit snugly between them. Always complete a back and forth journey of large daisies before filling in with smaller ones. This should give complete coverage. However, you may also add small No. 9 Back Stitches between the large daisies, as shown at A in DIAGRAM D.

DIAGRAM E shows a completed area. For a different effect, try working small daisies (and optional No. 9 Back Stitches) in a contrasting color.

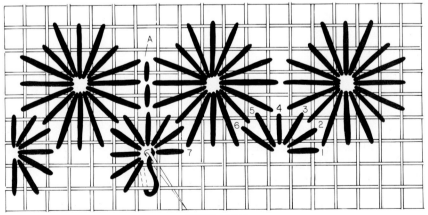

DIAGRAM D

DIAGRAM E

4 · ALGERIAN EYE DAISY STITCH NO. 2

CANVAS: #12 mono   NEEDLE: Size 18

TO COVER ONE SQUARE INCH: Just over 1 length Persian yarn

NUMBER OF THREADS: 2

This variation is in the small daisy used to fill the open spaces. It is almost necessary to use No. 9 Back Stitches with this for a finished appearance, especially if the yarn tightens up around the center opening as it tends to do.

DIAGRAM A shows the bottom half of a No. 3 Algerian Eye Daisy Stitch completed with the small daisies being worked. DIAGRAM B shows a completed area worked with No. 9 Back Stitches for full coverage. You can get many different effects by combining colors or shades of one color in individual stitches, or by working small daisies and Back Stitches in a contrasting color.

DIAGRAM A

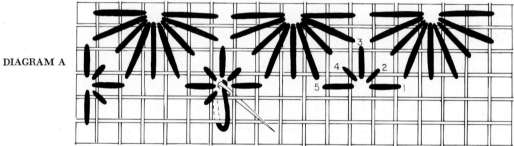

DIAGRAM B

5 · ALGERIAN EYE DAISY STITCH NO. 3

CANVAS: #12 mono   NEEDLE: Size 18

TO COVER ONE SQUARE INCH: Just over 1 length Persian yarn

NUMBER OF THREADS: 2

These daisies are worked on the diagonal. A combination of No. 59 Italian Cross Stitch and No. 11 Basketweave Stitch is used to fill.

Start the daisy at the lower right, with stitch as in DIAGRAM A. The pattern is worked alternately up and down so there are no special directions for left-handers. When working large areas, complete the first daisy before continuing.

The second daisy starts at stitch 17, to begin the second row which works diagonally up. Go halfway around the circle, through stitch 25, then continue with 26, and so on to the top of the row. The lower half of the daisy is worked on the return journey. Give the yarn a little yank after each stitch—this will leave four intersecting threads between each daisy.

Fill these spaces with No. 59 Italian Cross Stitches. In the final step, two small No. 11 Basketweave Stitches are worked on the four sides of the daisy, each slanting in the same direction as the stitches they lie between, as shown at A. (If the Basketweave Stitches fill in too snugly, work them with one less thread.)

DIAGRAM B shows a section of the completed pattern. Here too, combining colors can be really effective.

DIAGRAM A

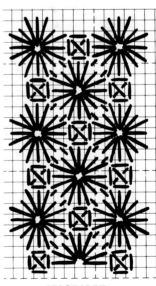

DIAGRAM B

6 · ALGERIAN STITCH, FILLING

CANVAS: #12 mono   NEEDLE: Size 18
TO COVER ONE SQUARE INCH: 1 length Persian yarn
NUMBER OF THREADS: 1 full strand

This is an upright stitch that gives a nice variety in texture and covers an area quickly.

DIAGRAM A shows the first stitch being worked. The left-hander can follow instructions as given since it is worked in both directions.

Beginning at 1, the needle is inserted at 2, and emerges at 3 (on the same level as 1). DIAGRAM B shows two finished stitches and a third being completed at 6, as the needle emerges at 7 to start the next group on a lower level. DIAGRAM C shows the second group of three stitches being completed. In order to raise the position of the next stitch, the needle emerges at 13 to start again on the upper level. A second row is worked from right to left into the base of the stitches on the first row.

DIAGRAM D shows a completed area with upper and lower edges finished with smaller stitches.

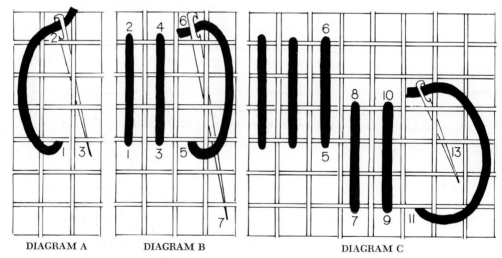

DIAGRAM A   DIAGRAM B   DIAGRAM C

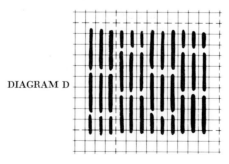

DIAGRAM D

7 · ALGERIAN STITCH, PLAITED

CANVAS: #12 mono   NEEDLE: Size 18

TO COVER ONE SQUARE INCH: About ½ length Persian yarn

NUMBER OF THREADS: 2

This is really a closer No. 116 Herringbone Stitch.

DIAGRAM A shows work beginning at the left edge at 1. Work moves back and forth, so left-handers follow directions as given.

From 1, the needle is inserted at 2, and emerges at 3. Next, the needle is inserted at 4, finally emerging at 5. The entire row is worked in this manner—alternating between upper and lower levels—until the edge is reached. Moving to the second row depends on whether the first row ends on the upper or lower level. If it ends on the upper level, the next row starts with the needle emerging below the lower edge of the previous row. When working from right to left, the needle is inserted five rows up and to the left of the yarn, and emerges two threads to the right. The same action is used on the lower level of this row. The needle on the upper level passes through the same openings as the stitches on the previous row. The third row is a repeat of the first; the fourth row is a repeat of the second.

Spaces left between rows can be filled with No. 9 Back Stitches worked over two threads in the same openings as the previously worked stitches, as shown in DIAGRAM B.

DIAGRAM A

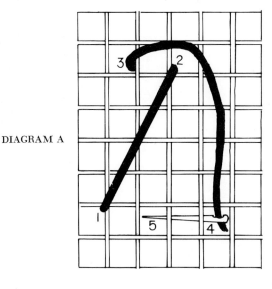

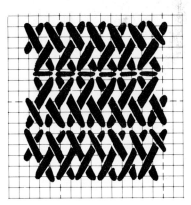

DIAGRAM B

8 · ASTRAKHAN VELVET STITCH (*Velvet Stitch*)

CANVAS: #12 mono   NEEDLE: Size 18

TO COVER ONE SQUARE INCH: Amount of Persian yarn varies with size of loops

NUMBER OF THREADS: 2

This stitch is excellent for making pile rugs as loops are formed and tied down very securely. Choose a yarn that fluffs out well and is strong enough to make a firm foundation. When the loops are cut and fluffed out, base stitches are no longer visible.

Before starting, practice the No. 47 Cross Stitch. Unlike most stitches, this is best worked from bottom to top because the long loops left on each row are awkward to keep out of the way if worked otherwise. Before you start, make sure your work is in the most comfortable position, because you can't change directions in the middle. Left-handers should start at the lower right and reverse the directions.

DIAGRAM A shows work beginning at the left, with the needle emerging at 1. Leaving a loop, the needle is inserted at 2, and emerges at 3. The loops can vary in length, but it is best to leave them longer than necessary, as they can always be trimmed. You can use a ruler or knitting needle to control their length, but once you are comfortable with the stitch, you can make uniform loops simply by using the thumb of your free hand to hold them. DIAGRAM B shows the needle inserted at 4 (in the same place as 2), and emerging at 5. Keep holding the loop while pulling the yarn up snugly. Next, DIAGRAM C shows the needle inserted at 6, and emerging at 7, in the same opening as 2 and 4. This completes the stitch, secures the loop, and puts you in position to start the next stitch.

DIAGRAM D shows three stitches completed. DIAGRAM E shows an area with part of the loops cut. Note that the stitch is also good for fringing the edges of a rug. If used for fringe, leave longer loops.

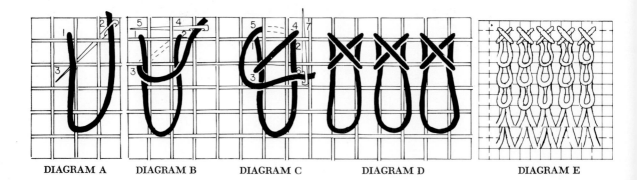

DIAGRAM A   DIAGRAM B   DIAGRAM C   DIAGRAM D   DIAGRAM E

9 · BACK STITCH

Because of its versatility, this stitch is used in all types of needle-work. It is a nice outline stitch, and can turn a corner or a curve nicely and change direction with ease. No measurements are given as amounts vary according to use. Normally you would use a full strand, but when working between stitches to outline an area, use only one thread of Persian yarn, or two threads of embroidery floss.

Normally it is worked over one or two canvas threads, but if you change directions, you also have to change the number of threads worked over. In DIAGRAM A, the needle emerges at 1, is inserted at 2, and reemerges at 3. This action is continued along the line. Left-handers should turn the diagrams upside down and work from left to right. DIAGRAM B shows the Back Stitch worked over two threads, with dotted lines showing the needle carried under four threads.

DIAGRAM C shows the action of the needle when turning corners and forming curves. Turning the canvas as you go, keep working from right to left.

This stitch is more important than it looks. Some stitches don't cover adequately, and the Back Stitch can be used to fill in open space and accent it. Another advantage is that it can be used to distinguish between shapes where colors may be too close to do so—as with flower petals. For this, work with finer yarn or embroidery floss in a contrasting color, and work lines right over existing stitches.

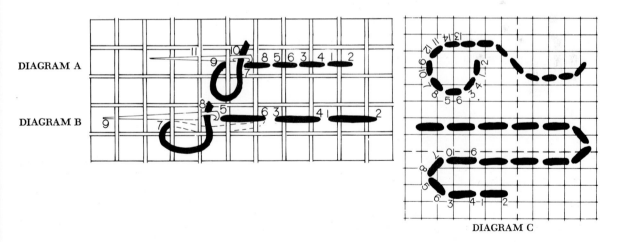

DIAGRAM A

DIAGRAM B

DIAGRAM C

10 · BARGELLO (*Florentine Stitch, Flame Stitch*)

CANVAS: #12 mono   NEEDLE: Size 18
NUMBER OF THREADS: 4

It is impossible to describe all of Bargello in one small section as there are so many varieties and patterns. This will start you off with the basic principles and some motifs to give an idea of the range.

Originally Bargello work was done on fine evenweave linen, with stitches as long as ten threads. Today it is done mostly on larger canvas, and stitches are rarely as long. The canvas and needle size suggested above are good for practice, but the finer the canvas the more effective the stitch will be. Any canvas larger than #10 mono will be difficult to cover. Bargello work needs fluffy yarn because the stitches are upright, covering only the horizontal threads. Stranded yarns, such as Persian or Appleton, are best although embroidery floss may be used on fine canvas. (Twisted yarns, such as mercerized cotton or rug wool, are not successful because with even the slightest tension, the canvas will show.)

Yarn requirements vary depending on a number of factors: the number of colors in the pattern; the size of canvas; whether you are going from dark to light with a complete color repeat—that is, from light to dark to light again; and whether the design is a line repeat or a pattern repeat. For a reliable yarn estimate, work a sample piece. First, outline the shape on canvas. Mark the center by folding it in half lengthwise, then crosswise, using the outlined shape as a guide. If you are doing a continuous line pattern, center the pattern on the canvas both horizontally and vertically and work an entire line of the pattern, starting at the center and working out in both directions. As you work, keep track of each length of yarn used. (Either leave the ends out in back and count afterwards, or keep notes as you go.) Then, starting at the left edge, work through one entire length of yarn in successive rows through the entire color range of your pattern. After working the entire color range, measure the length of your canvas. If the pattern is two inches long and your canvas is fourteen inches long, you will need seven times as much yarn of each color as you used in the original complete pattern row. (Once the pattern is established on the first row, all succeeding rows are worked from the edges straight across the canvas.) If your pattern consists of repeating motifs, work one motif in the center of the canvas. Measure how many will cover your canvas, then multiply your yarns by that number.

One of the important factors in any pattern is the stitch proportion. The one used most commonly today is four-two, which means that stitches are four canvas threads long, and the needle moves two threads up or down when changing levels. This is shown in DIAGRAM A: the needle emerges at 1, is inserted at 2 and emerges again at 3. DIAGRAM B shows the pattern starting with the needle emerging at 3, being inserted at 4 and reemerging at 5. Most Bargello work is symmetrical, and DIAGRAM C shows this sample pattern completed—after reaching a peak at 6, the two descending stitches match the two rising ones. DIAGRAM D shows how changing proportions change the pattern's appearance—gentle slopes become round curves.

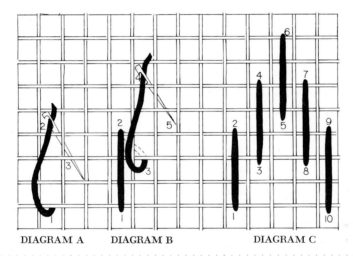

DIAGRAM A   DIAGRAM B   DIAGRAM C

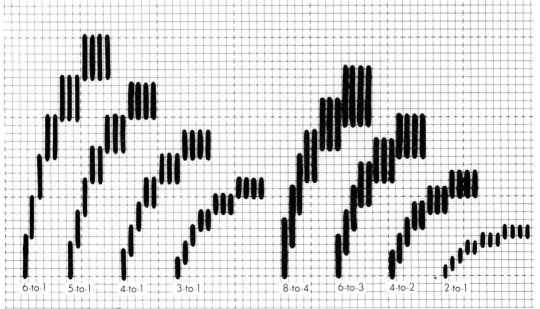

6-to-1   5-to-1   4-to-1   3-to-1   8-to-4   6-to-3   4-to-2   2-to-1

DIAGRAM D

Let's start with the motif in DIAGRAM E. This is a good beginning, as it contains both points and curves to practice on. As the work moves in both directions, left-handers can follow the directions as given. For ease of working you may find it comfortable to turn the work upside down after working the first half. A close look at the pattern—called a cartoon in Bargello work—shows that the entire pattern—from top to bottom—covers twenty horizontal canvas threads. Thus, the horizontal center runs between lines 10 and 11. The central scallop is six stitches wide, thus the vertical center line runs down the center of the scallop (with three stitches on each side).

DIAGRAM E shows the first journey, in which you work the downward half of the pattern—stitches 1 to 27.

Particularly on the first row, it helps to lay a ruler across the cartoon to keep your place. I usually work out a design on graph paper, and check off each part of the pattern as it is worked. It's also a good idea to pencil in guidelines across your canvas. If you don't come out on these lines, you'll catch the mistake at once and rip out a few stitches, instead of a whole area. It is also easy to slant a stitch without noticing; the guidelines will help you catch it quickly. Remember that a firm, not-too-tight stitch is best; you may have to loosen the tension slightly to cover the canvas.

To start stitch 1, the needle emerges between the sixth and

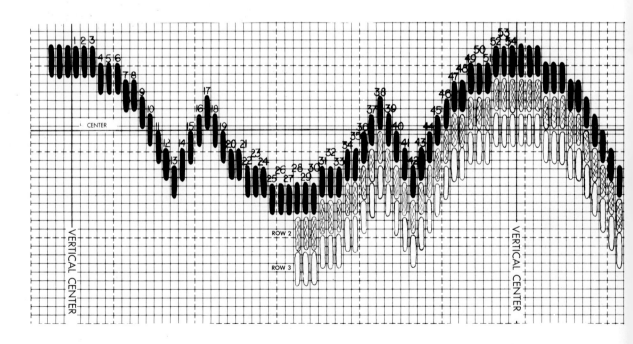

seventh threads above the center line and is inserted four threads above. Stitches 2 and 3 are worked alongside it. Then the stitch level is lowered two threads, and stitches 4, 5 and 6 are worked side by side. The level is lowered two threads as before, and stitches 7 and 8 are worked side by side. Then, lowering the level with each stitch, work stitches 9 to 13; 13 is the low point here. Stitches 14 to 17 are worked in a rising pattern, matching the levels of stitches 9 to 12. Stitches 18 and 19 start descending again—each matching the levels of 15 and 16. Again the level is lowered, and stitches 20 and 21 are worked side by side. The level is lowered, and 22, 23 and 24 are worked side by side. Once again the level is lowered, and stitches 25, 26 and 27 are worked side by side to complete one-half of the motif.

The full motif is completed by working stitches 28 to 54. As DIAGRAM E shows, these are exactly the reverse of stitches 1 to 27.

Remember that stitches always cover four horizontal canvas threads; the level always rises or descends two threads. The work is repeated until you reach the end of the canvas. As long as the middle scallop is centered, it doesn't matter how wide your area on each side of it—it will always be symmetrical no matter where the work stops.

Successive rows, worked identically under (and over) the first, may be in contrast colors or in shades of the same color (see lines 2 and 3 on DIAGRAM E).

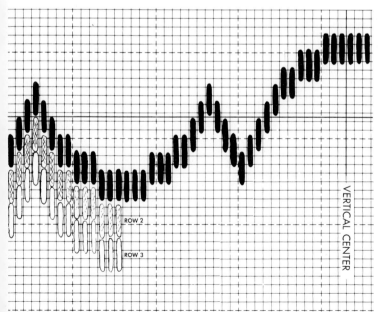

DIAGRAM E

A few other cartoons are included here. DIAGRAM F is similar to DIAGRAM E, but instead of descending it mounts to a still higher point. DIAGRAM G shows intersecting zigzag lines forming a repeated diamond pattern. This is a good allover pattern to be started at the center and worked outwards, or it can be an isolated piece.

Those interested in learning more about Bargello work should consult *Florentine Embroidery* by Barbara L. Snook (Charles Scribner's Sons, New York, 1947). This has many patterns to work and some very contemporary ideas. You can also buy design cartoons put out by the American Crewel Studio. These are diagrammed on graph paper and are easy to read. They can generally be purchased at good needlework stores or ordered by mail.

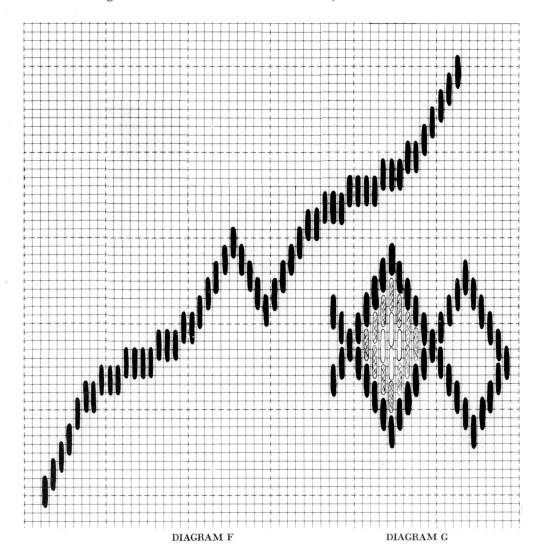

DIAGRAM F   DIAGRAM G

11 · BASKETWEAVE STITCH
(*Diagonal Tent, Gros Point, Petit Point, Tent*)

CANVAS: #12 mono or penelope   NEEDLE: Size 18
TO COVER ONE SQUARE INCH: 2 lengths Persian yarn
NUMBER OF THREADS: 2

This basic canvas embroidery stitch is a slanted or Tent Stitch covering one canvas intersection from lower left to upper right. There are two other Tent Stitches—No. 36 Continental and No. 54 Half Cross—but although they all look alike, each is worked differently. Other differences are yarn requirements and durability.

The Basketweave Stitch is named for the woven pattern it forms on the back of the canvas. It is a little harder to master than the others, but has considerable advantages. It is easily worked without turning the canvas and causes very little canvas distortion, making blocking simple. It can be cut without fraying. Perhaps best of all, the woven back makes it extremely strong and able to withstand heavy use. This is the best Tent Stitch for filling in backgrounds.

Basketweave is worked in diagonal rows. Try thinking of the canvas as a checkerboard, with all the red squares representing stitches worked in one direction, and black squares representing stitches in the opposite direction. It's best to master the working techniques before working a large area, or you may have a lot of picking-out to do, which isn't easy with a woven back. Large-count mono canvas, even rug canvas, is best for a practice piece.

To fill in a square area, begin at the upper right corner at A, leaving a short strand in back as indicated by the dotted line in DIAGRAM A. Note that the diagrams read from right to left for ease of working. Stitches are numbered to show sequence.

Left-handers work from lower left corner, and should follow special LEFT-HANDERS' DIAGRAMS A, B, C and D.

LEFT-HANDER DIAGRAMS

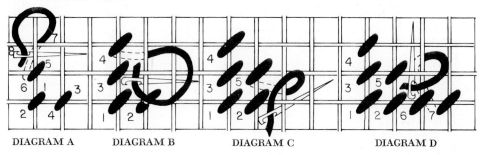

DIAGRAM A   DIAGRAM B   DIAGRAM C   DIAGRAM D

DIAGRAM D   DIAGRAM C   DIAGRAM B   DIAGRAM A

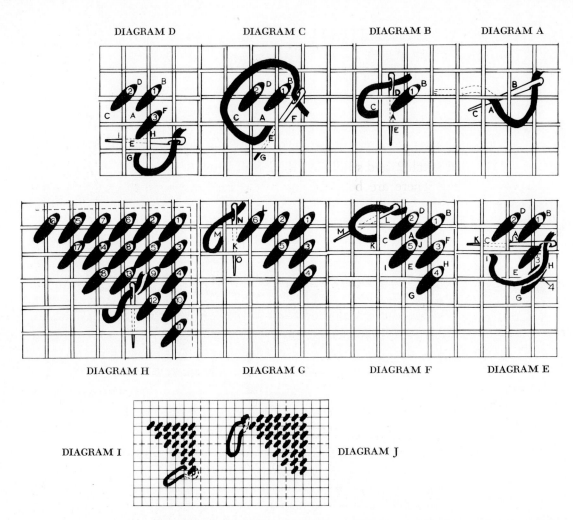

DIAGRAM H   DIAGRAM G   DIAGRAM F   DIAGRAM E

DIAGRAM I   DIAGRAM J

DIAGRAMS A to G show how to place stitches 1 to 7. For stitch 1, the needle emerges at A and is inserted diagonally up at B to re-emerge at C, ready to start stitch 2. Stitch 2, and all other stitches, will diagonally cover a single canvas intersection.

In working square areas, a stitch is added (or decreased) on each row to keep it squared off. DIAGRAMS I and J show stitches being squared off at lower right and upper left corners. It's a good idea to draw outside border lines on the canvas to give an edge to follow.

DIAGRAM H shows how the stitches move up and down diagonal rows, with stitch 19 being completed. After working a few rows the sawtooth edges of each diagonal row become visible, and it is easy to see where to place stitches between them on the next row. Keep in mind that the needle moves vertically on the down rows and horizontally on the up rows.

DIAGRAM C shows the final stitch in the down row completed at F, with the needle emerging at G to start the up row. At this point the needle action is the same as for No. 38 Vertical Continental Stitch, as it starts the up row with a diagonal stitch placed directly under stitch 1. DIAGRAM F shows the final stitch in the up row completed at L, with the needle emerging at M to start the down row. The action here is the same as for No. 36 Continental Stitch, placing stitch 6 to the left of stitch 2, and stitch 7 to the left of stitch 6.

There are bound to be odd-shaped areas which you will want to work in Basketweave Stitch. To fill irregular shapes, you have to figure out how to place the stitches and still keep the woven pattern on the back. DIAGRAM K shows how to start an irregular area. It shows an up row with two stitches worked and a third in progress. The dotted lines indicate how to pass the needle on the back. DIAGRAM L shows how to continue with a down row.

DIAGRAM K 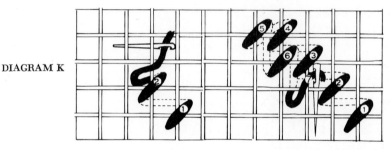 DIAGRAM L

For another hint on working odd shapes, notice the weave of the canvas and concentrate on the horizontal threads. On one row they go over the vertical ones, on the next row they go under them, and so on. Although this weave alternates horizontally, on the diagonal it is *always the same*—if you draw a diagonal line across the canvas, you will see that on this line the horizontal threads are always over, or always under, the vertical threads. What this means is that all up rows should be worked over the same kind of diagonal intersections; all down rows should be worked over the opposite. This may not seem important, but if two consecutive rows are worked in the same direction, a ridge will form that no amount of blocking will remove.

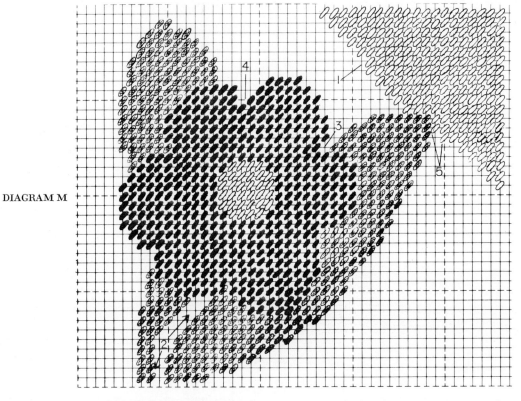

DIAGRAM M

If you stop work before an area is completed, end with a partly worked row as at 1 in DIAGRAM M. When you resume work, a quick look will show in which direction to continue. When beginning a new strand, always run the new yarn in with the weave—which means that it should pass either vertically or horizontally on the back of the work. As the needle moves vertically on the down rows and horizontally on the up rows, the direction of stitches on the reverse side will tell if you're working an up or down row.

The other part of DIAGRAM M shows a finished motif. Number 2 shows an area to be filled. Basketweave can be used for the background on the upper half, but a row of No. 38 Vertical Continental Stitch must be worked between the leaf and stem. Numbers 3 and 4 indicate the kind of spaces that can occur. These are simply filled with a few extra stitches. If the area is very small (not over half an inch), you can carry the yarn back to the original row and resume work always continuing in the direction of that row. But carrying yarn across a finished area is not a good practice, for the added bulk can show on the front and cause a pucker that won't block out. Number 5 shows how to continue filling after being interrupted by a leaf area.

12 · BASKETWEAVE STITCH, REVERSE

CANVAS: #12 mono   NEEDLE: Size 18

TO COVER ONE SQUARE INCH: 1⅔ lengths Persian yarn

NUMBER OF THREADS: full strand

As the name indicates, the woven pattern appears on the front and the Tent Stitch appears on the reverse. It is composed of straight stitches worked over two canvas threads in diagonal rows. The exceptions are the small edge-filling stitches that give a finished appearance.

Work begins at top right. Left-handers should turn the diagram upside down and begin at the lower left.

DIAGRAMS A to E show how to place the first five stitches, following numbers 1 through 11. DIAGRAMS F to I show Basketweave pattern emerging as successive stitches are worked, following the needle from 11 to 19. DIAGRAMS C and I show half-stitches finishing off an up row. DIAGRAMS F and G show half-stitches finishing off the side. DIAGRAM J shows a completed area, with all sides finished with half-stitches.

When working an irregular shape the adjustments are the same as for No. 11 Basketweave Stitch. It takes a little practice to see where short stitches are required.

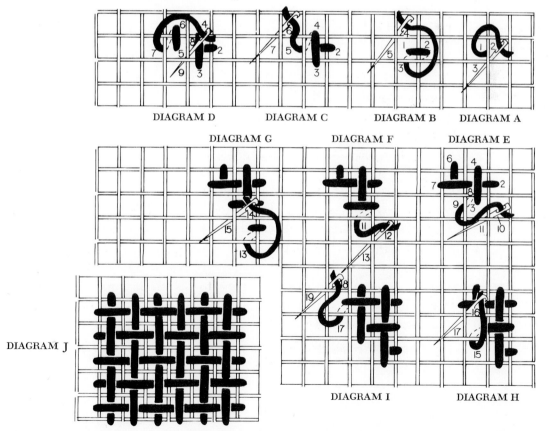

DIAGRAM D   DIAGRAM C   DIAGRAM B   DIAGRAM A

DIAGRAM G   DIAGRAM F   DIAGRAM E

DIAGRAM J

DIAGRAM I   DIAGRAM H

13 · BOKHARA COUCHING STITCH

CANVAS: #12 mono   NEEDLE: Size 18

TO COVER ONE SQUARE INCH: 2 lengths Persian yarn

NUMBER OF THREADS: 2

This versatile stitch has many variations. Just a few are given here, but do experiment and find more.

Work is done by laying a long stitch from left to right and working over it from right to left. Left-handers should work in the reverse way, laying the yarn from right to left and stitching from left to right.

DIAGRAM A shows the laid stitch worked from 1 to 2, and the first stitch being worked over it as the needle emerges at 3, is inserted at 4 and emerges at 5. Work continues in this manner. DIAGRAM B shows vertical stitches worked in every other opening across the row. DIAGRAM C shows how to move to the next row as a stitch is laid from 13 to 14, with the needle emerging at 15 in position to work across as before. DIAGRAM D shows the second row in progress, with stitches worked below the openings on the previous row.

DIAGRAM E shows a completed area with half-stitches inserted after the others are complete to give a finished edge.

This stitch gives a woven appearance and is good for backgrounds and for filling small areas. As with all couching stitches, laid yarn and stitches can be worked in contrasting colors for new effects.

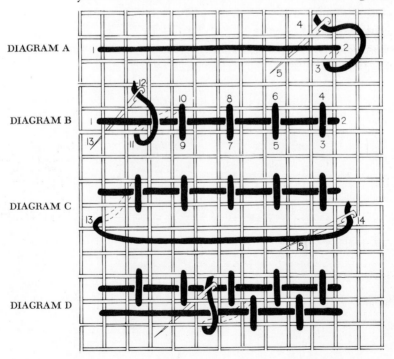

DIAGRAM A

DIAGRAM B

DIAGRAM C

DIAGRAM D

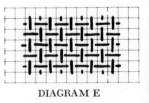

DIAGRAM E

14 · BOKHARA COUCHING STITCH, DIAGONAL

CANVAS: #12 mono   NEEDLE: Size 18
TO COVER ONE SQUARE INCH: 1½ lengths Persian yarn
NUMBER OF THREADS: 2

This is like No. 13 Bokhara Couching Stitch, with a variation in the placement of the vertical stitches.

DIAGRAM A shows the foundation stitch laid across the canvas and the first stitch being worked. Left-handers reverse the direction. DIAGRAM B shows vertical stitches continuing in every third opening over the laid yarn (numbers 5 to 12), while 13 and 14 lay another row of yarn alongside it. DIAGRAM C shows vertical stitches worked over both rows of laid yarn (numbers 15 to 22), while 23 and 24 lay down another long stitch beside them. DIAGRAM D shows vertical stitches being worked over two laid threads next to the stitches on the previous rows (numbers 25 to 31).

DIAGRAM E shows an area completed.

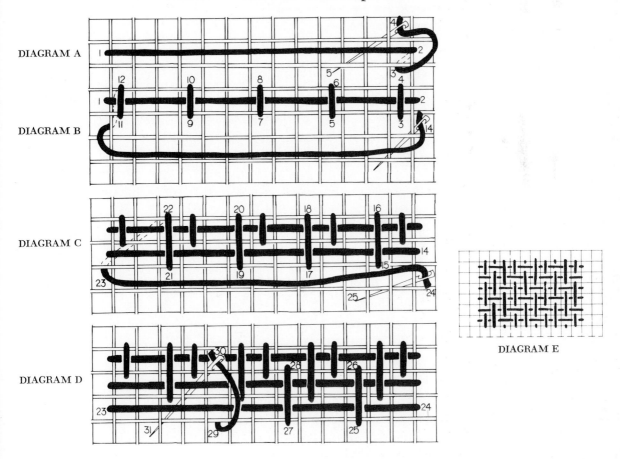

DIAGRAM A

DIAGRAM B

DIAGRAM C

DIAGRAM D

DIAGRAM E

15 · BOKHARA COUCHING STITCH, STAGGERED

CANVAS: #12 mono   NEEDLE: Size 18
TO COVER ONE SQUARE INCH: 1 length Persian yarn
NUMBER OF THREADS: 2

This gives a textured look rather than the woven appearance of the other couching stitches.

The diagram shows the finished effect. The base yarn is laid as in No. 13 Bokhara Couching Stitch. Left-handers reverse direction. The vertical stitches cover only one row of laid yarn, but their placement is staggered as shown.

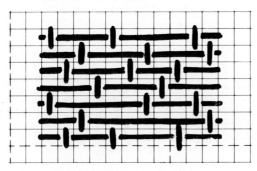

16 · BRAZILIAN STITCH (*Ponto Brasileiro*)

CANVAS: #12 mono   NEEDLE: Size 18
TO COVER ONE SQUARE INCH: 1⅓ lengths Persian yarn
NUMBER OF THREADS: 2

This stitch produces a nice textured look. It is useful for rug-making as the many crossings make it strong and secure. The diagrams look complicated, but after working a few squares you will find it is not very difficult.

Work begins at the upper left of the area to be covered. Work is done horizontally from left to right, beginning at least four canvas threads from the top. Left-handers should turn the diagrams upside down and begin at the lower right, following the numbers as given.

DIAGRAM A shows the first stitch being worked from 1 to 2, with the needle emerging at 3 to form the first half-cross stitch. DIAGRAM B shows the next stitch worked from 3 to 4, with the needle emerging at 5. DIAGRAM C shows the start of the upper part of the stitch with the needle inserted at 6 and emerging at 7, forming a long diagonal stitch. DIAGRAM D shows the start of the top crossing with the needle inserted at 8 and emerging at 9. DIAGRAM E shows the needle emerging at 9 and being inserted at 10, to emerge at 11. DIAGRAM F shows the upper right cross being finished as the needle is inserted at 12, and emerges at 13. DIAGRAM G shows the needle being inserted at 14, to emerge at 15. DIAGRAM H shows the fourth cross being completed as the needle is inserted at 16, and emerges at 17. DIAGRAM I shows the needle being inserted at 18, to emerge at 19 in position to begin again.

DIAGRAM J shows a completed area, but you must really see the stitch worked to get the full effect.

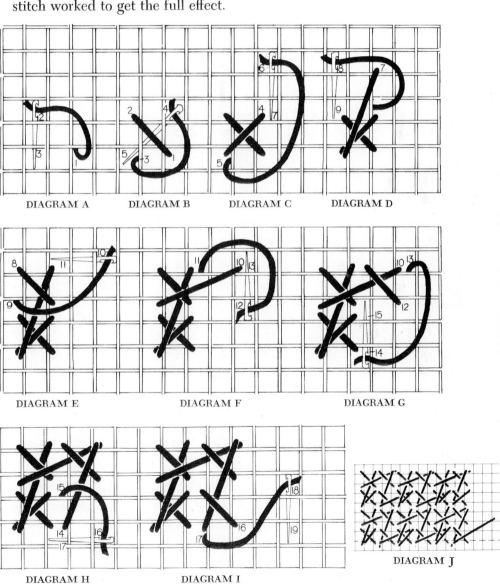

DIAGRAM A   DIAGRAM B   DIAGRAM C   DIAGRAM D

DIAGRAM E   DIAGRAM F   DIAGRAM G

DIAGRAM J

DIAGRAM H   DIAGRAM I

17 · BRICK STITCH (*Bricking Stitch*)

CANVAS: #12 mono   NEEDLE: Size 18

TO COVER ONE SQUARE INCH: 1 length Persian yarn (worked over
4 canvas threads)

NUMBER OF THREADS: 1 full strand

This is basically an upright stitch alternating in height. The height doesn't really matter as long as a good proportion is maintained, in this case two-one. This means that the stitches in each row are four canvas threads high, with two canvas threads between them.

Since it can be worked in both directions, there are no special instructions for left-handers. DIAGRAM A shows the work starting at 1 and continuing to the end of the row at 14. Stitches in the second row are worked two threads below, and between the stitches of the first row, as shown by numbers 15 to 21.

DIAGRAMS B and C show another method, with upper and lower stitches being completed in one row. The return is worked in the same way. (These stitches are two canvas threads high with one canvas thread between them, keeping the same two-one proportion.) DIAGRAM D shows the upper and lower edges being finished off with half-stitches.

DIAGRAM E shows a completed area worked over four threads, with edges finished with half-stitches. Regardless of stitch size, this gives a flat texture useful for backgrounds.

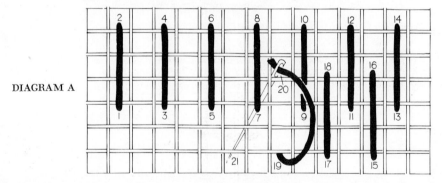

DIAGRAM A

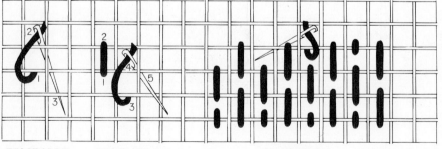

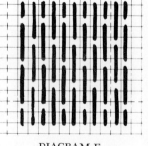

DIAGRAM B   DIAGRAM C   DIAGRAM D   DIAGRAM E

18 · BULLION KNOT

This is similar to the bullion knot used in regular embroidery. Canvas and yarn requirements are not given, as it can be worked on any size canvas, but it is rather difficult on a heavily sized canvas.

Here it is worked over four vertical canvas threads.

DIAGRAM A shows the work starting at the left, at 1. Left-handers start at the right edge and reverse the work throughout.

The needle emerges at 1 and is inserted at 2 to emerge again at 3 (same opening as 1)—but the needle is not pulled through. DIAGRAM B shows the yarn being twisted around the point of the needle. You want just enough to cover the distance of your stitch—from 1 to 2. Keep the tension fairly loose, for the next step is to give the needle a gentle pull, and ease it completely through the twists. Use the thumb and forefinger of your free hand to keep the twists in place as you do so, or they will slide over each other and look messy. DIAGRAM C shows the stitch completed, with the needle now reinserted at 4.

DIAGRAM D shows another method. Here the yarn is laid and twists sewn over it. This takes practice to keep an even tension, and it's best to use your free hand to hold the loops in place until the laid yarn is covered.

If working a circle or half circle, use the same opening for several stitches as shown in DIAGRAM E. One advantage of this stitch is that it can be worked over a background that is already stitched, in which case it is called "over embroidery."

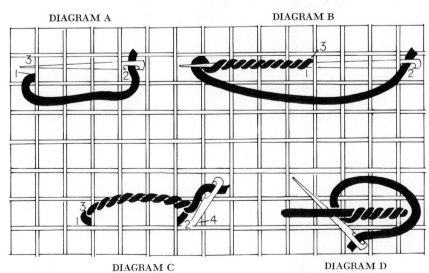

DIAGRAM A DIAGRAM B

DIAGRAM C DIAGRAM D

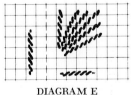

DIAGRAM E

19 · BUTTONHOLE STITCH

CANVAS: #12 mono NEEDLE: Size 18

TO COVER ONE INCH: ½ length Persian yarn (worked over 3 horizontal threads)

NUMBER OF THREADS: 1 full strand

This stitch is worked in the same way on canvas as on fabric, but the placement of the needle is dictated by the canvas weave. The length of the stitches may vary.

Work is done horizontally from left to right beginning at the lower left edge. Left-handers begin at the right edge and work to the left.

DIAGRAM A shows the first stitch being worked with the needle emerging at 1, inserted at 2, and reemerging at 3 over the working yarn. DIAGRAM B shows the next stitch being worked from 4 to 5 in the same way. As you continue, hold down the yarn with your free thumb as you work so it is always under the emerging needle. DIAGRAM C shows a completed row.

DIAGRAM D shows a row of Buttonhole Stitches worked in zigzagging lengths, with a return row worked by turning the canvas upside down so the loop edge is straight and the staggered stitches meet in the center. The return row can also be worked in a contrasting color.

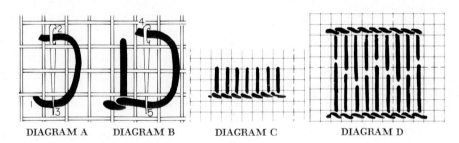

DIAGRAM A   DIAGRAM B   DIAGRAM C   DIAGRAM D

20 · BUTTONHOLE STITCH, DETACHED

CANVAS: #12 mono NEEDLE: Size 18

TO COVER ONE SQUARE INCH: 1½ lengths Persian yarn (with No. 9 Back Stitch edging)

NUMBER OF THREADS: 1 full strand

This is a filling stitch worked into a No. 9 Back Stitch edging, with the remainder of the stitches unattached to the canvas. It makes a nicely textured surface, but does not wear well and is not suitable for anything receiving a great deal of use.

Work is done horizontally in both directions, with No. 9 Back Stitches worked over two threads on all sides. There are no special directions for left-handers, but they might find it easier to start at the right and work left, following the action of row 2 in DIAGRAM B.

DIAGRAM A shows how Back Stitches are worked to anchor the first row of Detached Buttonhole Stitches. From here on, the needle works through the yarn on the surface and does not enter the canvas again. The needle emerges at 1, and is passed under the next Back Stitch from 2 to 3 without entering the canvas. Use your free thumb to form the loops and hold them in place. They should remain hanging loose, as they will be pulled down into place on the following row. DIAGRAM B shows the first row of loops completed and anchored through the Back Stitches edging the right side of the canvas. The next row is worked through the loops of the previous row, and so on.

When the area is completed, the final row of loops is passed under the Back Stitches edging the bottom of the canvas to pull all the work down into place and give the whole area a smooth finish.

DIAGRAM C shows the same stitch with the outside edges anchored directly into the canvas. The rest of the action remains the same. DIAGRAM D shows a completed area anchored through the canvas on the last row.

DIAGRAM E shows how to work the stitch to hold an object such as a stone or shell. Back Stitches outline the shape of the object, and a couple of rows are worked. Put the item in place (and secure it with a dot of white glue). Continue working until you have enough rows to hold it in place. Skip an occasional loop to draw in the rows as the stone becomes smaller.

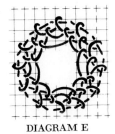

DIAGRAM E

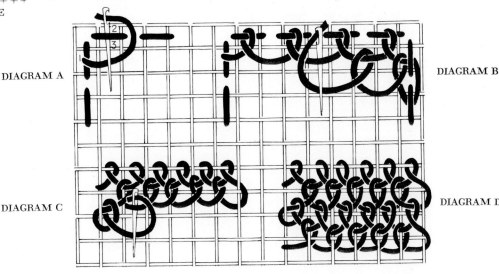

DIAGRAM A

DIAGRAM B

DIAGRAM C

DIAGRAM D

21 · BUTTONHOLE STITCH, DOUBLE

CANVAS: #12 mono   NEEDLE: Size 18
TO COVER ONE INCH: ½ length Persian yarn (worked over 3 threads)
NUMBER OF THREADS: 1 full strand

Because of its nicely finished edges, this makes a good border stitch. It is worked the same as No. 19 Buttonhole Stitch, with space left between stitches.

As DIAGRAM A shows, the stitch is completed in two rows. After the first row is done, turn the canvas upside down to work the second row in the spaces left by the first. Left-handers should work from right to left, also turning the canvas for the second row.

DIAGRAM B shows a completed area.

DIAGRAM A

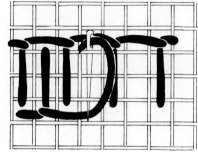

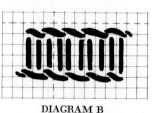
DIAGRAM B

22 · BUTTONHOLE STITCH, TAILORED

CANVAS: #12 mono   NEEDLE: Size 18
TO COVER ONE INCH: ⅔ length Persian yarn (worked over 3 threads)
NUMBER OF THREADS: 1 full strand

This stitch can be worked over any number of horizontal canvas threads, depending on how tall or short you want it. It has a nice firm edge that looks as if a row of No. 103 French Knots were worked in.

It begins like No. 19 Buttonhole Stitch, as shown in DIAGRAM A. Left-handers should start at the right and work left. DIAGRAM B shows the edging knot being made. Before pulling the needle through, hold it near the eye and pass the yarn under the needle from right to left near its point, pull up snugly and then pull the needle through.

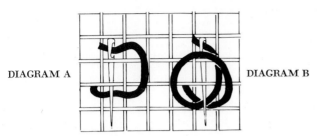

DIAGRAM A   DIAGRAM B

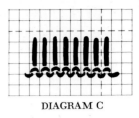

DIAGRAM C

To make a good edging for the canvas itself: fold under the canvas edges and work through the two layers. Work from the inside of the canvas, with the needle emerging outside the folded edge. At the corners, shorten stitches to fit; if necessary, work in a few extra stitches to fill. This makes a secure and good-looking border.

DIAGRAM C shows a completed area.

23 · BUTTONHOLE WHEEL STITCH

CANVAS: #12 mono   NEEDLE: Size 18

TO MAKE ONE WHEEL: ½ length Persian yarn (worked over 3 threads)

NUMBER OF THREADS: 1 full strand

This is worked exactly like No. 19 Buttonhole Stitch and can be worked over any number of canvas threads. The larger the wheel, the more stitches needed to complete it.

It can be worked in either direction. Left-handers should work clockwise.

DIAGRAM A shows a partially finished wheel done over two canvas threads. As you see, the needle is always inserted in the same center opening, while the outside moves in a circle around it. When the last stitch is completed, insert the needle over the original stitch for a smooth finish. Always use your free thumb to hold the loops.

DIAGRAM B shows a finished wheel.

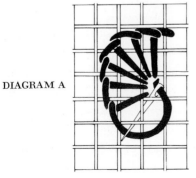

DIAGRAM A

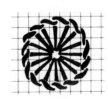

DIAGRAM B

24 · BUTTONHOLE STITCH, WHIPPED

CANVAS: #12 mono   NEEDLE: Size 18
TO COVER ONE INCH: 1¼ lengths Persian yarn
NUMBER OF THREADS: 1 full strand for Buttonhole Stitches;
                    1 or 2 threads for whipping

Complete a row of No. 19 Buttonhole Stitches. DIAGRAM A shows the whipping stitches progressing as the needle is inserted under the edge of each stitch (*not* into the canvas). Left-handers reverse direction.

DIAGRAM B shows a completed area. This makes an interesting edge, particularly if a contrasting color is used for whipping.

DIAGRAM A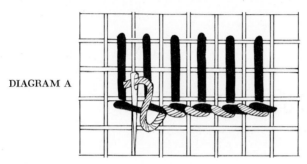

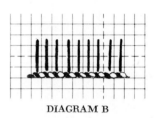

DIAGRAM B

25 · BYZANTINE STITCH

CANVAS: #12 mono   NEEDLE: Size 18
TO COVER ONE SQUARE INCH: 1 length Persian yarn (worked over 3
                          threads)
NUMBER OF THREADS: 1 full strand

This is similar to the No. 111 Slanting Gobelin Stitch. It gives a nicely textured zigzag effect good for backgrounds or area filling. The stitches can be any size as long as they cover an equal number of canvas threads horizontally and vertically to maintain a 45-degree angle. The number of stitches can vary also, as long as the same number is used in all directions (five are used here). Although some spaces are left between them, there is no need to fill in on the practice piece. Later on you will simply fill in wherever necessary.

Work begins at the upper left corner. Left-handers should begin at the lower right and turn the diagrams upside down. DIAGRAM A shows the needle emerging at 1 and being inserted at 2, to emerge at 3. Work continues across in this manner. DIAGRAM B shows a horizontal row with the needle beginning its down journey by emerging at 11, directly under 9. DIAGRAM C shows the placement of stitches as the pattern progresses. Working this way, a diagonal row is formed.

At the end of a row, stitches usually have to be gradually shortened to fit. DIAGRAM C shows this, along with stitches lengthened at the start of the second row.

The second row is worked from bottom to top under the first row. It is not necessary to turn the canvas around when changing direction.

DIAGRAM D shows a completed area. Note adjustments in stitch size at the corners and edges.

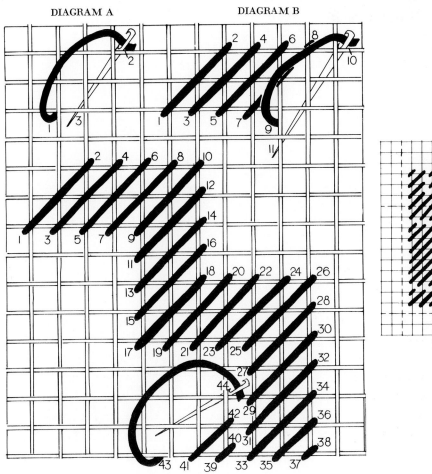

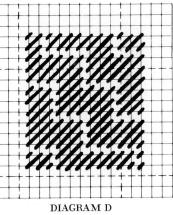

DIAGRAM A

DIAGRAM B

DIAGRAM C

DIAGRAM D

26 · CASHMERE STITCH NO. 1

CANVAS: #12 mono   NEEDLE: Size 18
TO COVER ONE SQUARE INCH: 1⅓ lengths Persian yarn
NUMBER OF THREADS: 1 full strand

This is a series of small stitches that form an oblong shape. There are several working methods; use the one most comfortable for you. The stitch sequence is always one short, two long, one short. The finished stitch has a nice flat texture suitable for any kind of filling. It distorts the canvas quite a bit, so be sure to outline the design on a piece of paper before starting (as described on p. 13), to aid in blocking.

Work is done horizontally from upper left to lower right. Left-handers turn the diagram upside down and begin at the lower right.

DIAGRAMS A to C show the first pattern being worked from 1 to 8, with the needle emerging at 9 in position to start the next stitch. DIAGRAM D shows the first pattern complete while the needle is working a second group in the same way.

DIAGRAM E shows a completed area.

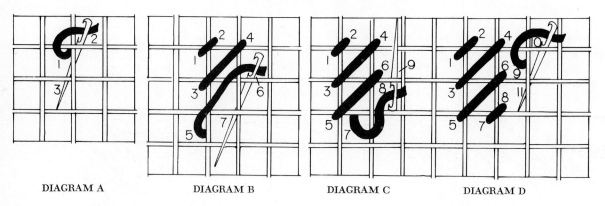

DIAGRAM A   DIAGRAM B   DIAGRAM C   DIAGRAM D

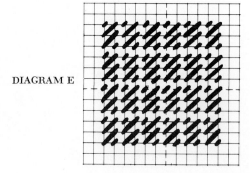

DIAGRAM E

27 · CASHMERE STITCH NO. 2

CANVAS: #12 mono   NEEDLE: Size 18

TO COVER ONE SQUARE INCH: 1⅓ lengths Persian yarn

NUMBER OF THREADS: 1 full strand

This looks exactly the same as No. 26 Cashmere Stitch, but it is worked in diagonal rows beginning at the upper right corner. Left-handers should begin at the lower left and turn the diagrams upside down.

DIAGRAM A shows the sequence of the first pattern, with the needle emerging below it at 9 to start the next group, which is worked from the bottom up. DIAGRAM B shows the first small stitch complete, with the needle emerging at 11. DIAGRAM C shows the second pattern completed at 16, and the third pattern started at 17 and moving up.

The down journey starts again as shown in DIAGRAM A for No. 28 Cashmere Stitch, following.

See DIAGRAM E for No. 26 Cashmere Stitch for a completed area.

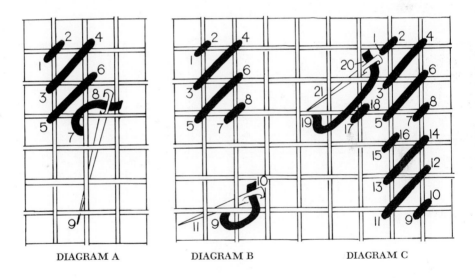

DIAGRAM A   DIAGRAM B   DIAGRAM C

28 · CASHMERE STITCH NO. 3

CANVAS: #12 mono   NEEDLE: Size 18

TO COVER ONE SQUARE INCH: 1⅓ lengths Persian yarn

NUMBER OF THREADS: 1 full strand

Again this looks like No. 26 Cashmere Stitch, but the patterns are worked in still another sequence. Work begins in the upper left corner. I find this the quickest method.

DIAGRAM A shows the first pattern being completed as the needle is inserted at 8, ready to start again at 9. Needle action on the final stitch is that of the "down" Basketweave. Left-handers should begin at lower right and turn diagrams upside down.

As DIAGRAM B shows, the second pattern continues diagonally under the first as the needle is inserted at 10 and emerges at 11. Work continues in this manner until time to start the up journey.

To work the up journey, follow DIAGRAMS B and C for No. 27 Cashmere Stitch.

See DIAGRAM E for No. 26 Cashmere Stitch for a completed area.

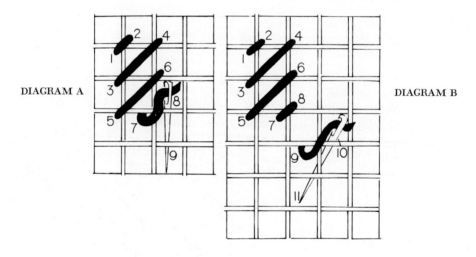

DIAGRAM A   DIAGRAM B

29 · CASHMERE STITCH, DIAGONAL

CANVAS: #12 mono   NEEDLE: Size 18

TO COVER ONE SQUARE INCH: 1⅓ lengths Persian yarn

NUMBER OF THREADS: 1 full strand

This is similar to No. 26 Cashmere Stitch, but gives the appearance of a textured zigzag line. It is equally good for backgrounds and area filling, but distorts the canvas quite a bit.

The action moves diagonally like No. 28 Cashmere Stitch, but after the first pattern is completed there is only one short stitch between patterns thereafter.

DIAGRAM A shows the first four stitches completed as the needle is inserted at 8, ready to emerge again at 9. DIAGRAM B shows the continued action of numbers 10 through 20 in a zigzag line to the bottom of the row.

Though the work is done in rows, the edges need filling in to keep them even. DIAGRAM B shows this at the lower edge. DIAGRAM B also shows the start of an up row with one short stitch and one long stitch worked before starting the regular pattern.

DIAGRAM C shows a completed area.

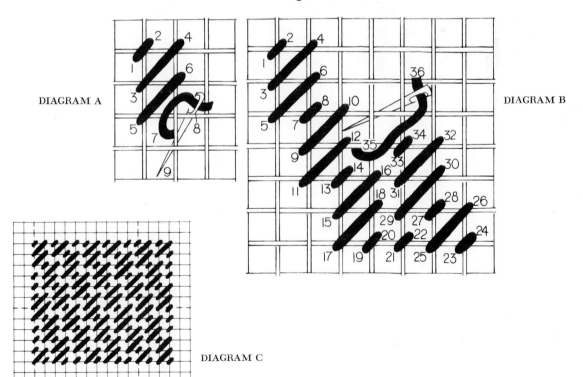

DIAGRAM A

DIAGRAM B

DIAGRAM C

30 · CHAIN STITCH

CANVAS: #12 mono   NEEDLE: Size 18

TO COVER ONE SQUARE INCH: 1½ lengths Persian yarn (worked over 2 mono canvas threads)

NUMBER OF THREADS: 1 full strand

This stitch is worked the same way on canvas as in regular embroidery. It is a versatile stitch, excellent for solid filling, and resembles knitting when covering an area. It takes curves nicely, which makes it useful for outlining uneven shapes. When working a smaller stitch over one thread, it is best to use penelope canvas. For a larger stitch, work over two threads on mono canvas. It is important always to keep a fairly loose, even tension.

The stitch is usually worked from top to bottom, or from right to left. Left-handers should work from the bottom up, or from left to right, reversing the directions.

DIAGRAM A shows the movement of the Chain Stitch. The needle emerges at 1, and a loop of yarn is held down below it by your free thumb while the needle is inserted again at 2 (in the same place as 1), and emerges at 3 over the loop of yarn.

DIAGRAM B shows a row of Chain Stitches continuing in the same manner. DIAGRAM C shows a line finished off with a small stitch, 1 and 2, at the base of the last chain.

DIAGRAM C also shows how to turn a corner: the needle simply emerges inside the last loop at 3, and continues in the new direction. The line may curve at will.

DIAGRAM D shows a solid area of Chain Stitch. If you are working over two horizontal canvas threads and using heavy yarn, you may be able to skip two vertical threads between rows—just be sure the yarn is fluffy enough to cover, and be sure not to pull loops too tight.

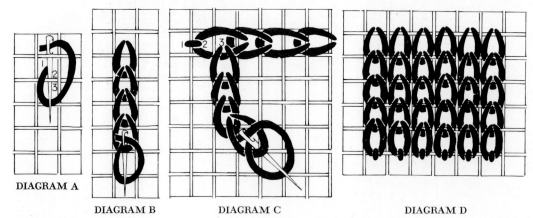

DIAGRAM A

DIAGRAM B   DIAGRAM C   DIAGRAM D

Rows can be worked back and forth for still another change in appearance. Do experiment with this stitch.

A charming variation is Magic Chain Stitch, which children love as it does appear to change colors like magic.

Using two contrasting colored threads of Persian yarn, it takes one-eighth length of each color to work a row one inch long on #12 mono canvas.

Thread a needle with both colors, and start as shown in DIAGRAM E. As for the regular Chain Stitch, the needle emerges at 1, but a loop of only one of your colors is held down below it by your free thumb. The needle is inserted at 2 (in the same place as 1), and emerges at 3 over the loop of yarn. Pull both colors evenly through, and the color you have not used will seem to disappear.

DIAGRAM F shows another chain being formed with the second color in exactly the same way. This time, as both colors are pulled evenly through, it is the first color that seems to disappear.

DIAGRAM G shows a line of Magic Chain Stitch with colors alternating every other Chain Stitch. DIAGRAM H shows a curving line, with colors alternating every two stitches.

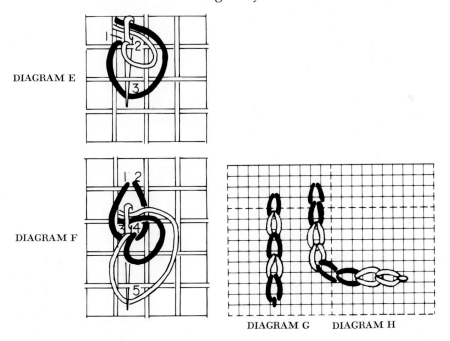

DIAGRAM E

DIAGRAM F

DIAGRAM G   DIAGRAM H

31 · CHAIN STITCH, BRAIDED

CANVAS: #12 mono   NEEDLE: Size 18
TO COVER ONE INCH: ½ length Persian yarn
NUMBER OF THREADS: 1 full strand

This is a useful decorative stitch that takes curves with ease. It should be worked with a looser tension than No. 30 Chain Stitch as the needle passes under stitches that are already worked.

Work is done vertically from top to bottom. Left-handers usually find this easy to work by the regular method, but passing the needle from left to right under the loops. Or they can start at the bottom and turn the diagrams upside down. DIAGRAM A shows how to begin by working a small stitch from 1 to 2, with the needle emerging at 3. The stitch must be secured firmly as it will have stitches pulling against it. DIAGRAM B shows the chain starting as the needle passes under the small stitch without being inserted in the canvas. Make sure not to pull the stitches too tightly. DIAGRAM C shows the next step, with the needle reinserted at 4 (in the same space as 3) and emerging at 5. DIAGRAM D shows another chain being formed in the same manner. DIAGRAM E shows how to continue, as the needle is carried up from 5 and slipped from left to right over the left leg of the previous chain, under both legs of the first chain and over the right leg of the previous chain, to be reinserted at 6. The next chain is formed as the needle emerges at 7 and is carried over the legs of the previous chain and under the legs of the inside chain as before. Work continues in this way. DIAGRAM F shows a completed area.

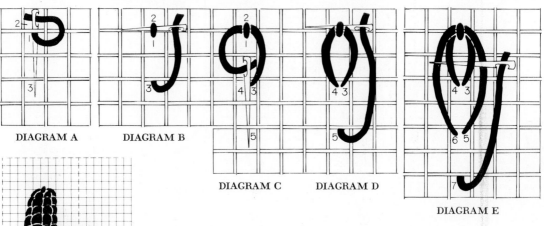

DIAGRAM A   DIAGRAM B

DIAGRAM C   DIAGRAM D

DIAGRAM E

DIAGRAM F

32 · CHAIN STITCH, HEAVY

CANVAS: #12 mono   NEEDLE: Size 18
TO COVER ONE INCH: ½ length Persian yarn
NUMBER OF THREADS: 1 full strand

This is worked like No. 31 Braided Chain Stitch, except for the last few steps. When finished it looks like rich braiding. Like the other Chain Stitches, it is useful both for curves and straight lines. A loose tension produces the best effect.

Work starts at the top. Left-handers can work as directed, but should pass the needle from left to right instead of from right to left. Begin by working a small stitch from 1 to 2, and emerging at 3. DIAGRAM A shows the needle slipped under the small stitch but not through the canvas. DIAGRAM B shows the needle reinserted at 4 (in the same space as 3) and emerging at 5. The next chain is formed in the same manner by slipping the needle under the first stitch, reinserting at 6, and emerging at 7. DIAGRAM C shows how to continue by carrying the needle up and slipping it under both previous stitches without inserting it in the canvas.

When used in combination with other stitches it is best to complete the rest of the work on a piece before working this stitch. It can also be worked in rows, in which case you should leave an extra vertical canvas thread between each row.

DIAGRAM D shows a completed area.

DIAGRAM A

DIAGRAM B

DIAGRAM C

DIAGRAM D

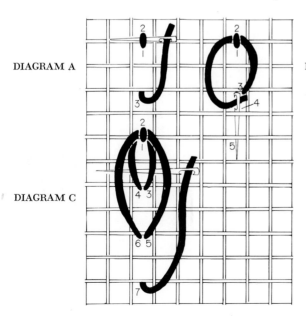

33 · CHAIN STITCH, INTERLACED

CANVAS: #12 mono   NEEDLE: Size 18

TO COVER ONE INCH: ⅜ length Persian yarn for chain;

1 length for interlacing (see below)

NUMBER OF THREADS: 1 full strand

This is a regular embroidery stitch that adapts itself well to canvas. It is strictly decorative and will not withstand any heavy wear. It is actually a row of No. 30 Chain Stitches, interlaced with contrasting yarn. In choosing yarn, note that the color used for the chain becomes unimportant once the interlacing is done. The lacing should be done with a firm thread like linen, mercerized cotton or even a metallic thread. Wool threads are usually too soft and the effect of the stitch is lost.

Work is done vertically from top to bottom. Left-handers can work as directed, but if it becomes awkward, just turn the diagrams upside down. DIAGRAM A shows a row of Chain Stitches finished and the interlacing starting at 1. The needle is slipped from right to left under the right leg of the second chain at 2. At no time is the needle inserted in the canvas except at the start and finish. DIAGRAM B shows the needle pulled through over the left leg of the chain, and slipped from left to right under the right leg of the first chain and the lacing thread at 3. DIAGRAM C shows how to continue. Complete the right side in this manner, inserting the needle in the canvas at the end of the row to anchor the yarn. DIAGRAM D shows the interlacing in progress on the left side. Work this as on the right side, reversing the procedure.

DIAGRAM E shows a completed area. Interlaced Chain Stitch works up quickly and can look quite elegant with metallic threads.

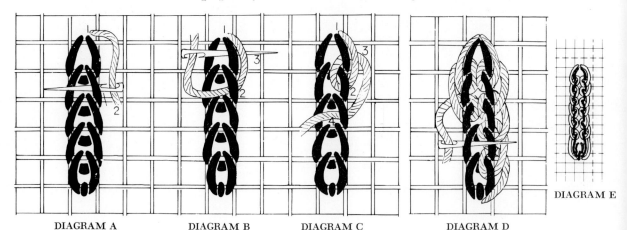

DIAGRAM A   DIAGRAM B   DIAGRAM C   DIAGRAM D   DIAGRAM E

34 · CHAIN STITCH, RAISED

CANVAS: #12 mono   NEEDLE: Size 18
TO COVER ONE INCH: ½ length Persian yarn (working 1 band over 2 threads)
NUMBER OF THREADS: 1 full strand

This stitch creates a nice textured look, but keep in mind that it can't take any heavy use. It is done by working a type of Chain Stitch over laid stitches.

Start by working the laid stitch from left to right. Left-handers can work the laid stitch as shown, but should reverse the procedure for working the chains. DIAGRAM A shows the foundation being laid as the needle moves from 1 to 5. Continue in this manner until the area is covered. Note that these stitches can be laid over any number of canvas threads to cover an area, and any number of rows of the stitches can be worked on the same foundation. On a large canvas you might want to leave one thread between stitches. The proportion diagrammed works well on #12 mono. DIAGRAM B shows how to start the chain. The needle emerges at 1, and is passed from 2 to 3 under the laid thread, but not through the canvas. Make sure not to pull any of the stitches too tight. DIAGRAM C shows how to continue by slipping the needle under the same laid stitch from 4 to 5 and emerging over the working yarn. It is easier if you hold the loop with your free thumb to let the needle pass over it. DIAGRAM D shows another chain worked over the next laid stitch. Emerging from inside the previous chain, the needle is slipped under the laid stitch from 6 to 7. The stitch is completed as before, and work continues down in this manner.

DIAGRAM E shows a completed area.

DIAGRAM A   DIAGRAM B   DIAGRAM C   DIAGRAM D   DIAGRAM E

35 · CHECKER STITCH (*Chequer Stitch*)

CANVAS: #12 mono   NEEDLE: Size 18

TO COVER ONE SQUARE INCH: 1⅔ lengths Persian yarn (with all
stitches the same color)

NUMBER OF THREADS: 1 full strand

This is a variation of No. 179 Scotch Stitch. There are several ways to work; the easiest is to work diagonal rows of Scotch Stitch first.

Work starts at the upper left. Left-handers should start at the lower right and turn the diagrams upside down. DIAGRAM A shows a small slanting stitch being worked from 1 to 2, with the needle emerging at 3. DIAGRAMS B through E show the rest of the stitches in the block being formed in the same manner. After completing the final stitch, the needle passes down, emerging finally at 11 in position to work the next pattern. Note that the first and fifth stitches are the same size, as are the second and fourth. Continue working patterns in this manner until the edge is reached. Adjustments in stitch size may be necessary at the bottom and sides.

To work the remaining rows, you can turn the canvas and work from the top again. You can also work without turning the canvas, as long as you leave the proper number of intersections between squares on the first row. DIAGRAM F shows how to do this. After working the last stitch, the needle emerges at 1, is inserted at 2 and reemerges at 3 in position to work the up row. When figuring out where to start the next row, note that all of the long stitches meet in the same openings.

DIAGRAM G shows how to work the Tent Stitch squares. They can be worked with either No. 54 Half Cross, No. 11 Basketweave or No. 36 Continental. I always use Basketweave as it causes the least distortion and is easy to work diagonally. Two squares at the upper left are completed and a third is started at the upper right. To do this, it is simplest to go from upper right to lower left, carrying the needle straight down from pattern to pattern. Left-handers should start at the lower right and reverse the procedure.

DIAGRAM H shows a completed area. Use contrasting colors for an interesting checkerboard effect. DIAGRAM I shows another area worked with No. 144 Mosaic Stitch, instead of Scotch Stitch, for a different look.

You can also vary the look by changing the size of the pattern squares. Note that the Scotch Stitch uses five stitches and the Mosaic Stitch uses three. Try using seven on fine canvas for an unusual effect.

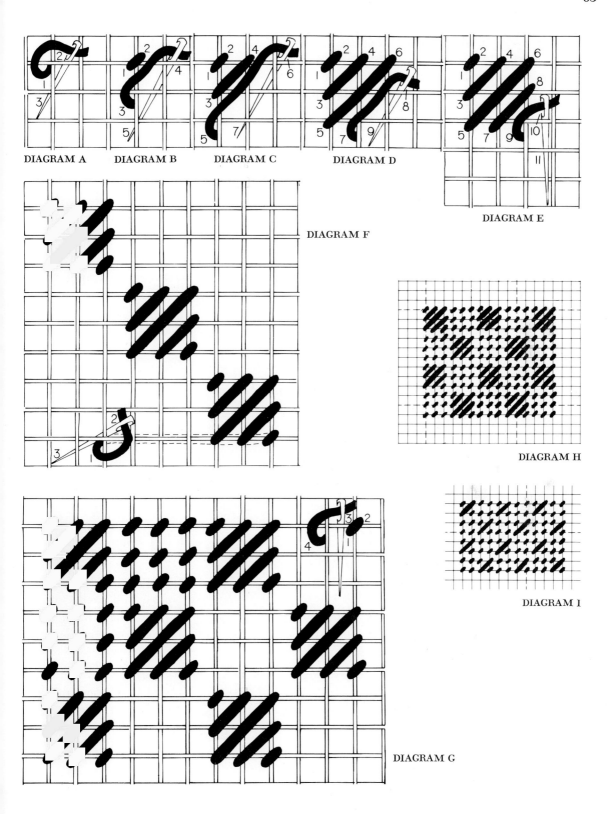

DIAGRAM A   DIAGRAM B   DIAGRAM C   DIAGRAM D

DIAGRAM E

DIAGRAM F

DIAGRAM H

DIAGRAM I

DIAGRAM G

36 · CONTINENTAL STITCH (*Tent Stitch, Gros Point*)

CANVAS: #12 mono   NEEDLE: Size 18
TO COVER ONE SQUARE INCH: 1½ lengths Persian yarn
NUMBER OF THREADS: 1 full strand

This stitch, along with No. 11 Basketweave and No. 54 Half Cross, is a basic slanting stitch used in canvas work. All three look the same, but each has its special advantages. Continental Stitch is best for filling spots where Basketweave can't go. It covers better than the Half Cross, and produces a smoother texture. But it does distort the canvas considerably, especially worked over a large area.

Work is done horizontally starting at the upper right. Left-handers should begin at the lower left and turn the diagrams upside down. DIAGRAM A shows how to begin, with the needle moving from 1 to 3. DIAGRAM B shows the next stitch worked from 3 to 4, with the needle emerging at 5. The canvas is turned bottom to top at the end of this and each successive row, so you always work from right to left. On this and all even rows, the needle emerges in the same opening as the base of the second stitch in the previous row. DIAGRAM C shows the second row starting exactly like the first as the needle emerges at 1. On this and all odd rows, the needle emerges diagonally under the base of the last stitch in the previous row. The needle is then inserted at 2, to emerge at 3. When row 2 is done, reverse the canvas and you're in position to start the third row. DIAGRAM D shows row 3 starting, as the needle moves from 1 to 3.

DIAGRAM E shows a completed area. Note that adjustments are necessary when filling irregular shapes or working around the edge of a design. These are simpler with this than with No. 11 Basketweave.

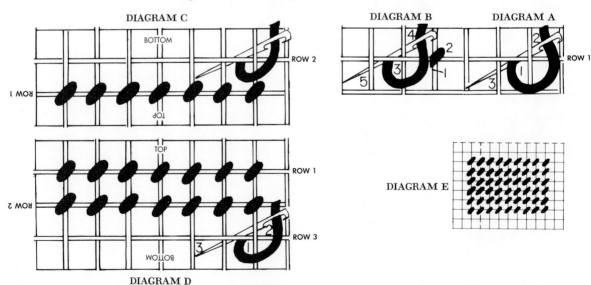

DIAGRAM C

DIAGRAM B   DIAGRAM A

DIAGRAM E

DIAGRAM D

37 · CONTINENTAL STITCH, DIAGONAL

You will need this stitch to work certain lines, parts of lines and circles, and for monogramming and some filling. Yarn requirements will vary accordingly.

Work is done from upper right to lower left, working rather like No. 9 Back Stitch. Left-handers should start at the lower left and turn the diagrams upside down.

DIAGRAM A shows how to begin. From 1, the needle is inserted at 2, and emerges at 3. DIAGRAM B shows the second stitch being worked from 3 to 4, with the needle emerging at 5. Work continues in this manner.

DIAGRAM C shows a cross with one line worked in Diagonal Continental and the other in No. 11 Basketweave. To do this requires some planning, as spaces are left on the Basketweave row, and it's sometimes necessary to work a second row of Basketweave for a solid appearance. On fine canvas, the irregular edge is hardly noticeable and the line looks much better.

DIAGRAM A 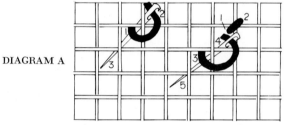 DIAGRAM B

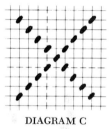

DIAGRAM C

38 · CONTINENTAL STITCH, VERTICAL

This stitch is particularly useful for parts of designs, borders and lettering. Yarn requirements will vary accordingly.

Work is done from top to bottom. Left-handers should start at the bottom and turn the diagrams upside down. DIAGRAM A shows the first stitch being formed from 1 to 2, with the needle emerging at 3. DIAGRAM B shows the next stitch worked in the same manner from 3 to 4, with the needle emerging at 5. Work continues down in this manner. (To move to an up row, use the same method as for No. 11 Basketweave.) DIAGRAM C shows a completed line.

DIAGRAM A 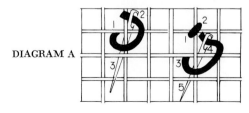 DIAGRAM B

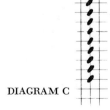

DIAGRAM C

39 · CONTINENTAL STITCH CIRCLE

DIAGRAM A

DIAGRAM A

DIAGRAMS A and B show that a combination of Nos. 36, 37 and 38 Continental Stitches is used to form a circle. Different combinations would also be used for lettering or monogramming or other curved shapes. Yarn requirements will vary accordingly.

DIAGRAM A also shows No. 11 Basketweave used at the upper right and lower left. DIAGRAM B is a larger circle which shows that different numbers of stitches in groups are necessary for a smooth appearance. The number needed depends on the size of the canvas as well as the shape. Obviously you will get a smoother curve on a finer canvas.

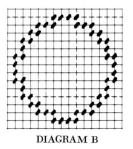

DIAGRAM B

Knowing just how to place the different stitches will come with experience. Left-handers should work the curved shapes in whatever way is most comfortable.

40 · CORAL KNOT STITCH

CANVAS: #12 mono   NEEDLE: Size 18
TO COVER ONE SQUARE INCH: 2 lengths Persian yarn (knotting in every other opening)
NUMBER OF THREADS: 1 full strand

This is a regular embroidery stitch that works well on canvas. It is good for solid filling and because it is constantly being tied down, it makes a good textured outline. It moves both horizontally and vertically and takes curves well.

Work starts at the right edge. Left-handers should begin at the left edge and reverse the procedure. DIAGRAM A shows how to begin. As the needle emerges at 1, the yarn is laid across from right to left and held with the free thumb. The needle is then inserted at 2 to pass under both yarn and canvas thread. It emerges at 3, passing over the working yarn as shown. DIAGRAM B shows a completed knot and a second in progress from 4 to 5. Work continues in this manner. If

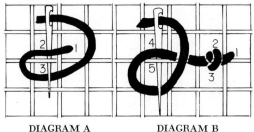

DIAGRAM A   DIAGRAM B

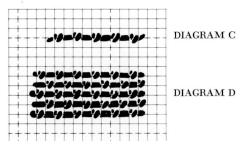

DIAGRAM C

DIAGRAM D

using this stitch for solid filling, turn the canvas at the end of every row and form knots in spaces left between knots on the previous row.

DIAGRAM C shows a completed line. DIAGRAM D shows an entire area completed.

41 · COUCHING STITCH

CANVAS: #12 mono   NEEDLE: Size 18
TO COVER ONE SQUARE INCH: ½ length Rug yarn or Persian yarn as base thread;
¾ length for couching
NUMBER OF THREADS: 1 full strand Rug yarn (or 2 of Persian) for
base; 1 or 2 threads for couching

Couching simply means laying down a strand of heavy yarn and working small tie-down stitches over it with a finer yarn. The yarn to be couched is laid across one or more canvas threads in the direction to be worked. The couching yarn emerges near the same opening and is worked across with small tie-down stitches. Work is done in both directions, so the left-hander can follow the instructions as given.

DIAGRAM A shows the laid yarn and the needle with the couching yarn forming the first stitch. Emerging at 1, the needle is inserted at 2 and emerges at 3. This action is repeated across the laid yarn. DIAGRAM B shows how to work successive rows for solid filling. The laid yarn is folded around to lie in the opposite direction under the row above, and a tie-down stitch is worked at the turning. Tie-down stitches on the next row are worked below the stitches of the row above. When work is completed, the ends of the laid yarn are anchored on the back with the couching yarn.

DIAGRAM C shows a completed row. DIAGRAM D shows a pattern called Brick Couching where the tie-down stitches are staggered. It uses the same amount of yarn as regular couching and is very effective worked in contrasting colors. Other effects can be achieved by varying the placement of the tie-down stitches and using contrasting colors. If couching a metallic thread, use a waxed silk thread for the tie-down stitches so they won't wear out too quickly.

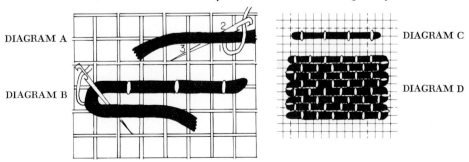

DIAGRAM A

DIAGRAM B

DIAGRAM C

DIAGRAM D

42 · COUCHING STITCH, BUTTONHOLE

CANVAS: #12 mono   NEEDLE: Size 18

TO COVER ONE INCH: Rug yarn sufficient to cover line and turn under; ½ length Persian yarn for Buttonhole Stitch couching

NUMBER OF THREADS: 1 full strand Rug yarn for base; 1 full strand or less for couching

Part of the effectiveness of this is to have the laid yarn show through by leaving space between the tie-down stitches.

Begin by laying a very heavy yarn. Often with such a yarn, the ends can't be inserted through just one opening. No matter what stitch is used for couching heavy yarn, the end where stitching begins is turned under and anchored to the right side of canvas by the couching thread so that just the smooth folded edge shows. DIAGRAM A shows small stitches anchoring the laid yarn. DIAGRAM B shows the laid yarn folded back, in position for couching with the needle ready to begin stitching. Left-handers work from right to left. DIAGRAM C shows the couching in progress. It is worked from left to right over the laid yarn with No. 19 Buttonhole Stitch, but the upright stitches are spaced out.

DIAGRAM D shows a completed area.

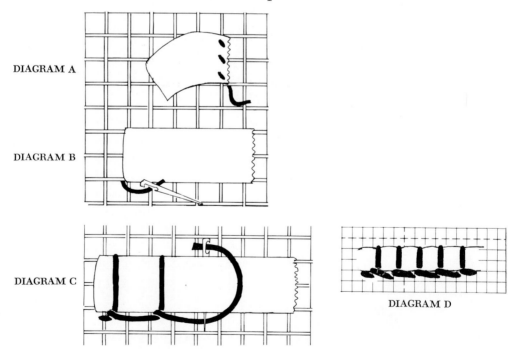

DIAGRAM A

DIAGRAM B

DIAGRAM C

DIAGRAM D

43 · COUCHING STITCH, HERRINGBONE

CANVAS: #12 mono   NEEDLE: Size 18

TO COVER ONE INCH: Rug yarn sufficient to cover line and turn under; Persian yarn for couching needs slightly larger amount than for No. 116 Herringbone Stitch

NUMBER OF THREADS: 1 full strand Rug yarn for base; 1 full strand or less for couching

This is another decorative Couching Stitch.

Work is done from left to right. Left-handers should work from right to left. Attach the yarn according to DIAGRAMS A and B of No. 42 Buttonhole Couching Stitch. DIAGRAM A shows how to work the couching. The action is the same as for No. 116 Herringbone Stitch.

DIAGRAM B shows a completed row.

DIAGRAM A

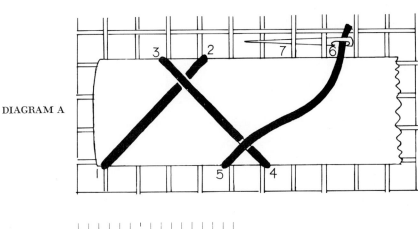

DIAGRAM B

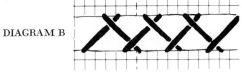

44 · COUCHING STITCH, OPEN CHAIN

CANVAS: #12 mono   NEEDLE: Size 18
TO COVER ONE INCH: Rug yarn sufficient to cover line and turn under;
⅓ length Persian yarn for couching
NUMBER OF THREADS: 1 full strand Rug yarn for base;
1 full strand for couching

DIAGRAM A

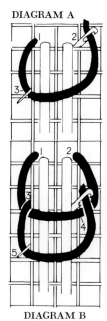

This stitch must be done with some care. It may be worked over a single heavy thread or several strands of yarn. Here it is worked over two vertically laid strands of yarn. A single in-and-out action completes one chain as it forms the loops of the next.

Work is done from the top down. Left-handers should turn the diagram upside down and work from the bottom up. Begin by securing the laid yarn as for No. 42 Buttonhole Couching Stitch. DIAGRAM A shows how to start the couching. The needle emerges at 1, is inserted at 2 and emerges at 3. Remember to hold the working yarn with your free thumb and let the needle pass over it. Always leave a little slack in the yarn as you pull it through. DIAGRAM B shows the second chain being formed. From 3, the needle is inserted at 4 (inside the first chain) and emerges at 5. Work continues in this manner. The last chain is anchored by making a small tie-down stitch over each side which gives it the same squared-off appearance as the others.

DIAGRAM C shows a completed row.

DIAGRAM B

DIAGRAM C

45 · CRETAN STITCH

CANVAS: #12 mono   NEEDLE: Size 18
TO COVER ONE INCH: ½ length Persian yarn when worked over 6 threads
NUMBER OF THREADS: 1 full strand

This stitch is effective for oblong areas or borders or irregular shapes worked so that the background doesn't show. It appears to have a braid running down the center of horizontal or slanting stitches, depending on the proportions used and the slant of the needle.

The action alternates from side to side, so where you start doesn't matter. Whether you are right- or left-handed, one side will always be awkward to do. DIAGRAM A shows how to begin. Emerging at 1, the needle is inserted at 2 and emerges over the working yarn at 3. Because it is a loop stitch, the yarn must be held in place so the emerging needle can pass over it. DIAGRAM B shows how to continue with the needle inserted at 4 and emerging at 5. Work is continued by alternating the action in both diagrams. The needle is inserted once from each side on the same level in order to cover completely. After a few stitches, you will see the braid start to form.

DIAGRAM C shows a completed area.

DIAGRAM A

DIAGRAM B

DIAGRAM C

DIAGRAMS D through H show how varying the length of the arms produces a leaf shape. First, a No. 30 Chain Stitch is worked from 1 to 2. The Cretan Stitch part is then worked from side to side following the numbers from 3 to 14 as shown. Note that you end up with the same two-two-two proportion as on the regular stitch. As a rule, the arms should not be any longer than those in DIAGRAM H. The diagram also shows that the needle emerges twice on each level to keep the stitches close enough to form a nice braid. DIAGRAM I shows a completed leaf. This method can be applied to the regular Cretan Stitch, varying the stitch lengths for a staggered edge effect. If using a fine canvas, try varying the proportions and working the stitches over a few more threads.

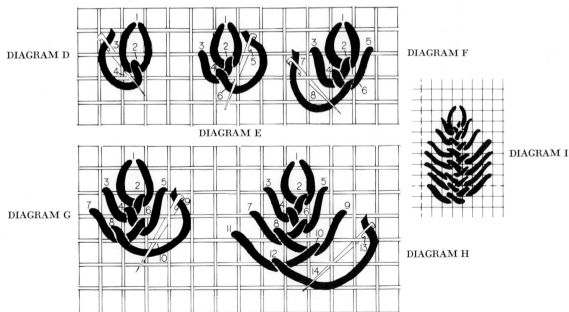

DIAGRAM D

DIAGRAM E

DIAGRAM F

DIAGRAM G

DIAGRAM H

DIAGRAM I

46 · CRETAN STITCH, DIAGONAL

CANVAS: #12 mono   NEEDLE: Size 18

TO COVER ONE SQUARE INCH: ½ length Persian yarn

NUMBER OF THREADS: 1 full strand

This doesn't cover as well as the No. 45 Cretan Stitch, and you may find that you'll need an extra thread.

The action alternates from side to side, and it doesn't matter which side you start on. For example, action here starts on the opposite side from No. 45 Cretan Stitch. Left-handers should work as directed. DIAGRAM A shows how to start with the needle emerging at 1, inserted at 2 and emerging at 3. DIAGRAM B shows the stitch continuing. From 3, the needle is inserted at 4 and emerges at 5. This action keeps the stitches close enough to cover. DIAGRAM C shows the next step as the needle is inserted at 6 and emerges at 7. Work alternates between DIAGRAMS B and C until the area is covered. You can vary outside stitch lengths here, too.

At the end, to give a finished appearance, the needle is inserted a couple of threads away from where it last emerged. This may be seen in DIAGRAM D showing a completed area.

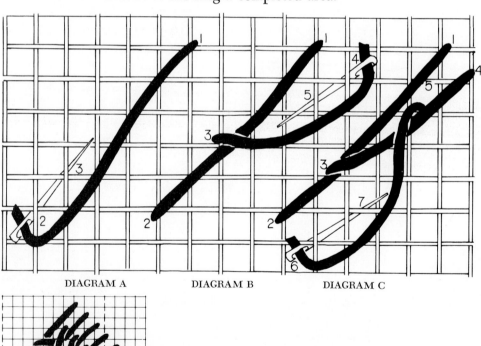

DIAGRAM A   DIAGRAM B   DIAGRAM C

DIAGRAM D

47 · CROSS STITCH NO. 1

CANVAS: #12 mono   NEEDLE: Size 18

TO COVER ONE SQUARE INCH: 1 length Persian yarn

NUMBER OF THREADS: 1

This is one of the oldest and most widely used stitches. For diagraming purposes mono canvas is shown, but it is most successfully worked on penelope. (On mono the threads tend to slip, and it's difficult to keep a smooth appearance.)

Work is done from right to left, and each cross is completed before moving on to the next one. Left-handers should work from left to right and reverse the directions. The important thing to remember is that all of the top stitches should slant in the same direction, or the work will look sloppy. DIAGRAM A shows how to begin. Emerging at 1, the needle is inserted at 2 and emerges at 3. DIAGRAM B shows how to complete the cross by working a stitch from 3 to 4 with the needle emerging at 5, in the same space as 3. DIAGRAM C shows the next stitch being worked, with the needle inserted at 6 and emerging at 7. Work continues in this manner. If working more than one row, turn the canvas and repeat the action in DIAGRAMS A and B.

This can also be worked diagonally from upper right to lower left, following the action in DIAGRAMS D and E. Left-handers should work from lower left to upper right.

DIAGRAM F shows a completed area.

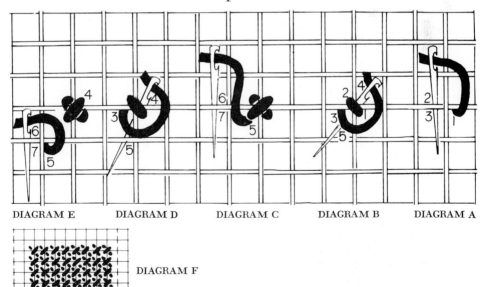

DIAGRAM E   DIAGRAM D   DIAGRAM C   DIAGRAM B   DIAGRAM A

DIAGRAM F

48 · CROSS STITCH NO. 2

CANVAS: #12 mono   NEEDLE: Size 18
TO COVER ONE SQUARE INCH: 1⅛ lengths Persian yarn
NUMBER OF THREADS: 1 full strand

This is quicker than No. 47 Cross Stitch. All the bottom stitches are worked on one journey and crossed on the return trip. Be sure to use enough threads to cover. Remember that with a fluffy yarn, the bottom stitches will hardly show.

Work starts at the left edge. The stitch is worked in two directions, so left-handers can work as directed. DIAGRAM A shows how to begin. The needle emerges at 1, is inserted at 2 and emerges at 3. This action is repeated across the area. DIAGRAM B shows how to work the return journey. From 1, the needle is inserted at 2 and emerges at 3, completing the cross. From there, the needle is inserted at 4 and emerges at 5, and so on across the row. Remember to keep all the top stitches slanting in the same direction. Because two journeys complete a row, the work needn't be turned between rows.

DIAGRAM C shows a completed area. You can vary this by having the top stitches going in different directions in adjacent areas. For a different texture, drop down only one thread and work rows next to completed areas. This can be effective on two halves of a leaf, different areas of a house, or for a textured ground surface. The top stitch direction can be reversed in adjoining areas, which will make the thread appear to be a different shade.

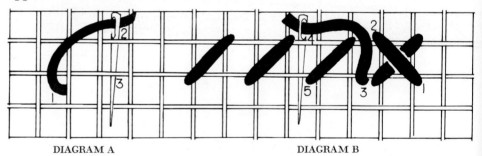

DIAGRAM A   DIAGRAM B

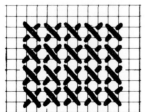

DIAGRAM C

49 · CROSS STITCH, BOUND

CANVAS: #12 mono   NEEDLE: Size 18
TO COVER ONE SQUARE INCH: 1½ lengths Persian yarn
NUMBER OF THREADS: 1 full strand

This is really a series of diagonal No. 176 Satin Stitches worked first in one direction, then the other. When repeated, it forms little square patterns. It can be worked in rows, or used as an isolated design.

Work is done from left to right. Left-handers should start at the left and turn the diagrams upside down. DIAGRAM A shows the first stitch in a group being made from 1 to 2, with the needle emerging at 3. DIAGRAM B shows the second stitch being worked from 3 to 4, with the needle emerging at 5. DIAGRAM C shows the first group completed, and the first stitch in the second group being worked from 7 to 8, with the needle emerging at 9. DIAGRAM D shows the second stitch in this group worked, and the third in progress. To complete the group, the needle emerges at the same spot as it began, at 11 and 13 in the diagram.

DIAGRAM E shows a completed area.

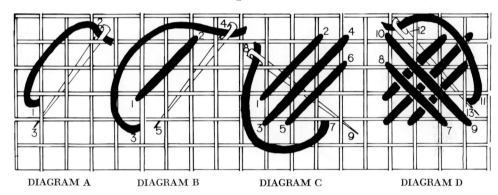

DIAGRAM A   DIAGRAM B   DIAGRAM C   DIAGRAM D

DIAGRAM E

50 · CROSS STITCH, DIAGONAL

CANVAS: #12 mono   NEEDLE: Size 18
TO COVER ONE SQUARE INCH: 2 lengths Persian yarn
NUMBER OF THREADS: 1 full strand

This is a combination of No. 75 Upright Cross Stitch and No. 54 Half Cross. It has a heavy textured look and is extremely durable as it covers both sides of the canvas.

Work is done from lower right to upper left, beginning two threads in from the edge. Left-handers should start at the upper left and turn the diagrams upside down.

DIAGRAM A shows a vertical stitch being worked from 1 to 2, with the needle emerging at 3. DIAGRAM B shows the diagonal stitch being formed as the needle is inserted at 4 and emerges at 5. DIAGRAM C shows a completed pattern and another in progress. Work continues along the row in this manner.

DIAGRAM D shows a completed area with stitches adjusted at the edges for a finished look. In squaring off, usually the best rule is common sense. Let your eyes determine the necessary stitches.

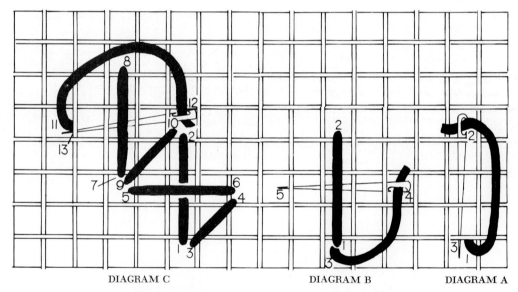

DIAGRAM C   DIAGRAM B   DIAGRAM A

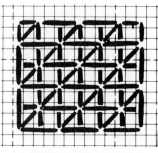

DIAGRAM D

51 · CROSS STITCH, DOUBLE (*Leviathan, Smyrna*)

CANVAS: #12 mono   NEEDLE: Size 18
TO COVER ONE SQUARE INCH: 1 length Persian yarn
NUMBER OF THREADS: 1 full strand

This is a combination of No. 75 Upright Cross Stitch and No. 47 Cross Stitch. It is usually worked over an area four canvas threads square.

Work is done from left to right. Left-handers should work from right to left. DIAGRAM A shows how to begin by working the first stitch from 1 to 2, with the needle emerging at 3. DIAGRAM B shows the cross completed as the needle moves from 3 to 4 and emerges finally at 5. DIAGRAMS C and D show how to work the upright part as the needle moves from 5 to 8 and emerges at 9. Work continues across the row in this manner. Remember to keep all the crosses slanting in the same direction.

DIAGRAM E shows a completed area. Because this is a large stitch, you will have to adjust some stitches for angles, curves and squared-off areas. Small vertical, horizontal or slanting stitches would be used for these adjustments.

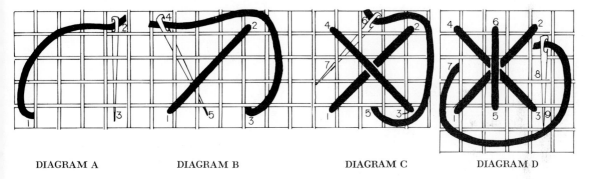

DIAGRAM A   DIAGRAM B   DIAGRAM C   DIAGRAM D

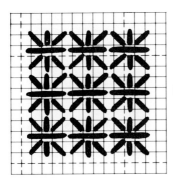

DIAGRAM E

52 · CROSS STITCH, DOUBLE, REVERSED

CANVAS: #12 mono   NEEDLE: Size 18

TO COVER ONE SQUARE INCH: 1 length Persian yarn for foundation; 1 length for overstitching

NUMBER OF THREADS: 2 for foundation; 1 for overstitching

The foundation gives this Cross Stitch an interesting appearance. The overstitching should be done with a finer yarn, perhaps even a metallic thread. On #12 mono or finer canvas, it shows up best if silk or embroidery floss is used. Wools are effective only on larger canvas. Unless the overstitching is done in a contrasting color as well, the entire effect will be lost. Work alternates between one row of No. 47 Cross Stitch and one row of No. 75 Upright Cross Stitch.

Work is done diagonally from upper left to lower right. Left-handers should start at the lower right and turn the diagrams upside down. DIAGRAM A shows a No. 47 Cross Stitch being worked from 1, with the needle emerging finally at 5. DIAGRAMS B and C show how to work down diagonally. Work continues down in this manner. To complete the final cross in the down row, the needle is inserted at 8 and emerges at 9, in position to start the next portion of the pattern.

DIAGRAM A   DIAGRAM B   DIAGRAM C

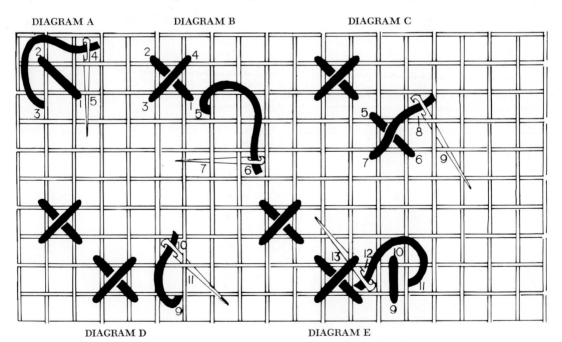

DIAGRAM D   DIAGRAM E

DIAGRAM D shows how to start the row of No. 75 Upright Cross Stitches. From 9, the needle is inserted at 10 and emerges at 11. DIAGRAM E shows the vertical stitch formed and the horizontal one being completed as the needle is inserted at 12 and emerges at 13. From 13, another Upright Cross is worked above in the same manner. Work alternate rows over the area to complete the foundation.

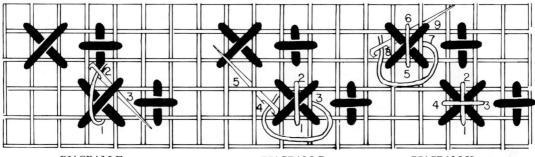

DIAGRAM F   DIAGRAM G   DIAGRAM H

DIAGRAM F shows the overstitching beginning. This is really the reverse of the foundation. The needle emerges at 1, is inserted at 2 and emerges at 3. DIAGRAM G shows the horizontal stitch being formed from 3 to 4, with the needle emerging at 5. DIAGRAM H shows the overstitching being worked on the top cross, with the needle moving from 5 through 8, to emerge finally at 9 in position to work No. 47 Cross Stitches over the Upright Crosses. These are worked in the same manner as the foundation stitches in DIAGRAMS B and C.

DIAGRAM I shows a completed area.

DIAGRAM I

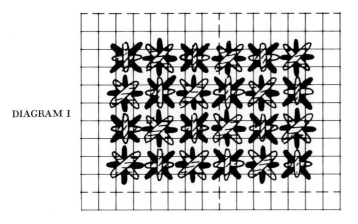

53 · CROSS STITCH, DOUBLE STRAIGHT

CANVAS: #12 mono   NEEDLE: Size 18
TO COVER ONE SQUARE INCH: 1½ lengths Persian yarn
NUMBER OF THREADS: 1 full strand

This is done by working a row of No. 47 Cross Stitches over a foundation of No. 75 Upright Cross Stitches. You will have to use good judgment in deciding how heavy a yarn to use. If it is too heavy, the effect will be lost. Sometimes a full strand of Persian is too much, while two threads won't cover. This varies somewhat with color, since lighter yarns tend to be fluffier, in which case two threads cover nicely. English crewel yarns sometimes work the best with this stitch. Two colors are also effective.

Work is done from left to right. Left-handers should work from right to left. DIAGRAMS A and B show an Upright Cross being worked in the usual manner from 1 to 5. DIAGRAMS C and D show the No. 47 Cross Stitch worked over the Upright Cross from 5, with the needle emerging finally at 9, in position to work the next pattern. Work continues across in this manner. Successive rows are worked in the spaces left. This stitch can be worked in horizontal rows, but make sure that all the top stitches slant in the same direction. It may be necessary to do short stitches at edges for a squared-off appearance.

DIAGRAM E shows a completed area.

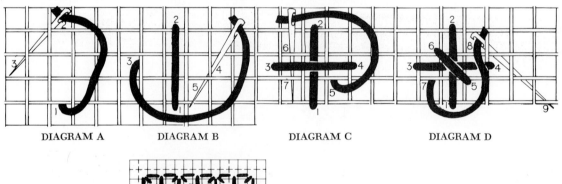

DIAGRAM A   DIAGRAM B   DIAGRAM C   DIAGRAM D

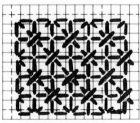

DIAGRAM E

54 · CROSS STITCH, HALF (*Tent Stitch, Gros Point*)

CANVAS: #10 penelope   NEEDLE: Size 18
TO COVER ONE SQUARE INCH: ¾ length Persian yarn
NUMBER OF THREADS: 1 full strand

This is the third of the basic Tent Stitches. It looks the same as No. 11 Basketweave and No. 36 Continental, but uses much less yarn. Aside from this, there is little to say in its favor. Because of the needle action, it is difficult to get a smooth rhythm, and therefore a smooth texture. It's impossible to work on mono canvas as the weave permits the yarn to slip. Note that the double penelope canvas thread is treated like a single thread.

Work is done from left to right starting at the upper left. Left-handers should start at the lower right and turn the diagrams upside down. DIAGRAM A shows how to anchor the yarn by the "waste knot" method. The yarn is knotted at one end, and the needle is inserted from the top at 1, leaving the knot out. The needle emerges at 2, is reinserted at 3 completing the first stitch, and emerges at 4. DIAGRAM B shows the needle inserted at 5 and emerging at 6 forming a second stitch, covering the underneath yarn in the same manner. When the knot is reached, clip it off, and pass the loose end to the back. At the end of this and successive rows, turn the canvas bottom to top so you always work from left to right. At the end of the first row, reverse the canvas and work the second row exactly like the first. On the final stitch of this and all even rows, the needle is not brought up until the canvas has been turned. It then emerges one thread directly below the final stitch of the previous row.

DIAGRAM C shows the canvas reversed and row 2 starting. DIAGRAM D shows direction of following rows, with row 5 starting.

DIAGRAM E shows a completed area.

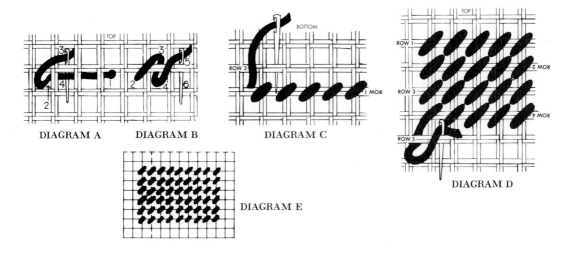

DIAGRAM A   DIAGRAM B   DIAGRAM C   DIAGRAM D

DIAGRAM E

55 · CROSS STITCH, HALF VERTICAL

CANVAS: #12 mono   NEEDLE: Size 18

TO COVER ONE SQUARE INCH: ¾ length Persian yarn

NUMBER OF THREADS: 1 full strand

This looks the same as No. 54 Half Cross, but may be a little easier to work. It doesn't distort the canvas quite as much, and it gives the smoothest appearance possible for a Half Cross Stitch. Although they can be used in combination on borders, you should always stick to one or the other when working areas of half crosses, or ridges will develop that can't be blocked out.

Work begins at the lower right and moves up. Left-handers should begin at the upper left and turn the diagrams upside down. DIAGRAM A shows how to start, as the first stitch is worked from 1 to 3. DIAGRAM B shows the next stitch being worked in the same manner from 3 to 5. Continue this way along the row, turning the canvas upside down at the end of each successive row. DIAGRAM C shows how to start row 2.

DIAGRAM D shows a completed area.

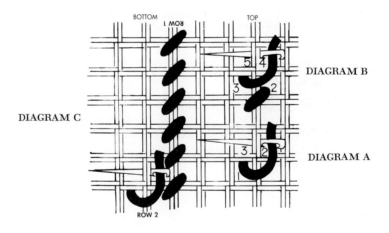

DIAGRAM B

DIAGRAM C

DIAGRAM A

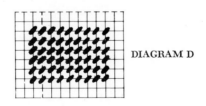

DIAGRAM D

56 · CROSS STITCH, HALF, with LAID THREAD

CANVAS: #12 mono   NEEDLE: Size 18

TO COVER ONE SQUARE INCH: 1⅔ lengths Persian yarn

NUMBER OF THREADS: 2

This is the only Half Cross Stitch that can be worked on mono canvas. The laid thread gives it a raised effect, something like the ridges on corduroy.

Work begins a few threads in from the upper left edge. It is worked back and forth without turning the canvas. Left-handers should begin at the lower right and turn the diagram upside down. DIAGRAM A shows how to start, as the needle is brought to the front by splitting the canvas intersection or thread at 1, at the right of the canvas thread to be covered. The yarn is laid across and inserted just above the thread being covered at 2, and emerges directly below at 3. DIAGRAM B shows the first stitch being worked over the laid yarn in No. 54 Half Cross Stitch, following numbers 3 to 5. DIAGRAM C shows the laid thread covered with Half Cross Stitches (numbers 3 to 12), and the start of the next row, with the needle splitting the canvas threads just below the first row. The final stitch on each row will cover the split canvas intersection.

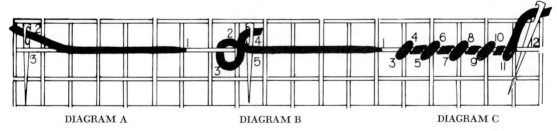

DIAGRAM A   DIAGRAM B   DIAGRAM C

57 · CROSS STITCH, HEAVY

CANVAS: #12 mono   NEEDLE: Size 18
TO COVER ONE SQUARE INCH: 1 length Persian yarn
NUMBER OF THREADS: 1 full strand

This stitch should be worked only on medium to fine canvas as the individual stitches are long and can snag easily. It is made by working three long No. 176 Satin Stitches, and crossing them with three others.

Work is done in horizontal rows and in both directions, so left-handers can work as directed. DIAGRAMS A and B show the three foundation stitches being worked from 1 to 6, with the needle emerging at 7 in position to work the crossing stitches. DIAGRAM C shows two crossing stitches completed and a third in progress from 11 to 12, with the needle emerging at 13 in position to start the next pattern. On the return row, the vertical stitches are worked in the spaces left between patterns on the first row. Successive rows are worked in the same manner.

DIAGRAM D shows a completed area. For a squared-off appearance, do extra stitches to cover any spots of canvas still showing.

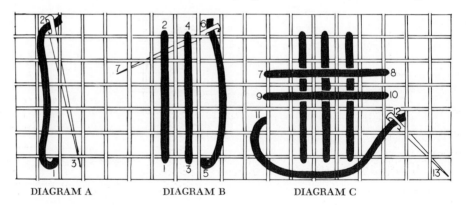

DIAGRAM A   DIAGRAM B   DIAGRAM C

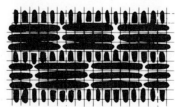

DIAGRAM D

58 · CROSS STITCH, HOUNDSTOOTH

CANVAS: #12 mono   NEEDLE: Size 18

TO COVER ONE SQUARE INCH: 3 lengths Persian yarn worked over 2
threads; 2 lengths worked over 3 threads

NUMBER OF THREADS: 2 (over 2 threads); 1 full strand (over 3 threads)

This stitch produces a delightful rough texture. By keeping the tension loose, the yarn will fluff out and cover the entire background.

Work is done in horizontal rows beginning at the left edge. Left-handers should begin at the right and turn the diagrams upside down. DIAGRAM A shows a No. 54 Half Cross Stitch worked over three canvas threads, from 1 to 3. DIAGRAM B shows the needle slipping under the first stitch to form a loop. DIAGRAM C shows the needle inserted at 4 to emerge at 5. DIAGRAM D shows a second loop being formed as the needle slips under the previous stitch and the top part of the first loop. DIAGRAM E shows the needle reinserted at 6 to complete the pattern, and emerging at 7 to start the next.

DIAGRAM F shows a completed area.

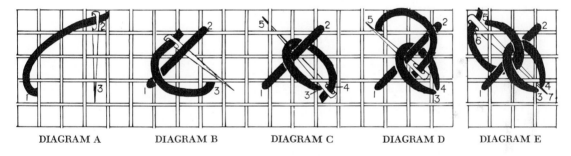

DIAGRAM A   DIAGRAM B   DIAGRAM C   DIAGRAM D   DIAGRAM E

DIAGRAM F

59 · CROSS STITCH, ITALIAN
(*Two-Sided Cross Stitch, Arrowhead Cross*)

CANVAS: #12 mono   NEEDLE: Size 18

TO COVER ONE SQUARE INCH: 1⅓ lengths Persian yarn

NUMBER OF THREADS: 2

This stitch covers well on both front and back, which makes it able to withstand all kinds of heavy use.

It is worked horizontally, starting at the bottom left. Each row is worked in the same direction. Left-handers should hold a mirror next to the diagrams to see how to work in reverse. DIAGRAM A shows the base being worked from 1 to 2, with the needle emerging at 3. DIAGRAM B shows the first part of the cross being worked to upper right at 4, with the needle finally emerging at 5. DIAGRAM C shows a vertical stitch worked on the left side from 5 to 6, with the needle emerging at 7. DIAGRAM D shows the cross completed as the needle is inserted at 8 and emerges at 9. This completes the procedure. The right side of the square is completed by the next pattern, and the top is completed by the row above. Continue working in this manner across the row, making an extra vertical stitch at the end to complete the last pattern.

DIAGRAM E shows how to work the final row; when the needle is inserted at 8 (as in DIAGRAM D) it emerges at the top at 9, and completes the top at 10. It then emerges at 11 to start the next stitch. Work continues across until the top row is covered.

DIAGRAM F shows a completed area.

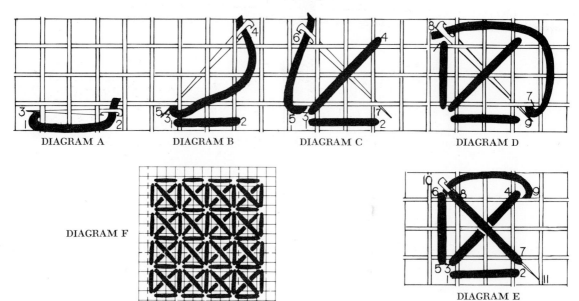

DIAGRAM A   DIAGRAM B   DIAGRAM C   DIAGRAM D

DIAGRAM F

DIAGRAM E

60 · CROSS STITCH, LONG-ARMED
(*Long-Legged Cross, Plaited Slav, Portuguese Cross*)

CANVAS: #12 mono   NEEDLE: Size 18

TO COVER ONE SQUARE INCH: 1½ lengths Persian yarn

NUMBER OF THREADS: 2

This is a very old canvas stitch used today for making rugs.

Work is done horizontally, starting at the left edge. It can be worked in either direction, so left-handers need no special instructions. DIAGRAMS A and B show how to begin by working a No. 47 Cross Stitch following numbers 1 to 4, with the needle emerging at 5. This is not part of the pattern, but it gives the edge a finished appearance. DIAGRAM C shows a long slanting stitch being worked from 5 to 6, with the needle emerging at 7. DIAGRAM D shows the long stitch crossed from 7 to 8, with the needle emerging at 9. DIAGRAM E shows another long stitch being worked from 9 to 10, with the needle emerging at 11. Work continues by repeating the action in DIAGRAMS D and E to the end of the row. DIAGRAM F shows how to finish off a row by working a small stitch from 13 to 14.

DIAGRAM G shows a completed area.

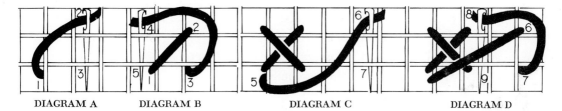

DIAGRAM A   DIAGRAM B   DIAGRAM C   DIAGRAM D

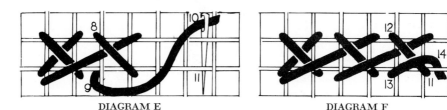

DIAGRAM E   DIAGRAM F

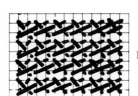

DIAGRAM G

61 · CROSS STITCH, LONG-ARMED REVERSE (*Greek Stitch*)

CANVAS: #12 mono   NEEDLE: Size 18
TO COVER ONE SQUARE INCH: 1½ lengths Persian yarn
NUMBER OF THREADS: 2

This is the same as No. 60 Long-Armed Cross Stitch except that it is worked from right to left. Left-handers can follow the directions as given. DIAGRAMS A and B show a small Cross Stitch worked from 1 to 4, with the needle emerging at 5. DIAGRAM C shows the stitch being worked from 5 to 6, with the needle emerging at 7. Work is continued by alternating the action in DIAGRAMS B and C.

To finish the row, see DIAGRAM F of No. 60 Long-Armed Cross Stitch, and reverse the action.

DIAGRAM D shows a completed area. DIAGRAM E shows an area worked by alternating this stitch with No. 60 Long-Armed Cross Stitches, producing a braidlike texture.

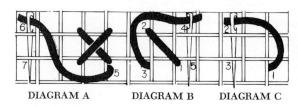

DIAGRAM A   DIAGRAM B   DIAGRAM C

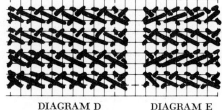

DIAGRAM D   DIAGRAM E

62 · CROSS STITCH, LONG-ARMED CORNER

CANVAS: #12 mono   NEEDLE: Size 18
TO COVER ONE SQUARE INCH: 1½ lengths Persian yarn
NUMBER OF THREADS: 2

Turning a corner with this is basically a matter of taking an extra stitch to give a finished appearance. DIAGRAM A shows a completed No. 60 Long-Armed Cross Stitch, with the needle emerging at 1, ready to turn the corner. DIAGRAM B shows the small stitch being made, with the needle inserted at 2 and emerging at 3. DIAGRAM C shows the first long stitch being worked in the new direction, from 3 to 4, with the needle emerging at 5. Work continues as for No. 60 Long-Armed Cross Stitch.

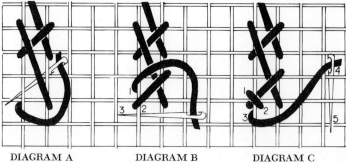

DIAGRAM A   DIAGRAM B   DIAGRAM C

63 · CROSS STITCH, LONG-ARMED DIAGONAL

CANVAS: #12 mono   NEEDLE: Size 18

TO COVER ONE INCH: 1½ lengths Persian yarn

NUMBER OF THREADS: 2

This is worked diagonally from lower left to upper right in the same manner as No. 60 Long-Armed Cross Stitch. Left-handers should start at the upper right and turn the diagrams upside down. The upright stitches may be worked over two or four canvas threads, depending on the size canvas and type of yarn.

DIAGRAMS A and B show the first stitch being worked from 1 to 2 and the second in progress from 3 to 4, with the needle emerging at 5. Work is continued in this manner, alternating the action in DIAGRAMS A and B.

DIAGRAM C shows how to turn a corner as a long slanting stitch is worked in a different direction from 1 to 2, with the needle emerging at 3. From 3, the needle would be inserted four threads down and emerge two threads up and two to the left to be in position for the next slanting stitch. Work continues in this manner.

DIAGRAM D shows an area worked in both directions with a small stitch worked at each end for a finished appearance.

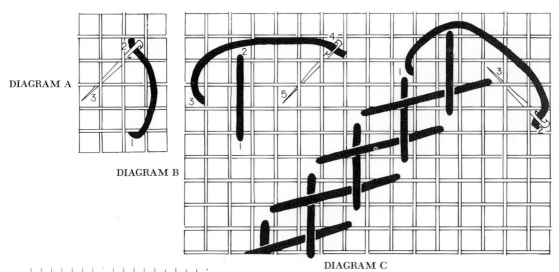

DIAGRAM A

DIAGRAM B

DIAGRAM C

DIAGRAM D

64 · CROSS STITCH, MONTENEGRIN
(*Two-Sided Montenegrin, Montenegrin Stitch*)

CANVAS: #12 mono   NEEDLE: Size 18

TO COVER ONE SQUARE INCH: 1 length Persian yarn worked over 4 threads

NUMBER OF THREADS: 1 full strand

This stitch is most successful worked over four threads on #12 mono. It can also be worked over two threads, but is not as dramatic.

Work is done horizontally from left to right. Left-handers should start at the right and reverse the procedure. DIAGRAM A shows how to start by working a slanting stitch from 1 to 2, with the needle emerging at 3. DIAGRAM B shows an upright stitch worked from 3 to 4, with the needle emerging at 5. These are not part of the pattern, but are used to give the edge a finished look. DIAGRAM C shows a long slanting stitch being worked from 5 to 6, with the needle emerging at 7. DIAGRAM D shows a shorter slanting stitch worked in the opposite direction from 7 to 8, with the needle emerging at 9. DIAGRAM E shows an upright stitch being worked from 9 to 10, with the needle emerging at 11. Work is continued by repeating the action in DIAGRAMS C, D and E. DIAGRAM F shows an upright stitch being worked to finish off a line.

DIAGRAM G shows a completed area.

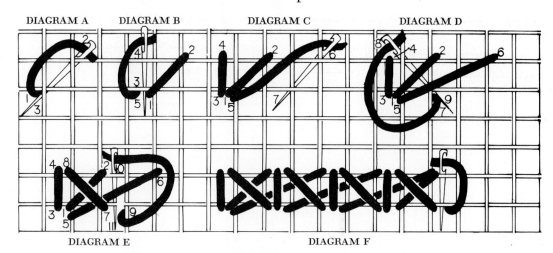

DIAGRAM A   DIAGRAM B   DIAGRAM C   DIAGRAM D

DIAGRAM E   DIAGRAM F

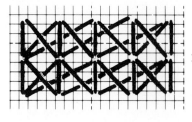

DIAGRAM G

65 · CROSS STITCH, OBLONG

CANVAS: #12 mono   NEEDLE: Size 18

TO COVER ONE SQUARE INCH: 1 length Persian yarn (for a 2-to-4
proportion)

NUMBER OF THREADS: 1 full strand

This is worked the same as No. 47 Cross Stitch, but the length of the stitches is greater than the width. It is diagrammed with a two-four proportion, but you may work over any number of threads as long as the proportion remains the same.

Work is done in horizontal rows beginning at the upper left. Left-handers should begin at the lower right and reverse the procedure. DIAGRAM A shows the first stitch being worked from 1 to 2, with the needle emerging at 3. Work continues across in this manner. DIAGRAM B shows how to work the return journey as the first stitch is formed from 1 to 2, with the needle emerging at 3. Remember to keep all the top stitches slanting in the same direction. Successive rows are worked in the same openings as the base of these stitches.

DIAGRAM C shows a completed area worked with No. 9 Back Stitches between rows. This gives a nice finished look, but uses a little more yarn.

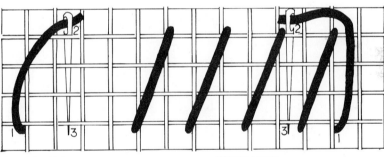

DIAGRAM A   DIAGRAM B

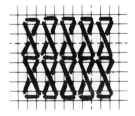

DIAGRAM C

66 · CROSS STITCH, OBLONG with BACK STITCH

CANVAS: #12 mono   NEEDLE: Size 18

TO COVER ONE SQUARE INCH: 1¼ lengths Persian yarn

NUMBER OF THREADS: 1 full strand

This is a combination of No. 65 Oblong Cross Stitches with overstitching in No. 9 Back Stitches, which makes it more durable. Unless you plan to work the Back Stitches in another color, complete one entire pattern before moving to the next.

Work is done horizontally from left to right. Left-handers should start at the right and reverse the procedure. DIAGRAM A shows a Cross Stitch being worked, with the needle emerging at 5 in position to work the Back Stitch. DIAGRAM B shows the Back Stitch being worked from 5 to 6, with the needle emerging at 7 in position to work the next pattern.

DIAGRAM C shows a completed area. Back Stitches can also be worked between rows if desired.

DIAGRAM A 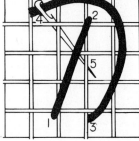  DIAGRAM B

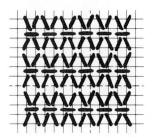 DIAGRAM C

67 · CROSS STITCH, PLAITED (*Braided Cross Stitch*)

CANVAS: #12 mono   NEEDLE: Size 18

TO COVER ONE SQUARE INCH: ⅞ length Persian yarn

NUMBER OF THREADS: 2

This stitch is worked back and forth in overlapping rows producing a braided appearance. It covers both sides well, which makes it very durable. The long stitches are secured by small ones, so there is no danger of snagging. Worked on #12 mono with a six-four proportion, some detail is lost, but this is a good proportion for larger canvas.

Work starts six canvas threads below the left edge. It is worked in both directions so left-handers need no special instructions. Diagram A shows how to begin by working a long slanted stitch from 1 to 2, with the needle emerging at 3. Diagram B shows a short cross worked from 3 to 4, with the needle emerging at 5. Work is continued by alternating the action in Diagrams A and B.

Diagram C shows how to start the return journey by working a long stitch from 9 to 10, with the needle emerging at 11. Diagram D shows a short cross formed from 11 to 12, with the needle emerging at 13. Work on this journey is continued by alternating the action in Diagrams C and D. The remaining odd rows are worked from left to right, even rows from right to left. On the final row it is best to work small stitches in the opposite direction to those on the previous row.

Diagram E shows a completed area with the extra slanting stitches worked on the last row.

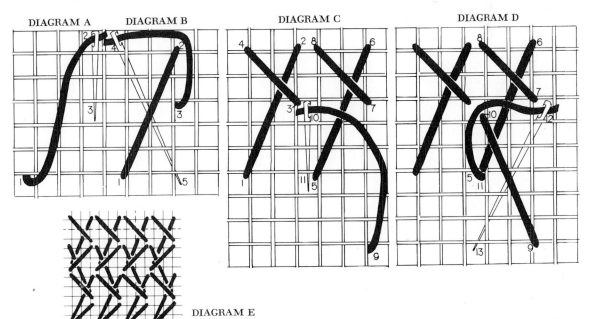

DIAGRAM A   DIAGRAM B   DIAGRAM C   DIAGRAM D

DIAGRAM E

68 · CROSS STITCH, REINFORCED

CANVAS: #12 mono   NEEDLE: Size 18

TO COVER ONE SQUARE INCH: 2 lengths Persian yarn worked over 2 threads

NUMBER OF THREADS: 2

The overall effect of this stitch can best be appreciated when it is worked on a large canvas. On fine canvas it looks like No. 47 Cross Stitch with a slightly raised effect.

Work is done horizontally starting at the upper left. Left-handers should start at the lower right and reverse the procedure. DIAGRAMS A and B show a Cross Stitch being worked, with the needle emerging finally at 5. DIAGRAMS C and D show a second cross being formed in the same direction as the original stitch. From 5, the needle is slipped under the stitch worked from 3 to 4, inserted at 6, and emerges at 7 in position to work the next stitch. Work continues in this manner.

DIAGRAM E shows a completed area.

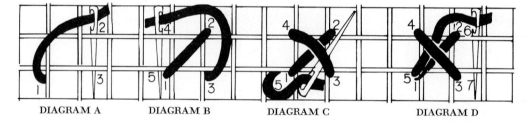

DIAGRAM A   DIAGRAM B   DIAGRAM C   DIAGRAM D

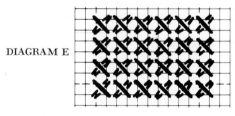

DIAGRAM E

69 · CROSS STITCH, REVERSED

CANVAS: #12 mono   NEEDLE: Size 18

TO COVER ONE SQUARE INCH: 1⅓ lengths Persian yarn worked over 2 threads; 3 lengths worked over 1 thread

NUMBER OF THREADS: 2 (over 2 threads); 1 (over 1 thread)

This stitch can be done by either of the methods diagrammed here. It is worked by reversing the direction of the cross on alternate stitches both horizontally and vertically. Each method is worked in both directions, so left-handers can work as directed.

DIAGRAM A shows how to start the first method by working a Cross Stitch, with the needle emerging at 5 in position to work the next stitch. DIAGRAM B shows the next stitch being worked from 5 to 6, with the needle emerging at 7. DIAGRAM C shows the stitch being crossed from 7 to 8, with the needle emerging at 9. Note that it has been worked in the opposite direction from the first stitch. Work is continued by alternating these two stitches. DIAGRAM D shows how to start the next row, with the first stitch worked in the opposite direction from the stitch above.

The second method is to lay the base stitches on one journey and cross them on the return trip. DIAGRAMS E and F show the first slanting stitches being made. These alternate across the row. DIAGRAM G shows how to work the return journey by reversing the procedure. The first is worked from 1 to 2, with the needle emerging at 3. The next is worked by reinserting the needle at 1 and proceeding as before.

DIAGRAM H shows a completed area. Both methods produce the same finished appearance.

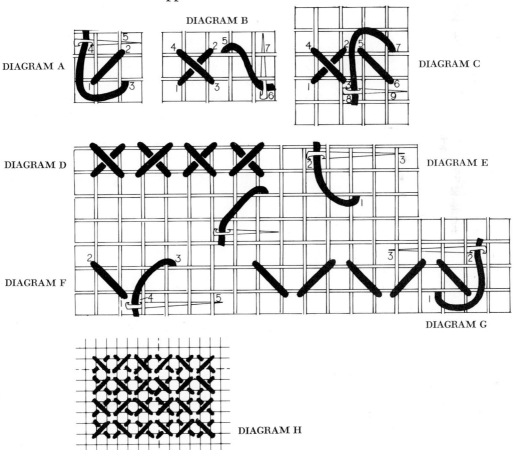

70 · CROSS STITCH, STAGGERED

CANVAS: #12 mono   NEEDLE: Size 18

TO COVER ONE SQUARE INCH: 1⅓ lengths Persian yarn for large cross;
1 length for small cross

NUMBER OF THREADS: 2 for large cross; 1 for small cross

These stitches are staggered to give the rows a diagonal appearance.

Work is done horizontally, beginning at the upper left. Left-handers should start at the lower right and turn the diagrams upside down. DIAGRAM A shows the first large cross being made, with the needle emerging at 5. Note that this is one thread below the usual emerging point. DIAGRAMS B and C show the second large cross worked in the usual manner, with the needle emerging at 9. DIAGRAM D shows how to finish the edge. Small slanting stitches are made in each direction beside the last Cross Stitch. These give a good finish and should be worked before the small crosses. The needle emerges one intersection away to work the next Cross Stitch on the return journey from 1 to 5. The up journey is continued in the same way.

DIAGRAM E shows the first small cross being worked, with the needle emerging at 5 to work the next stitch. Work is continued on up and down rows by working small crosses over all intersections left between the large crosses.

DIAGRAM F shows a completed area. A different effect is produced by using a contrasting color for the small crosses. Another variation is to use the same color for the small cross but a different yarn, such as mercerized cotton or floss whose glossy finish provides an interesting contrast.

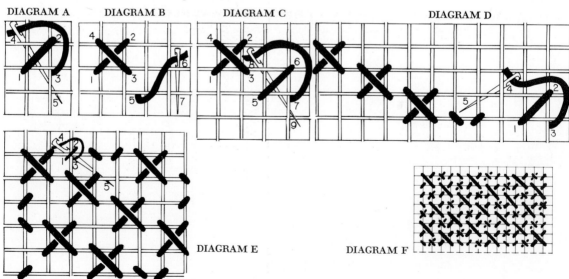

DIAGRAM A   DIAGRAM B   DIAGRAM C   DIAGRAM D

DIAGRAM E   DIAGRAM F

71 · CROSS STITCH, ST. GEORGE and ST. ANDREW

CANVAS: #12 mono   NEEDLE: Size 18

TO COVER ONE SQUARE INCH: 1½ lengths Persian yarn if working in 1 color;

⅞ length Persian yarn for regular cross,

and ⅔ length for upright cross if working in 2 colors

NUMBER OF THREADS: 1 full strand

This is one of the oldest of the Cross Stitch variations, and it is particularly effective in two colors. As the diagrams show, the stitch is formed by checkerboard rows of No. 47 Cross Stitch, with No. 75 Upright Crosses worked in the empty spaces between them.

Work diagonal rows of regular Cross Stitch first. You can finish each cross completely before moving on to the next. DIAGRAM A shows the beginning of the first row, with one Cross Stitch done from 1 to 4, and the needle emerging at 5, ready to start the second Cross Stitch in the diagonal row, just below and to the right of the first. Work continues in this way to the end of the area. DIAGRAM B shows the second diagonal row starting at the top, on the same level as the top Cross Stitch on row one, with two empty canvas intersections between them. Work continues down to the end in this and all subsequent rows. Rows may be worked up and down as well as from the top.

The Upright Crosses are worked in diagonal rows from the bottom up in the spaces left between the Cross Stitch rows. DIAGRAM C shows the first Upright Cross completed from 1 to 4, with the needle emerging at 5, ready to start the second Upright Cross in the row. These rows also may be worked up and down as well as all from the bottom. Work continues in diagonal rows until all spaces are filled.

Just remember to have the top crossing of all stitches going in the same direction. DIAGRAM D shows a finished area.

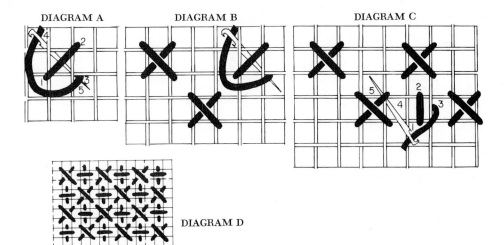

DIAGRAM A   DIAGRAM B   DIAGRAM C

DIAGRAM D

72 · CROSS STITCH, TRAMÉ

CANVAS: #12 mono   NEEDLE: Size 18

TO COVER ONE SQUARE INCH: 1⅝ lengths Persian yarn

NUMBER OF THREADS: 2

This is made with No. 47 Cross Stitches over a laid or tramé yarn.

Work is done horizontally starting at the upper left. Left-handers can do laid stitches as directed and work the Cross Stitches in whatever way is most comfortable. DIAGRAM A shows the yarn woven through several vertical threads before it emerges at 1. The stitch is then laid from 1 to 2, with the needle emerging at 3. DIAGRAM B shows a horizontal row of the laid work, while Cross Stitches are worked over them. The first journey is worked from 1 to 6, and the needle is beginning the return journey from 7 to complete the crosses.

DIAGRAM C shows a completed area. When done, the laid work gives a raised texture but doesn't show.

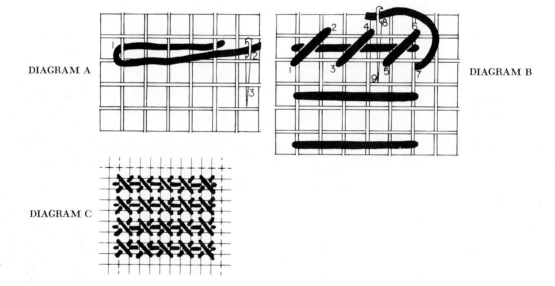

DIAGRAM A

DIAGRAM B

DIAGRAM C

73 · CROSS STITCH, TRIPLE

CANVAS: #12 mono NEEDLE: Size 18
TO COVER ONE SQUARE INCH: 1½ lengths Persian yarn
NUMBER OF THREADS: 2

This is formed by working two No. 65 Oblong Cross Stitches over a large No. 47 Cross Stitch. It covers the canvas well and looks best when the yarn used is not too heavy.

Work is done from left to right. Left-handers should start at the right and reverse the procedure. DIAGRAM A shows the large cross being worked, with the needle emerging at 5. DIAGRAM B shows the next stitch being worked from 5 to 6, with the needle emerging at 7. DIAGRAM C shows the next stitch being worked, with the needle emerging at 9. DIAGRAMS D and E show how to cross the last two stitches as the needle moves from 9, emerging finally at 13 in position to work the next pattern.

DIAGRAM F shows a completed area.

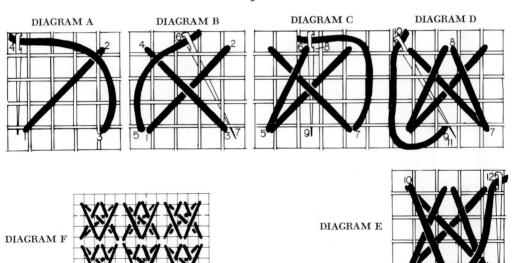

DIAGRAM A   DIAGRAM B   DIAGRAM C   DIAGRAM D

DIAGRAM F   DIAGRAM E

74 · CROSS STITCH, TWO-SIDED

CANVAS: #12 mono   NEEDLE: Size 18
TO COVER ONE SQUARE INCH: ¾ length Persian yarn
NUMBER OF THREADS: 2 full strands

As the name indicates, this stitch looks the same on both sides of the canvas. It must be worked over at least four canvas threads to do this. It was originally used on linens that would be seen or used on both sides.

DIAGRAM A shows the first journey in progress with the dotted lines indicating the yarn on the back. At the end of the row, the needle is inserted in the same opening as usual, but passes back to the left before emerging again. DIAGRAM B shows the next step with the needle forming a small diagonal stitch. When actually working on a design, the needle is brought to the far side of the canvas to start the return journey. DIAGRAM C shows the return journey in progress with dotted lines indicating crosses being formed on the back. DIAGRAM D shows the last cross being worked with the needle emerging in position to continue back across the same row in the spaces left on the previous journeys. DIAGRAM E shows the next journey worked across, with the needle ready to complete the row of crosses.

No diagram is given for the finished stitch as it looks exactly like No. 47 Cross Stitch worked over four canvas threads.

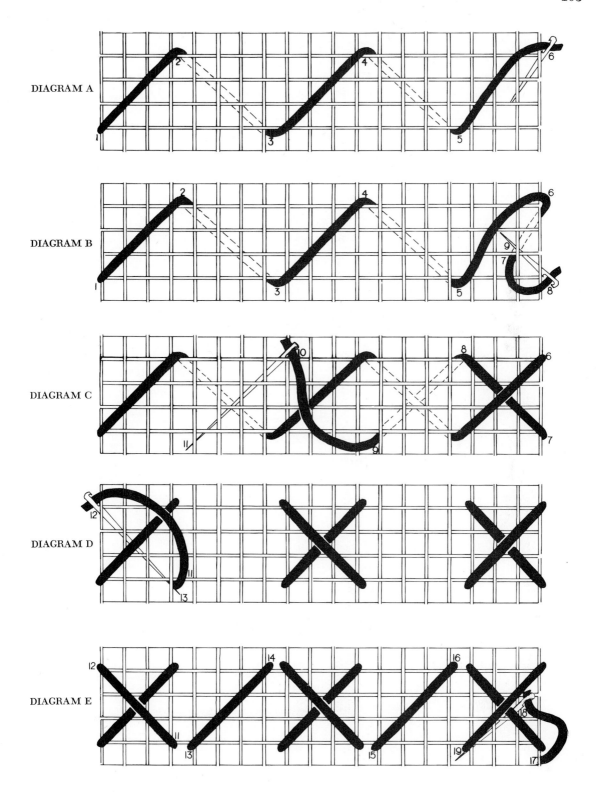

DIAGRAM A

DIAGRAM B

DIAGRAM C

DIAGRAM D

DIAGRAM E

75 · CROSS STITCH, UPRIGHT

CANVAS: #12 mono   NEEDLE: Size 18
TO COVER ONE SQUARE INCH: 1½ lengths Persian yarn
NUMBER OF THREADS: 2

This stitch looks exactly like a plus sign in arithmetic.

Rows are worked back and forth from top to bottom. Left-handers can follow the directions as given, but might be more comfortable working the stitches from the bottom up. DIAGRAM A shows the vertical stitch being made from 1 to 2 with the needle emerging at 3. DIAGRAM B shows the stitch being completed, with the needle inserted at 4 and emerging at 5 in position to start the next stitch. Work continues across in this manner. DIAGRAM C shows how to start the next row, which is worked in the spaces left on the first row. The needle emerges at 1, is inserted at 2, and emerges at 3 in position to work the next stitch. DIAGRAM D shows the cross being completed, with the needle emerging at 5. The row continues in this manner.

DIAGRAM E shows a completed area, with small stitches worked at the edges for a finished appearance. If the area has a diagonal edge, these stitches won't be necessary.

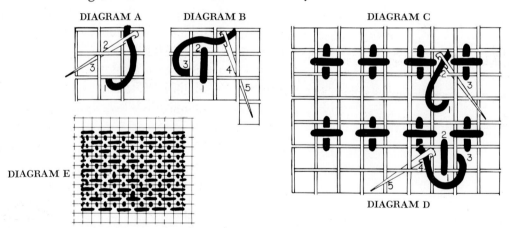

DIAGRAM A   DIAGRAM B   DIAGRAM C

DIAGRAM E

DIAGRAM D

76 · CROSS STITCH WITH BAR

CANVAS: #12 mono   NEEDLE: Size 18
TO COVER ONE SQUARE INCH: 1½ lengths Persian yarn
NUMBER OF THREADS: 2

This stitch covers the canvas well and produces an interesting texture.

Work is done in horizontal rows from left to right. Left-handers should start at the bottom right and turn the diagrams upside down.

DIAGRAM A shows a No. 47 Cross Stitch worked, with the needle emerging at 5. It is then inserted at 6 and emerges at 7 forming the bar. Work continues across the row in this manner.

DIAGRAM B shows a completed area. See No. 50 Diagonal Cross Stitch for a diagonal variation of this.

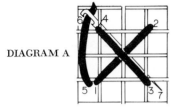 DIAGRAM A

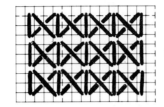 DIAGRAM B

77 · CROSS STITCH, WOVEN NO. 1

CANVAS: #12 mono   NEEDLE: Size 18
TO COVER ONE SQUARE INCH: ⅞ length Persian yarn
NUMBER OF THREADS: 1 full strand

With this method, the yarn is automatically woven in as the stitches are worked.

Work is done horizontally beginning at the top left. Left-handers should start at the lower right and turn the diagrams upside down. DIAGRAM A shows how to work the first stitch from 1 to 2, with the needle emerging at 3. DIAGRAM B shows a cross worked from 3 to 4, with the needle emerging at 5. DIAGRAM C shows the action from 5 to 7. DIAGRAMS D and E show the final stitch being worked. The yarn is slipped under the first stitch, inserted at 8 and emerges at 9 in position to work the next pattern. Work continues across in this manner and in the following rows. DIAGRAM F shows a completed area.

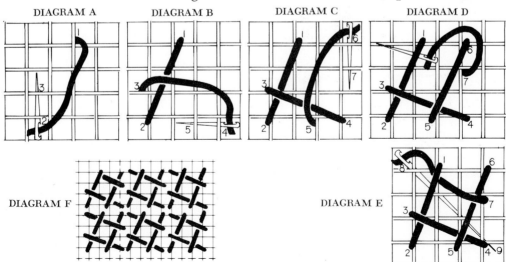

78 · CROSS STITCH, WOVEN NO. 2

CANVAS: #12 mono   NEEDLE: Size 18

TO COVER ONE SQUARE INCH: 1¼ lengths Persian yarn

NUMBER OF THREADS: 1 full strand

This makes a nice bulky stitch that can be used either as an overall pattern or as an isolated design.

Stitches are done horizontally from the top left, and are placed in horizontal rows. Left-handers should start at the bottom right and reverse the procedure. DIAGRAM A shows a Cross Stitch worked from 1 to 4, with the needle emerging at 5. DIAGRAM B shows the next stitch worked from 5 to 6, with the needle emerging at 7. DIAGRAM C shows two stitches being crossed from 7 to 8, with the needle emerging at 9. DIAGRAM D shows another crossing from 9 to 10, with the needle emerging at 11. DIAGRAM E shows the pattern being completed. As the needle moves from 11 to 12, it is slipped under the stitch already worked from 5 to 6 as shown, emerging finally at 13 in position to work the next pattern.

DIAGRAM F shows a completed area.

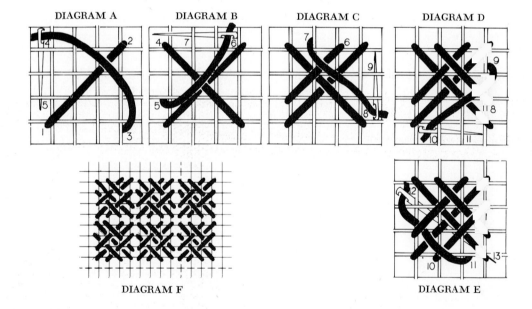

DIAGRAM A   DIAGRAM B   DIAGRAM C   DIAGRAM D

DIAGRAM F   DIAGRAM E

79 · CROSS STITCH, WOVEN NO. 3

CANVAS: #12 mono   NEEDLE: Size 18
TO COVER ONE SQUARE INCH: 1½ lengths Persian yarn
NUMBER OF THREADS: 1 full strand

The action of this stitch is similar to the top layer of No. 78 Woven Cross Stitch, but the basic large Cross Stitch is eliminated.

Stitches are worked horizontally from left to right. Left-handers should work from right to left and reverse the procedure. DIAGRAMS A, B, C and D show how to work the pattern as for the top layer of No. 78 Woven Cross Stitch. The needle emerging at 9 is in position to work the next pattern. DIAGRAM E shows how to work the second row in the spaces left by the first row, following numbers 1 to 7, so that no canvas shows. Spaces left around the edges should be filled with a few small stitches.

DIAGRAM F shows a completed area. DIAGRAM G shows a variation in which No. 47 Cross Stitches are worked in a contrasting color between the large crosses. It is easiest to work all the large crosses first in diagonal rows. To do this, after completing the first cross insert the needle five threads down and four to the left to start the next cross. Afterwards, fill in with small crosses.

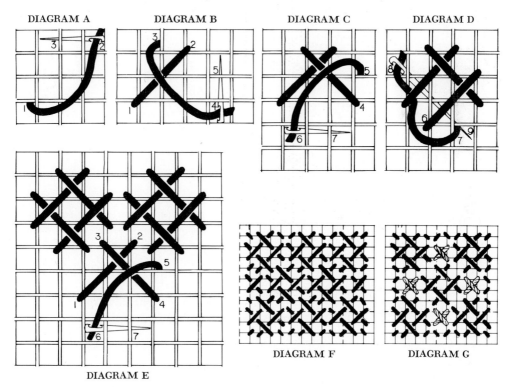

DIAGRAM A   DIAGRAM B   DIAGRAM C   DIAGRAM D

DIAGRAM E

DIAGRAM F   DIAGRAM G

80 · CUSHION STITCH NO. 1

CANVAS: #12 mono   NEEDLE: Size 18

This is one of two very old stitches that have the same name but are completely different. This one is very much the same as No. 10 Bargello (or Florentine) Stitch. The main difference (as described in 1880 in the *Handbook of Embroidery* by Lady Marion Alford) is that it used to be worked over very fine evenweave linen. Yarn requirements vary according to the length of the stitches.

Its beauty consists in its perfect regularity. Stitches are uniform in length across the design; each row starts half the height above (or below) the stitches of the preceding row, and is kept the same length throughout.

The diagram shows placement of stitches along a row. When worked very fine, the finished effect is that of a woven fabric.

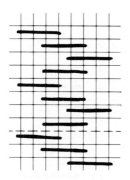

81 · CUSHION STITCH NO. 2

CANVAS: #12 mono   NEEDLE: Size 18

TO COVER ONE SQUARE INCH: 1⅔ lengths Persian yarn if worked in 1 color

NUMBER OF THREADS: 1 full strand

This stitch is a more common version which makes a nice background covering as well as a good isolated design. Although it looks like No. 179 Scotch Stitch, it doesn't distort the canvas as much, since it doesn't have all stitches slanting in the same direction.

Work is done diagonally. Left-handers should reverse the procedure, which means slanting the long laid stitch from lower right to upper left. DIAGRAMS A to E show the first five stitches being worked, all slanting from lower left to upper right, with the needle emerging at 11. The needle is now in position to work another group of five stitches in the same manner. Work continues this way until the area is covered. Alternate rows can be worked from the bottom up as long as care is taken to slant all the stitches in the same direction. Note that three vertical and three horizontal canvas threads are left between rows.

DIAGRAM F shows how to start the next step as a long stitch is placed between two patterns from 1 to 2, with the needle emerging at 3. DIAGRAM G shows how to work the last step as a five-stitch pattern, slanting in the opposite direction, is worked over the laid thread following numbers 3 to 13. At 13 the needle is in position to work the next five-stitch pattern over the rest of the laid thread.

DIAGRAM H shows a completed area. An interesting effect is achieved by working the long stitch in a contrasting color. Even if worked in the same color, the stitch appears to have different shadings because of the slants.

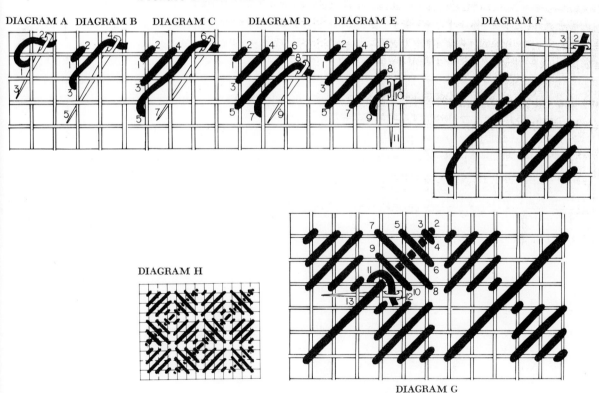

DIAGRAM A   DIAGRAM B   DIAGRAM C   DIAGRAM D   DIAGRAM E   DIAGRAM F

DIAGRAM H

DIAGRAM G

82 · DARNING STITCH

CANVAS: #12 mono   NEEDLE: Size 18

TO COVER ONE SQUARE INCH: 1 length Persian yarn

NUMBER OF THREADS: 1 full strand

This can be varied in many ways. The main thing to remember is that it does form a pattern so be sure there is enough yarn in the needle to cover the canvas. It covers both sides equally which makes it very durable. Stitch proportion is determined by the canvas size. On a larger canvas it is not advisable to carry the yarn over too many threads as it may snag.

Work is done in both directions so the left-hander can use the instructions as given. DIAGRAM A shows the action moving from 1 to 5. This is repeated across the row. DIAGRAM B shows how to work the return journey as the needle moves from 5 to 7, covering the canvas left unworked on the first journey. This action is repeated until all the spaces have been covered.

DIAGRAM C shows a completed area. There are innumerable variations. DIAGRAM D shows one worked at right angles to give a woven look. You can also stagger the stitches so the finished pattern looks like No. 17 Brick Stitch. Create your own variations by working out designs on graph paper and applying them to canvas.

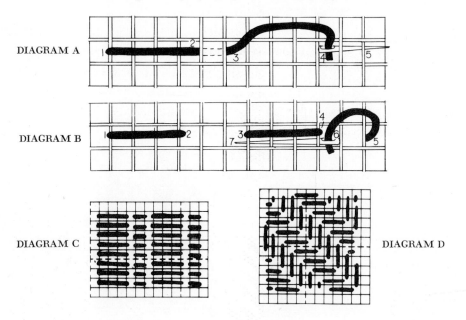

DIAGRAM A

DIAGRAM B

DIAGRAM C

DIAGRAM D

83 · DIAGONAL STITCH

CANVAS: #12 mono   NEEDLE: Size 18

TO COVER ONE SQUARE INCH: 1½ lengths Persian yarn

NUMBER OF THREADS: 1 full strand

This uses a great deal of yarn, but it covers the back well and is very durable. Tension should be kept loose in order to cover completely. It distorts the canvas somewhat, and it is best to outline the piece beforehand to help in blocking.

Work is done diagonally from top to bottom. Since it is done in both directions, left-handers should work as directed. If it's more comfortable, left-handers can also turn the diagrams upside down and reverse the procedure. DIAGRAMS A to C show the first five stitches being worked, following the numbers from 1 to 11. Note that the first and fifth stitches are the same size, as are the second and fourth. DIAGRAM D shows how to continue as the next four stitches are worked from 11 to 18. The diagram also shows how to start the up row. From 18, the needle emerges at 19, is inserted at 20, and emerges at 21. The dotted lines indicate the yarn on the back. DIAGRAM E shows how to work the next three stitches at the lower edge from 22, with the needle emerging at 29, in position to work the first long stitch in the row. Work continues up, with adjusting stitches taken at the top as for the down row.

DIAGRAM F shows a completed area with adjusting stitches worked on all four edges. If tension is tight there may be spaces left between rows. These can be filled with No. 9 Back Stitches.

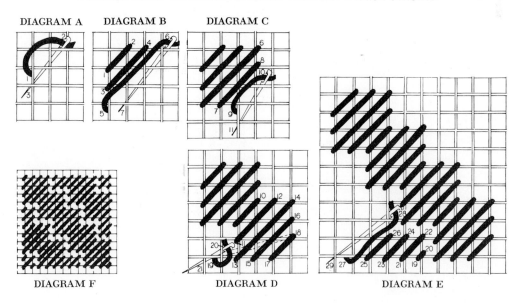

DIAGRAM A   DIAGRAM B   DIAGRAM C

DIAGRAM F   DIAGRAM D   DIAGRAM E

84 · DIAMOND EYELET STITCH

CANVAS: #12 mono   NEEDLE: Size 18

TO FORM ONE PATTERN: ½ length Persian yarn without No. 9 Back
Stitches; 1⅔ lengths with Back Stitches

NUMBER OF THREADS: 2

This works well either as an isolated stitch or overall pattern. It uses a lot of yarn and a sample piece should be worked first. Fifteen stitches are inserted at the center opening so the yarn must be fine enough to pass through easily. At the same time, it must be heavy enough to cover at the outer edges where the stitches are spaced apart. Two threads of Persian yarn cover #12 mono nicely if a loose tension is maintained.

Work is done in either horizontal or diagonal rows. Left-handers should work in whatever way is most comfortable. This resembles No. 4 Algerian Eye Daisy Stitch. Consult those diagrams for specific working instructions. The stitch makes a true 45-degree angle. The needle is always inserted in the center and emerges at the outer edge. Remember to give a little yank each time the yarn is inserted so that

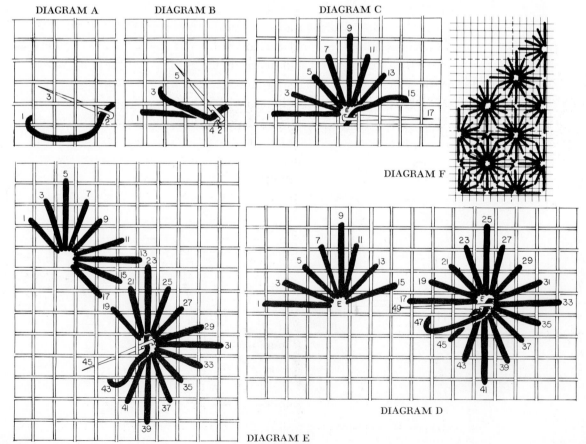

DIAGRAM A   DIAGRAM B   DIAGRAM C

DIAGRAM F

DIAGRAM D

DIAGRAM E

openings are left. These will be filled by No. 9 Back Stitches. Diagram A shows how to work horizontally from 1, with the needle emerging at 17 in position to work the return half of the pattern. Diagram B shows the return journey, and Diagram C the top half of the second row. Diagram D shows two half patterns worked and the progression used to work the bottom half of the second. Emerging at 49, the needle is ready to work the bottom of the next pattern in the same manner.

Diagram E shows two patterns being worked diagonally with the needle completing patterns on the up journey.

Diagram F shows a completed area with No. 9 Back Stitches.

85 · DIAMOND EYELET STITCH—VARIATION

CANVAS: #12 mono   NEEDLE: Size 18

TO FORM ONE PATTERN: ⅓ length Persian yarn, with small amount of contrasting yarn for Cross Stitch

NUMBER OF THREADS: 2

This stitch can be used as an isolated stitch or an area covering. The variation is in the length of the stitches and the fact that the needle never enters the center opening.

Work is done horizontally in both directions, with the top half worked on one journey and the lower half completed on the return journey. Left-handers should work as directed, but might be more comfortable starting at the right edge. Diagram A shows how to begin the pattern as the needle moves from 1 to 7. Diagram B shows the top half completed and the return journey in progress. There are four groups of three stitches each, with a short slanting stitch between groups, all done around the unworked center opening.

Diagram C shows a completed area with the center opening filled with a No. 47 Cross Stitch and No. 9 Back Stitches worked around the pattern.

DIAGRAM A   DIAGRAM B   DIAGRAM C

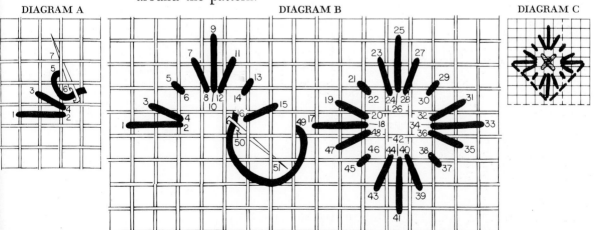

86 · DIAPER PATTERN STITCH

CANVAS: #12 mono   NEEDLE: Size 18

TO COVER ONE SQUARE INCH: ½ length Persian yarn in light color;
¾ length in dark color

NUMBER OF THREADS: 1 full strand

This is an old stitch that adapts itself nicely to canvas work. Make sure to use sharply contrasting colors, or the effect will be lost.

Work is done diagonally from the upper left to lower right. Left-handers should work from lower right to upper left and turn the diagrams upside down. The needle action is similar to No. 10 Bargello, with stitches worked in groups of three. DIAGRAM A shows a group of stitches being worked from 1 to 6, with the needle emerging at 7 in position to work another group. Work continues down in this manner. DIAGRAM B shows the first row completed and the second being worked in a contrasting color. Work continues by alternating these two rows.

DIAGRAM C shows a completed area, with long stitches filling between groups of stitches for a finished appearance.

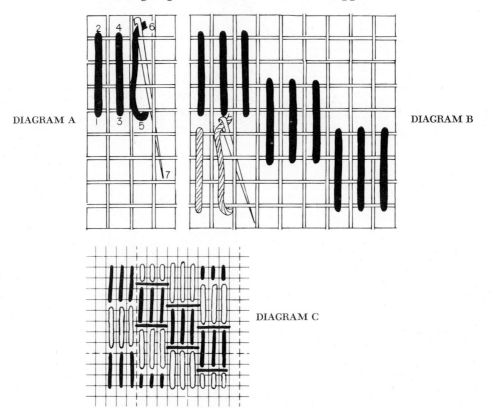

DIAGRAM A

DIAGRAM B

DIAGRAM C

87 · DOUBLE KNOT STITCH (*Palestrina Stitch*)

CANVAS: #12 mono   NEEDLE: Size 18
TO COVER ONE SQUARE INCH: ⅓ length Persian yarn
NUMBER OF THREADS: 1 full strand

This stitch is used mainly for outlining or area filling. It can also be used for solid filling by working the knots on each row between the knots on the previous row.

Work is done horizontally from left to right. Left-handers should reverse the procedure and work from right to left. DIAGRAM A shows how to begin by working a stitch from 1 to 2, with the needle emerging at 3. DIAGRAM B shows the needle carried up and slipped under the stitch (but not into the canvas). DIAGRAM C shows the needle slipped under the same stitch again, but to the right of the loop just formed. Hold the loop of yarn down with your free thumb so the needle passes over it. DIAGRAM D shows the knot completed, with the needle inserted at 4 and emerging at 5 in position to work the next knot.

DIAGRAM E shows a completed area. For an attractive variation, work with a soft cotton yarn. It shows off the stitch nicely and gives an interesting finish.

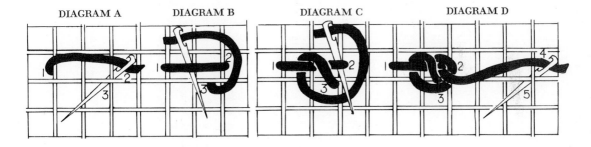

DIAGRAM A   DIAGRAM B   DIAGRAM C   DIAGRAM D

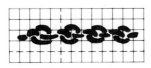

DIAGRAM E

88 · DOUBLE STAR STITCH

CANVAS: #12 mono   NEEDLE: Size 18

TO FORM ONE PATTERN: ⅞ length Persian yarn

NUMBER OF THREADS: 1 full strand

This is more of a design than a stitch. It can be used as a single motif or as a central pattern with other stitches worked around it.

Work is similar to No. 10 Bargello patterns, but this uses both horizontal and vertical stitches. The needle moves in counterclockwise direction in working the groups of stitches. Left-handers should work in the direction most comfortable.

DIAGRAM A shows the first four horizontal stitches being worked from 1 to 8. The needle then emerges at 9, in position to start the vertical stitches. DIAGRAM B shows the vertical stitches worked from 9 to the center at 16. This begins the up journey, which ends at the same height as 9. Work continues by turning the canvas to complete the other sides in the same manner.

DIAGRAM C shows a completed Double Star with a small No. 47 Cross Stitch worked in the center. A variation popular in the nineteenth century was to attach a bead to the center.

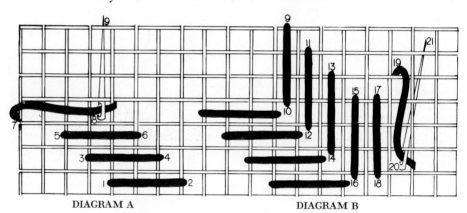

DIAGRAM A   DIAGRAM B

DIAGRAM C

89 · DOUBLE STITCH

CANVAS: #12 mono   NEEDLE: Size 18

TO COVER ONE SQUARE INCH: 1¼ lengths Persian yarn

NUMBER OF THREADS: 1 full strand

This is actually a Cross Stitch variation which alternates rows of No. 65 Oblong Cross Stitch with rows of small No. 47 Cross Stitch.

Work is done horizontally, with each row worked from left to right. Left-handers should start at the right and reverse the procedure. DIAGRAMS A and B show the first Oblong Cross Stitch being worked from 1 to 5. DIAGRAMS C and D show the small Cross Stitch being worked from 5, with the needle emerging at 9 in position to work the next Oblong Cross. Work continues across by repeating these two stitches. On the next row, small Cross Stitches are worked under Oblong Crosses and vice versa.

DIAGRAM E shows a completed area. DIAGRAM F shows the Oblong Crosses worked over three canvas threads and the small Cross Stitches worked over one thread. This can be done only on penelope canvas.

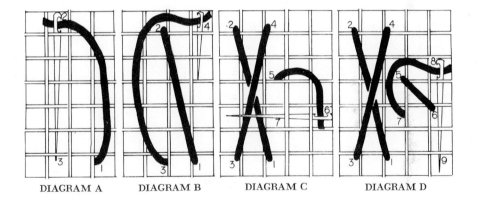

DIAGRAM A   DIAGRAM B   DIAGRAM C   DIAGRAM D

DIAGRAM E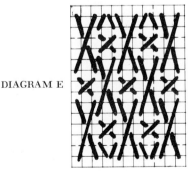

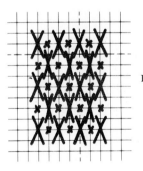 DIAGRAM F

90 · EASTERN STITCH (*Egyptian Stitch*)

CANVAS: #12 mono   NEEDLE: Size 18

TO COVER ONE SQUARE INCH: 1¾ lengths Persian yarn worked over 3
threads; 3 lengths worked over 2 threads

NUMBER OF THREADS: 2 (over 3 threads); 1 (over 2 threads)

This stitch has an interesting texture, especially good for rug designs. The back is covered well which also makes it good for any heavy-duty piece. The stitch size doesn't really matter, but working over three threads seems best on #12 mono.

Work is done horizontally from left to right starting at the upper left. Left-handers should start at the lower right and turn the diagrams upside down. DIAGRAM A shows how to begin by working a stitch from 1 to 2, with the needle emerging at 3. DIAGRAM B shows the next stitch worked from 3 to 4, with the needle emerging at 5. DIAGRAMS C to E show the next two loops worked over the two completed stitches. Hold the working yarn in place with your free thumb when forming loops. The needle is not inserted in the canvas until the end at 6, when it emerges at 7 in position to work the next pattern. Work continues in this manner. Note that the overstitches are actually No. 19 Buttonhole Stitches.

DIAGRAM F shows a completed area.

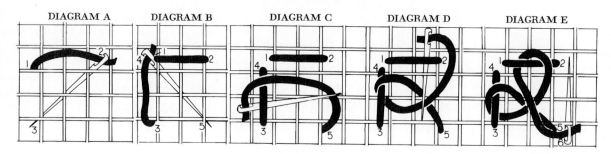

| DIAGRAM A | DIAGRAM B | DIAGRAM C | DIAGRAM D | DIAGRAM E |

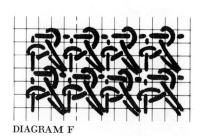

DIAGRAM F

91 · ECONOMIC STITCH (*Czar Stitch*)

CANVAS: #12 mono   NEEDLE: Size 18
TO COVER AN AREA ONE INCH LONG AND EIGHT CANVAS THREADS WIDE:
⅔ length Persian yarn
NUMBER OF THREADS: 1 full strand

This is actually a No. 65 Oblong Cross Stitch worked in vertical rows.

A series of slanting stitches is made in one direction and crossed on the return journey. Consult the diagrams for No. 65 for the working action. Left-handers should work as directed.

The diagram shows a completed area.

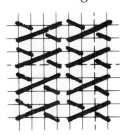

92 · FANCY STITCH

CANVAS: #12 mono   NEEDLE: Size 18
TO FORM ONE PATTERN: ¾ length Persian yarn
NUMBER OF THREADS: 1 full strand

This stitch is actually a pattern formed by slanting and horizontal stitches. It is not suitable for an entire area, but makes an unusual point of interest when combined with another stitch.

Work should be done in whatever way is most comfortable. I find it easiest to start at the upper left and work all the diagonal stitches clockwise. Fill the center with horizontal stitches starting at the top, with the first stitch worked over two canvas threads.

The diagram shows a completed area.

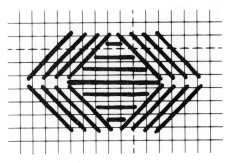

93 · FERN STITCH

CANVAS: #12 mono   NEEDLE: Size 18

TO COVER AN AREA ONE INCH LONG AND FOUR CANVAS THREADS WIDE:

¾ length Persian yarn

NUMBER OF THREADS: 2

This can be worked in a variety of ways depending on the desired effect. By varying the length of the arms, it can be used to fill irregular spaces.

Work is done from top to bottom with the needle sliding from right to left. Left-handers should slide the needle from left to right and reverse the procedure. DIAGRAM A shows how to begin by working a No. 47 Cross Stitch from 1 to 4, with the needle emerging at 5. It is not part of the actual pattern, but serves to give the edge a finished look. DIAGRAM B shows how to start the pattern by working a stitch from 5 to 6, with the needle emerging at 7. DIAGRAM C shows how to continue. From 7, the needle is inserted at 8 and emerges at 9. Work continues by alternating the action in DIAGRAMS B and C.

DIAGRAM D shows a completed area, with two stitches worked at each edge for a finished appearance. DIAGRAM E shows the stitch in a different proportion. This can be done only on penelope canvas.

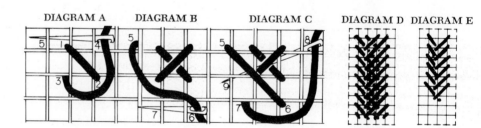

DIAGRAM A   DIAGRAM B   DIAGRAM C   DIAGRAM D   DIAGRAM E

94 · FERN STITCH, LEAF

This stitch produces a neat-looking leaf effect. Yarn requirements vary with canvas and stitch size.

Work begins with a single upright stitch. The rest is worked as for No. 93 Fern Stitch, but the stitches are varied in length to produce the leaflike appearance.

The diagram shows a completed area.

95 · FISHBONE STITCH (*Long and Short Oblique Stitch*)

CANVAS: #12 mono   NEEDLE: Size 18

TO COVER ONE SQUARE INCH: 1 length Persian yarn

NUMBER OF THREADS: 2

Essentially this is composed of diagonal stitches tied down at top or bottom. It is done in rows alternately slanting up and down to give the fishbone effect. For practice purposes requirements are given for mono canvas, but it is most successfully worked on penelope.

There are several methods of working this, all producing the same finished appearance.

One method is to work from the bottom up. Left-handers should reverse the procedure, using a mirror next to the diagrams if necessary. DIAGRAM A shows the first stitch being formed as the needle moves from 1 to 4, with the needle emerging at 5 in position to work the next stitch in the row above it.

In the second method, work is done from top to bottom. Left-handers should reverse the procedure as before. DIAGRAM B shows the first stitch being formed from 1 to 4, with the needle emerging at 5 in position to work the next stitch in the row below it. DIAGRAM C shows small stitches worked to square off the rows at top and bottom. Note that each row, whether down or up, begins with a small No. 47 Cross Stitch worked over one canvas intersection. No tie-down stitches are made at the end of rows. Note also in DIAGRAM C that the second row of stitches slants in the opposite direction. DIAGRAM D shows a completed area.

DIAGRAM E shows a variation. Following the numbers from 1 to 12, you can see that the long stitches are worked separately, before the tie-down stitches. DIAGRAM F shows a completed area worked in this manner. This is a good method if you are using contrasting yarn for the tie-down stitches.

DIAGRAM A

DIAGRAM B

DIAGRAM C

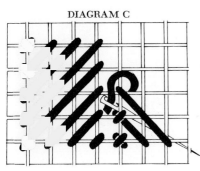

DIAGRAM D

DIAGRAM E

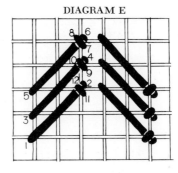

DIAGRAM F

96 · FISHBONE STITCH, DIAGONAL

CANVAS: #12 mono   NEEDLE: Size 18
TO COVER ONE SQUARE INCH: 1 length Persian yarn
NUMBER OF THREADS: 2

This is composed of horizontal and vertical stitches as opposed to No. 95 Fishbone Stitch.

Work is begun in the upper left corner and goes down and to the left. Space must be left for the number of stitches in the row. Left-handers should work as directed. DIAGRAMS A and B show the first horizontal stitches being worked from 1 to 4, with the needle emerging at 5. DIAGRAM C shows several more horizontal stitches worked in the same manner. A No. 75 Upright Cross Stitch has been worked at the upper left to square off. Another is worked on the lower level, numbers 1 to 4, with the needle emerging at 5 to start the first vertical stitch from 5 to 7. DIAGRAM D shows the vertical stitches being worked from 5 to 12, with the needle emerging at 13, ready to continue the upward row. Work continues in this manner, alternating downward rows of horizontal stitches and upward rows of vertical stitches.

DIAGRAM E shows a completed area, which is difficult to square off and needs a number of adjusting stitches to do so.

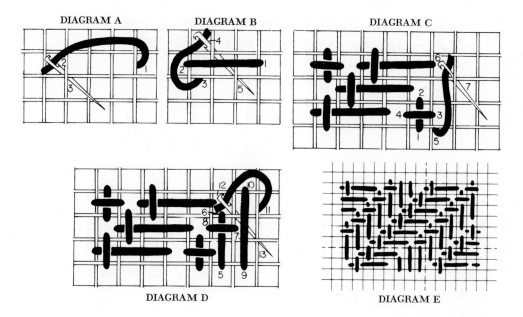

DIAGRAM A   DIAGRAM B   DIAGRAM C

DIAGRAM D   DIAGRAM E

97 · FLAT STITCH NO. 1

CANVAS: #12 mono   NEEDLE: Size 18

TO COVER ONE SQUARE INCH: 1½ lengths Persian yarn

NUMBER OF THREADS: 2

This is a variation of No. 179 Scotch Stitch, with alternating squares slanting in opposite directions.

Work is done from top to bottom starting at the upper left. Left-handers should start at the lower right and turn the diagrams upside down. A loose tension should be maintained throughout. It is easiest to work diagonal rows of all the squares slanting in one direction, and then work those slanting in the opposite direction. DIAGRAM A shows how to form the first square of five slanting stitches from 1 to 10, with the needle emerging in position to continue with the next square diagonally below it at 11. Work continues in this manner. DIAGRAM B shows how to work a square in the opposite direction from 1 to 10, with the needle emerging in position to continue with the next square at 11.

DIAGRAM C shows a completed area. If the yarn covers well, it should have a nice squared-off appearance.

DIAGRAM A

DIAGRAM B

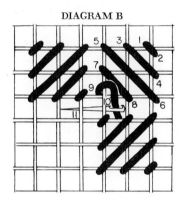

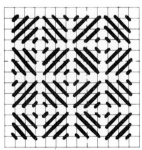

DIAGRAM C

124

98 · FLAT STITCH NO. 2

CANVAS: #12 mono   NEEDLE: Size 18

TO COVER AN AREA ONE INCH LONG AND EIGHT CANVAS THREADS WIDE:

⅔ length Persian yarn

NUMBER OF THREADS: 1 full strand

This is a surface embroidery stitch that adapts well to canvas. The length of the stitches can be varied for a leaf effect.

Work is done horizontally or vertically in both directions. Left-handers should work as directed. DIAGRAM A shows how to begin by working a stitch from 1 to 2, with the needle emerging at 3. DIAGRAMS B to D show how to continue following numbers 3 to 9, as the stitches alternate from side to side and cross at the center. Note that the width of the arms varies. Stitches should be shortened at the base to maintain the leaf shape.

DIAGRAM E shows a completed area with shortened stitches at the top and bottom.

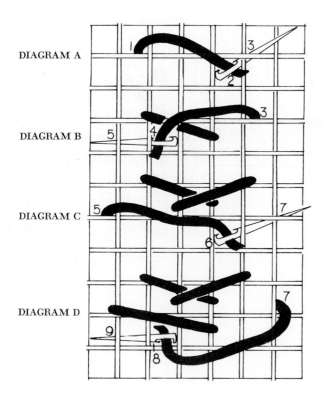

DIAGRAM A

DIAGRAM B

DIAGRAM C

DIAGRAM D

DIAGRAM E

99 · FLORENCE STITCH

CANVAS: #12 mono   NEEDLE: Size 18
TO COVER ONE SQUARE INCH: 1 length Persian yarn
NUMBER OF THREADS: 1 full strand

This is similar to No. 144 Mosaic Stitch.

Work is done diagonally from upper left to lower right. Left-handers should begin at the lower right and turn the diagrams upside down. DIAGRAMS A and B show the first two stitches being worked from 1 to 4, with the needle emerging at 5 in position to work the next short stitch. Work continues down in this manner, alternating long and short stitches. DIAGRAM C shows how to work the return journey. An extra short stitch is worked at A to square off the area before moving on. The first two stitches of the next row are worked from 1 to 4, with the needle emerging at 5. Work continues up in this manner.

DIAGRAM D shows a completed area with short stitches taken at all the edges.

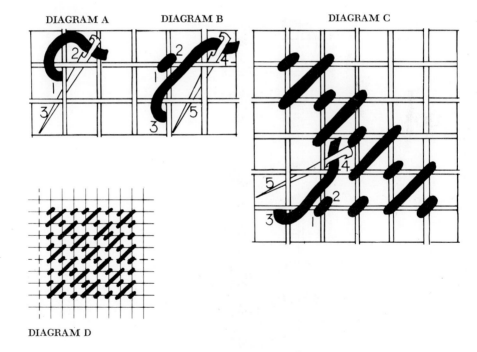

DIAGRAM A   DIAGRAM B   DIAGRAM C

DIAGRAM D

100 · FLORENTINE STITCH, OLD

CANVAS: #12 mono   NEEDLE: Size 18
TO COVER ONE SQUARE INCH: 1 length Persian yarn
NUMBER OF THREADS: 1 full strand

This stitch consists of pairs of upright stitches of equal length grouped to form a pattern.

Work is done back and forth horizontally. Left-handers should follow the directions as given. DIAGRAMS A to C show the first two pairs of stitches being worked from 1 to 8, with the needle emerging at 9 in position to work the next pair. Continue across in this manner, alternating pairs of long and short stitches. On the return journey, work the long stitches under the short ones and vice versa.

DIAGRAM D shows a completed area with adjusting stitches on the upper and lower edges for a finished look.

DIAGRAM A   DIAGRAM B   DIAGRAM C

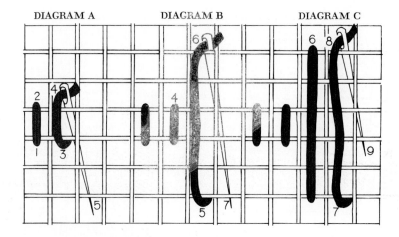

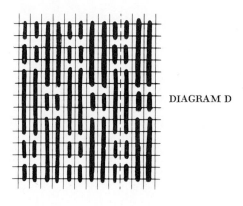

DIAGRAM D

101 · FLORENTINE STITCH, SPLIT

This stitch has the advantage of covering the canvas completely. It can be used only on very large canvas, or rug canvas, where No. 10 Bargello can't be used effectively. Because the stitches have to be split, it is best to work out designs on graph paper, as adjusting stitches must be worked first on the top of the piece. Yarn requirements vary according to canvas and stitch size.

Work is done back and forth as for Bargello. Left-handers should work as directed. DIAGRAM A shows the work in progress. The first row is a series of staggered upright stitches. On succeeding rows, stitches are worked with the needle emerging through the yarn at the base of stitches on previous rows, as from 1 to 3.

DIAGRAM B shows a completed area worked in several colors.

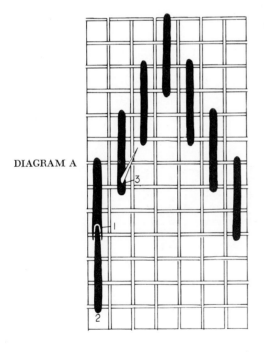

DIAGRAM A

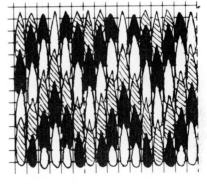

DIAGRAM B

102 · FLY STITCH, CLOSED

CANVAS: #12 mono   NEEDLE: Size 18
TO MAKE A ONE-INCH LEAF: ⅔ length Persian yarn
NUMBER OF THREADS: 1 full strand

This is a regular embroidery stitch that lends itself well to canvas work. It is most effective when used as a leaf shape, but can be used for borders as well.

Work is done from right to left, starting at the top. Left-handers should reverse the procedure and work from left to right. DIAGRAM A shows how to begin by working an upright stitch from 1 to 2, with the needle emerging at 3. DIAGRAM B shows a long loop stitch worked from 3 to 4, with the needle emerging and passing over the yarn at 5. It is best to hold the yarn in place with your free thumb as the needle passes over it. DIAGRAM C shows the loop being anchored by a small stitch worked from 5 to 6, with the needle emerging at 7 in position to work the next loop. DIAGRAM D shows how to continue, as another loop is worked from 7 to 8, with the needle emerging at 9 in position to anchor the loop.

DIAGRAM E shows a completed area. Note that the arms should not extend more than three canvas intersections on either side of the tie-down stitch, or they will tend to snag.

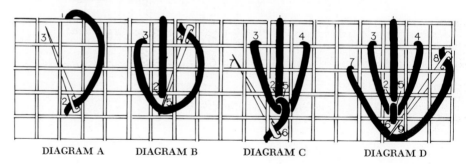

DIAGRAM A   DIAGRAM B   DIAGRAM C   DIAGRAM D

DIAGRAM E

103 · FRENCH KNOT

This stitch is the same on canvas as on regular embroidery. It can be used alone to accent another stitch, or several can be worked in a group for a textured surface. Yarn requirements vary according to use. The main thing to remember is that a good tight knot should be formed with only a single twist of yarn. Extra twists will make a floppy knot. For a bulkier knot, use an extra thread.

Work is done by slipping the needle from right to left. An entire area would begin at the upper right. Left-handers should reverse the procedure. DIAGRAM A shows how to begin by twisting the yarn once around the needle as it emerges at 1. The loose yarn should be held firmly near the emerging point as you continue. DIAGRAM B shows the needle inserted at 2. The working yarn should be held until it is pulled through completely. DIAGRAM C shows a completed knot. The needle reemerges wherever you plan to work the next knot. When working from knot to knot, pass the needle as for No. 11 Basketweave Stitch or No. 36 Continental Stitch, rather than to one side or up or down.

DIAGRAM D shows a completed area.

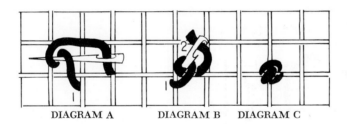

DIAGRAM A   DIAGRAM B   DIAGRAM C

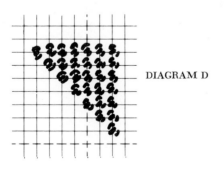

DIAGRAM D

104 · FRENCH STITCH

CANVAS: #12 mono   NEEDLE: Size 18
TO COVER ONE SQUARE INCH: 2⅛ lengths Persian yarn
NUMBER OF THREADS: 2

This is a versatile stitch, good for backgrounds, filling and rugs. Worked horizontally, it is good for shading; diagonally it can produce either a stripe or a zigzag line. It can be used alone or as an overall pattern, but it also blends nicely with No. 84 Diamond Eyelet Stitch or No. 172 Rococo Stitch. Regardless of direction, the needle action is always the same.

This method is done horizontally from left to right. Left-handers should start at the right and reverse the procedure. DIAGRAM A shows how to begin by working a long upright stitch from 1 to 2, with the needle emerging at 3. DIAGRAMS B and C show how to continue as two more stitches are worked from 3 to 6, with the needle emerging at 7. DIAGRAM D shows how to complete the stitch with the needle inserted at 8 and emerging at 9. Work continues across in this manner. Note that as you work across, spaces are left between the long stitches, and the tie-down stitches meet in a continuous row. Successive rows are worked in the spaces left on each row.

DIAGRAM E shows a completed area with extra half-stitches taken along the sides, while straight stitches are worked in empty spaces on upper and lower edges for a finished appearance.

DIAGRAM A   DIAGRAM B   DIAGRAM C   DIAGRAM D

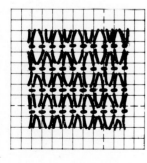

DIAGRAM E

105 · FRENCH STITCH—VARIATIONS

CANVAS: #12 mono   NEEDLE: Size 18

TO COVER ONE SQUARE INCH: 2⅛ lengths Persian yarn

NUMBER OF THREADS: 2

These are methods of working No. 104 French Stitch diagonally and sideways.

Work for a single stitch is done with the same needle action as No. 104. Left-handers should reverse the procedure as before. DIAGRAM A shows one pattern completed as for No. 104, but when completing the stitch the needle emerges down at 9 to start the next pattern. This is worked from 9 to 16, with the needle emerging at 17 in position to work the next pattern on the diagonal row. DIAGRAM B shows the needle action used to complete a stitch if you wish to work diagonally to the left. See DIAGRAM E of No. 104 French Stitch for a picture of the completed area, worked in either direction diagonally or sideways, with the same adjusting stitches.

DIAGRAM C shows how to work the stitch sideways from top to bottom. To work in other directions, the needle should emerge in the direction you want to work.

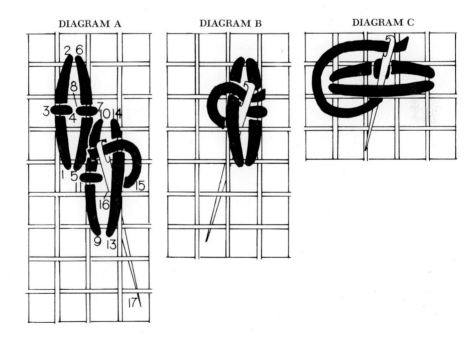

DIAGRAM A   DIAGRAM B   DIAGRAM C

106 · GOBELIN STITCH, DIAGONAL

CANVAS: #12 mono   NEEDLE: Size 18
TO COVER ONE SQUARE INCH: 1⅛ lengths Persian yarn
NUMBER OF THREADS: 2

Gobelin Stitches derive their name from seventeenth-century tapestries. Worked on fine evenweave linen they will resemble the old tapestries. This particular variation resembles No. 17 Brick Stitch.

Work is done up and down diagonally starting at the upper left. Left-handers can work as directed, but may find it easier to start at the upper right and reverse the procedure. DIAGRAM A shows the first short stitch being worked from 1 to 2, with the needle emerging at 3. DIAGRAM B shows the first long stitch being worked directly below from 3 to 4, with the needle emerging at 5. DIAGRAM C shows the following stitch formed in the same manner from 5 to 6, with the needle emerging at 7. DIAGRAM D shows another short stitch formed from 7 to 8, with the needle emerging at 9. DIAGRAM E shows the next stitch worked from 9 to 10, with the needle emerging at 11 in position to start the down journey. When the bottom is reached, the upward journey should be worked as before, with an extra short stitch worked at the top.

DIAGRAM F shows a completed area with extra stitches worked for a finished appearance.

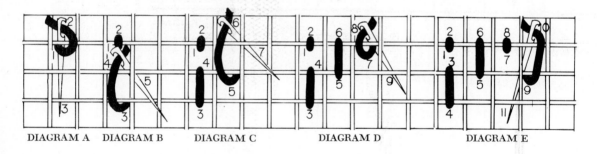

DIAGRAM A   DIAGRAM B   DIAGRAM C   DIAGRAM D   DIAGRAM E

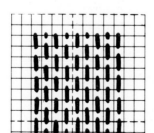

DIAGRAM F

107 · GOBELIN STITCH, DIAGONAL with LAID THREAD

CANVAS: #12 mono   NEEDLE: Size 18

TO COVER ONE SQUARE INCH: 2 lengths Persian yarn

NUMBER OF THREADS: 2

This stitch gives a nice diagonally ridged effect when covering an area.

It is done in the same manner as No. 106 Diagonal Gobelin Stitch but over a laid thread. Left-handers do not need special directions but might be more comfortable placing the laid thread from lower right to upper left and reversing the procedure. DIAGRAM A shows the first stitch laid from 1 to 2, with the needle emerging at 3. DIAGRAM B shows the first short stitch being formed from 3 to 4, with the needle emerging at 5. DIAGRAM C shows the next stitch worked over the laid yarn from 5 to 6, with the needle emerging at 7, in position to work the next laid stitch. DIAGRAM D shows the laid stitch from 7 to 8, with the needle emerging at 9 in position to start the downward journey.

DIAGRAM F for No. 106 Gobelin Stitch shows a completed area. Note that the laid stitches do not show, but simply give a raised appearance.

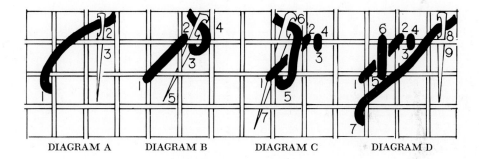

DIAGRAM A   DIAGRAM B   DIAGRAM C   DIAGRAM D

108 · GOBELIN STITCH, ENCROACHING
(*Interlocking Gobelin*)

CANVAS: #12 mono   NEEDLE: Size 18
TO COVER ONE SQUARE INCH: 1⅓ lengths Persian yarn
NUMBER OF THREADS: 1 full strand

This can be worked over any number of canvas threads. On #12 mono it is most effective worked over three.

Work is done horizontally in both directions starting at the upper left. Left-handers need no special directions. DIAGRAM A shows the first stitch being worked from 1 to 2, with the needle emerging at 3. Work continues across in this manner. DIAGRAM B shows how to work the second row as the first two stitches are formed from 1 to 4. The needle emerges at 5 in position to work across in the same manner. Always insert the needle between the stitches on the previous row so the yarn passes over the lower canvas thread covered by those stitches.

DIAGRAM C shows a completed area.

DIAGRAM A 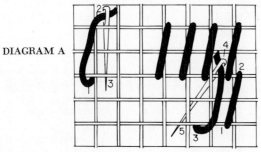 DIAGRAM B

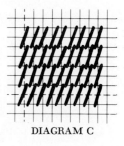

DIAGRAM C

109 · GOBELIN STITCH, FILLING

This resembles No. 17 Brick Stitch and No. 106 Gobelin Stitch. The needle action is basically the same as for the two stitches; only the stitch proportions differ.

It is worked over six canvas threads, keeping a two-one stitch proportion. Use the diagram as a pattern guide.

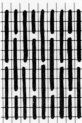

110 · GOBELIN STITCH, PLAITED

CANVAS: #12 mono   NEEDLE: Size 18
TO COVER ONE SQUARE INCH: 1⅓ lengths Persian yarn
NUMBER OF THREADS: 1 full strand

This is different from the other Gobelin Stitches in that it produces a woven appearance. It is popular for rugs because the interlocking stitches make it strong, and it works up rapidly. It is diagrammed on mono canvas. To work on penelope, keep the same proportion by working over two threads and coming back over one.

Work is done in both directions, either horizontally or vertically. Left-handers should work as directed. DIAGRAM A shows the first stitch worked from 1 to 2, with the needle emerging at 3. Work continues across in this manner. DIAGRAM B shows how to work the second row. After completing the last stitch on the first row, the needle emerges at 1 and is inserted at 2. Work continues across in this manner, with stitches slanting in the opposite direction and crossing the stitches on the previous row as shown. Continue by alternating these two rows.

DIAGRAM C shows a completed area with stitches taken on each edge to maintain the pattern. An interesting effect can be achieved by changing colors from row to row. It is not really a shading stitch, but will give that effect because stitches slant in both directions.

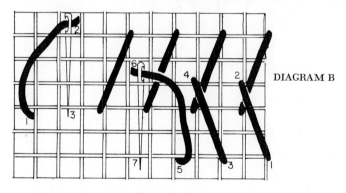

DIAGRAM B

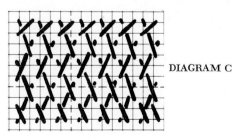

DIAGRAM C

111 · GOBELIN STITCH, SLANTING
(*Gobelin Stitch, Oblique Gobelin Stitch*)

CANVAS: #12 mono   NEEDLE: Size 18

TO COVER ONE SQUARE INCH: 1 length Persian yarn (worked over
3 canvas threads)

NUMBER OF THREADS: 1 full strand

This, like some other Gobelin Stitches, was meant to resemble the old seventeenth-century tapestries originally worked on fine evenweave linen. It is particularly effective when worked in many colors. Its slightly ridged appearance is good for background or area filling.

Work is done horizontally in both directions. Left-handers should work as directed. DIAGRAM A shows the first slanting stitch being worked from 1 to 2, with the needle emerging at 3. Work continues across in this manner. DIAGRAM B shows how to begin the second row so that it slants at the same angle as the first. The first stitch is worked from 1 to 2, with the needle emerging at 3. Work continues across in this manner. Continue by alternating these two rows.

DIAGRAM C shows a completed area.

DIAGRAM A

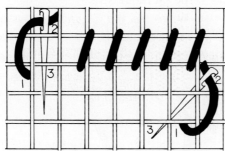

DIAGRAM B

DIAGRAM C

112 · GOBELIN STITCH, STRAIGHT *(Upright Stitch, Droit Stitch)*

CANVAS: #12 mono   NEEDLE: Size 18

TO COVER ONE SQUARE INCH: Just over 1 length Persian yarn
(worked over 2 canvas threads)

NUMBER OF THREADS: 1 full strand

The stitches can vary in size as long as care is taken to cover the canvas well. If worked over more than two threads on #12 mono, an extra thread may be needed to cover.

Work is done horizontally in both directions. Left-handers should work as directed, but if it's more comfortable to insert the needle from the bottom up, turn the diagrams upside down and work accordingly. DIAGRAM A shows the first stitch worked from 1 to 2, with the needle emerging at 3. Work continues across the row. On the final stitch the needle passes four canvas threads down to start the next row. DIAGRAM B shows how to work the first stitch on the next row from 11 to 12, with the needle emerging at 13. Work continues across in this manner. Continue by alternating these two rows.

DIAGRAM C shows a completed area. The two bottom rows illustrate No. 113 Straight Tramé Gobelin Stitch.

DIAGRAM D shows how to use the stitch for borders or oblong areas. Adjustments are shown at the corners. These are mainly a matter of common sense. Simply work in the neatest way possible to maintain the pattern. Work a border from left to right, turning at each corner. Left-handers should work from right to left.

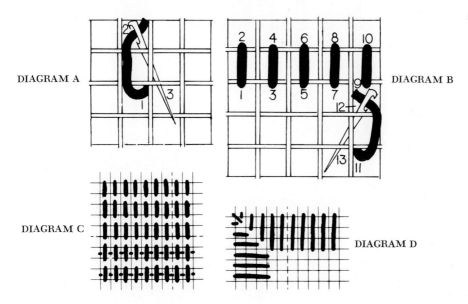

DIAGRAM A

DIAGRAM B

DIAGRAM C

DIAGRAM D

113 · GOBELIN STITCH, STRAIGHT TRAMÉ
(*Straight Gobelin with Laid Thread*)

CANVAS: #12 mono   NEEDLE: Size 18
TO COVER ONE SQUARE INCH: 1½ lengths Persian yarn
NUMBER OF THREADS: 2

This is exactly the same as No. 112 Straight Gobelin Stitch, except that it is worked over a laid thread. Left-handers should work as directed.

The diagram shows how to work the laid stitches and start the overstitching. On large areas the laid stitches should be done as for No. 205 Tramé. Consult the diagrams for No. 112 for the remaining working action.

The two bottom rows of DIAGRAM C of No. 112 show a completed area. This can also be worked as a border in the same way as No. 112. Work the laid stitches first, and use DIAGRAM D of No. 112 as guide.

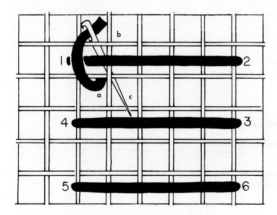

114 · GOBELIN STITCH, UPRIGHT (*Gobelin Stitch*)

CANVAS: #12 mono   NEEDLE: Size 18

TO COVER ONE SQUARE INCH: 1 length Persian yarn

NUMBER OF THREADS: 1 full strand

The difference between this and No. 112 Straight Gobelin Stitch is that No. 112 is similar to No. 176 Satin Stitch, and this is similar to No. 17 Brick Stitch although it is worked over three canvas threads.

Work is done horizontally in both directions. Left-handers should work as directed. DIAGRAM A shows the first stitch being worked from 1 to 2, with the needle emerging at 3. Note that a space is left between each stitch. Work continues across in this manner. Then the needle drops down only two threads to start the next row. DIAGRAM B shows the first row completed and the second row in progress. The first stitch is worked from 1 to 2, with the needle emerging at 3. Work continues across in this manner. Continue by alternating these two rows.

DIAGRAM C shows a completed area with short stitches taken in the top and bottom empty spaces for a finished appearance.

DIAGRAM A

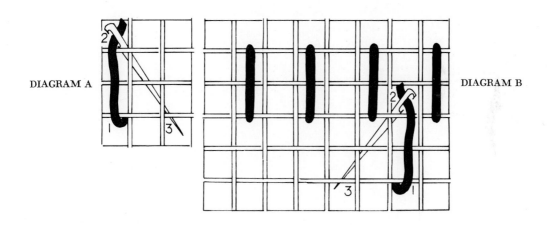

DIAGRAM B

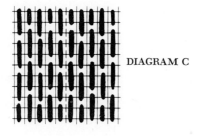

DIAGRAM C

115 · GOBELIN STITCH, WIDE

CANVAS: #12 mono   NEEDLE: Size 18

TO COVER ONE SQUARE INCH: 1¼ lengths Persian yarn

NUMBER OF THREADS: 1 full strand

This is similar to No. 111 Slanting Gobelin Stitch, but has a more pronounced slant.

Work is done horizontally in both directions. Left-handers can work as directed, but if it's more comfortable to insert the needle from the bottom up, turn the diagrams upside down and work accordingly. DIAGRAM A shows the first stitch being worked from 1 to 2, with the needle emerging at 3. Work continues across in this manner. Small adjusting stitches are necessary at the beginning and end of each row. DIAGRAM B shows a small stitch taken to fill the space at the end of the row. DIAGRAM C shows how to start the next row, by first working a small stitch from 1 to 2 and then a regular stitch from 3 to 4, with the needle emerging at 5. Work continues across in this manner. Continue by alternating these two rows.

DIAGRAM D shows a completed area with small adjusting stitches taken at both ends of each row.

DIAGRAM A

DIAGRAM B

DIAGRAM C

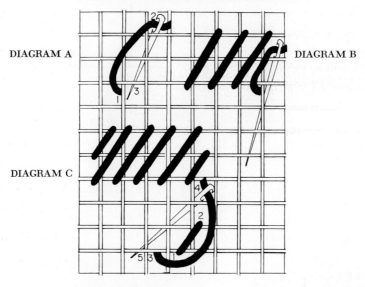

DIAGRAM D

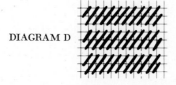

116 · HERRINGBONE STITCH

CANVAS: #12 mono   NEEDLE: Size 18
TO COVER ONE SQUARE INCH: 1½ lengths Persian yarn
NUMBER OF THREADS: 1 full strand

This stitch is done in the same way as for regular embroidery. It can be worked on either mono or penelope canvas. On penelope, cut the proportions in half, or count each double thread as one. The length of the individual stitches can vary, but always keep the same spacing between stitches.

Work moves horizontally from left to right, starting at upper left. Left-handers should reverse the procedure and work from right to left. DIAGRAM A shows a small slanting stitch worked from 1 to 2, with the needle emerging at 3. This is not part of the pattern, but is used to begin and end rows for a finished appearance. DIAGRAMS B and C show the action of the stitch from 3 to 7. Work continues across by alternating the action in DIAGRAMS B and C. DIAGRAM D shows one row completed, and another being started from 1 to 5. Note the small slanting stitch at A that ends the first row. Succeeding rows are worked like the first row, starting with the small slanting stitch. After the first row, hold the previous row's yarn out of the way when working the tops of the stitches. Make sure that the top stitches always cross in the same direction.

DIAGRAM E shows a completed area with filling stitches worked wherever necessary.

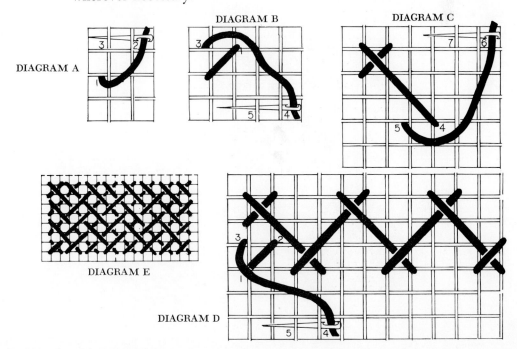

DIAGRAM A

DIAGRAM B

DIAGRAM C

DIAGRAM E

DIAGRAM D

117 · HERRINGBONE STITCH, DOUBLE

CANVAS: #12 mono   NEEDLE: Size 18

TO COVER ONE SQUARE INCH: ⅝ length of each of 2 colors Persian yarn

NUMBER OF THREADS: 1 full strand

This stitch makes a very attractive border, but is not really effective unless worked in two colors or shades.

Work is done from left to right in the same manner as No. 116 Herringbone Stitch. Left-handers should work from right to left. First work a row of No. 116 Herringbone in one color. DIAGRAMS A and B show this first row worked and the second color worked in the empty spaces across it. The small filling stitch is worked from 1 to 2, with the Herringbone being worked from 3 to 7.

DIAGRAM C shows the interesting final effect.

DIAGRAM D shows what can be done by reversing the position of the colors. The colors meet on the edges of rows to make a completely different pattern.

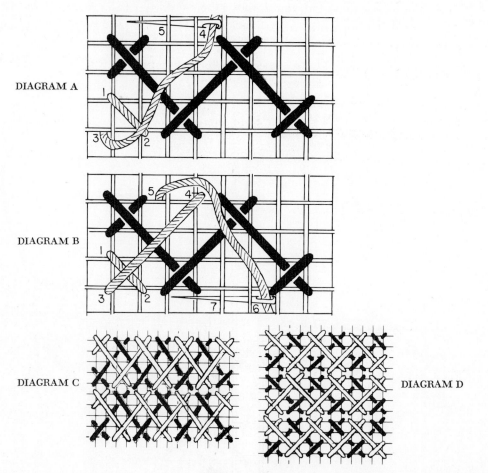

DIAGRAM A

DIAGRAM B

DIAGRAM C   DIAGRAM D

118 · HERRINGBONE STITCH, GONE WRONG

CANVAS: #12 mono   NEEDLE: Size 18
TO COVER ONE SQUARE INCH: 1 length Persian yarn
NUMBER OF THREADS: 1 full strand

This is worked the same as No. 116 Herringbone Stitch, except that the canvas is turned after every row, producing a double weave texture good for background or area covering.

Work is done horizontally from left to right. Left-handers should reverse the procedure and work from right to left. DIAGRAM A shows a row of Herringbone Stitch worked in the usual manner from 1 to 11. Note that this time the small filling stitch is worked on the lower level, at 1 and 2. At the end of the row, another small stitch is worked from 11 to 12, with the needle emerging at 13 in position to start the next row. Work is turned completely around at this point. DIAGRAM B shows how to start the second row as the needle moves from 13 to 14 to form the small filling stitch. Next, the needle moves from 15 to 16 and emerges at 17, in position to work across in the usual manner. Continue by alternating these two rows. After the first row, hold the previous row's yarn aside when working the tops of stitches.

DIAGRAM C shows a completed area with filling stitches worked wherever necessary.

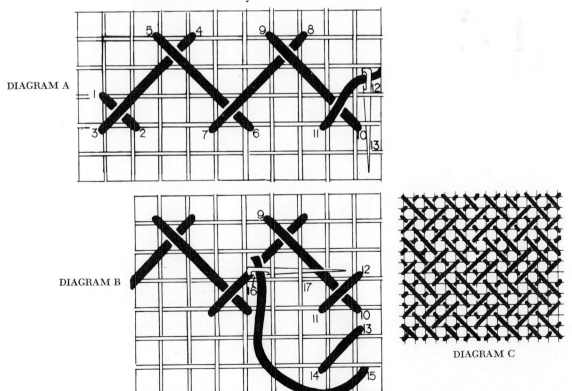

DIAGRAM A

DIAGRAM B

DIAGRAM C

119 · HERRINGBONE STITCH, SIX STEP (*Bazaar Stitch*)

This stitch makes a delightful border or overall covering. It can be worked only on penelope canvas. Yarn amounts vary according to the size of the piece and the number of colors used. Estimate total requirements as follows: Work an entire row across, keeping track of the amount of yarn used. This stitch is worked in six layers per row, and approximately the same amount of yarn is needed for each layer. Therefore the number of layers used of a color will determine the total amount for that color per row. Next, measure the height of a row and the height of the entire canvas. If your row is one inch high, and your canvas is 14 inches high, you will need 14 times the amount of each color used on the practice row.

Work is done horizontally from left to right. Left-handers should reverse the procedure and work from right to left. DIAGRAM A shows how to work the small slanting stitch that begins the first row. DIAGRAMS B and C show how to work two long slanting stitches from 3 to 6, with the needle emerging at 7. Work continues across by alternating these two stitches, ending with a small slanting stitch. DIAGRAM D shows the first row completed and the second in progress. It is worked in the same color as the first, again beginning and ending with a small slanting stitch. The remaining stitches are worked under the vertical canvas threads to the right of the stitches in the first row. DIAGRAM E shows how to start the next row. Another color is usually introduced at this point. Note that the slanting stitches at the beginning and end are varying in size. DIAGRAM F shows the fourth row in progress. It is worked in the same color as the third. A small slanting stitch is worked from 1 to 2 at the upper edge, then a long slanting stitch from 3 to 4, with the needle emerging at 5 in position to continue across. DIAGRAM G shows the fifth row in progress. Start another new color here, and proceed according to the numbers. DIAGRAM H shows the final row worked according to the numbers in the same color as the previous row.

DIAGRAM I shows one row completed and a second row starting.

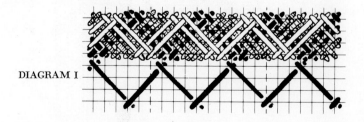

DIAGRAM I

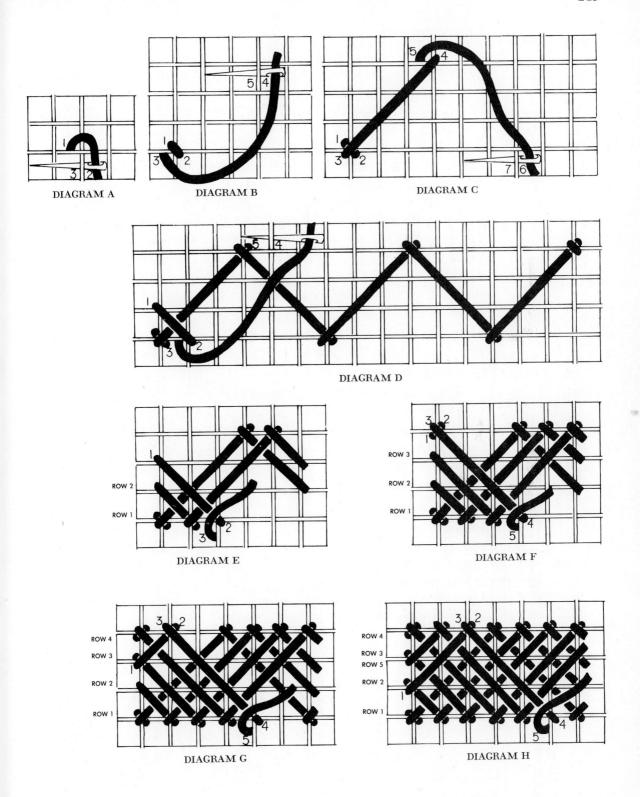

DIAGRAM A

DIAGRAM B

DIAGRAM C

DIAGRAM D

DIAGRAM E

DIAGRAM F

DIAGRAM G

DIAGRAM H

120 · HOBNAIL STITCH

CANVAS: #12 mono   NEEDLE: Size 18

TO COVER ONE SQUARE INCH: 2½ lengths Persian yarn; 3 lengths for the variation

NUMBER OF THREADS: 2

This resembles No. 68 Reinforced Cross Stitch, with No. 11 Basketweave Stitches in between. It produces a nice texture, but takes some practice.

Work is done diagonally starting at the upper right. Left-handers should start at the lower left and turn the diagrams upside down. DIAGRAM A shows how to begin by working a stitch from 1 to 2, with the needle emerging at 3. DIAGRAM B shows the intersection being re-covered from 3 to 4, with the needle emerging at 5. DIAGRAM C shows these two stitches crossed by a stitch slanting in the opposite direction from 5 to 6. DIAGRAM D shows how to begin the up row which will consist of No. 11 Basketweave Stitches. The first is worked from 7 to 8, with the needle emerging at 9. DIAGRAM E shows the final stitch in the up row worked from 9 to 10, with the needle emerging at 11. The down row begins at 11 and is worked as in DIAGRAMS A to C. Work continues by alternating these two rows.

DIAGRAM F shows a completed area. DIAGRAM G shows a variation where the down rows are worked entirely in the fancy Cross Stitch. This will not show up on fine canvas but works well on #7 penelope or rug canvas.

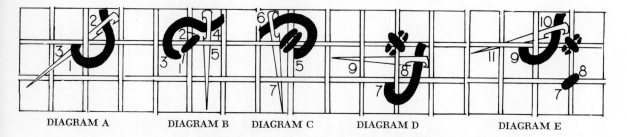

DIAGRAM A   DIAGRAM B   DIAGRAM C   DIAGRAM D   DIAGRAM E

DIAGRAM F 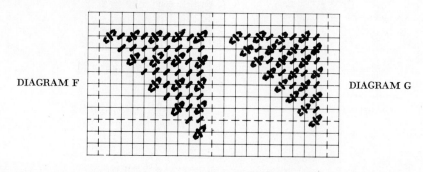 DIAGRAM G

121 · HUNGARIAN POINT

This is a very old embroidery technique developed around the same time as No. 10 Bargello. It should not be attempted until Bargello has been mastered. Yarn amounts vary and should be calculated as for No. 10 Bargello.

The needle action is similar to No. 10 Bargello, but the stitches are not of uniform length. Left-handers should turn the diagram upside down in order to work properly.

The diagram does not show a complete pattern, but is an example of how this type of work proceeds. The long stitches are always carried over six canvas threads, the short ones over two. As the pattern progresses, each row is varied slightly until it comes back to the original pattern row. At that point, the most common procedure is to reverse the color scheme. A complete repeat could also be worked if desired.

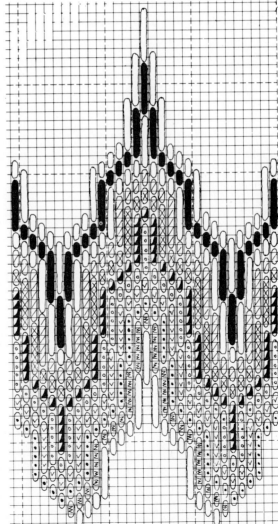

122 · HUNGARIAN STITCH

CANVAS: #12 mono   NEEDLE: Size 18

TO COVER ONE SQUARE INCH: 1⅓ lengths Persian yarn (worked in
1 color)

NUMBER OF THREADS: 1 full strand

This very old stitch also resembles No. 10 Bargello, with basically the same needle action. Worked in one color, it makes an interesting area covering. Worked by rows in two or more colors, it has a nice textured look.

Work is done horizontally in both directions. Left-handers should work as directed. Each row consists of groups of three stitches—short, long, short—with space between groups. DIAGRAMS A to C show the first group of stitches being worked from 1 to 6, with the needle emerging at 7. Work continues across in this manner. DIAGRAM D shows how to pass the needle to start the next row. After completing the last stitch on the first row, it emerges at 1. The position of stitches on the second row depends on the first row. DIAGRAMS E and F show the second row in progress. A short stitch is worked from 1 to 2, then a space is skipped because of the long stitch on the first row. A complete group starts with the stitches worked from 3 to 7. Work continues across in this manner.

DIAGRAM G (next page) shows a completed area worked in two colors, with adjusted stitches worked on the top and bottom edges.

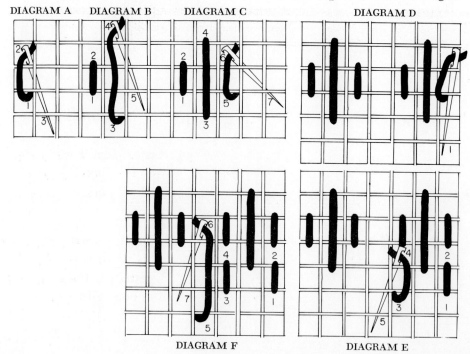

DIAGRAM A   DIAGRAM B   DIAGRAM C   DIAGRAM D

DIAGRAM F   DIAGRAM E

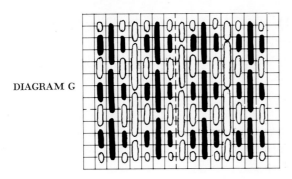

DIAGRAM G

123 · HUNGARIAN STITCH, DIAMOND (*Diamond Stitch*)

CANVAS: #12 mono   NEEDLE: Size 18

TO COVER ONE SQUARE INCH: 1⅓ lengths Persian yarn

NUMBER OF THREADS: 1 full strand

This is the same as No. 122 Hungarian Stitch, except that large diamond shapes are formed. Consult No. 122 for the working action and use the diagram here as a pattern guide.

Many different effects can be achieved by varying the colors.

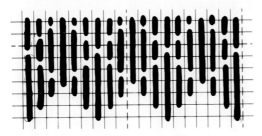

124 · HUNGARIAN GROUND STITCH (*Grounding Stitch*)

CANVAS: #12 mono   NEEDLE: Size 18

TO COVER ONE SQUARE INCH: 1⅓ lengths Persian yarn if worked in 1 color; ⅔ length for zigzag line and ½ length for stitch if worked in 2 colors

NUMBER OF THREADS: 1 full strand

The terms "ground" or "grounding" are used in English needlework to refer to background filling. This stitch is excellent for that as well as for area covering. The basic pattern is the same as No. 122 Hungarian Stitch. It can be worked in one or two colors.

Work is done in both directions. Left-handers should work as directed. Start by working a row of No. 122 Hungarian Stitches. DIA-GRAM A shows how to start the second, or filling, row by working a stitch from 1 to 2, with the needle emerging at 3. The stitches in this row are all the same size, following the pattern established by No. 122 Hungarian Stitch. DIAGRAMS B to D show the next three stitches being worked from 3 to 8, with the needle emerging at 9. Work continues across by repeating the action in these four diagrams. DIAGRAM E shows two rows of Hungarian Stitch completed with the grounding row in between. The needle emerges in position to work the next row.

DIAGRAM F shows a completed area worked in two colors with adjusting stitches worked at the top and bottom edges.

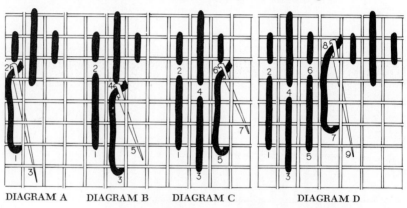

DIAGRAM A   DIAGRAM B   DIAGRAM C   DIAGRAM D

DIAGRAM E

DIAGRAM F

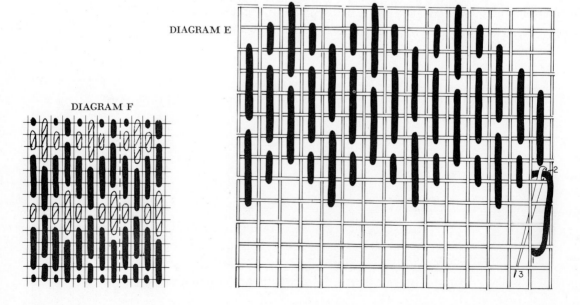

125 · HUNGARIAN GROUND STITCH, DIAGONAL

CANVAS: #12 mono   NEEDLE: Size 18

TO COVER ONE SQUARE INCH: 1½ lengths Persian yarn

NUMBER OF THREADS: 1 full strand

This is worked like No. 124 Hungarian Ground Stitch. When finished, it looks the same as No. 144 Mosaic Stitch.

Work is done diagonally from upper left to lower right. Left-handers should start at the lower right and turn the diagrams upside down. DIAGRAMS A to C show the first group of three stitches being formed from 1 to 6, with the needle emerging at 7, in position to work the next group on the down row. DIAGRAM D shows how to begin the up row with a short stitch worked from 1 to 2, with the needle emerging at 3. The lower portion of DIAGRAM E shows the up row in progress, following the numbers. The action on the upper portion of the diagram shows how to work the down row, once the top is reached.

DIAGRAM F shows a completed area done in two colors with adjusting stitches taken wherever necessary. Other variations can be achieved by varying the color patterns.

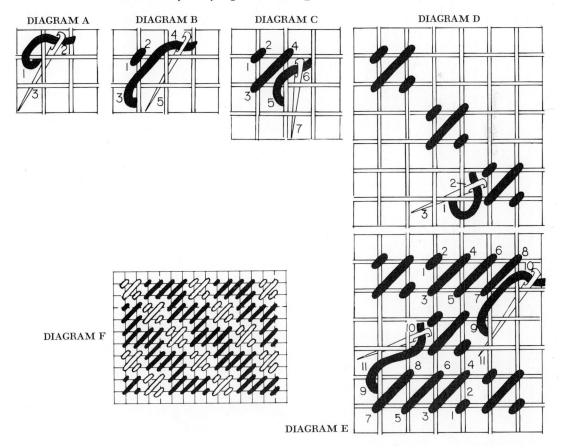

DIAGRAM A   DIAGRAM B   DIAGRAM C   DIAGRAM D

DIAGRAM F

DIAGRAM E

126 · JACQUARD STITCH

CANVAS: #12 mono   NEEDLE: Size 18

TO COVER ONE SQUARE INCH: 1⅓ lengths Persian yarn

NUMBER OF THREADS: 1 full strand

The Jacquard is a good background stitch that is especially effective worked with two different types of yarn of the same color. A good combination, on #14 mono canvas, is two threads of Persian yarn for the large stitches and a full strand (six threads) of embroidery floss for the small ones. It resembles No. 25 Byzantine Stitch in that the patterns can vary as long as the number and slant are consistent.

Work is done horizontally and vertically, starting at the upper left. Left-handers should start at the lower right and turn the diagrams upside down. DIAGRAM A shows the first two stitches being formed from 1 to 4, with the needle emerging at 5. Note that the first stitch, a Tent Stitch, is not part of the pattern, but gives the edge a finished appearance. DIAGRAM B shows how to continue across from 5 to 10, with the needle emerging at 11 in position to start the vertical row. The last stitch in this direction is the first stitch in the other direction. Next, the same number of stitches is worked down. When completing the last stitch of the group, the needle should emerge beside the base of the last stitch in order to work horizontally as in DIAGRAM A. DIAGRAM C shows how to work the small Tent Stitches following the pattern established by the large stitches. They are shown worked on both sides of the basic row. The canvas must be turned each time you change the direction of the Tent Stitch. At the base of the diagram they are worked from right to left as for the horizontal No. 36 Continental Stitch. At the completion of the row it is simplest to turn the work and continue with No. 38 Vertical Continental Stitches. At the top edge, Vertical Continental Stitches are worked first, then the canvas is turned and work is continued with horizontal Continental Stitches.

DIAGRAM D shows a completed area with adjusting stitches taken wherever necessary.

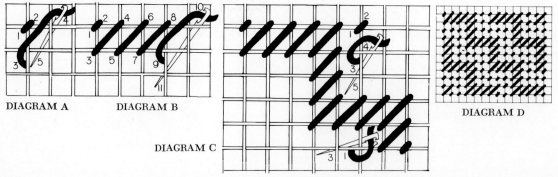

DIAGRAM A   DIAGRAM B

DIAGRAM C

DIAGRAM D

127 · KALEM STITCH (*Kilim Stitch, Kelim Stitch*)

CANVAS: #12 mono   NEEDLE: Size 18

TO COVER ONE SQUARE INCH: 2 lengths Persian yarn

NUMBER OF THREADS: 2

This stitch was originally used to imitate old weaving techniques for tapestry rugs. It resembles No. 187 Soumak Stitch and one form of No. 130 Knitting Stitch. It is especially suitable for rugs.

Work is done vertically from top to bottom starting at the left edge. Left-handers should start at the right and work from the bottom, turning the diagrams upside down. After trying the stitch, right- and left-handers may find it easier to hold the canvas horizontally while working. DIAGRAM A shows the first stitch being worked from 1 to 2, with the needle emerging at 3. It is not really part of the pattern, but is used to give a finished look. DIAGRAM B shows the first pattern stitch worked from 3 to 4, with the needle emerging at 5. Work continues down in this manner. DIAGRAM C shows how to start the up journey; the dotted lines indicate the yarn at the back. The needle emerges at 1, is inserted at 2 and emerges again at 3. Work continues up in this manner with a small stitch worked at the end to complete the row. When working a large area, a small stitch is also worked between the two halves of the stitch.

DIAGRAM D shows a completed area with the extra stitch between halves.

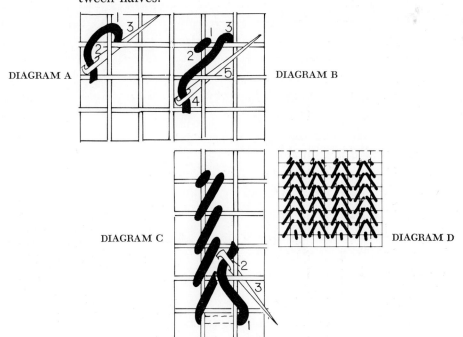

DIAGRAM A   DIAGRAM B

DIAGRAM C   DIAGRAM D

128 · KNITTING STITCH NO. 1

CANVAS: #10 penelope   NEEDLE: Size 18
TO COVER ONE SQUARE INCH: 2 lengths Persian yarn
NUMBER OF THREADS: 2

When done, this old stitch does resemble knitting. It must be done on penelope canvas. Work is done between a pair of threads, and a row is completed when worked in both directions.

Work is done vertically in both directions starting at the lower right. Left-handers should start at the upper left and turn the diagrams upside down. DIAGRAM A shows how to begin by bringing the needle up between a pair of double canvas threads at 1, inserting it at 2 and emerging at 3. Work continues to the top in this manner. DIAGRAM B shows how to complete the stitch on the down journey. To complete the last stitch of the up journey, the needle emerges at 1, is inserted at 2 (the same spot as the last stitch) and emerges at 3. Work continues down in this manner. At the bottom the needle is passed to the left from the middle of one pair of double threads to the middle of the adjoining pair, to start the next row.

DIAGRAM C shows a completed area with extra stitches taken to fill the bottom spaces.

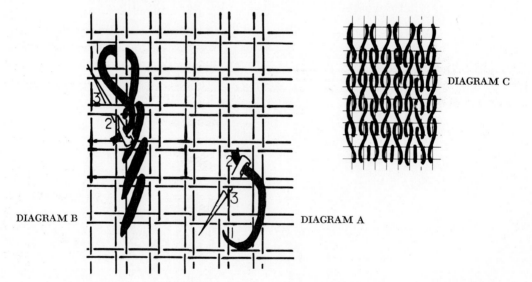

DIAGRAM C

DIAGRAM B

DIAGRAM A

129 · KNITTING STITCH NO. 2

CANVAS: #12 mono   NEEDLE: Size 18

TO COVER ONE SQUARE INCH: 2 lengths Persian yarn

NUMBER OF THREADS: 1 full strand

This stitch actually resembles braided or plaited stitches more than it resembles knitting. It covers the back well, which makes it strong and suitable for rugs and other heavy-duty items.

Work is done horizontally from left to right starting at the upper left edge. Left-handers should start at the right and reverse the procedure. Although it is not shown, begin by working a small stitch to give the row a finished appearance. The first pattern stitch will cross it. DIAGRAM A shows the first stitch worked from 1 to 2, with the needle emerging at 3. DIAGRAM B shows the second stitch crossing it in the opposite direction from 3 to 4, with the needle emerging at 5. DIAGRAM C shows the next stitch worked in the same manner as the first from 5 to 6, with the needle emerging at 7. DIAGRAM D shows the next stitch worked in the same manner as the second stitch from 7 to 8, with the needle emerging at 9. Work continues by alternating the action in DIAGRAMS C and D. End the row by working a small stitch the reverse of the one done at the start, and over a stitch that has already been worked. Turn the canvas between each row so that you always work in the same direction.

DIAGRAM E shows a completed area with the finishing stitches at the ends of each row. A different appearance can be achieved by working all the rows in the same direction without turning the canvas.

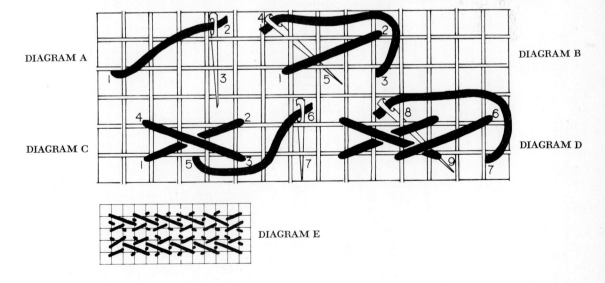

DIAGRAM A

DIAGRAM B

DIAGRAM C

DIAGRAM D

DIAGRAM E

130 · KNITTING STITCH, DIAGONAL (*Reverse Bargello*)

This stitch is more like No. 10 Bargello than No. 129 Knitting Stitch. The advantage is that the slanted stitches cover the canvas better, using less yarn than the upright Bargello Stitches. Two yarn threads cover well on #12 mono canvas. Yarn amounts vary according to the number of colors, canvas size, etc. Estimate requirements as for No. 10 Bargello.

Diagonal zigzag rows are worked diagonally starting at the lower left. Left-handers should reverse the procedure by starting at the upper right and using a mirror or tracing paper. It is best to work a sample piece to determine how many stitches are needed in the pattern row. Although there is a pattern, there are no scallops or large pattern areas as in Bargello so it is not necessary to start in the middle of the area. DIAGRAM A shows the first stitch being worked from 1 to 2, with the needle emerging at 3. Work continues up in this manner. The first stitch in the down row should technically start in the same opening as the end of the final stitch in the up row. DIAGRAM B shows how to start the down row working from 1 to 2 and emerging at 3. The dotted lines indicate how to pass the needle on the back to start the row. Work continues down in this manner. If the action is awkward, turn the canvas.

DIAGRAM C shows a completed area worked in several colors. There is an equal number of stitches up and down. Interesting effects are achieved by varying the number of stitches on the up and down journeys. Another variation is to work a solid color row across the pattern every few rows, changing colors in between, either at a point in the zigzag or wherever you run out of thread.

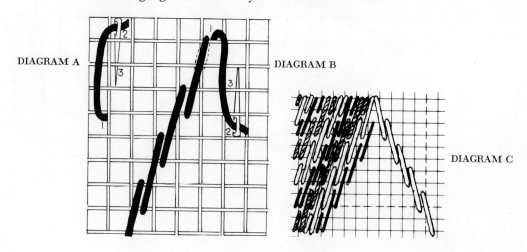

DIAGRAM A

DIAGRAM B

DIAGRAM C

131 · KNOTTED STITCH

CANVAS: #12 mono   NEEDLE: Size 18

TO COVER ONE SQUARE INCH: 2 lengths Persian yarn

NUMBER OF THREADS: 2

This is a nice tight stitch that also works well on rug canvas. It can sometimes be used for shading as the rows do encroach. The long stitches can vary in length provided they always cover an odd number of canvas intersections. This is because the tie-down stitch must always be worked over the center intersection.

Work is done horizontally in either or both directions. Left-handers should work as directed, unless they prefer to turn the diagrams upside down and reverse right and left. DIAGRAM A shows the first slanting stitch already worked from 1 to 2, with the needle emerging at 3. DIAGRAM B shows the tie-down stitch worked from 3 to 4, with the needle emerging at 5 to start the next stitch. Work continues by alternating the action in these two diagrams. DIAGRAM C shows the needle emerging below at 1 to start the second row. It is inserted at 2 and emerges at 3 in position to work the tie-down stitch. On this row the needle moves one canvas thread to the left for each long stitch, and work continues across in this manner. Continue by alternating these two rows.

DIAGRAM D shows a completed area with adjusting stitches taken on the lower edges. These will be needed on top and bottom, particularly on large canvas.

DIAGRAM A   DIAGRAM B   DIAGRAM C   DIAGRAM D

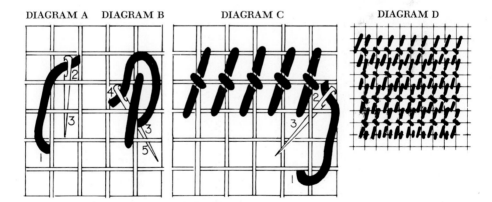

132 · KNOTTED STITCH, SINGLE

This stitch is used to produce a tufted effect. The yarn crosses itself in the back, which makes a good firm knot. Yarn requirements vary depending on canvas size, type of yarn, etc. A full strand of Persian works well on #12 mono.

Work is begun at the bottom when an area is being covered. The knots can be worked in either direction, but are diagrammed from left to right. Left-handers should reverse the procedure and work the knots from right to left. DIAGRAM A shows the first step, with the needle inserted at 1 and emerging at 2, leaving the end of the working yarn hanging loose. DIAGRAM B shows the second step, with the needle inserted at 3 and emerging at 4. After being pulled through, the yarn is cut to the desired length. Work continues in this manner with each stitch two canvas threads to the right and one up from the previous stitch. The ends left after forming the knot should fluff out and cover the top of the knot on the previous row. To prevent crowding, leave a horizontal canvas thread between rows.

DIAGRAM C shows a completed area.

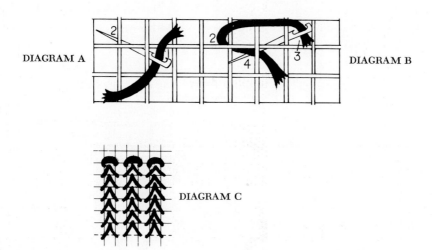

DIAGRAM A

DIAGRAM B

DIAGRAM C

133 · LADDER STITCH

CANVAS: #12 mono   NEEDLE: Size 18

TO COVER AN AREA ONE INCH LONG AND EIGHT CANVAS THREADS WIDE:

1 length Persian yarn

NUMBER OF THREADS: 1 full strand

This is a good border or line stitch. The width can be varied which also makes it useful for working shapes.

Work is done from the top down, alternating from side to side. Left-handers should work as directed. DIAGRAM A shows how to work the first stitch from 1 to 2, with the needle emerging at 3. DIAGRAM B shows a slanting stitch worked from 3 to 4, with the needle emerging at 5. DIAGRAM C shows the needle carried up and slipped under the long straight stitch from the top down, keeping the working yarn to the right without being inserted in the canvas. DIAGRAM D shows the next long stitch being formed as the needle is carried from 5 and slipped up from right to left under the crossed stitches, but not inserted in the canvas. DIAGRAM E shows the needle finally inserted at 6 and emerging at 7. From 7 the needle is carried up and slipped under the crossed stitches on the left side but not inserted. Work continues by alternating the action in DIAGRAMS D and E. The needle is always inserted on the right and emerges on the left when doing the surface work.

DIAGRAM F shows a completed area.

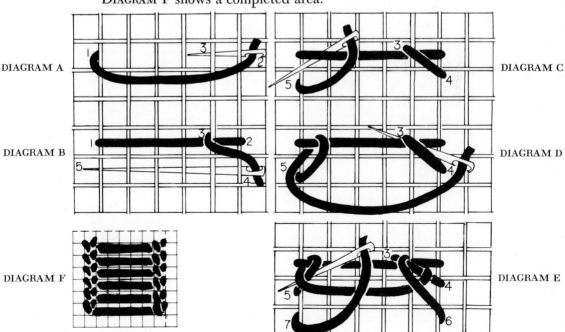

DIAGRAM A

DIAGRAM B

DIAGRAM C

DIAGRAM D

DIAGRAM E

DIAGRAM F

134 · LEAF STITCH

CANVAS: #12 mono   NEEDLE: Size 18

TO FORM ONE LEAF AS DIAGRAMMED: ¼ length Persian yarn

NUMBER OF THREADS: 1 full strand

This is not the same as the embroidery stitch of the same name. It is formed by a series of long stitches worked in several directions. The size and length can vary, the only restrictions being the size of the canvas and the intended use of the piece. Very long stitches tend to snag and are not suitable for heavy-duty items.

Work starts at the bottom left of each individual leaf, and the patterns are worked in horizontal rows from left to right. Left-handers start work at lower right of each leaf and work pattern rows from right to left.

DIAGRAM A shows the first stitch being worked from 1 to 2, with the needle emerging at 3. Work continues up in this manner. DIAGRAM B shows the left side being completed with the needle inserted at 8 and emerging at 9, in position to work an upright stitch. DIAGRAM C shows the upright stitch formed from 9 to 10, and the first stitch on the down journey on the right side formed from 11 to 12. The needle emerges at 13 in position to continue down. Don't pull the stitches too tightly, or spaces will show on the canvas.

DIAGRAMS D and E show completed areas worked with slightly different proportions. DIAGRAM F shows a completed area with adjusting stitches to give a squared-off appearance.

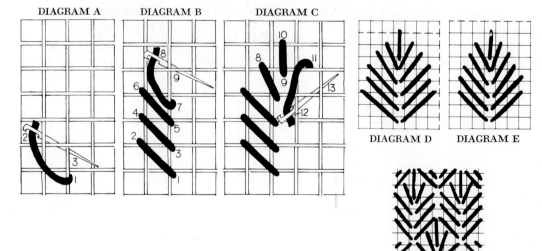

DIAGRAM A   DIAGRAM B   DIAGRAM C

DIAGRAM D   DIAGRAM E

DIAGRAM F

135 · LEAF STITCH, DIAGONAL

CANVAS: #12 mono   NEEDLE: Size 18

TO FORM ONE LEAF AS DIAGRAMMED: ¼ length Persian yarn

NUMBER OF THREADS: 1 full strand

This is worked like No. 134 Leaf Stitch, except that stitches at the base are worked horizontally and vertically.

Work starts at the lower right. Left-handers should work as directed, or reverse the action if more comfortable. DIAGRAM A shows the first stitch being worked from 1 to 2, with the needle emerging at 3. DIAGRAM B shows the first two horizontal stitches worked from 1 to 4 and the next two stitches from 5 to 8 worked in the same center space. The needle emerges at 9 to start curving to the top. DIAGRAM C shows the upward journey continuing. At 12, the high point, the action is reversed as the downward journey starts on the outside at 13. The needle is shown emerging at 17, ready for three vertical stitches that complete this leaf pattern.

DIAGRAM D shows a completed area with adjusting stitches taken where needed to square off.

DIAGRAM A   DIAGRAM B   DIAGRAM C

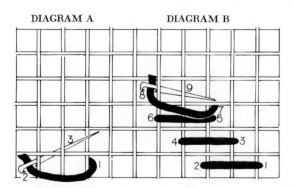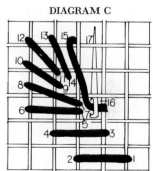

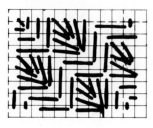

DIAGRAM D

136 · LEVIATHAN STITCH, DOUBLE

CANVAS: #12 mono   NEEDLE: Size 18

TO COVER ONE SQUARE INCH: ¼ length Persian yarn (worked over 4 canvas threads)

NUMBER OF THREADS: 2

This stitch produces an interesting raised texture. It is actually a series of Cross Stitches worked over each other. It can be worked over any even number of canvas threads, though four is the most common. It makes a good isolated stitch or area covering, but is not suitable for backgrounds.

Work moves horizontally from left to right. Left-handers should work from right to left, reversing right and left in the text. DIAGRAM A shows the first cross being formed from 1 to 4, with the needle emerging at 5. DIAGRAMS B and C show the next cross being formed from 5 to 8, with the needle emerging at 9. DIAGRAMS D and E show the third cross being formed from 9 to 12, with the needle emerging at 13. DIAGRAM F shows the final cross being formed from 13 to 16, with the needle emerging at 17 in position to work the next pattern. Work continues across in this manner.

DIAGRAM G shows a completed area.

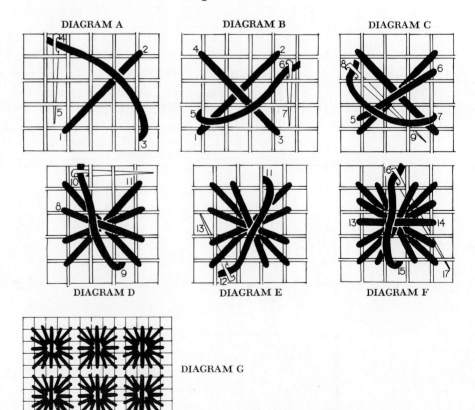

DIAGRAM A   DIAGRAM B   DIAGRAM C

DIAGRAM D   DIAGRAM E   DIAGRAM F

DIAGRAM G

137 · LEVIATHAN STITCH, TRIPLE

CANVAS: #12 mono   NEEDLE: Size 18

TO FORM ONE PATTERN: ¼ length Persian yarn for base stitches;
⅕ length for top stitches

NUMBER OF THREADS: 2

This stitch is usually worked in combination with others but makes a good overall covering as well. It is both snagproof and durable and will stand up to any use. It is a combination of No. 75 Upright Cross Stitches and groups of slanting stitches worked in the same manner as Eyelet Stitches. They can be worked in one color or with contrasting Upright Cross Stitches. When worked over a large area, it has a completely different appearance.

Work is done horizontally from left to right starting at the top left. Left-handers should reverse the procedure and work from right to left. DIAGRAM A shows the first stitch worked from 1 to 2, with the needle emerging at 3. DIAGRAMS B and C show slanting stitches filling the upper left corner from 3 to 8, with the needle emerging at 9. Note that all even numbers are inserted in the same opening represented by E. DIAGRAM D shows all the corners worked from 9 to 23, with the needle emerging at 25 in position to start the Upright Crosses. DIAGRAM E shows the first Upright Cross worked from 25 to 28, with the needle emerging at 29. Work continues counterclockwise with Upright Crosses worked in the openings around the square. The last Upright Cross is worked in the center opening.

DIAGRAM F shows a completed area with adjusting stitches taken wherever necessary. DIAGRAM G shows a variation worked in the same manner, but filled with three stitches—two short and one long—instead of Upright Crosses.

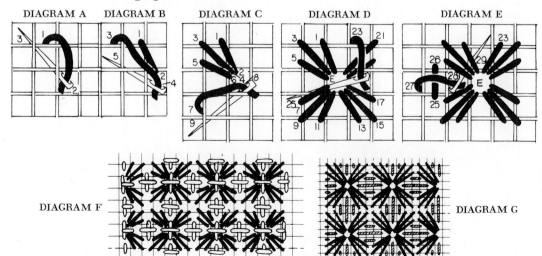

DIAGRAM A   DIAGRAM B   DIAGRAM C   DIAGRAM D   DIAGRAM E

DIAGRAM F   DIAGRAM G

138 · LONG AND SHORT STITCH

CANVAS: #12 mono   NEEDLE: Size 18
NUMBER OF THREADS: 1 full strand or more

This is an embroidery stitch that works equally well on canvas if a full enough yarn is used. It is particularly good for shading. The yarn requirements depend on stitch size and number of colors. It is normally used with other stitches, and it is best to work the background first and then work the outer edges of this stitch over it, making sure no canvas remains exposed. It can be worked horizontally, vertically and diagonally, so it can adapt to almost any shape of background.

Work is done horizontally and can be worked in both directions. Left-handers should work as directed. DIAGRAM A shows the basic long and short action as the needle moves across from 1 to 9. DIAGRAM B shows how to work the next row. The needle always emerges through the stitches on the previous row as from 1 to 9. Note that all the stitches in this row are the same size. Work continues in this manner until the last row, where the stitches are varied in length as on the first row.

If working irregular shapes rather than straight lines, the stitch size will vary within the rows. DIAGRAM C shows a completed irregular-shaped area. Note the varying stitch sizes. Adjusting stitches are taken wherever necessary to maintain the desired shape.

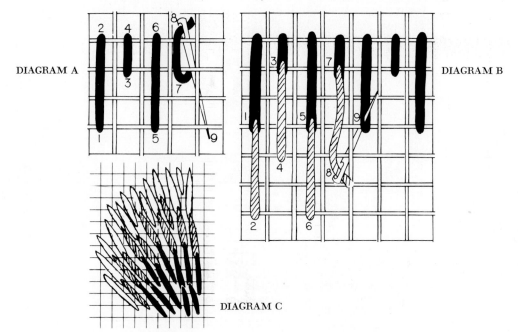

DIAGRAM A

DIAGRAM B

DIAGRAM C

139 · LOOP STITCH

CANVAS: #12 mono   NEEDLE: Size 18

TO COVER ONE INCH: ⅓ length Persian yarn (worked over 4 canvas threads)

NUMBER OF THREADS: 1 full strand

This is a regular embroidery stitch that adapts well to canvas. It makes a nice line or border stitch and looks well with other stitches as well. It can be worked over any even number of canvas threads. The loop has a knotted appearance.

Work is done horizontally from right to left. Left-handers should work from left to right. DIAGRAM A shows the first stitch being worked from 1 to 2, with the needle emerging at 3. DIAGRAM B shows the loop being formed as the needle is carried up from 3 and slipped from right to left under the original stitch, passing over the working thread without entering the canvas. DIAGRAM C shows the needle inserted at 4 and emerging at 5 in position to work the next pattern. Work continues across in this manner.

DIAGRAM D shows a completed area. DIAGRAM E shows a variation in which the loops are worked first, leaving space between the upright stitches. No. 19 Buttonhole Stitches are then worked in the spaces. This gives a nice smooth edge, suitable for borders, if the Buttonhole Stitch is worked on both sides of the loops. It's particularly nice worked in two colors.

DIAGRAM C   DIAGRAM B   DIAGRAM A

DIAGRAM D 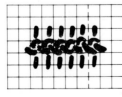 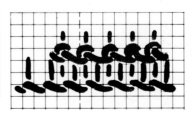 DIAGRAM E

140 · MILANESE STITCH NO. 1

CANVAS: #12 mono   NEEDLE: Size 18
TO COVER ONE SQUARE INCH: 2 lengths Persian yarn
NUMBER OF THREADS: 1 full strand

Work is begun in the upper left corner, but rows are worked diagonally from upper right down. It consists of No. 9 Back Stitches of varying sizes. Because of the length of the stitches, a large area must be worked in order to get the full effect. It distorts the canvas quite a bit, so make an outline of the piece before working to help in blocking.

Work is done diagonally starting at the upper left. Left-handers should start at the lower right and turn the diagrams upside down. DIAGRAM A shows how to work the first two stitches from 1 to 4, with the needle emerging at 5 in position to work the next stitch. The dotted lines indicate the yarn on the back. Note that the entire corner is not shown being covered as the stitch must be mastered before this can be done. DIAGRAM B shows three rows completed and a fourth in progress, with the needle at 23 in position to work the last stitch. Note how the size of the stitches changes on each row, with the fourth row being the complete reverse of the first. Work continues by repeating these four rows.

DIAGRAM C shows a completed area with adjusting stitches taken to square off.

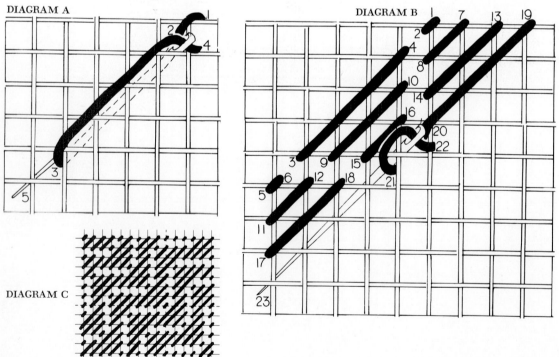

DIAGRAM A

DIAGRAM B

DIAGRAM C

141 · MILANESE STITCH NO. 2

CANVAS: #12 mono   NEEDLE: Size 18

TO COVER ONE SQUARE INCH: 1½ lengths Persian yarn

NUMBER OF THREADS: 1 full strand

This looks exactly like No. 140 Milanese Stitch, but is worked somewhat differently. It is easier, as durable and uses less yarn. The only disadvantage is that the stitches tend to snag when worked on larger canvas.

Work is done diagonally starting at the upper left. Left-handers should start at the lower right and turn the diagrams upside down. DIAGRAMS A to D show four stitches being worked from 1 to 8, with the needle emerging at 9. Work continues down diagonally by repeating these four stitches. On reaching the bottom, turn the canvas and work the return journey in the same manner, which means working the shortest stitch next to the longest stitch.

DIAGRAM C for No. 140 Milanese Stitch shows a completed area.

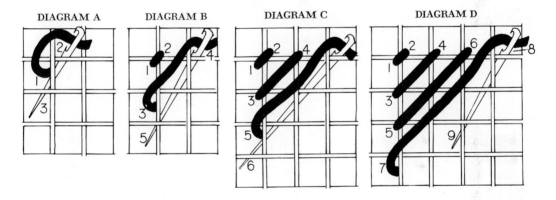

DIAGRAM A   DIAGRAM B   DIAGRAM C   DIAGRAM D

142 · MONTENEGRIN STITCH

CANVAS: #12 mono   NEEDLE: Size 18

TO COVER ONE SQUARE INCH: 1½ lengths Persian yarn (worked over 3 canvas threads)

NUMBER OF THREADS: 2

Although similar, this should not be confused with No. 64 Montenegrin Cross Stitch. This has an extra stitch which increases the bulk and durability. It is effective only on large canvas.

Work can be done horizontally in both directions. Left-handers should work as directed. Right- and left-handers may have trouble working from right to left and if so, should place a mirror next to the diagrams to see the proper working action. DIAGRAMS A to C show the first three stitches being worked from 1 to 6, with the needle emerging at 7. DIAGRAM D shows the final stitch crossing the two slanting stitches from 7 to 8, with the needle emerging at 9 in position to work the next pattern. Work continues across in this manner.

DIAGRAM E shows a completed area with adjusting stitches taken wherever necessary. Some of these may have to be slipped under the Cross Stitches already worked.

DIAGRAM A   DIAGRAM B   DIAGRAM C   DIAGRAM D

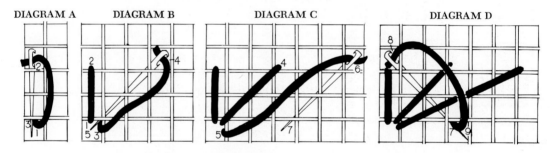

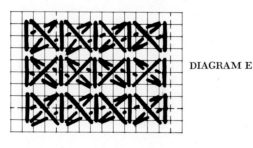

DIAGRAM E

143 · MOORISH STITCH

CANVAS: #12 mono   NEEDLE: Size 18
TO COVER ONE SQUARE INCH: 1½ lengths Persian yarn
NUMBER OF THREADS: 1 full strand

This is a stitch formed by two distinct patterns. It is easiest to work the portion with varying sizes of stitches first.

Work is done diagonally starting at the upper left. Left-handers should start at the lower right and turn the diagrams upside down. Although not shown, it is best to start with a slanting stitch worked over one canvas intersection. DIAGRAMS A to D show the five-stitch pattern being formed from 1 to 10, with the needle emerging at 11 in position to continue the pattern. Work continues down in this manner. Note that the row ends with a slanting stitch worked over one intersection. DIAGRAM E shows how to work the up row of the second pattern, with the dotted lines indicating the yarn in the back. The numbers on the lower portion of the diagram indicate how to work up diagonally; the upper numbers indicate how to fill the corner above the first pattern.

DIAGRAM F shows a completed area with adjusting stitches taken wherever necessary.

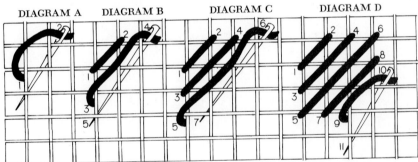

DIAGRAM A   DIAGRAM B   DIAGRAM C   DIAGRAM D

DIAGRAM E

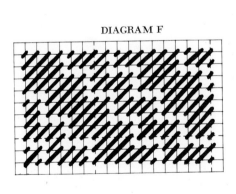

DIAGRAM F

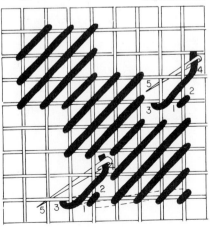

144 · MOSAIC STITCH

CANVAS: #12 mono   NEEDLE: Size 18

TO COVER ONE SQUARE INCH: 1⅔ lengths Persian yarn

NUMBER OF THREADS: 1 full strand

Worked horizontally or diagonally, either method produces the same flat textured appearance. A complete pattern always consists of three stitches—two short and one long. Work begins at upper left.

The diagonal method is by far the most comfortable to work. Left-handers should start at the lower right and turn the diagrams upside down. DIAGRAMS A to C show one pattern being formed from 1 to 6, with the needle passing under two canvas threads as in No. 11 Basketweave Stitch. Be sure to leave a space between squares. The needle emerges at 7 in position to work the next pattern. Work continues down in this manner. DIAGRAMS D to F show how to work the first pattern on the up row as the needle moves from 1 to 6 and emerges at 7 in position to continue up. The dotted lines on DIAGRAM D indicate the yarn on the back.

The horizontal method also starts at the upper left. Left-handers should start at the right and reverse the procedure. DIAGRAMS G to I show how to work one pattern from 1 to 6, with the needle emerging at 7 in position to work the next pattern, and so on across.

DIAGRAM J shows a completed area. The vertical row of slanting stitches on the right shows how to finish an area if complete patterns cannot be worked.

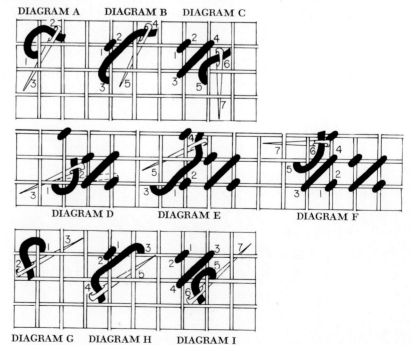

DIAGRAM A   DIAGRAM B   DIAGRAM C

DIAGRAM D   DIAGRAM E   DIAGRAM F

DIAGRAM G   DIAGRAM H   DIAGRAM I

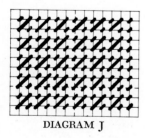

DIAGRAM J

145 · MOSAIC STITCH, CROSSED

CANVAS: #12 mono NEEDLE: Size 18
TO COVER ONE SQUARE INCH: 2 lengths Persian yarn
NUMBER OF THREADS: 2

This is effective only on large canvas.

Work is done in horizontal rows from right to left. Left-handers should reverse the procedure and turn the diagrams upside down. DIAGRAMS A to C show the first three stitches being worked from 1 to 6, with the needle emerging at 7. Note that the appearance is the same as No. 144 Mosaic Stitch. DIAGRAM D shows the three stitches being crossed from 7 to 8, with the needle emerging at 9 in position to work the next pattern. Work continues across in this manner.

DIAGRAM E shows a completed area.

DIAGRAM A   DIAGRAM B   DIAGRAM C   DIAGRAM D

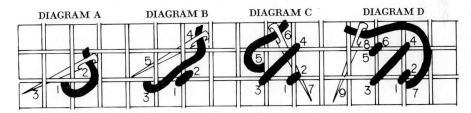

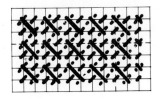

DIAGRAM E

146 · MOUND STITCH (*Raised Stitch*)

CANVAS: #12 mono NEEDLE: Size 18
TO COVER ONE SQUARE INCH: ½ length of each of 2 colors Persian yarn
NUMBER OF THREADS: 2

This consists of No. 9 Back Stitches which give the appearance of Tent Stitches. In addition, each Mound Stitch is worked in four directions, and the pulling action as you take the stitches produces a raised pyramid effect.

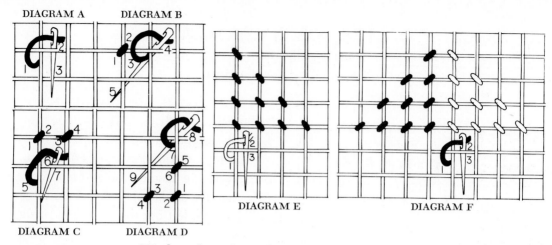

DIAGRAM A   DIAGRAM B

DIAGRAM E   DIAGRAM F

DIAGRAM C   DIAGRAM D

DIAGRAM G

Work is done from the center out. DIAGRAM A shows the beginning stitch taken from 1 to 2, with the needle emerging at 3 in position to begin the second row. DIAGRAM B shows the second row beginning as a diagonal Back Stitch is taken from 3 to 4, with the needle emerging at 5. DIAGRAM C shows the final Back Stitch being taken in this row from 5 to 6, with the needle emerging at 7 in position to start the third row. The canvas is now turned before starting the third row. DIAGRAM D shows the first Back Stitch being taken in the third row from 7 to 8, with the needle emerging at 9 in position to complete the third row with two more Back Stitches. The final stitch in this and every row is taken as shown in DIAGRAM C, putting the needle in position to start a new row.

DIAGRAM E shows a completed triangle of four rows. However, you can make the triangles as large as desired.

When a triangle is completed, give the canvas a half-turn so the triangle just completed is above the area you are about to work on.

DIAGRAM E also shows the second triangle begun in a different color, as the needle moves from 1 to 3, exactly as shown in DIAGRAM A. Then follow DIAGRAMS A to E, to complete the second triangle.

As DIAGRAM F shows, the canvas has been given a half-turn, and the third triangle is being started below the second as the needle moves from 1 to 3. Note the position of triangle one.

DIAGRAM G shows a completed Mound Stitch, with Tent Stitches worked to square off the area. The three-dimensional effect can only be appreciated after the stitch is actually worked.

To maintain the pyramid when blocking and keep it from being flattened, place a push pin upside down at the center of each pyramid to keep it raised. When mounting, the pyramids may be padded with cotton batting.

147 · OBLIQUE STITCH (*Oblique Slav Stitch*)

CANVAS: #12 mono   NEEDLE: Size 18

TO COVER ONE SQUARE INCH: 1 length Persian yarn

NUMBER OF THREADS: 1 full strand

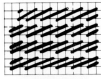

DIAGRAM C

DIAGRAM D

Work is always done horizontally from left to right, in much the same way as the Stem Stitch in surface embroidery. Left-handers should work from right to left. DIAGRAMS A and B show the first two stitches being worked from 1 to 4, with the needle emerging at 5. Work continues across in this way to the end of the row. Start the second row two canvas threads below 1, on the left edge.

DIAGRAM C shows a completed area with adjusting stitches taken wherever necessary. DIAGRAM D shows the stitch with rows worked only one thread apart. This gives a tighter finish and may need only two threads to cover.

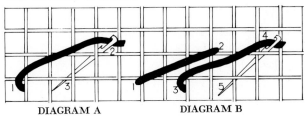

DIAGRAM A   DIAGRAM B

148 · OBLIQUE STITCH, DIAGONAL

CANVAS: #12 mono   NEEDLE: Size 18

TO COVER ONE SQUARE INCH: 1 length Persian yarn

NUMBER OF THREADS: 1 full strand

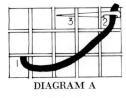

DIAGRAM A

DIAGRAM B

This has the same finished appearance as No. 147 Oblique Stitch, but is useful if you plan to work with two colors, or to maintain a continuous diagonal pattern. It is most useful for working a tubular shape with a hidden seam (like the eyeglass case shown in photograph 35, page 287).

Work is done diagonally starting at the lower left. Left-handers should start at the upper right and turn the diagrams upside down. DIAGRAM A shows the first stitch worked from 1 to 2, with the needle emerging at 3. DIAGRAM B shows the next stitch worked from 3 to 4, with the needle emerging at 5. Work continues diagonally up in this manner. Succeeding rows are worked on either side of the original, in the same way.

DIAGRAM C for No. 147 Oblique Stitch shows a completed area.

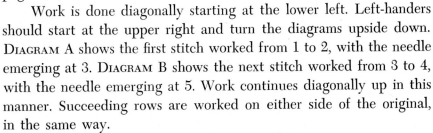

149 · OBLIQUE STITCH, REVERSE

CANVAS: #12 mono   NEEDLE: Size 18

TO COVER ONE SQUARE INCH: 1 length Persian yarn

NUMBER OF THREADS: 1 full strand

This looks like No. 147 Oblique Stitch, with the stitches slanting in the opposite direction.

Work is done horizontally in both directions. Left-handers should work as directed. DIAGRAM A shows the first stitch being worked from 1 to 2, with the needle emerging at 3. Work continues across in this manner. DIAGRAM B shows how to start the second row as the needle moves from 10 on the first row to 11 on the second row, where it is inserted at 12 and emerges at 13. The dotted lines indicate the yarn on back. Work on across, and continue by alternating these two rows.

DIAGRAM C shows a completed area with adjusting stitches taken wherever necessary. The bottom row of the diagram shows the stitch worked with a slightly different slant.

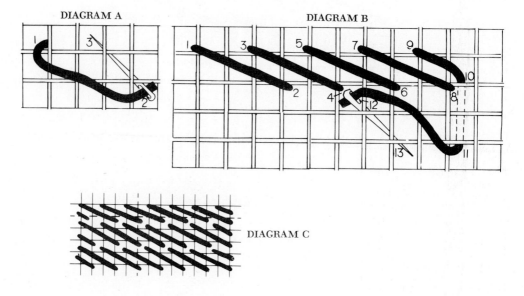

DIAGRAM A

DIAGRAM B

DIAGRAM C

150 · ORIENTAL STITCH

CANVAS: #12 mono   NEEDLE: Size 18

TO COVER ONE SQUARE INCH: 1½ lengths Persian yarn if worked in 1 color; ½ length for the diamonds and 1 length for the triangles if worked in 2 colors

NUMBER OF THREADS: 1 full strand

This is an old embroidery pattern formed by two types of stitches worked to produce diamond and triangle shapes. The working action of the triangle shapes is similar to No. 140 Milanese Stitch.

Work is done diagonally starting at the upper left. Left-handers should start at the lower right and turn the diagrams upside down. It is easiest to work all the triangles first. DIAGRAMS A to D show the first four stitches, forming the first triangle, being worked from 1 to 8, with the needle emerging at 9. Note that the first automatically fills the corner of the pattern. Work continues down in this manner. The rows of triangles on each side are worked in the opposite direction, following the numbers at lower left in DIAGRAM E. Work the remaining triangles up and down, spacing them so the long stitches meet in the same openings. DIAGRAM E shows an area of completed triangles with the diamond-shaped spaces at both upper and lower portions of the diagram filled horizontally and vertically with groups of slanting stitches in contrasting color, according to the numbers.

DIAGRAM F shows a completed area with adjusting stitches taken wherever necessary.

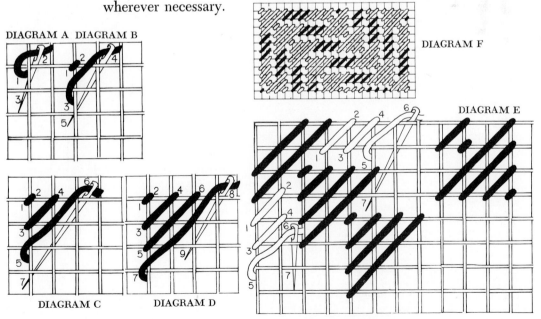

DIAGRAM A   DIAGRAM B

DIAGRAM F

DIAGRAM E

DIAGRAM C   DIAGRAM D

151 · OUTLINE STITCH (*Cable Stitch, Stem Stitch*)

CANVAS: #12 mono NEEDLE: Size 18
TO COVER ONE INCH: ⅛ length Persian yarn
NUMBER OF THREADS: 1 full strand

This stitch is used mainly for outlining, but can be an effective solid filling. It changes direction and takes curves nicely. Stitches can be of any size, depending on the desired effect. Four canvas threads is the best length on #12 mono.

Work is done horizontally in any direction, but is shown from left to right. Left-handers should work from right to left. DIAGRAM A shows the first stitch worked from 1 to 2, with the needle emerging at 3. Hold the yarn out of the way with your free thumb as you work, to prevent splitting it. Stitches can be done with the yarn lying above or below the needle, depending on how you want the stitches to flow. Just be sure to be consistent throughout. DIAGRAM B shows the second stitch being formed from 3 to 4, with the needle emerging at 5. DIAGRAM C shows how to continue the line and work around a curve as the needle moves from 5 to 10 and emerges at 11. Note how the stitches change in size to keep the curve smooth.

DIAGRAM D shows a completed area with the curve started in DIAGRAM C completed. It is easiest to turn the canvas as you change direction. To work solid filling, all rows are done from left to right with the yarn always held in the same position.

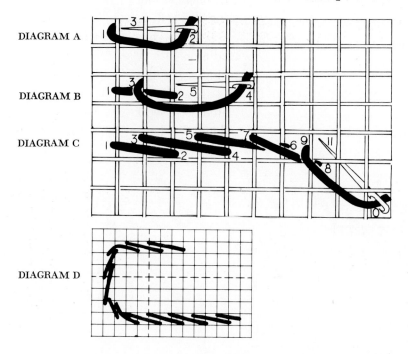

DIAGRAM A

DIAGRAM B

DIAGRAM C

DIAGRAM D

152 · PALACE PATTERN

CANVAS: #12 mono   NEEDLE: Size 18
TO COVER ONE PATTERN: 1 length Persian yarn
NUMBER OF THREADS: 1 full strand

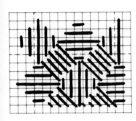

This is a pattern made with straight stitches going in different directions. It produces a nice texture worked in one color or alternating colors. Both right- and left-handers should work whichever way is most comfortable, using the diagram as a guide. The bottom and right edges show the adjusting stitches that have to be worked. Remember that the longer stitches can tend to snag. On fine or evenweave canvas, stitches may be added to enlarge the size of the diamonds.

153 · PARIS STITCH (*Double Stitch, Tie Stitch*)

CANVAS: #12 mono   NEEDLE: Size 18
TO COVER ONE SQUARE INCH: 2 lengths Persian yarn
NUMBER OF THREADS: 2

This resembles No. 104 French Stitch in texture. It covers the back well, making it a good rug stitch.

Work is done diagonally starting at the upper left. Left-handers should start at the lower right and turn the diagrams upside down. DIAGRAMS A and B show the first two stitches being worked in the same opening from 1 to 4, with the needle emerging at 5. DIAGRAM C shows the tie-down stitch being worked from 5 to 6, with the needle emerging at 7 in position to work the next pattern.

DIAGRAM D shows a completed area with adjusting stitches on all four edges. On the vertical edges, single upright stitches are tied down. On the upper edge, two upright stitches are worked in each space. On the lower edge, two upright stitches are worked in each space, and horizontal stitches are worked along the base. These may also be worked on the upper edge if you wish.

DIAGRAM B   DIAGRAM C

DIAGRAM A

DIAGRAM D

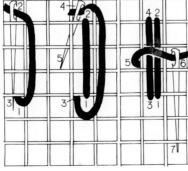

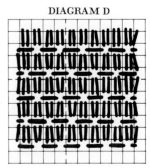

154 · PARISIAN STITCH (*Pavillion Stitch*)

CANVAS: #12 mono   NEEDLE: Size 18

TO COVER ONE SQUARE INCH: 1 length Persian yarn

NUMBER OF THREADS: 1 full strand

This is similar to No. 114 Upright Gobelin Stitch with a pattern consisting of alternating short and long stitches.

Work is done horizontally in both directions. Left-handers should work as directed. DIAGRAMS A and B show the first two stitches being worked from 1 to 4, with the needle emerging at 5. Work continues across in this manner. DIAGRAM C shows how to work the return journey. At the completion of the first row, the needle emerges at 1, is inserted at 2 and emerges at 3. Work continues across in this manner, with long stitches under short stitches, and vice versa.

DIAGRAM D shows a completed area with adjusting stitches taken wherever necessary. DIAGRAM E shows a completed area worked with a different proportion. DIAGRAM F shows a two-color variation that actually alternates rows of Parisian Stitch with No. 114 Upright Gobelin Stitch. Note that the long stitches meet between rows. Adjusting stitches are taken at the upper and lower edges wherever necessary.

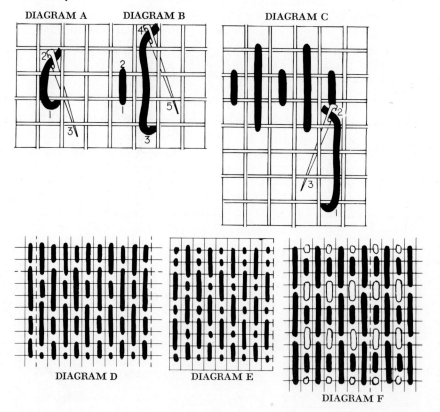

DIAGRAM A   DIAGRAM B   DIAGRAM C

DIAGRAM D   DIAGRAM E

DIAGRAM F

155 · PERSPECTIVE STITCH

CANVAS: #12 mono   NEEDLE: Size 18
TO COVER ONE SQUARE INCH: ⅞ length Persian yarn in each color
NUMBER OF THREADS: 1 full strand

This is done with slanting stitches which give the appearance of depth due to the contrasting colors. For best results, the bottom color should be darker.

Work is done horizontally from left to right. Left-handers should reverse the procedure and work from right to left, using a mirror next to the diagrams if necessary. DIAGRAMS A to C show the first three stitches being worked to form half of the pattern from 1 to 6, with the needle emerging at 7. DIAGRAMS D and E show the second side being worked from 7 to 12, with the needle emerging at 13 in position to work the next pattern. DIAGRAM F shows the first contrasting stitch being worked from 1 to 2, with the needle emerging at 3. Note that the contrasting stitches slant in the opposite direction. DIAGRAM G shows the contrasting pattern completed and the next row starting with the original color, as the needle moves from 1 to 2 and emerges at 3. These stitches slant in the same direction as the previous row, but do not cross them. Work continues on the four rows in the order shown in the diagrams.

DIAGRAM H shows a completed area with adjusting stitches taken wherever necessary. It is best to plan the pattern so that no adjusting stitches will be needed at the sides.

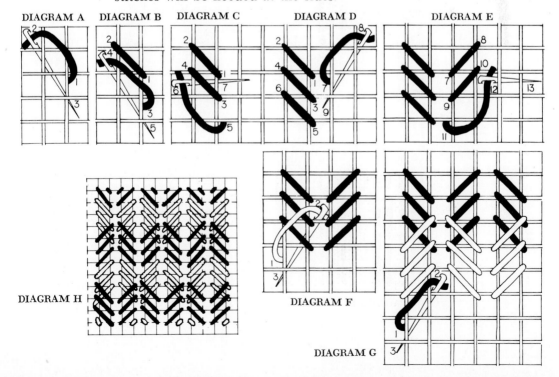

DIAGRAM A   DIAGRAM B   DIAGRAM C   DIAGRAM D   DIAGRAM E

DIAGRAM H

DIAGRAM F

DIAGRAM G

156 · PETIT POINT

CANVAS: #10 penelope   NEEDLE: Size 18
TO COVER ONE SQUARE INCH: 1 length Persian yarn
NUMBER OF THREADS: 1 full strand

This is a term rather than a stitch. Originally a French term meaning small stitch, it has come to refer to small No. 11 Basketweave or No. 36 Continental Stitch worked on penelope canvas, or 20-to-the-inch (or finer) mono canvas. It is used most often to work fine detail and shading. Left-handers should work this stitch the same way they work the Basketweave Stitch.

Before working on penelope canvas, separate the double threads with the blunt end of the needle so that you can work more easily. The diagram shows an area being done in Petit Point Basketweave. The first two stitches are worked and the third stitch is being formed with the needle emerging in position to work the next stitch.

157 · PLAIT STITCH (*Spanish Stitch*)

CANVAS: #12 mono   NEEDLE: Size 18
TO COVER ONE SQUARE INCH: 2 lengths Persian yarn
NUMBER OF THREADS: 2

This stitch gives a tightly woven, ridged appearance. It covers the back well, making it a suitable rug stitch. The stitches can be of any length, as long as the number of canvas threads between stitches remains the same.

Work can be done horizontally in both directions. Left-handers should work as directed. DIAGRAMS A and B show the first two stitches being formed from 1 to 4, with the needle emerging at 5. Work continues across in this manner. DIAGRAMS C and D show how to work in the opposite direction.

DIAGRAM E shows a completed area with the first two rows worked from left to right and the third row worked from right to left. Adjusting stitches are taken at the ends of each row.

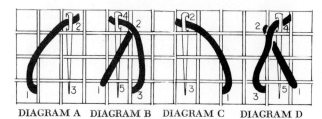

DIAGRAM A   DIAGRAM B   DIAGRAM C   DIAGRAM D

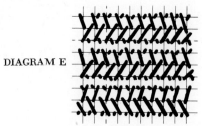

DIAGRAM E

158 · PLAIT STITCH, CROSSED (*Mexican Cross Stitch*)

CANVAS: #12 mono   NEEDLE: Size 18
TO FORM ONE PATTERN: ¾ length Persian yarn
NUMBER OF THREADS: 2

This stitch creates a large square woven pattern with a diamond-shaped center. It must be worked over at least seven canvas threads to be effective. It makes a nice focal point and can also be used for area filling.

Work is done all around the square. Left-handers should reverse the procedure, using a mirror next to the diagram to see the needle action. DIAGRAM A shows one large cross formed and a second being worked as the needle moves from 1 to 8 and emerges at 9. The next stitch slants from lower left to upper right, as the needle emerging at 9 is inserted just below 2, to emerge just above 3. The final stitch of this layer would be made across the top of the square. Work continues around all four sides in this manner. On the final row the needle is slipped under a single thread on each side and inserted in opening 36 to complete the last stitch.

DIAGRAM B shows a completed area. DIAGRAM C shows the pattern worked on an angle, creating a diamond shape. Interesting variations are made by using contrasting colors within squares or from square to square.

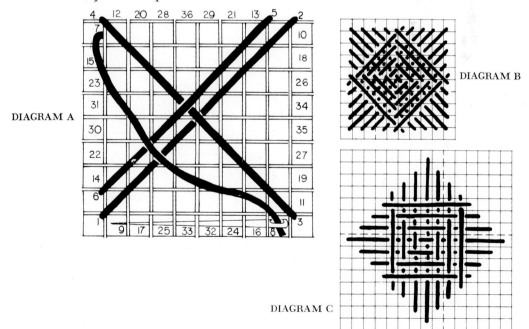

DIAGRAM A

DIAGRAM B

DIAGRAM C

159 · PLAIT STITCH, SQUARE (*Woven Band*)

CANVAS: #12 mono   NEEDLE: Size 18

TO COVER ONE INCH WITH CORNER AS DIAGRAMMED: ⅓ length of each
of 2 colors Persian yarn

NUMBER OF THREADS: 1 full strand

This takes corners nicely, making it a good border stitch. It can be
worked over an odd or even number of canvas threads.

Work can be done in any direction in straight lines or surrounding
a squared-off area. Left-handers should reverse the procedure. DIA-
GRAM A shows how to begin at the top left of a square area with the
first stitch worked from 1 to 2, and the needle emerging at 3. Work
continues across in this manner. DIAGRAM B shows how to work down
once the right edge is reached as the needle is inserted at 6 and
emerges at 7, in position to work the vertical row. Work continues
down in this manner. Note that this action would also be used at the
lower left if the corner is turned upside down. DIAGRAM C shows how
to work the lower right corner, and when turned upside down it shows
how to work the upper left corner. DIAGRAM D shows the second layer
of contrasting stitches in progress. It is easiest to begin these in the
middle of any of the straight edges. They slant in the opposite direction
and are woven over and then under the base stitches, starting at the
outside edge.

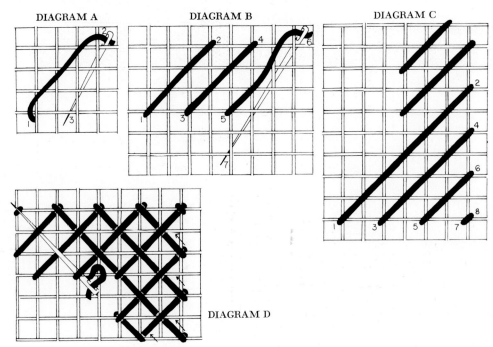

DIAGRAM A

DIAGRAM B

DIAGRAM C

DIAGRAM D

160 · PLAITED STITCH (*Spanish Plaited Stitch*)

CANVAS: #12 mono; #10 penelope   NEEDLE: Size 18

TO COVER ONE SQUARE INCH: 2 lengths Persian yarn on mono;
2½ lengths on penelope

NUMBER OF THREADS: 1 full strand on mono; 2 threads on penelope

This is a very old stitch which is worked much like No. 93 Fern Stitch, but resembles No. 110 Plaited Gobelin Stitch when completed.

Work is always done vertically from top to bottom, starting at the upper left. Left-handers should start at the lower right and turn the diagrams upside down. DIAGRAM A shows the first row completed following numbers from 1 to 12. The second row has started, with the needle emerging at the top again to start the next row following numbers 13 to 15. DIAGRAM B shows the next row in progress, with the first stitch being completed from numbers 15 to 16, and the needle emerging at 17 to start the second stitch. Work continues down in this manner. Note overlapping of the stitches of the previous row.

DIAGRAM C shows a completed area with adjusting stitches taken at the ends of each row. DIAGRAM D shows a completed area worked in the proportion for penelope canvas. Each stitch is three canvas threads wide and one deep, as opposed to the four-two proportion used on mono canvas.

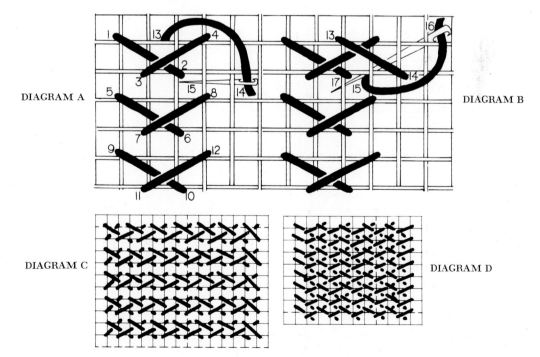

DIAGRAM A   DIAGRAM B

DIAGRAM C   DIAGRAM D

161 · PLAITED EDGE STITCH (*Rug Binding Stitch*)

CANVAS: #12 mono   NEEDLE: Size 18

TO COVER THREE INCHES ON THE EDGE: 1 length Persian yarn

NUMBER OF THREADS: 2

As the name indicates, this stitch is worked on an edge or to join two edges together for a seam. It can be worked in any direction and forms curves and turns corners easily. It is especially useful as it not only makes a neat edge but the triple layer wears very well.

Whether for an edge or a seam, work always begins by turning under at least one inch of the raw edge of the canvas. On penelope canvas, the fold would be right on the double thread. On mono, make the fold so a row of holes is left on the edge. For large areas, it's a good idea to baste the fold in place.

As work is done in either direction, left-handers should work as directed. Right- and left-handers should place a mirror next to the diagrams to see how to proceed in the opposite direction. It makes a neater edge if worked with the wrong side of the canvas facing you. DIAGRAM A shows how to begin by leaving a short end lying loose on the top—this will be anchored by the first few stitches. The dotted lines in the diagrams indicate the double fold of canvas. The needle emerges at 1 and is carried to the other side of the canvas, to emerge at 2. DIAGRAM B shows the needle emerging through the first opening again at 3, thus securing the original stitch. DIAGRAMS C and D show the working action as the needle moves on both sides of the canvas through number 7. Work continues across, with each stitch moving three canvas threads forward and two back. (You may have to hold the worked stitches out of the way as you go along, as each area is covered several times.) Note that the needle always moves from the back to the front of the canvas.

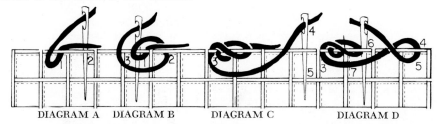

DIAGRAM A   DIAGRAM B   DIAGRAM C   DIAGRAM D

When nearing a corner, the procedure is a little different because you usually add an extra stitch to cover the corner before moving on. DIAGRAM E shows the needle emerging at 5 to take this little corner stitch from 6 to 7. The needle then moves on to 8 and 9. DIAGRAM F shows the corner turn being completed following numbers 10 to 15. Work then proceeds as before, repeating DIAGRAMS A through D until the next corner.

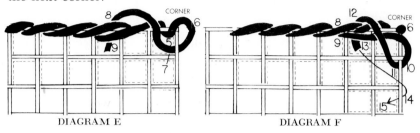

DIAGRAM E   DIAGRAM F

162 · PORTUGUESE STEM STITCH

CANVAS: #12 mono   NEEDLE: Size 18
TO COVER ONE INCH: 1 length Persian yarn
NUMBER OF THREADS: 2

This is a good outline stitch. It can be done in any direction and takes corners and curves nicely. It looks best worked in pearl cotton or any other tightly twisted thread.

The stitch is worked from the bottom up. Left-handers should start at the top and turn the diagrams upside down. DIAGRAM A shows the first stitch taken from 1 to 2, with the needle emerging at 3. DIAGRAMS B and C show two loops formed as the needle slips under the stitch twice without being inserted in the canvas. DIAGRAM D shows the second vertical stitch being formed as the needle is inserted at 4 and emerges at 5. DIAGRAM E shows the loops being started, this time with the needle passing under both threads. After the second loop, work continues up for the next vertical stitch, and so on. Be sure to keep the needle to the left of the working yarn throughout.

DIAGRAM F shows a completed area. Note that in rounding a curve, the long stitches are worked over canvas intersections rather than over horizontal or vertical threads.

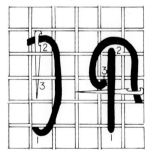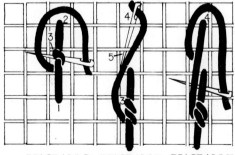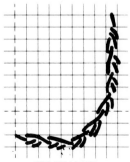

DIAGRAM A   DIAGRAM B   DIAGRAM C   DIAGRAM D   DIAGRAM E   DIAGRAM F

163 · PRINCESS PATTERN

CANVAS: #12 mono   NEEDLE: Size 18

TO FORM ONE PATTERN: ¾ length Persian yarn

NUMBER OF THREADS: 1 full strand

This is a pattern made up of horizontal and vertical stitches.

The diagram shows a completed pattern. Note that the vertical stitches are worked over two, four and six canvas threads in a symmetrical pattern from the center. The horizontal stitches are No. 9 Back Stitches worked over two threads. The second row of vertical stitches is a mirror image of the first.

Nineteenth-century needlework books suggest filling in with beads instead of No. 9 Back Stitches.

164 · QUICK POINT

This is a fairly new addition to needlework language and it refers to embroidery done on large, or rug, canvas. Almost any regular canvas stitches can be worked on rug canvas, though not all stitches are suitable for rugs.

Since almost all of these canvases are double weave, the basic method is to alternate rows of No. 54 Half Cross Stitch with No. 36 Continental Stitch. Working in this manner, the canvas does not have to be turned. The result on the front is the same as for any of the Tent Stitches, but an even tension cannot be achieved with alternating methods. The result tends to be sloppy, and the stitch is not recommended. The diagram shows the back of the canvas.

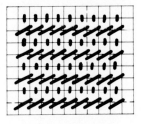

165 · RAISED STITCH (*Pyramid Stitch*)

CANVAS: #12 mono   NEEDLE: Size 18

TO COVER AN AREA EIGHT CANVAS THREADS SQUARE:

1 length Persian yarn

NUMBER OF THREADS: 2

This stitch forms an interesting textured square pattern. All of the stitches cross in the center so that it becomes higher as each stitch is worked. Although the stitches can be of any length, it is not advisable to make too large a square. Too many crossings can get bulky and very long stitches tend to snag.

Work is done counterclockwise around the square. Left-handers should work clockwise, using a mirror next to the diagram if necessary. DIAGRAM A shows the first two stitches in progress from 1 to 4, with the needle emerging at 5. Continue in this manner, always inserting the needle to the left of the previous insertion, and emerging to the right of the previous emerging point.

DIAGRAM B shows a completed area. DIAGRAM C shows the stitch worked on the diagonal to produce a diamond-shaped pattern. Patterns may be worked side by side in the same or different sizes for various textured effects.

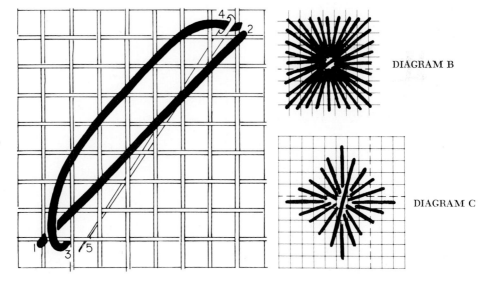

DIAGRAM A

DIAGRAM B

DIAGRAM C

166 · RAY STITCH (*Fan Stitch*)

CANVAS: #12 mono   NEEDLE: Size 18
TO COVER ONE SQUARE INCH: 2 lengths Persian yarn
NUMBER OF THREADS: 2

This is formed in the same basic manner as the No. 1 Algerian Eye Stitch. It forms a square pattern that can be worked in all four directions, and changing directions within a piece can produce really interesting effects. It is usually worked over a four-thread intersection but stitches can vary in size. Just remember that this enlarges or decreases the size of the finished pattern.

Work is shown with the stitches radiating diagonally from the upper left. Give the diagrams a quarter-turn to the right or to the left, or give a half-turn to see how to work the other directions. Left-handers should reverse each procedure, using a mirror next to the diagrams if necessary. DIAGRAMS A to C show the working action as the needle moves from 1 to 15, starting with a horizontal stitch and ending with a vertical one. All even numbers are inserted in the same opening, indicated by E. The needle at 15 is in position to work the next pattern, directly below. Note that to work stitches in this direction, vertical rows are the simplest. For other directions work in the direction indicated by the emerging needle.

DIAGRAM D shows a completed area, with each row worked in a different direction. Other interesting effects are achieved by changing the type but not the color of yarn—using mercerized cotton, for instance, to contrast with wool.

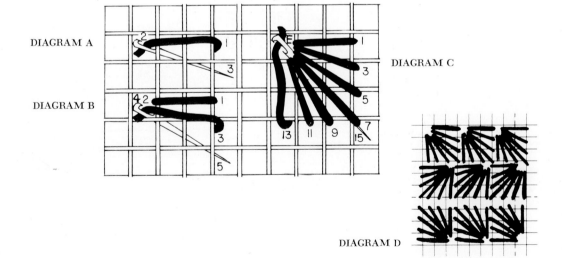

DIAGRAM A

DIAGRAM B

DIAGRAM C

DIAGRAM D

167 · RENAISSANCE STITCH

CANVAS: #12 mono   NEEDLE: Size 18

TO COVER ONE SQUARE INCH: 2 lengths Persian yarn

NUMBER OF THREADS: 2

This resembles No. 178 Padded Satin Stitch. It covers well on both sides, making it extremely durable. It is not highly recommended, however, because it is awkward to work.

Work is done vertically in both directions starting at the top. Left-handers should start at the bottom and turn the diagrams upside down. DIAGRAM A shows the first stitch worked horizontally from 1 to 2, with the needle emerging at 3. DIAGRAM B shows the next stitch worked vertically from 3 to 4, with the needle emerging at 5. DIAGRAM C shows the pattern completed with a second vertical stitch worked from 5 to 6. The dotted lines indicate the yarn on back. The needle emerges at 7 in position to work the next pattern. Work continues down in this manner.

DIAGRAM D shows a completed area. Note that when actually worked, the horizontal threads do not show, but merely give the stitch a raised appearance.

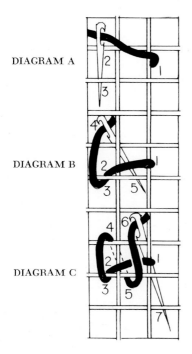

DIAGRAM A

DIAGRAM B

DIAGRAM C

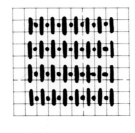

DIAGRAM D

168 · REP STITCH

CANVAS: #10 penelope   NEEDLE: Size 18

TO COVER ONE SQUARE INCH: 2½ lengths Persian yarn

NUMBER OF THREADS: 1

This resembles very fine corduroy and must be done on penelope canvas. Worked on mono in these proportions, it would be the same as No. 111 Slanting Gobelin Stitch or No. 176 Satin Stitch.

Work is done vertically from top to bottom. Left-handers should work from bottom to top and turn the diagrams upside down. Before beginning, separate the horizontal double canvas threads with the blunt end of the needle to make work easier. DIAGRAM A shows the first stitch being worked with the needle emerging between the threads at 1, inserted at 2 and emerging at 3. DIAGRAM B shows the next stitch with the needle inserted between the threads at 4 and emerging between the threads at 5. Work continues down in this manner, alternating the two stitches. Succeeding rows are worked beside the first one. This delicate stitch makes a nice contrast to other stitches worked on penelope canvas.

DIAGRAM A

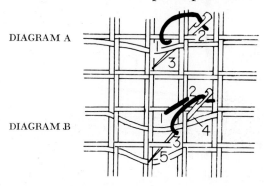

DIAGRAM B

169 · RICE STITCH NO. 1

(*William and Mary Stitch, Crossed Corners Stitch*)

CANVAS: #12 mono   NEEDLE: Size 18

TO COVER ONE SQUARE INCH: 1½ lengths Perisan yarn

NUMBER OF THREADS: 1 full strand

This stitch can have a variety of appearances if different colors, weights and textures of yarn are used. The extra padding created by the tie-down stitches makes it durable and suitable for rugs. Stitches can be as long as desired since the tie-down stitches will prevent snagging. Working over four canvas threads is best on #12 mono.

Work is done horizontally from left to right. Left-handers should reverse the procedure and work from right to left. DIAGRAMS A and B show a large cross stitch worked from 1 to 4, and a tie-down stitch being worked from 5 to 6. The needle emerges at 7 in position to work the next tie-down stitch. DIAGRAMS C to E show how to work the remaining tie-down stitches from 7 to 12, with the needle emerging at 13 ready to work the next pattern. Work continues across in this way.

DIAGRAM F shows a completed area. DIAGRAMS G, H and I illustrate a variation in which the tie-down stitches are worked in a contrasting color over a row of worked crosses. Work progresses according to the numbers from 1 to 9. Left-handers should reverse the procedure to work this. Another variation that changes the look completely is to alternate the colors of the base and tie-down stitches from pattern to pattern across the piece.

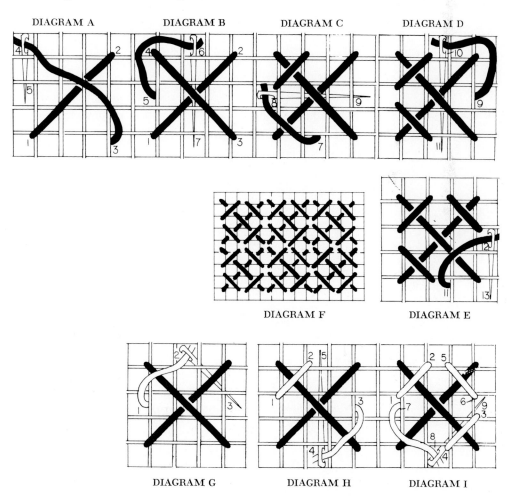

DIAGRAM A   DIAGRAM B   DIAGRAM C   DIAGRAM D

DIAGRAM F   DIAGRAM E

DIAGRAM G   DIAGRAM H   DIAGRAM I

170 · RICE STITCH NO. 2

CANVAS: #12 mono   NEEDLE: Size 18

TO COVER ONE SQUARE INCH: ⅔ length Persian yarn in main color;
½ length in contrasting color

NUMBER OF THREADS: 1 full strand

This variation has an extra tie-down stitch worked in a contrasting color. The large cross forming the foundation must be made larger to accommodate it.

Work is done horizontally from left to right. Left-handers should reverse the procedure and work from right to left. DIAGRAMS A and B show the foundation cross worked, and the first four tie-down stitches being worked in the principal color from 1 to 13. Work continues across in this manner. Note that these tie-down stitches do not go to the edges of the square formed by the large cross. DIAGRAM C shows how to work the row of contrasting tie-down stitches. These stitches are formed from 1 to 8, with the needle emerging finally at 9 in position to work over the next pattern. Note that these stitches reach the edges of the square formed by the large cross.

DIAGRAM D shows a completed area. A possible variation, if you work with a fine enough yarn, is to work a third row of tie-down stitches the same size as on the first row, but crossing at the extreme ends of the foundation cross. Do experiment with colors and threads.

DIAGRAM A

DIAGRAM B

DIAGRAM C

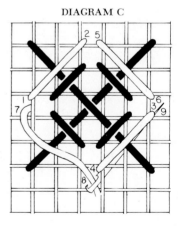

DIAGRAM D

171 · RICE STITCH, PADDED

CANVAS: #12 mono   NEEDLE: Size 18

TO COVER ONE SQUARE INCH: 1 length Persian yarn for padding;
1½ lengths for Rice Stitch

NUMBER OF THREADS: 1 full strand for padding;
1 or 2 threads for Rice Stitch

This is done the same as No. 169 Rice Stitch except that the stitches are worked over laid padding threads. Make sure that the yarn used for the Rice Stitch is finer than the padding yarn.

Work is done by laying the padding stitches vertically from top to bottom and working the Rice Stitch over them from left to right. Left-handers should reverse both procedures and work the padding from bottom to top and the Rice Stitch from right to left. DIAGRAMS A and B show the padding stitches being laid from 1 to 7. Work continues down in this manner. DIAGRAM C shows No. 169 Rice Stitch being worked over the laid threads. The action continues across in this manner.

DIAGRAM F for No. 169 Rice Stitch shows a completed area. The laid stitches, if worked in the same color, do not show but add to the texture by raising the stitches. For a different effect, work the padding stitches in one color and the Rice Stitch in two other colors.

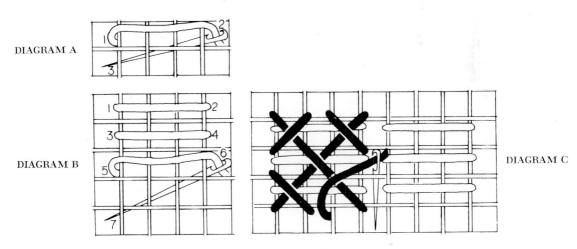

DIAGRAM A

DIAGRAM B

DIAGRAM C

172 · ROCOCO STITCH NO. 1

CANVAS: #12 mono   NEEDLE: Size 18
TO COVER ONE SQUARE INCH: 2½ lengths Persian yarn
NUMBER OF THREADS: 2

This is similar to No. 104 French Stitch. The stitches can vary in size according to the area being filled.

Work in this method is done diagonally starting at the upper left. Left-handers should start at the lower right and turn the diagrams upside down. DIAGRAM A shows the first long stitch being worked from 1 to 2, with the needle emerging at 3. Note that the working yarn is left slack to the left of the needle so that it remains to the left when the needle emerges. DIAGRAM B shows the first tie-down stitch worked from 3 to 4, with the needle emerging at 5. DIAGRAMS C to G show the remaining stitches being worked from 5 to 16, with the needle emerging at 17 in position to work the next pattern. Work continues down diagonally in this manner. Succeeding rows can be worked from the top—or you can turn the canvas and work back in the same manner, starting the first stitch two threads down and three to the left instead of at 17.

DIAGRAM H shows a completed area. Two slanting stitches and an upright stitch are worked to fill each space on top and bottom edges; half a pattern is worked on every other row to finish the right edge; and a row of No. 9 Back Stitches completes the bottom edge.

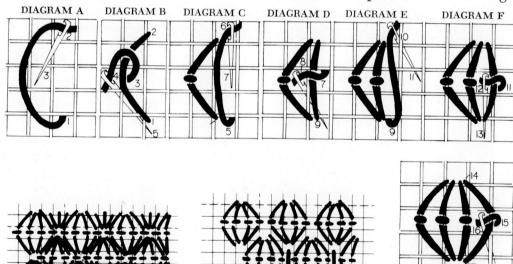

DIAGRAM A   DIAGRAM B   DIAGRAM C   DIAGRAM D   DIAGRAM E   DIAGRAM F

DIAGRAM H   DIAGRAM I   DIAGRAM G

DIAGRAM I is a variation in which the canvas thread is left between the tie-down stitches of one row and the long stitches on the next row instead of working them in one opening. Note that upright stitches are worked between patterns to fill in on the second and third rows. Half patterns or upright stitches are worked at the right edge if necessary, as on rows 2 and 3. Upper and lower edges can be filled with slanting stitches as shown on the lower edge of the diagram. This variation allows a heavier yarn to be used.

173 · ROCOCO STITCH NO. 2

CANVAS: #12 mono   NEEDLE: Size 18

TO COVER ONE SQUARE INCH: 1¼ lengths Persian yarn

NUMBER OF THREADS: 2

This stitch produces an interesting openwork pattern. If you work it on fine canvas, it will look best in a twisted thread such as mercerized cotton or silk. There is some preparation involved, which makes it unsuitable for working large areas. The rest of the canvas should be completed before doing this.

First the canvas area must be opened up by removing some of the threads. DIAGRAM A shows an area marked to indicate which threads to clip. Leave two horizontal and two vertical threads bordering the area, then clip the remaining threads, leaving every third thread in each direction intact. DIAGRAM B shows the canvas with the clipped threads pulled out. These are carried to the back and woven with a needle to the edges of the previously worked area, following the weave of the canvas. This woven line can be covered with a single row of any filling stitch before or after working the Rococo Stitch. DIAGRAM C shows the stitch being worked as for No. 172 Rococo Stitch, but from upper right to lower left. Use a mirror next to those diagrams to see the proper working action. Note that only the two outer tie-down stitches of each pattern are worked over canvas threads. The center two are worked over the upright stitches.

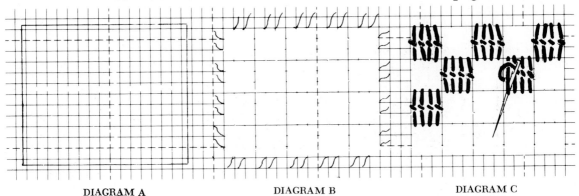

DIAGRAM A   DIAGRAM B   DIAGRAM C

174 · ROPE STITCH

CANVAS: #12 mono   NEEDLE: Size 18
TO COVER ONE INCH: ¼ length Persian yarn
NUMBER OF THREADS: 1 full strand

This is a line stitch that can be worked horizontally and vertically and goes around curves with ease. When worked, it has a nice raised appearance on one edge.

If work is done vertically, it moves from the top down. Left-handers should start at the bottom and turn the diagrams upside down. DIAGRAM A shows how to begin as the needle emerges at 1 and is inserted in the same opening at 2. As the needle emerges at 3, the working yarn is passed over it from left to right and then under it from right to left. It is easiest if the working yarn is held by the free thumb. Work continues down in this way, with the needle inserted one thread lower each time. DIAGRAM B shows the second stitch worked from 3 to 5. DIAGRAM C shows how to change directions and work to the left. Note that this widens the rope. When changing directions, the stitch is worked over one less intersection than the number of threads worked over vertically to keep the stitch size uniform.

DIAGRAM D shows a completed area with each row worked in different proportions producing ropes of different widths. A small tie-down stitch is worked at the bottom of each row for a finished look.

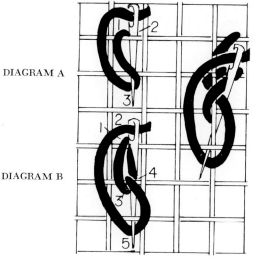

DIAGRAM A

DIAGRAM B

DIAGRAM C

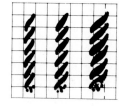

DIAGRAM D

175 · ROUMANIAN STITCH (*Roman Stitch*)

CANVAS: #12 mono   NEEDLE: Size 18

TO COVER ONE SQUARE INCH: 1 length Persian yarn (worked over
6 canvas threads)

NUMBER OF THREADS: 1 full strand

This stitch is good for borders or filling in irregular shapes. It can be worked square or adapted to any shape by varying the stitch size.

Work is done vertically from the top down. Left-handers should reverse the procedure and turn the diagrams upside down. DIAGRAM A shows a long stitch worked from 1 to 2, with the needle emerging at 3. Be sure to hold the working yarn with your free thumb below the area where the needle is inserted and emerges. DIAGRAM B shows a slanting tie-down stitch worked over the long stitch from 3 to 4, with the needle emerging at 5 in position to work the next pattern. If filling irregular areas, vary the length of the long stitches as necessary, but keep the tie-down stitches the same size unless the base stitch is extremely long.

DIAGRAM C shows a completed area with straight edges. Experiment with different stitch sizes and yarns for different effects. But remember that tightly twisted yarns are not suitable.

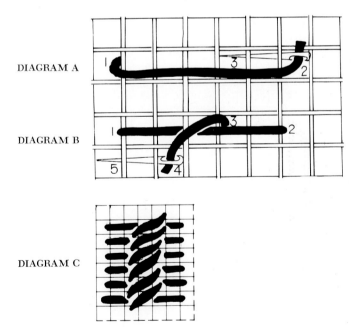

DIAGRAM A

DIAGRAM B

DIAGRAM C

176 · SATIN STITCH

CANVAS: #12 mono   NEEDLE: Size 18
TO COVER ONE SQUARE INCH: 1 length Persian yarn
NUMBER OF THREADS: 1 full strand

This is similar to the various Gobelin Stitches in appearance and working action. The stitches can vary in size and be either upright or slanting, the only limit being length. Extra-long stitches can snag and are unsuitable on pieces that will receive heavy wear.

Work is done horizontally in both directions. Left-handers should work as directed. DIAGRAM A shows how to work the upright Satin Stitch as the needle moves from 1 to 6, and emerges at 7 in position to work the next stitch. Work continues across in this manner. DIAGRAM B shows how to work a slanting Satin Stitch as the needle moves from 1 to 2 and emerges at 3, in position to continue across.

DIAGRAM C shows two completed rows, with upright stitches on top and slanting stitches below. DIAGRAM D shows an area worked with slanting stitches of varying lengths. This is useful for background filling. Changing colors from row to row or within rows can produce many different looks.

DIAGRAM E shows just how versatile this stitch is as a large geometric shape is filled with upright and slanting stitches of different lengths and colors. The canvas should be turned to work each section.

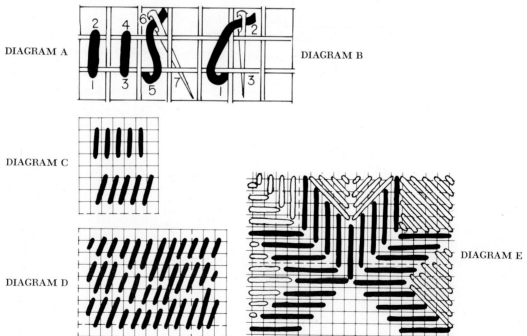

DIAGRAM A

DIAGRAM B

DIAGRAM C

DIAGRAM D

DIAGRAM E

177 · SATIN STITCH, ALTERNATING

CANVAS: #12 mono   NEEDLE: Size 18

TO COVER ONE SQUARE INCH: 1¼ lengths Persian yarn

NUMBER OF THREADS: 1 full strand

This consists of rows of slanting stitches worked in opposite directions from row to row.

Work is done either horizontally or vertically in both directions. Left-handers should work as directed. DIAGRAM A shows how to work a slanting stitch in left-to-right horizontal rows as the needle moves from 1 to 2 and emerges at 3. Work continues across in this manner. DIAGRAM B shows one horizontal row completed and a second in progress as the needle moves from 1 to 5. Work continues across in this manner. Horizontal work continues by alternating these two rows.

DIAGRAM C shows how to work a slanting stitch for vertical rows from 1 to 3. DIAGRAM D shows one vertical row completed and a second in progress from 1 to 5. Vertical work continues by alternating these two rows. Note the small slanting stitches that begin and end rows in both methods. These are not part of the pattern, but give the area a finished appearance.

DIAGRAM E shows completed areas of horizontal and vertical rows.

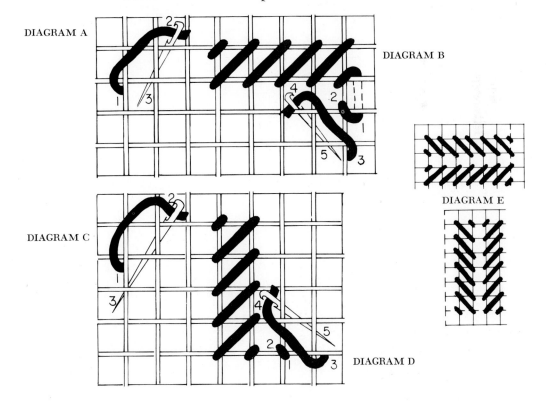

DIAGRAM A

DIAGRAM B

DIAGRAM C

DIAGRAM D

DIAGRAM E

178 · SATIN STITCH, PADDED

CANVAS: #12 mono   NEEDLE: Size 18
TO COVER ONE SQUARE INCH: 1⅓ lengths Persian yarn
NUMBER OF THREADS: 2

This stitch has a nice flat texture made extremely durable by the extra padding. It is worked over a laid padding thread in the same manner as No. 176 Satin Stitch.

Work is done in horizontal rows worked from right to left for the padding stitches and from left to right for the Satin Stitch. Left-handers should work the laid stitches from left to right and the Satin Stitches from right to left. DIAGRAM A shows a long padding stitch worked from 1 to 2, with the needle emerging at 3. DIAGRAM B shows No. 176 Satin Stitches worked over the canvas and padding threads. Consult the diagrams for No. 176 for the proper working action. At the end of the row, the needle emerges at 11 in position to work the next padding stitch.

DIAGRAM C shows a completed area. When actually worked, the padding stitches don't show.

DIAGRAM A	DIAGRAM B	DIAGRAM C

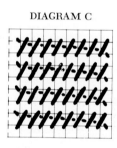

179 · SCOTCH STITCH (*Scottish Stitch*)

CANVAS: #12 mono   NEEDLE: Size 18
TO COVER ONE SQUARE INCH: 1½ lengths Perisan yarn
NUMBER OF THREADS: 1 full strand

This is basically an expanded No. 144 Mosaic Stitch, and has a similar working action. It is useful for borders and background or area filling. It also distorts the canvas somewhat.

Work is done diagonally from upper left to lower right. Left-handers should start at the lower right and turn the diagrams upside down. DIAGRAMS A to C show the five slanting stitches that form each pattern being worked from 1 to 10, with the needle emerging at 11 in position to work the next pattern, and so on diagonally down. Note that the first and fifth stitches are the same size, as are the second and fourth. DIAGRAM D shows how to work an up row as one complete pattern is formed from 1 to 10, with the needle emerging at 11 in position to continue up.

This can also be worked horizontally from right to left (left to right for left-handers). To do so, use DIAGRAM D as a guide, but instead of emerging at 11, emerge three threads down and two to the left of 10, and continue across.

DIAGRAM E gives a completed area, showing how to adjust at the right edge if it doesn't end with a full pattern.

A new variation on this stitch produces a gingham pattern that is good as an all-over effect or as area filling. You should use two sharply contrasting colors to achieve the full effect. A third color is formed by using an equal number of threads of each of the two colors.

First thread your needle with the mixed colors. On #14 mono canvas you would use one thread of each color of Persian yarn. On #10 mono, use two threads of each color.

Starting at upper left, first work a diagonal row of Scotch Stitch. Then work another diagonal row leaving three canvas threads between it and the first row. Work successive diagonal rows leaving three canvas spaces between them until your area is covered. Work all these diagonal rows first.

Starting at top right work horizontal rows of the two solid colors in the empty spaces. When working horizontally start your Scotch Stitches at the bottom, beginning one thread in from the right edge, and work up. Work completely across each row alternating the solid colors in each row.

DIAGRAM F shows a completed gingham pattern area.

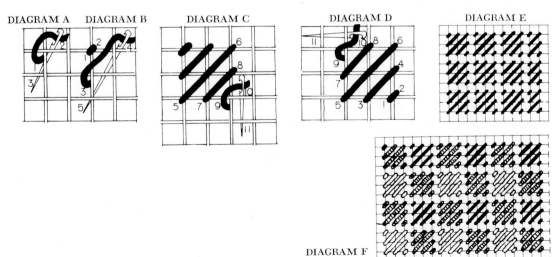

DIAGRAM A   DIAGRAM B   DIAGRAM C   DIAGRAM D   DIAGRAM E

DIAGRAM F

180 · SCOTCH STITCH, ALTERNATING

CANVAS: #12 mono   NEEDLE: Size 18

TO COVER ONE SQUARE INCH: 1⅗ lengths Persian yarn

NUMBER OF THREADS: 1 full strand

This consists of No. 179 Scotch Stitches worked in opposite directions in horizontal rows.

As work is done in both directions, left-handers should work as directed. DIAGRAM A shows a pattern in progress. One No. 179 Scotch Stitch is completed and a second is being started with stitches slanting in the opposite direction. The needle moves from 1 to 10, emerging at 11 in position to work the next pattern. Work continues across in this manner, alternating the slant of the stitches in each pattern. This stitch can be worked in diagonal rows as well.

DIAGRAM B shows a completed area.

DIAGRAM A

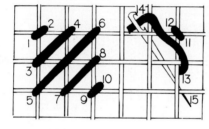

DIAGRAM B

181 · SCOTCH STITCH, CROSSED

CANVAS: #12 mono   NEEDLE: Size 18

TO COVER ONE SQUARE INCH: 2 lengths Persian yarn

NUMBER OF THREADS: 1 full strand

This stitch is an interesting textured variation of No. 179 Scotch Stitch. This also shows up well on large canvas.

DIAGRAM A

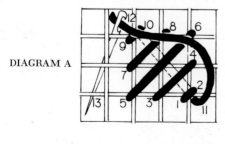

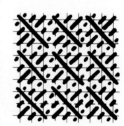

DIAGRAM C

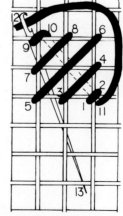

DIAGRAM B

Work is done horizontally from right to left or vertically from top to bottom. Left-handers should turn diagrams upside down and work horizontal rows from left to right and vertical rows from bottom to top. DIAGRAM A shows how to work horizontally. A No. 179 Scotch Stitch is worked from 1 to 10. From 10 the needle emerges at 11, and, crossing the pattern in the opposite direction, is inserted at 12 to emerge at 13 in position to work the next pattern. Work continues across in this manner. DIAGRAM B shows how to work vertically. The action is exactly the same as for horizontal work, but instead of emerging to the left, the needle emerges below at 13 to work the next pattern, and so on down.

DIAGRAM C shows a completed area.

182 · SCOTCH STITCH, WOVEN

CANVAS: #12 mono   NEEDLE: Size 18

TO COVER ONE SQUARE INCH: 2 lengths Persian yarn

NUMBER OF THREADS: 1 full strand

This variation is similar to No. 181 Crossed Scotch Stitch, but the final stitch is woven through the No. 179 Scotch Stitch foundation rather than crossing over it.

Work moves horizontally from right to left or vertically from top to bottom. Left-handers should turn the diagram upside down and work from left to right horizontally, and from bottom to top vertically. Follow DIAGRAMS A to C for No. 179, and complete a Scotch Stitch from 1 to 10. Now follow DIAGRAM A for No. 182, for the weaving. From 10 the needle emerges at 11. Then it is woven over the first stitch, under the second, over the third, under the fourth, over the fifth, and inserted at 12. To continue on, the needle emerges as for DIAGRAM A or B of No. 181 Crossed Scotch Stitch, depending on the direction you wish to take.

DIAGRAM B shows a completed area with adjusting stitches worked across the bottom.

DIAGRAM A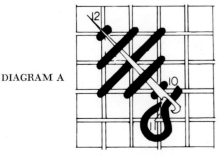

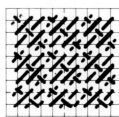 DIAGRAM B

183 · SCOTCH STITCH with TENT STITCH

CANVAS: #10 mono   NEEDLE: Size 18
TO COVER ONE SQUARE INCH: 1⅔ lengths Persian yarn
NUMBER OF THREADS: 1 full strand

This alternates No. 179 Scotch Stitch squares with Tent Stitch squares.
No. 11 Basketweave or No. 37 Continental can be used for the Tent
Stitches. Since Scotch Stitch distorts the canvas somewhat, No. 11
Basketweave may keep the shape a little better.

Work is done diagonally with the Scotch Stitches moving from
upper left to lower right and Tent Stitches moving from upper right
to lower left. Left-handers should work in whatever manner is most
comfortable. It is easiest to work the Scotch Stitches first, leaving
bare canvas intersections between rows, and then filling in with Tent
Stitches. DIAGRAM A shows square being completed. Consult diagrams
for No. 179 Scotch Stitch for the working action, and work the Tent
Stitches as shown from 1 to 18. The needle emerging at 19 is in position to work the next Tent Stitch square.

DIAGRAM B shows a completed area.

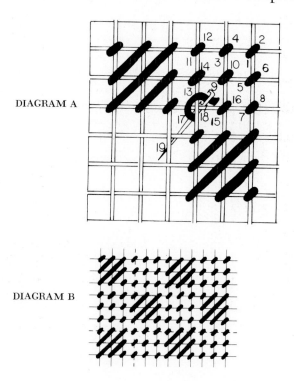

DIAGRAM A

DIAGRAM B

184 · SHELL STITCH

CANVAS: #12 mono   NEEDLE: Size 18

TO COVER ONE SQUARE INCH: ¾ length main color Persian yarn for bundle;

⅓ length contrasting color for lacing

NUMBER OF THREADS: 1 full strand (for both)

This stitch makes an attractive border or area covering.

Work is done horizontally from left to right, then laced with a contrasting color, also from left to right. Left-handers should reverse both procedures and work from right to left, using a mirror next to the diagrams if necessary. DIAGRAM A shows how to work the four upright stitches of one bundle from 1 to 8, with the needle emerging at 9 in position to gather the stitches together. Note that the needle should be on the right of the last stitch after emerging. If necessary, push the four stitches to the left with your free thumb. DIAGRAM B shows the upright stitches gathered into a bundle by a stitch worked from 9 to 10. The needle emerging at 11 is in position to work the next bundle. Work continues across in this manner. DIAGRAM C shows how to do the lacing. The needle is brought up in the middle of a bundle and not inserted again until the end of the row. It is wound around the horizontal stitches from 1 to 4, then slipped below the second horizontal stitch in order to continue the journey.

DIAGRAM D shows a completed area. No. 9 Back Stitches are used to fill between rows on the right side. Spaces can be filled with the same or contrasting color.

DIAGRAM A   DIAGRAM B   DIAGRAM C

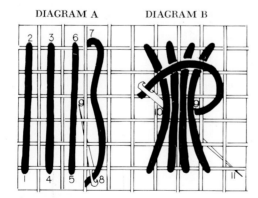 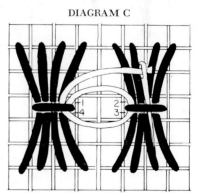

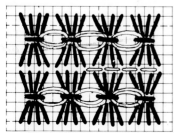

DIAGRAM D

185 · SHELL STITCH, DIAGONAL

CANVAS: #12 mono   NEEDLE: Size 18

TO COVER ONE SQUARE INCH: ⅔ length main color Persian yarn
for bundle; ⅓ length contrasting
color for lacing

NUMBER OF THREADS: 1 full strand (for both)

This has too many spaces between stitches and rows to be suitable for overall covering. It is best used to lend interest to a larger area. Only three long stitches are used for the bundle.

Work is done diagonally from upper left to lower right. Left-handers should turn the diagrams upside down and work from lower right to upper left. DIAGRAM A shows the three long stitches being worked from 1 to 6, with the needle emerging at 7 in position to tie down the bundle. DIAGRAM B shows the tie-down stitch worked from 7 to 8, with the needle emerging at 9 in position to work the next bundle. When the row is completed, work the lacing as for No. 184 Shell Stitch.

DIAGRAM C shows a completed area. If working more than one row, fill in between rows with No. 9 Back Stitches.

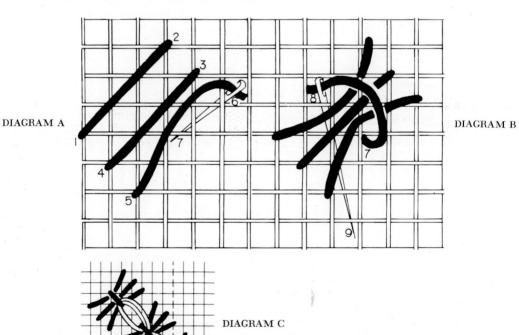

DIAGRAM A

DIAGRAM B

DIAGRAM C

186 · SORBELLO STITCH

CANVAS: #12 mono   NEEDLE: Size 18

TO COVER ONE SQUARE INCH: 1⅓ lengths Persian yarn worked over
3 canvas intersections;
2 lengths worked over 2 intersections

NUMBER OF THREADS: 4 (over 3 intersections); 1 full strand (over 2 intersections)

This very old stitch has Neapolitan origins. Working with wool produces a nice texture, but it also looks well worked with a tightly twisted thread such as pearl cotton.

Work is done horizontally from left to right. Left-handers should reverse the procedure and work from right to left. DIAGRAM A shows the first stitch worked from 1 to 2, with the needle emerging at 3. DIAGRAM B shows a loop being formed as the needle is carried up over the worked stitch and slipped under it, but not inserted in the canvas. The needle passes over the working yarn as it emerges. DIAGRAM C shows a second loop formed in the same manner. Loops should not be pulled too tightly, but they should be firm. DIAGRAM D shows the needle inserted at 4 and emerging at 5 in position to work the next pattern. Work continues across in this manner. This can also be worked in vertical rows with the needle emerging at 3 to start a square below the original one.

DIAGRAM E shows a completed area.

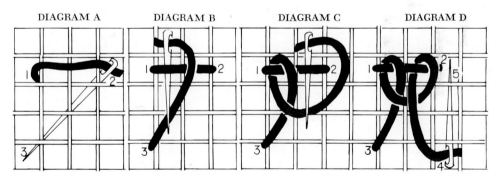

DIAGRAM A   DIAGRAM B   DIAGRAM C   DIAGRAM D

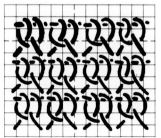

DIAGRAM E

187 · SOUMAK STITCH

CANVAS: #10 penelope   NEEDLE: Size 18
TO COVER ONE SQUARE INCH: 2½ lengths Persian yarn
NUMBER OF THREADS: 1

DIAGRAM A
DIAGRAM B

This resembles No. 128 Knitting Stitch but is easier to work and more durable. It is an excellent rug stitch, deriving its name from the Soumak rugs woven in the East. It looks well combined with other stitches, but is easier to design when used alone.

Work is generally done vertically from top to bottom and right to left. Left-handers can keep the diagrams as is, but interchange right and left in the directions. It is easiest to work if the selvage edge of the canvas is horizontal. DIAGRAMS A and B show how to complete one stitch as the needle emerges between the double threads at 1, is inserted at 2, emerges at 3, is reinserted between the double threads at 4 and emerges between the threads at 5. DIAGRAM C shows how to continue the vertical row with each stitch passing behind the base of the previous stitch. Successive rows are also worked from the top.

Sometimes the shape of a design requires working in other directions. DIAGRAM D shows how to work horizontally. DIAGRAM E shows how to work down diagonally. DIAGRAM F shows how to work up diagonally. The dotted lines in all three diagrams indicate the yarn on the back. Left-handers should reverse each procedure.

DIAGRAM C   DIAGRAM D   DIAGRAM E   DIAGRAM F

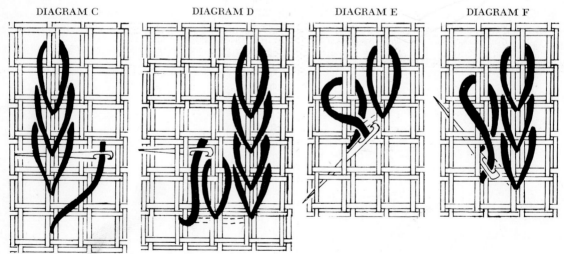

188 · SPIDER WEB FOUNDATIONS

Spider Web Stitches are isolated patterns used as accent points in conjunction with other stitches. There are several methods of laying the foundations. Once these are mastered, you can go ahead and work any of the Spider Web Stitches.

Because they receive a lot of pull, the foundations must be anchored firmly either on the front or back of the work but preferably on the front. The stitches are raised so a knot will not spoil the finished appearance.

DIAGRAM A shows one foundation being worked. The dotted lines at the right indicate the knot on the back. The first stitch from 1 to 2 is anchoring the knot. The stitch from 3 to 4 starts the actual foundation. Work continues counterclockwise in this manner, with all even numbers inserted in the same center opening at E. There can be an odd or even number of spokes. As shown, it's a good idea to sketch an outline of the area before working it. Left-handers should work clockwise. DIAGRAM B shows a completed foundation.

DIAGRAM C shows a foundation worked with the same counterclockwise needle action, but the stitches do not all meet in the same center opening. There can be an odd or even number of spokes, and it's a good idea to outline the area first as with the previous method. When done, a No. 75 Upright Cross Stitch is worked to cover the center. DIAGRAM D shows a completed foundation.

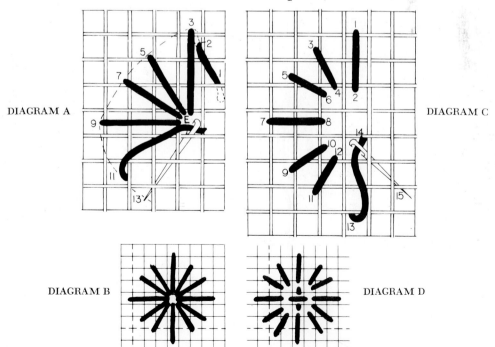

DIAGRAM A

DIAGRAM C

DIAGRAM B

DIAGRAM D

DIAGRAMS E and F show a third foundation which always has an odd number of spokes. First, outline the area, making one half of the "circle" larger than the other. The first stitch is worked from 1 to 2, intentionally not bisecting the circle. The needle emerges at 3 about one-fourth of the way around the larger portion of the circle and is inserted at 4. A third stitch is worked from 5 to 6. The needle, emerging at 7, is in position to work the last spoke, at the same time gathering the other stitches and making a knot. The needle is slipped under all three stitches and emerges over the working yarn. Note that the stitches do not cross at the same point as none of them bisect the circle. After the loop is formed, the stitches can be shifted around until the loop is in the exact center. DIAGRAM G shows a completed foundation.

DIAGRAM E	DIAGRAM F	DIAGRAM G

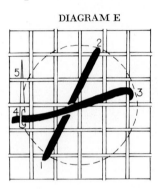  

189 · SPIDER WEB STITCH, RAISED

CANVAS: #12 mono   NEEDLE: Size 18
TO FORM A ONE-INCH WEB (WITHOUT RAISING): 1 length Persian yarn
NUMBER OF THREADS: 1 full strand

This method produces an oval shape due to different-sized spokes. It is a little difficult to master as it requires both hands. Use a piece of yarn long enough to complete the pattern with a continuous thread.

The raised effect is achieved by first working a foundation according to the third method described in No. 188 Spider Web Foundations. DIAGRAM A shows a small piece of yarn slipped under the entire group of stitches. This separates the spokes so that the center will be considerably higher. It is held by the free hand as work is done. The needle emerges between two spokes, is carried back to the right over two spokes and forward to the left under one spoke. Work continues around in concentric circles in this manner. Left-handers reverse directions and right and left in the text.

DIAGRAM B shows a completed area.

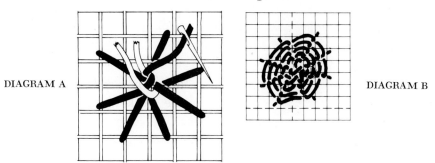

DIAGRAM A   DIAGRAM B

190 · SPIDER WEB STITCH, WHIPPED

This stitch can be worked over an odd or even number of spokes. Yarn requirements vary according to the size of the pattern.

Work is done clockwise. Left-handers should work counterclockwise. DIAGRAM A shows the whipping progress. The needle emerges between two spokes, is carried back over one spoke to the right and forward under it and the next spoke. Work continues around in this manner in concentric circles.

DIAGRAM B shows a completed area. DIAGRAM C shows how to work if the yarn between spokes becomes too long and starts to snag. Note that short spokes are worked on the outside edges. These are whipped along with the others on the outside rows. This is a good way to work a large area without the center getting too tight or the edges getting too loose.

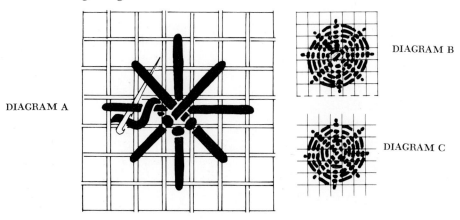

DIAGRAM A

DIAGRAM B

DIAGRAM C

191 · SPIDER WEB STITCH, WOVEN

This stitch must be worked over an odd number of spokes, so lay the foundation as for the third method described in No. 188 Spider Web Foundations.

Weaving is done either clockwise or counterclockwise. Left-handers should work in whatever manner is most comfortable. DIAGRAM A shows how to do the weaving. After the foundation is laid, the needle moves around in concentric circles in a simple under-over manner.

DIAGRAM B shows a completed area with the spokes worked in different lengths. Two extra rows are worked at the lower right, with the weaving action continued.

DIAGRAM A   DIAGRAM B

192 · SPLIT STITCH

CANVAS: #12 mono   NEEDLE: Size 18

TO COVER ONE INCH: ⅛ length Persian yarn (worked over 2 canvas threads)

NUMBER OF THREADS: 1 full strand

This looks like a small No. 32 Chain Stitch. It produces a nice flat line suitable for outlining and takes curves and corners nicely. It also makes a good area filling.

Work is done horizontally from left to right. Left-handers should reverse the procedure and work from right to left, using a mirror next to the diagrams if necessary. DIAGRAM A shows how to begin as the needle emerges at 1, is inserted to the right at 2 and emerges back to the left at 3, splitting the working yarn in the process. This is easier if you hold the working yarn with your free thumb. Work continues

DIAGRAM A   DIAGRAM B   DIAGRAM C

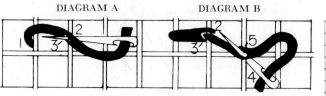
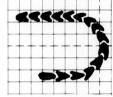

across in this manner. DIAGRAM B shows how to work a curve, also splitting the working yarn. To keep a smooth curve, the stitches going around it are shorter than straight horizontal or vertical stitches. In going around curves and corners, turn the canvas as you work.

DIAGRAM C shows a completed curve.

193 · SPRATS HEAD STITCH

CANVAS: #12 mono   NEEDLE: Size 18
TO FORM ONE PATTERN: ⅔ length Persian yarn
NUMBER OF THREADS: 1 full strand

This is actually a tailoring stitch adapted for canvas. It is ideally worked as an equilateral triangle, but due to the restrictions of the canvas, it is easier to make the height about half of the width at the base. It is diagrammed nine threads high and twelve threads wide.

Work is done by slipping the needle from right to left. Left-handers should slip the needle from left to right, using a mirror next to the diagrams if necessary. DIAGRAMS A and B show the first two stitches being worked from 1 to 4, with the needle emerging at 5. These form the basic triangle shape with both stitches meeting in the same opening at the top. DIAGRAMS C and D show the action used to continue as the needle moves from 5, emerging finally at 9. Continue by alternating the action in these two diagrams, always moving one thread in at the base and one thread down at the top. DIAGRAM E shows the process continuing as the next stitch is formed from 9 to 10 and emerges at 11.

DIAGRAM F shows a completed area.

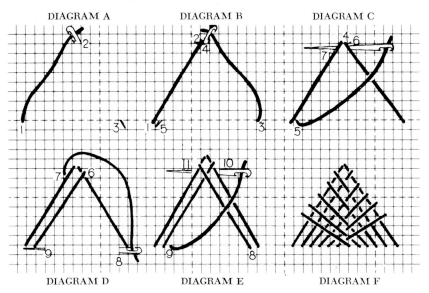

DIAGRAM A   DIAGRAM B   DIAGRAM C

DIAGRAM D   DIAGRAM E   DIAGRAM F

194 · STEM STITCH (*Feather Stitch*)

CANVAS: #12 mono   NEEDLE: Size 18

TO COVER ONE SQUARE INCH: 2 lengths Persian yarn for Stem Stitch;
⅔ length for No. 9 Back Stitches

NUMBER OF THREADS: 1 full strand for Stem Stitch; 2 threads for
Back Stitches

This consists of rows of slanting stitches with No. 9 Back Stitches worked between. Stitch size can vary, but working over two canvas intersections is best on #12 mono.

Work is done vertically from top to bottom and left to right. Left-handers should turn the diagrams upside down and work from bottom to top and right to left. For a squared-off appearance, each row begins and ends with a slanting stitch worked over one canvas intersection. DIAGRAM A shows the slanting stitch and a regular stitch being formed as the needle moves from 1 to 4, and emerges at 5. Work continues down in this manner, ending with another small slanting stitch. DIAGRAM B shows one row completed and the second row starting. Note that it starts with a small slanting stitch and the remaining stitches slant in the opposite direction. Work continues by alternating these two rows. At the end, DIAGRAM C shows No. 9 Back Stitches worked between rows as the needle moves from 1 to 4, and emerges at 5.

DIAGRAM D shows a completed area.

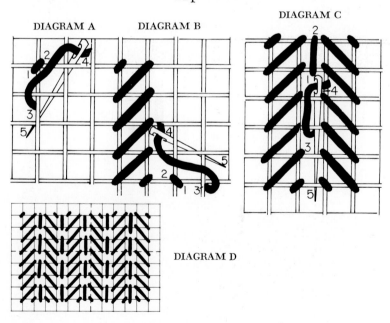

DIAGRAM A   DIAGRAM B   DIAGRAM C

DIAGRAM D

195 · STEM STITCH, DIAGONAL

CANVAS: #12 mono   NEEDLE: Size 18

TO COVER ONE SQUARE INCH: 1⅓ lengths Persian yarn for Stem Stitch;
⅔ length for No. 9 Back Stitches

NUMBER OF THREADS: 1 full strand for Stem Stitch;
1 thread for Back Stitches

This is worked the same as No. 194 Stem Stitch, but since it is done diagonally the stitches formed are horizontal and vertical.

Work is done diagonally from upper left to lower right. Left-handers should turn the diagrams upside down and work from lower left to upper right. DIAGRAM A shows the first row of vertical stitches completed following numbers 1 to 14, and the next row of horizontal stitches beginning. Note that the last two stitches on the vertical row are shortened to keep a square edge. Horizontal stitches are all worked as from 15 to 17 in the diagram. The last two stitches in the horizontal row are also shortened to make a square edge. Work continues by alternating these two rows. When the area is covered, work No. 9 Back Stitches between rows as in No. 194 Stem Stitch.

DIAGRAM B shows a completed area.

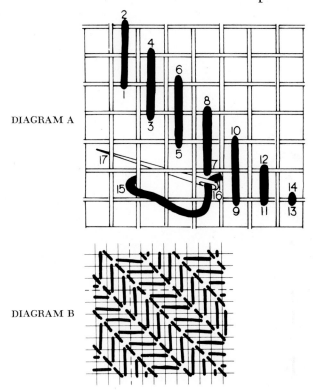

DIAGRAM A

DIAGRAM B

196 · STITCH À LA VAN DYKE

CANVAS: #12 mono NEEDLE: Size 18

TO COVER ONE SQUARE INCH: ⅗ length Persian yarn in main color;
½ length in contrasting color

NUMBER OF THREADS: 2

This consists of upright stitches worked in groups of different size and color stitches to form patterns.

Work is done horizontally from left to right. Left-handers should always work from right to left, using a mirror next to the diagrams if necessary. DIAGRAMS A to C show the first group of three stitches being worked from 1 to 6, with the needle emerging at 7 in position to work the next group. Work continues across in this manner. It is best to work all stitches of one color first. Work the second row in the same manner, with the long stitches of each row meeting in the same openings. When these rows are done, fill the spaces with upright stitches worked in the contrasting color.

DIAGRAM D shows a completed area with adjusting stitches at the upper and lower edges.

DIAGRAM A   DIAGRAM B   DIAGRAM C

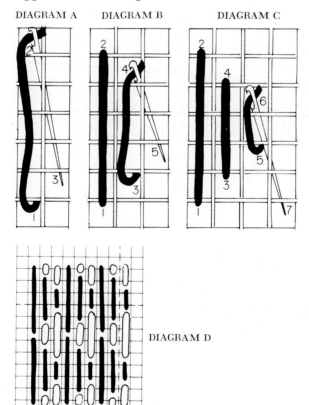

DIAGRAM D

197 · SURREY STITCH

CANVAS: #10 penelope   NEEDLE: Size 18

TO COVER ONE SQUARE INCH: 5 lengths Persian yarn (worked with ½-inch loops)

NUMBER OF THREADS: 1 full strand

This is a good rug stitch that must be worked on penelope canvas. It is worked with a nice tight knot that gives a tufted look.

Work is done from the bottom up in horizontal rows moving from left to right. Left-handers should reverse the procedure and work from right to left. DIAGRAM A shows how to begin. The yarn is not anchored on the back, as the stitch is always cut. A short length is left on top of the canvas as the needle is inserted at 1 and emerges at 2. The length is then folded down over the working yarn and held in place with the free thumb until the first stitch is completed. DIAGRAM B shows the needle inserted at 3 and emerging over the working yarn at 4. DIAGRAM C shows the first knot completed and a second in progress with the needle inserted at 5 and emerging over the working yarn at 6 forming a loop. Work continues in this manner. To get uniform loops, work over a ruler or your thumb. When the area is completed, cut the loops for a piled effect.

DIAGRAM D shows a completed area with the loops cut. Note that the ends of one row cover the knots on the next.

DIAGRAM A   DIAGRAM B   DIAGRAM C

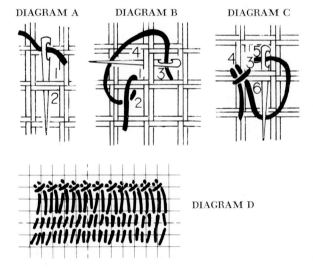

DIAGRAM D

198 · SUTHERLAND PATTERN

CANVAS: #10 mono   NEEDLE: Size 18
TO FORM ONE PATTERN: ½ length Persian yarn
NUMBER OF THREADS: 1 full strand

This is a very old pattern worked with a combination of straight and cross stitches. It is nice for overall covering or an isolated pattern.

Use the diagram as a working guide. It is easiest first to work the horizontal rows of stitches. Then continue by turning the canvas and repeating the process on all four sides. At the end, fill in the center spaces with No. 48 Cross Stitches.

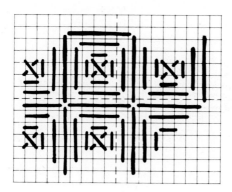

199 · TENT STITCH, ALTERNATING NO. 1

CANVAS: #10 mono   NEEDLE: Size 18
TO COVER ONE SQUARE INCH: 1½ lengths Persian yarn
NUMBER OF THREADS: 2

This is an extremely useful stitch worked very much like No. 12 Basketweave Stitch, the difference being that every other diagonal canvas intersection is skipped. Its interesting, rather flat texture shows up best with a large canvas and heavy yarn. It can also be worked on #12 mono, but it won't be nearly as effective.

The first step is to master No. 12 Basketweave Stitch, so learn and practice it before starting this. Left-handers should turn the diagram upside down and begin at the lower left.

DIAGRAM A shows the first two stitches worked as in the Basketweave Stitch. DIAGRAM B shows the Basketweave Stitches continuing with one down row completed at 8, and the needle starting the up row as it emerges at 9 and is inserted at 10. The needle then reemerges at 11, continuing the basketweave action to the top of the row. DIAGRAM C shows this square of Basketweave Stitches completed at 26,

The canvas is then given a quarter-turn, and DIAGRAM C also shows the second square of Basketweave Stitches being done at right angles to the first in exactly the same way. As the corners have been filled on the first square, work starts at the bottom of the up row. DIAGRAM C shows the up row completed from A to D. The first two stitches of the down row have been completed from E to H, with the needle emerging at I to continue the row. Up and down rows of Basketweave Stitch are continued until the square is filled. Make sure that all stitches slant in the same direction.

DIAGRAM D shows a completed stitch. DIAGRAM E shows the inner area worked in contrasting color.

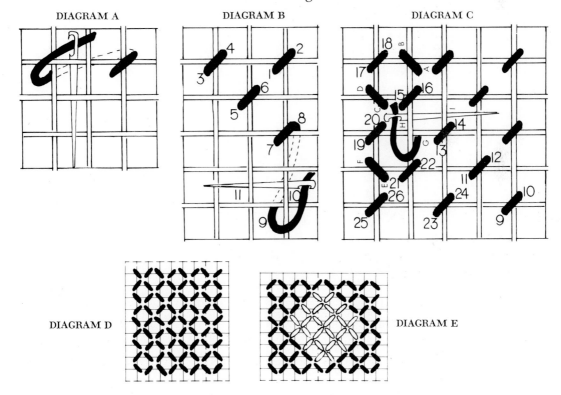

DIAGRAM A   DIAGRAM B   DIAGRAM C

DIAGRAM D   DIAGRAM E

200 · TENT STITCH, ALTERNATING NO. 2

CANVAS: #10 mono   NEEDLE: Size 18
TO COVER ONE SQUARE INCH: 1½ lengths Persian yarn
NUMBER OF THREADS: 2

This is worked like No. 199 Alternating Tent Stitch until it is ready to be turned. Left-handers should turn diagram upside down and begin at the lower left.

Complete the first step as directed for No. 199 Alternating Tent Stitch. When this is completed, lay a strand of yarn diagonally across the canvas intersections omitted by the first step, 1 to 2 in DIAGRAM A. Next, the needle emerges one thread below, and work continues back over the laid yarn with stitches slanting in the opposite direction from those worked on the first journey to complete stitches 3 and 4. These continue until you reach the beginning of the laid yarn. Then, bypassing 1, the needle emerges out to the edge at 5. You will add two more diagonal stitches to every succeeding row until the area is covered. Repeat this process.

The laid yarn covers the canvas so well that you may be able to use one thread less in working those rows. They may also be worked in a different color.

DIAGRAM B shows a completed area.

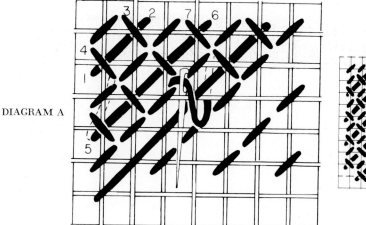

DIAGRAM A

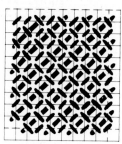

DIAGRAM B

201 · TENT STITCH, DIAGONAL MOSAIC

CANVAS: #12 mono   NEEDLE: Size 18

TO COVER ONE SQUARE INCH: 1½ lengths Persian yarn

NUMBER OF THREADS: 1 full strand

This is an interesting Tent Stitch variation.

Work is done diagonally from upper left to lower right. Left-handers should start at the lower right and turn the diagrams upside down. Since the Tent Stitches can be worked in either direction, the area can be filled on either side of the original row. DIAGRAMS A to C show the first three stitches being worked from 1 to 6, forming the first Diagonal Mosaic pattern. The needle emerges at 7 in position to work the next pattern. Work continues in this manner. DIAGRAM D shows how to work the stitch in contrasting colors. To do this, keep two needles going, each threaded with a different color. The needle with the first color emerges at 9. The contrasting color follows the route indicated by the numbers from 1 to 3. Note the extra stitch taken to square off at the upper left.

DIAGRAM E shows a completed area with adjusting stitches taken wherever necessary. The upper right of the diagram is worked in one color, the lower left in two.

DIAGRAM A   DIAGRAM B   DIAGRAM C   DIAGRAM D

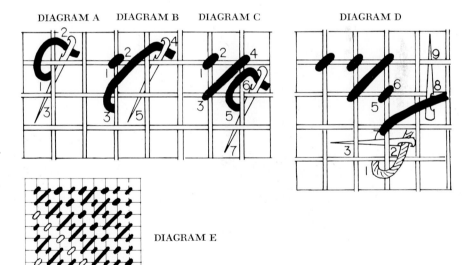

DIAGRAM E

202 · TENT STITCH, REVERSED ALTERNATING

CANVAS: #12 mono   NEEDLE: Size 18

TO COVER ONE SQUARE INCH: 2 lengths Persian yarn

NUMBER OF THREADS: 1 full strand

No. 36 Continental Stitch is the only Tent Stitch suitable for this.

Work is done horizontally in both directions. Left-handers should work as directed. DIAGRAM A shows how to work the first stitch from 1 to 2, with the needle emerging at 3. Work continues across in this manner. DIAGRAM B shows the first row completed with the needle emerging at 9 in position to work the next row. DIAGRAM C shows how to work the first stitch on the next row from 1 to 3. Work continues across in this manner by alternating these two rows.

DIAGRAM D shows a completed area.

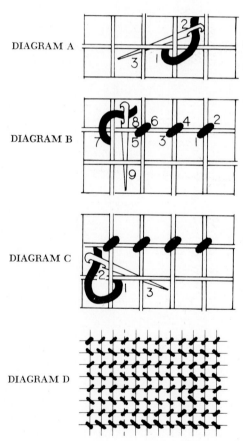

DIAGRAM A

DIAGRAM B

DIAGRAM C

DIAGRAM D

203 · TENT STITCH, TEXTURED NO. 1

CANVAS: #12 mono   NEEDLE: Size 18

TO COVER ONE SQUARE INCH: 1⅔ lengths Persian yarn

NUMBER OF THREADS: 1 full strand

This is a combination of Eyelet and Tent Stitches.

Work is done diagonally from upper left to lower right. Left-handers should start at the lower right and turn the diagrams upside down. Work all the Eyelet Stitches first. DIAGRAMS A to C show one corner of an eyelet being worked from 1 to 7. All the stitches are inserted in the same center opening indicated by an E for even numbers. DIAGRAM D shows the eyelet completed with the needle emerging at 25 in position to work the next eyelet. The diagram also shows how to work the Tent Stitch filling with No. 11 Basketweave Stitches worked from 1 to 17.

DIAGRAM E shows a completed area. Different effects can be achieved by varying the placement of the eyelets.

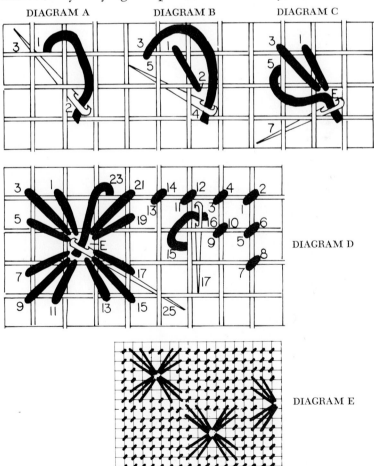

DIAGRAM A   DIAGRAM B   DIAGRAM C

DIAGRAM D

DIAGRAM E

224

204 · TENT STITCH, TEXTURED NO. 2

CANVAS: #12 mono   NEEDLE: Size 18

TO COVER ONE SQUARE INCH: 1 length Persian yarn for Tent Stitch;
½ length for No. 176 Satin Stitch

NUMBER OF THREADS: 1 full strand

To work this, groups of four No. 176 Satin Stitches are worked horizontally and vertically with Tent Stitch filling.

Work is done in zigzag rows starting at the upper right. Left-handers should start at the lower right and turn the diagrams upside down. DIAGRAM A shows three Satin Stitches worked vertically and the fourth being completed with the needle inserted at 8 and emerging at 9 in position to work a horizontal group. DIAGRAM B shows the vertical group completed and the horizontal group being completed as the needle is inserted at 16. It emerges at 17 in position to work the next vertical group. Work continues down in this manner, alternating vertical and horizontal groups. Continue either by working Tent Stitch filling and then another zigzag row, or work all the zigzag rows first, leaving two canvas threads between groups, and then fill.

DIAGRAM C shows a completed area with adjusting stitches worked around the edges.

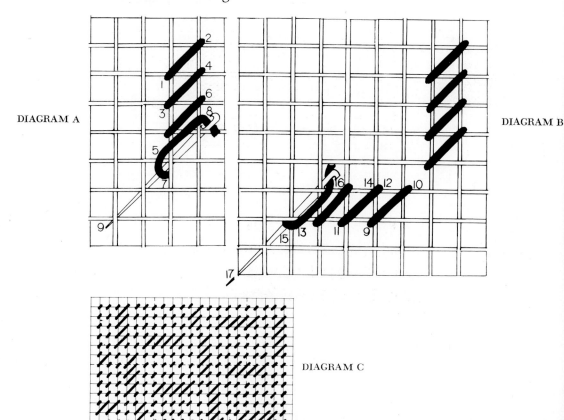

DIAGRAM A

DIAGRAM B

DIAGRAM C

205 · TRAMÉ

CANVAS: #12 mono   NEEDLE: Size 18

TO COVER ONE SQUARE INCH: ⅓ length Persian yarn

NUMBER OF THREADS: 1 full strand or 2 threads

This is an old European method of padding stitches. It is never used by itself, but as a foundation for other stitches.

Work is done horizontally in both directions. Left-handers should work as directed. The main thing to remember is to vary the length of the stitches from row to row to prevent ridges in the finished piece. The stitches can be longer than is usually practical as they will be covered. DIAGRAM A shows the first stitch worked over four canvas threads. The needle emerges at 1, is inserted to the right at 2 and emerges back to the left at 3, splitting the working yarn in the process. Work continues across in this manner. DIAGRAM B shows how to work the last stitch on a row and proceed to the next row as the needle is inserted at 6 and emerges at 7 in position to work across to the left, splitting the working yarn with each stitch.

DIAGRAM C shows a completed area. Note how the stitch size is varied, with no stitch placed directly below another.

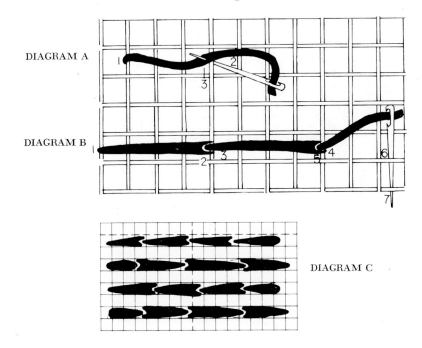

DIAGRAM A

DIAGRAM B

DIAGRAM C

206 · TRIANGLE PATTERN

CANVAS: #12 mono   NEEDLE: Size 18
TO FORM ONE PATTERN: ⅞ length Persian yarn
NUMBER OF THREADS: 1 full strand

This pattern, formed by horizontal and vertical stitches, was popular in the nineteenth century.

Work is done clockwise around the square. Left-handers should reverse the procedure, using a mirror next to the diagrams if necessary. DIAGRAMS A and B show the first two stitches worked from 1 to 4, with the needle emerging at 5 in position to work the next stitch. Stitch proportion is important. The first stitch is worked over two canvas threads, with the next three stitches increasing one thread in height, then decreasing in the same manner. DIAGRAM C shows this with six stitches worked and the seventh in progress as the needle moves from 13 to 14. At this point the canvas is turned one-quarter of the way around and another group of seven stitches is worked in the same manner, starting at 15. Work continues around the square in this manner.

DIAGRAM D shows a completed area. Spaces at each corner are filled with Cross Stitches. They may also be filled with Tent Stitches.

DIAGRAM A   DIAGRAM B

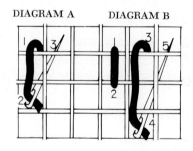

DIAGRAM C

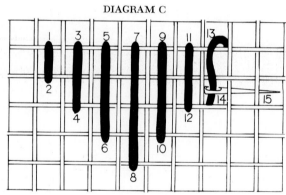

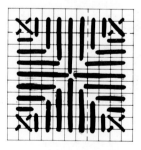

DIAGRAM D

207 · TURKEY STITCH (*Ghiordes Knot, Tufting Stitch*)

CANVAS: #12 mono or #10 penelope   NEEDLE: Size 18

TO COVER ONE SQUARE INCH: 3 lengths Persian yarn
(when making ½ inch loops)

NUMBER OF THREADS: 1 full strand

This is one of the earliest known rug stitches, which used to be done with the fingers while the rug was being woven. It can be done on mono or penelope canvas; the method differs slightly, but the finished effect is the same.

For both methods work is done horizontally from left to right, starting at the lower left. Left-handers should reverse the procedure, using a mirror next to the diagrams if necessary, and reversing right and left in the text.

When working on mono canvas; the yarn is not anchored on the back, as each stitch knots itself. As DIAGRAM A shows, the stitch is started on the front of the canvas, with a length of yarn left hanging loose. Hold this with your free thumb until the first stitch is knotted. The needle is inserted at 1 and emerges diagonally up at 2. It is then inserted at 3 and emerges diagonally down at 4, in the same hole as 1. Pull tightly, and this will anchor the knot. DIAGRAM B shows the next stitch in progress. The first stitch has been completed at 4, and a loop has been left hanging. This is held down firmly with the free thumb until the next stitch is completed. DIAGRAM B shows this starting as the needle is inserted at 5 and emerges diagonally up at 6. Action continues as in DIAGRAM A. Work continues across, and successive rows are worked in the same manner. Hold the loops down firmly between stitches, and be sure to pull each stitch up tightly.

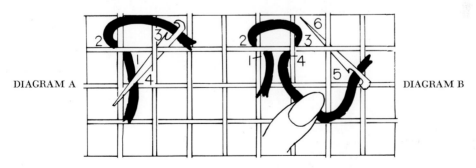

DIAGRAM A   DIAGRAM B

228

To work on penelope canvas; begin work on the outside of the canvas in the same way as for mono (see Diagram C); this time, however, the needle passes horizontally under a pair of canvas threads, being inserted at 1 and emerging at 2. Diagram D shows the stitch being completed as the needle then moves horizontally from 3 to 4, emerging in the same hole as 1. Hold down a loop of yarn between stitches, just as in Diagram B, and pull up each stitch tightly. Successive rows are worked in the same way.

For both methods, cut the loops to the desired size after the area is covered.

Diagram E shows a completed area with the loops cut. When clipped closely, this resembles Oriental rugs.

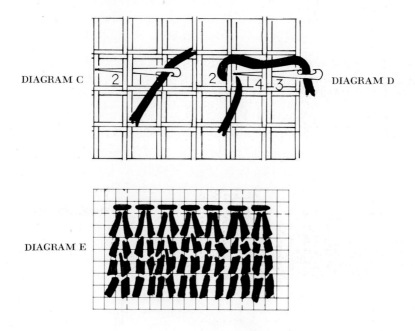

DIAGRAM C

DIAGRAM D

DIAGRAM E

208 · TWO, FOUR, SIX, EIGHT AND TIE (*Tie Stitch*)

CANVAS: #12 mono   NEEDLE: Size 18

TO COVER ONE SQUARE INCH: 1 length Persian yarn (without No. 9
Back Stitches)

NUMBER OF THREADS: 1 full strand

This stitch gives the effect of quilting. If care is taken in stitching, No. 9 Back Stitches will not be necessary.

Work is done horizontally from left to right in groups of seven stitches. Left-handers should work from right to left, using a mirror next to the diagrams if necessary. DIAGRAM A shows the first three stitches worked from 1 to 7, and the fourth (center) stitch being completed as the needle is inserted at 8 and emerges at 9. DIAGRAM B shows a tie-down stitch worked from 9 to 10, with the needle emerging at 11 in position to work the next three stitches, which decrease in size to correspond to the first three. Work continues across in this manner, with two canvas threads left between diamond patterns. Patterns on the next row are worked so that the long center stitches fall in the spaces between patterns on the previous row.

DIAGRAM C shows a completed area with adjusting stitches around the edges. No. 9 Back Stitches are worked between patterns on the lower portion of the diagram. These are optional, but will emphasize the quilted effect if worked with a finer yarn in a contrasting color.

DIAGRAM A   DIAGRAM B

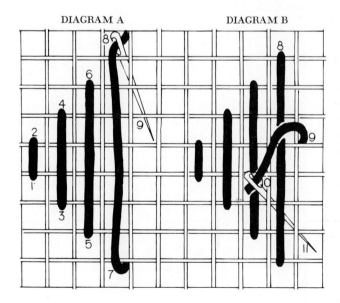

DIAGRAM C

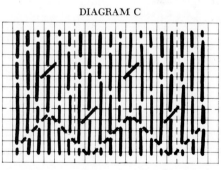

209 · VAN DYKE STITCH

CANVAS: #12 mono   NEEDLE: Size 18

TO COVER ONE SQUARE INCH: ⅔ length Persian yarn

(when worked over 6 canvas threads)

NUMBER OF THREADS: 1 full strand

Although this is commonly thought of as an embroidery stitch, it lends itself to canvas work very nicely. It is very adaptable in that lengths of the legs can be varied to form a leaf or similar shape, as well as an interesting border or contemporary staggered effect.

DIAGRAM A shows the first action completed and the second in work. Left-handers should use a mirror or tracing paper and reverse the procedure, sliding the needle from left to right.

Work begins with the needle emerging at 1. It is inserted at 2 to emerge at 3, and then crosses over the first leg as it completes the second leg at 4. The next action continues with the needle emerging at 5 directly under 1, to repeat the first action as the needle is inserted at 6 and emerges at 7. DIAGRAM B shows the action completed at 8 with the third action continuing from 9 to 11.

The central braided portion can also be done by passing the needle under the crossing of the preceding stitch only, without inserting the needle into the canvas. However, the slant of the long stitches tends to get lost in a line of any length. Pass the needle directly into the canvas every third or fourth stitch to maintain the slant.

DIAGRAM C shows a completed line with all legs the same size. DIAGRAM D shows a completed line with legs of varying lengths. The diagrams don't really show the effectiveness of the Van Dyke Stitch, which is well worth experimenting with. It combines well with other long-legged stitches, such as No. 19 Buttonhole Stitch and No. 139 Loop Stitch. It can also be worked diagonally, passing the needle under a single canvas intersection.

DIAGRAM C

DIAGRAM D

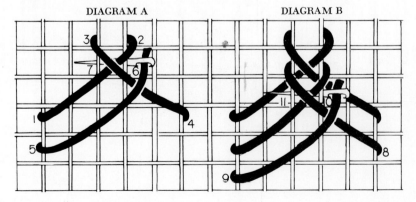

DIAGRAM A   DIAGRAM B

210 · VELVET STITCH

CANVAS: #10 penelope NEEDLE: Size 18

TO COVER ONE INCH: 1 length Persian yarn

(when making ½ inch loops)

NUMBER OF THREADS: 1 full strand

This is a very durable loop stitch that is somewhat difficult to work. You'll do better with one of the other loop stitches, unless the piece you plan must be extremely strong.

Work is done horizontally from left to right starting at the lower left. Left-handers should start at the lower right and work from right to left, using a mirror next to the diagrams if necessary. DIAGRAM A shows how to begin as a small slanting stitch is worked from 1 to 2, with the needle emerging at 3. DIAGRAM B shows how to form the loop as the yarn emerging at 3 is held down with the free thumb while the needle is inserted at 4 and emerges at 5. DIAGRAM C shows how to complete the stitch: still holding the loop, the needle is inserted at 6 and emerges at 7, where it is pulled up snugly. Successive rows are worked in this manner.

DIAGRAM D shows a completed area with the loops of one row covering the crosses of the previous one.

DIAGRAM A   DIAGRAM B   DIAGRAM C

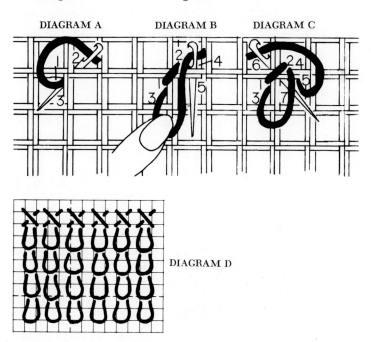

DIAGRAM D

211 · WAVE STITCH, CLOSED

CANVAS: #12 mono   NEEDLE: Size 18

TO COVER ONE SQUARE INCH: 1⅛ lengths Persian yarn

NUMBER OF THREADS: 1 full strand

This stitch resembles knitting. It is strictly decorative as it is not durable and the loops tend to snag.

Work is done horizontally in both directions. Left-handers should work as directed. Begin by working a row of small upright stitches to use as a base for the first row of loops. DIAGRAM A shows the upright stitches worked and the Wave Stitch beginning as the needle is inserted at 14 and emerges at 15. DIAGRAMS B and C show the first whole stitch completed as the needle skips the next upright stitch and is slipped under the following upright stitch, then is inserted at 16 and emerges at 17, in position to work the next loop. The yarn should be left a little slack so that it will fluff out to cover the canvas. Work continues across in this manner, with Wave Stitches worked through every other upright stitch. DIAGRAM D shows how to pass the needle to work the next row. From 18, the needle emerges at 19, is slipped under the right leg of the last loop, inserted at 20 and emerges at 21. DIAGRAM E shows how to continue the row by slipping the needle under the left leg of one loop and the right leg of the adjacent loop before inserting it. All succeeding rows are worked in this manner with the needle passing under the legs of two adjacent loops.

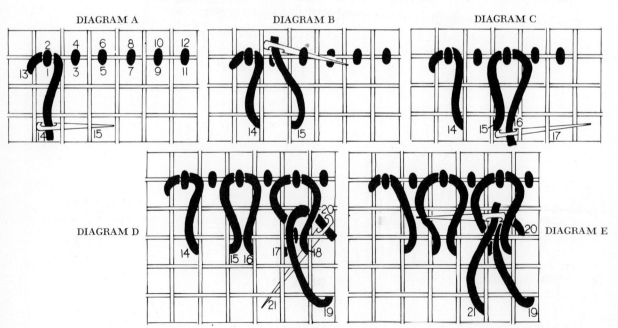

DIAGRAM A   DIAGRAM B   DIAGRAM C

DIAGRAM D   DIAGRAM E

DIAGRAM F shows a completed area with upright stitches filling the lower edge. Extra legs are added at the lower portion to increase the width. If the area being covered gets narrower, decrease legs as necessary.

DIAGRAM F

212 · WAVE STITCH, OPEN

CANVAS: #12 mono   NEEDLE: Size 18

TO COVER ONE SQUARE INCH: ⅓ length Persian yarn for laid stitches;
¾ length for Wave Stitch

NUMBER OF THREADS: 1 full strand

This is worked over laid stitches in the same manner as No. 211 Wave Stitch, but the spacing of the stitches is different. It can be worked in contrasting colors as shown, or all in one color.

Work is done by laying the long stitches vertically and stitching over them in both directions. Left-handers should work as directed. The laid threads can be placed over every opening or every other opening as long as the yarn fluffs out enough to cover. DIAGRAM A shows the laid stitches taken and work started over them. Note that small slanting stitches, numbers 1 to 4, are used to tie down on the first row. We see work progressing from 5 to 12, with the needle emerging at 13 in position to continue across. Work continues back and forth in this manner.

DIAGRAM B shows a completed area with rows symmetrically decreasing in size.

DIAGRAM A   DIAGRAM B

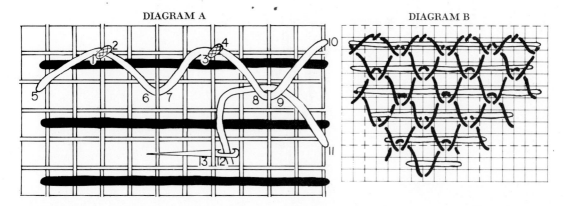

213 · WEB STITCH

CANVAS: #12 mono or #10 penelope   NEEDLE: Size 18

TO COVER ONE SQUARE INCH: 2⅛ lengths Persian yarn

NUMBER OF THREADS: 2

This stitch produces a tight covering if stitches are worked in every opening, but is most effective with stitches in every other opening.

Work is done diagonally from upper left to lower right. Left-handers should start at the lower right and turn the diagrams upside down. DIAGRAM A shows the first two stitches being worked from 1 to 4, with the needle emerging at 5 in position to work a tie-down stitch. DIAGRAM B shows a tie-down stitch worked from 5 to 6, with the needle emerging at 7 in position to work another long stitch. DIAGRAM C shows a long stitch worked from 7 to 8, and a tie-down stitch worked from 9 to 10, with the needle emerging at 11 in position to work the next tie-down stitch. Work continues in this manner with tie-down stitches worked over long stitches. The dotted lines on DIAGRAM C indicate the Tent Stitch filling that can be worked to square off the edges once the area is covered. These are not needed if work is done without space between rows.

DIAGRAM A   DIAGRAM B   DIAGRAM C

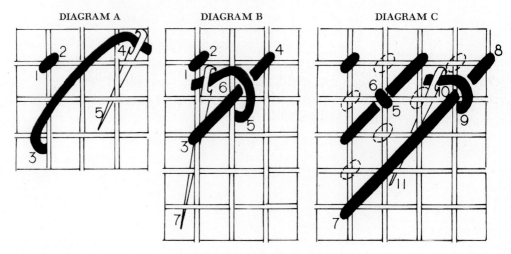

235

This can also be worked on penelope canvas. The action is the same, except that the tie-down stitches are worked between the double threads at canvas intersections. DIAGRAM D shows the first two stitches being worked from 1 to 4, with the needle splitting the canvas intersection as it emerges at 5, in position to work the tie-down stitch. DIAGRAM E shows the tie-down stitch being completed with the needle splitting the canvas intersection at 6. The needle emerges at 7 ready to take the next long stitch. Here the long stitches are taken in every opening, so filling stitches are not needed.

DIAGRAM F shows a completed area with Tent Stitches taken to fill wherever necessary.

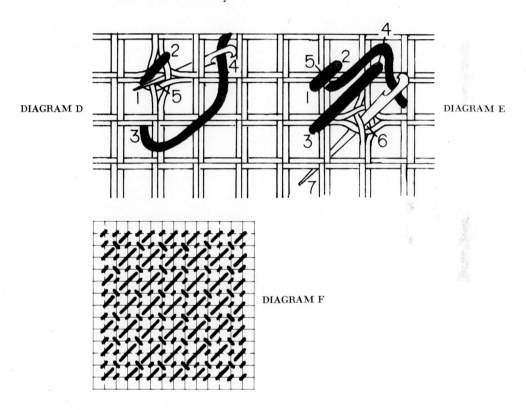

DIAGRAM D

DIAGRAM E

DIAGRAM F

214 · WHEAT SHEAF STITCH (*Interlocking Wheat Sheaf Stitch*)

CANVAS: #12 mono   NEEDLE: Size 18

TO COVER ONE SQUARE INCH: 2 lengths Persian yarn

NUMBER OF THREADS: 2

This stitch is good for both area filling and isolated designs. The upright stitches can be of any length as long as they are worked over an even number of canvas threads.

Work is done horizontally in both directions. Left-handers should work as directed. DIAGRAM A shows how to work the upright stitch from 1 to 3. Each sheaf consists of four stitches worked in this manner. DIAGRAM B shows the upright stitches completed, with the needle emerging at 9 in position to work the horizontal stitch. Hold the stitches to the left so that the needle emerges to the right of the group. DIAGRAM C shows the horizontal stitch worked from 9 to 10, with the needle emerging at 11 in position to work the next pattern. Work continues across in this manner. DIAGRAM D shows how to work the patterns on the next row up into the spaces left by the preceding row as the needle moves from 1 to 10 and emerges at 11 in position to continue across. Work continues by alternating these two rows.

DIAGRAM E shows a completed area with adjusting stitches taken wherever necessary. No. 9 Back Stitches are used to fill between patterns, as shown at the base of the fourth row.

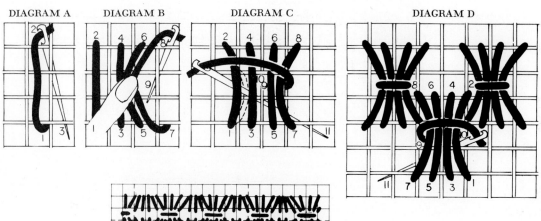

DIAGRAM A   DIAGRAM B   DIAGRAM C   DIAGRAM D

DIAGRAM E

215 · WOVEN PATTERN (*Weaving Stitch*)

CANVAS: #12 mono   NEEDLE: Size 18

TO COVER ONE SQUARE INCH: 1½ lengths Persian yarn (worked over 2 canvas threads)

NUMBER OF THREADS: 1 full strand

This is similar in appearance to No. 12 Reverse Basketweave Stitch and is worked something like No. 110 Plaited Gobelin Stitch. Adjusting stitches for a squared-off appearance are done as you go.

Work is done horizontally in both directions. Left-handers should work as directed. DIAGRAM A shows the first row in progress with stitches worked from 1 to 4, with the needle emerging at 5. The action continues across in this manner with stitches worked over every other canvas intersection. If there is an even number of intersections on the row, begin and end each left-to-right journey with a Tent Stitch, and work right-to-left rows as usual. If there is an odd number of intersections, work a Tent Stitch at the end of every row. DIAGRAM B shows the next row in progress from 9 to 12, with the needle emerging at 13 in position to work across. DIAGRAM C shows the next row in progress from 1 to 5. Work continues by alternating the last two rows. The last row consists of Tent Stitches worked over every other intersection and slanting in the opposite direction from the row above.

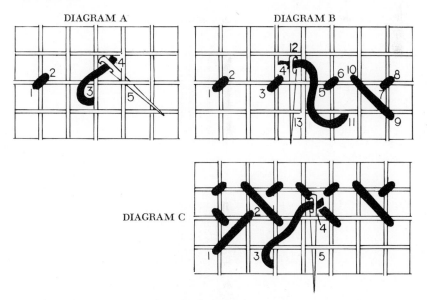

DIAGRAM A   DIAGRAM B

DIAGRAM C

DIAGRAM D shows how to work with two colors at the same time. To do this, thread two separate needles and keep them going. The diagram shows the row of Tent Stitches and the first pattern row worked in contrasting colors. The next row is worked in the original color with the dotted lines indicating how the needle is passed from the end of the first row. The next row is worked from left to right in the contrasting color, and so on, alternating colors with each row.

DIAGRAM E shows a completed area with the top half worked in one color and the bottom half worked in two colors.

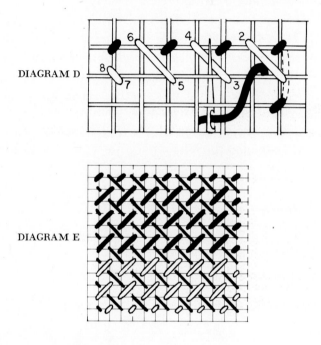

DIAGRAM D

DIAGRAM E

Three Special Stitches

The following are three very special new stitches from England, the invention of Dr. John L. Gleave, and they are reproduced here from *Embroidery*, the English needlework magazine, by courtesy of The Embroiderers' Guild of London, England.

Dr. Gleave, who contributes regularly to *Embroidery* and who teaches at the Embroiderers' Guild, shows these delightful results of experimenting with the basic needlepoint stitches.

INTERLACED CROSS STITCH

CANVAS: #12 mono   NEEDLE: Size 18
TO COVER ONE SQUARE INCH: 2⅓ lengths Persian yarn
NUMBER OF THREADS: 1 full strand

This stitch gives a very interesting texture, although it is not recommended for items that will have to withstand hard wear. Different threads will also give different textures—a firmly twisted thread such as perle cotton, for instance, will show up the interlacing to advantage.

DIAGRAM A shows the start, with the needle emerging at 1, being inserted at 2 to emerge again at 3. DIAGRAM B shows the interlaced cross being made as the needle is slipped under the first stitch without going through the canvas. DIAGRAM C shows the needle then being inserted at 4 to emerge at 5, in the same opening as 3. The left-hander would probably be more comfortable working from right to left, so the mirror or tracing paper method should be used. Work across the row repeating these three steps.

The stitch can be worked over any number of canvas intersections, so long as you keep length and width equal. However, the larger the area covered, the heavier your working yarn would have to be.

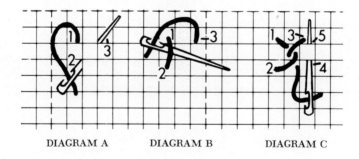

DIAGRAM A   DIAGRAM B   DIAGRAM C

ALTERNATE STITCH

CANVAS: #12 mono   NEEDLE: Size 18
TO COVER ONE SQUARE INCH: 2 lengths Persian yarn
NUMBER OF THREADS: 2

This is really a short length of the Long-Armed Cross Stitch, and it is worked from right to left across the canvas. Left-handers should turn the diagrams upside down and work from left to right. DIAGRAMS A through D show how to complete the first sequence of the stitch as the needle moves from A through H, and then emerges at 1, ready to start the next sequence, which moves just in reverse. DIAGRAMS E through H show how to complete the second sequence of the stitch as the needle moves from 1 through 8, and then emerges again at A, ready to start the first sequence again.

Alternate the two sequences, moving across the canvas until your area is covered. There will be empty spaces to fill in at upper and lower levels. These are filled in with Cross Stitches made in the same direction as the last stitch in their particular row. DIAGRAM I shows a completed row of Alternate Stitch with the finishing Cross Stitches in place at top and bottom.

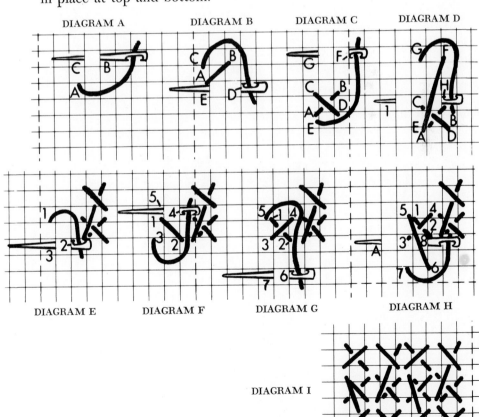

DIAGRAM A   DIAGRAM B   DIAGRAM C   DIAGRAM D

DIAGRAM E   DIAGRAM F   DIAGRAM G   DIAGRAM H

DIAGRAM I

INTERLACE STITCH

CANVAS: #12 mono   NEEDLE: Size 18
TO COVER ONE SQUARE INCH: 1¾ lengths Persian yarn
NUMBER OF THREADS: 1 full strand

This is a beautifully textured stitch. Its appearance will vary considerably depending on the number of canvas threads you work over. It gives a very heavy texture when worked over one or two threads; when worked over three or four canvas threads (as shown here) the effect is very rich. (It is not a good idea to work over longer distances as the threads will snag.)

The stitch is worked in rows in both directions, so left-handers follow directions as given. DIAGRAMS A, B and C show the action of the needle and yarn when working from left to right.

Empty spaces will be left between stitches above and below the interlacing. DIAGRAM D shows the upper spaces filled in with upright stitches; these will also be done to fill in spaces below the lacing.

DIAGRAM D also shows the beginning of a row worked from right to left, with the needle emerging at 1, to be inserted at 2 and emerging again at 3. As you work in this opposite direction, the interlacing on this row will also be reversed as the needle now slips under the stitch from right to left.

Interlace Stitch can be done vertically, horizontally or diagonally, so do experiment.

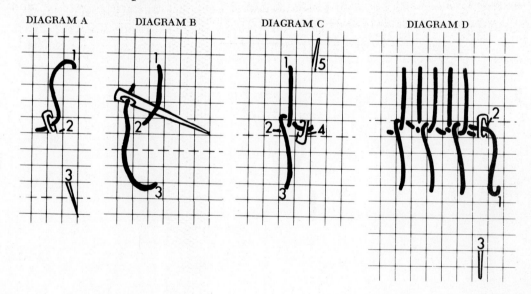

DIAGRAM A   DIAGRAM B   DIAGRAM C   DIAGRAM D

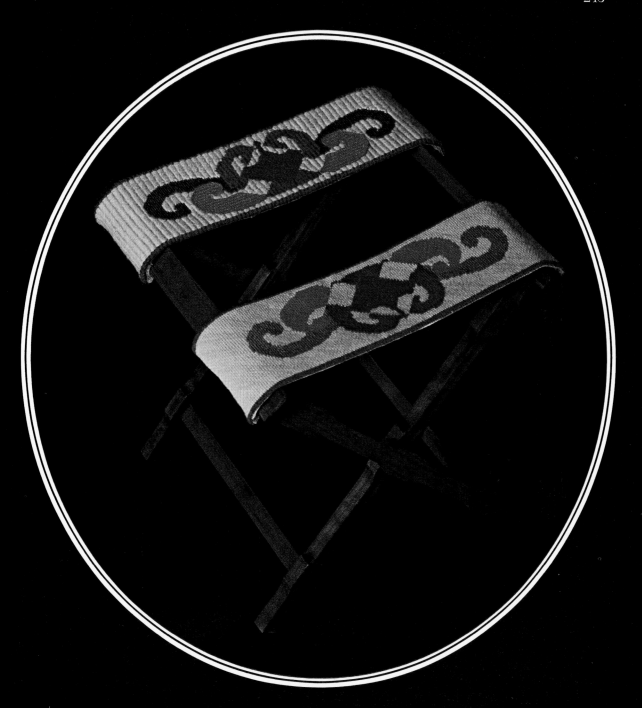

13 This handsome luggage rack has two six-inch straps done on #12 mono canvas using a full strand of Persian yarn. One strap is worked entirely in No. 11 Basketweave Stitch; the other strap has the same design worked in No. 132 Knot Stitch, No. 53 and No. 75 Cross Stitches, and No. 36 Continental Stitch against a background of No. 112 Gobelin Stitch.

How to Do
Special Needlepoint Techniques

Once you have acquired a working knowledge of some stitches in Part II (or simply the various Tent Stitches) you will want to create special or unusual effects, and here are the special techniques that will enable you to do so. In this section you will learn how to apply one terrific needlepoint initial to enhance a gift, or weave a small-size detail into the heart of a flower, or beautify an accessory or a gown with single needlepointed motifs. You will also learn how to make your own cording, tassels and pompoms with which to decorate pillows, boxes and cases, and the other pretty things your needlepointing produces.

14 *Top:* This elegant bag, set in an antique silver frame, is done in the waste canvas technique described on page 249, using Persian and crewel yarns and linen and metallic threads.

Stitches are: No. 162 Portuguese Stem, No. 36 Continental, No. 30 Chain, No. 190 Spider Web, No. 19 Buttonhole, No. 104 French, No. 172 Rococco, No. 4 Algerian Eye Daisy, No. 103 French Knot, No. 31 Chain, No. 126 Jacquard, No. 87 Double Knot, No. 10 Bargello, No. 112 Gobelin, No. 194 Stem.

Center: The No. 147 Oblique Stitch is worked on #12 mono canvas with mixed threads of Persian yarn to create a handsome Bermuda bag. The stitch's natural twist gives a tweedy appearance to the mixed yarn.

Bottom: This Bermuda bag is done on #12 mono canvas using a full strand of Persian yarn. Its woven design is worked in No. 10 Bargello Stitch.

Two-Size Canvas Technique

There are times when you want to work a detail of the design on finer canvas—perhaps to show the heart of a flower, or a face or a delicate motif. This can be done in one of two ways.

The easiest is to use penelope canvas, and work the detail in Petit Point over single canvas intersections, then work the surrounding area over the double canvas intersections as usual, either in Tent Stitch or some other background stitch. (See No. 156 Petit Point diagram (page 180) for using this method.) Just be sure no single intersections remain uncovered between the detail and the larger work. This can be checked by holding the canvas up to the light. If so, they should be filled in with Petit Point in the background color, so they fade into it.

The second method is more versatile, as any size of canvas can be used to achieve your effect. Photograph 15 shows the several stages of this work. The detail is first worked on fine canvas—even as fine as 30 threads to the inch—and then blocked. The detail is then trimmed to leave one inch or more of unworked canvas around it.

Next, unravel all vertical canvas threads on right and left sides, and all horizontal threads on top and bottom.

On your large canvas mark off the area to be covered by the detail. Put a few dabs of white glue on it, then place the detail in position. Put a weight on it and allow the glue to dry.

When dry, use a needle or fine crochet hook to weave the unworked detail-canvas threads in and out of the surrounding larger canvas. There will be more threads in the detail canvas, so work them in two threads at a time, with perhaps every third or fourth thread a single. Be sure to end all threads in the back of the work.

Secure the detail by working at least a row or two of stitches around it, covering both the larger canvas and the detail threads woven through it, as shown in the photograph. Tent Stitch is best for this.

If applying more than one small detail, each of them should be secured into the background with one or two rows of Tent Stitch around it. The rest of the surrounding canvas can then be completed as usual.

15

Shading

You can achieve interesting shading effects by doing a central detail on very fine canvas, the surrounding area on slightly larger canvas, and a border on even larger canvas. This is very effective and eliminates filling in large areas of fine background stitches. I suggest a little practice with this method before working on large or expensive projects.

Shading

An excellent way to achieve shaded effects in needlepoint is by mixing different shades of threads in your color as you work over the area to be shaded. You will be working with three shades: dark, medium and light.

Start work with the darkest area, working completely in the dark shade thread. For the next area, mix two threads of dark and one thread of the medium shade. Next, mix two threads of medium and one thread of the dark shade. After that, mix two threads of medium with one thread of the light shade. Then mix two threads of light with one thread of the medium shade. And finally, your last area will be worked entirely in the light shade.

This is a simple but unique way of shading leaves, flowers, grass, or anything where a shaded or mottled effect is desired. The same kind of gradual shading can be achieved on piled rugs, using the No. 207 Turkey Stitch.

One great advantage to this method is that with three shades you achieve six gradations that would require buying six different shades of yarn—if, indeed, you could match the perfect shades to suit your particular effect. Mixing your own colors assures that the shading will blend in perfectly, particularly if you change colors as you shade—if, for example, your light shade is a cream, your medium shade yellow and your dark shade

green. There is no end to the variations you can achieve.

Applying Spot Designs

Needlepoint spots—small motifs or initials—can be glued or sewn onto a wide variety of items to enrich them with a personal touch. They can be added to handbags, to wastebaskets, telephone and address books; they even make effective small emblems for the pockets of sports jackets.

The smaller the item the smaller the design should be and the finer the canvas you will use. Designs need not necessarily be squared off. The motif or initial may have a border incorporated into the needlework design, or various borders may be provided after the piece is blocked.

Block the finished design as usual (see page 264), then trim away excess canvas to half an inch all around. Go around all edges lightly with white glue. At this point the excess canvas may be folded back and a border of No. 161 Plaited Edge Stitch worked all around to give a finished look.

Mounting can be done in several ways. For woven handbaskets and wastebaskets and for fabric handbags, the motifs should have raw edges glued with the corners mitered, and then the motif glued into place. When the glue is dry, the motif should also be slip-stitched to the background if this is possible. (Remember always to use Sobo or another white glue of this type, as it does not stain fabric or yarn and dries quickly.)

Or you can glue down the motif with the unworked canvas out flat (as shown at right in photograph 40, page 294), and then frame the motif with braid, also glued down, to cover the excess canvas.

The uses of these small needlepointed spots are unending, and provide a delightful way of making personalized gifts with very little time and money.

16

Waste Canvas Technique
for needle pointing onto fabric

There are times when it is nice to have needlepointed motifs worked right into a fabric background. For this you need a special kind of disposable canvas meant for this work—it is lightweight and the cross-threads pull out easily. It is placed over the fabric area to be needlepointed. When stitching is completed, the disposable canvas threads are pulled out, leaving the needlework directly on the fabric.

The top handbag shown in photograph 14, page 246, was made of white wool with needlepointed motifs done in this way. This bag was later mounted onto a handsome antique silver frame.

The first step is to mark the design onto the disposable canvas, with the size and shape of the finished article outlined around it. The disposable canvas is then carefully basted to the fabric. It might be well first to pin the two pieces together, making sure the weaves of both pieces are going in the same direction. Baste across diagonally from corner to corner in both directions, making sure that both pieces lie smooth with no puckering. If necessary, use a frame to keep fabric taut. If the project is a large one, it may need a few more rows of basting. Next, machine-stitch around the outline, using a contrasting color and the largest stitch possible.

Photograph 16 shows this completed and the needlework begun. Note that the stitches are worked through *both* layers—the canvas and the background fabric as well. The needle is kept vertical when entering and emerging to make sure it goes straight down and up through both layers. If you find it hard to do this holding the piece in the hand, by all means use a frame. Finish working the needlepoint spots completely.

After all the needlework has been completed, you may have to block the piece (see page 264); this will not be necessary if work has been done on a frame.

The next step is to trim the canvas around the needlepointed spots, being careful not to cut into the background fabric. The canvas between spots can be cut away almost entirely, leaving one-quarter to one-half inch around spots, as shown in photograph 17.

The next stage is to pull out the canvas threads, leaving the needlepoint on the fabric only. Photograph 17 shows the canvas threads being pulled out, one at a time, with a pair of tweezers. Start with the unworked canvas between spots, and gradually work up to the spots. Always pull the canvas threads *in the direction of the weave*, starting with the shortest threads—in this case, those in the narrow portion of the paisley shape. Photograph 17 shows a thread firmly clamped with the tweezers. It is now eased through, as a quick tug might break it before it has come completely out. When all canvas threads have been pulled out, the needlework remains embroidered onto the background fabric.

This technique is good for handbags, as shown, and also for adding designs to fabric belts, or onto a man's velvet slippers. It would also make a beautiful center design for the bodice of a simple evening dress.

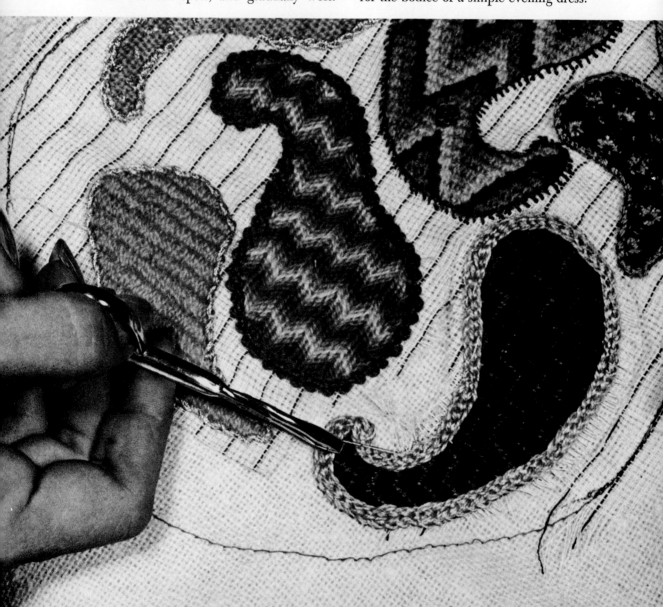

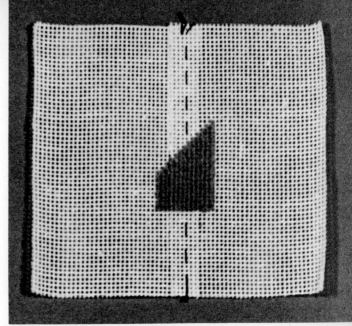

Enlarging Canvas

There are times when you will want to enlarge your canvas, either because not enough canvas has been allowed, or because you may decide to extend it for mounting.

One way is to use the weaving method, as in the Two-Size Canvas Technique shown in photograph 15, page 247. This works just as well with canvases of equal mesh size, and it is a good way to enlarge your canvas on all sides.

Another way to enlarge canvas is shown in photograph 18. Here the canvas is extended by overlapping it with another piece of the same length. The overlap is held firm by basting, with the canvas openings of both pieces carefully matched. Needlepoint is then worked through both layers.

It can also be enlarged by seaming, as shown in photograph 19. In this case, the seam allowances are then basted back, and needlework is done through both layers.

Still another method is to sew a fabric frame around your worked canvas. If the joining must be strong, machine-stitching is advisable. Mark off, in the center of your piece of fabric, the exact outline of the worked canvas—this is the stitching line. Add a one-inch seam allowance to the inner edge of the fabric, and cut along this seam-allowance line. Clip in at each corner, to the stitching line. Diagram A shows this done.

Then place the fabric over the canvas—right sides together—and machine-stitch, one side at a time, with the canvas side up. Stitch carefully, as close as you can get to the worked area of the canvas. When stitching is completed, trim off excess canvas and touch the edges with white glue. Then turn back the frame, as shown in Diagram B, and press into place.

The entire piece may now be mounted into a pillow, or framed, or used for upholstery.

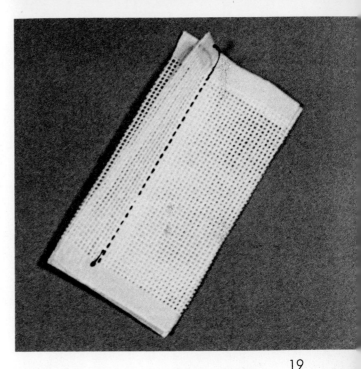

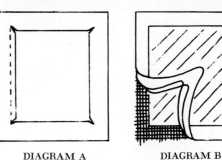

DIAGRAM A   DIAGRAM B

Working Mitered Corners into Needlepoint Borders and Designs

Often you will want to work a needlepoint border around an interior design. As with any frame, neatly mitered corners are essential. Photograph 20 shows, at the left, four mitered corners worked in various needlework stitches. These were worked on a lovely piece of wool evenweave, but the method is the same for canvas.

The first step is to rule in a 45-degree angle bisecting the canvas corner before you start work. Use either a very light pencil line or a basting thread. This will serve as a guide to adjusting the stitches as work progresses.

Straight and upright stitches are really no problem. As these corners show, the stitch size is decreased (or increased) as the corner is approached.

Slanting stitches work very nicely around corners. Work them up to the borderline of the 45-degree angle on each side, and the adjustments will be a matter of common sense.

Stitches forming a square are also easily worked into the corner of a border. Plan beforehand, counting off canvas threads to make sure the stitch comes out even when the corner is reached. The adjustments will be obvious row by row as you work.

Mitering can also be carried beyond a border—clear across the canvas—to create an entirely new and exciting effect. The Bargello pillow at the right of photograph 20 shows how a simple Bargello pattern has been transformed into a vivid geometric design, simply by increasing (or decreasing) the length of each row to fit within the lines formed by the basting threads that run across the canvas and bisect the angles from corner to corner.

Work is done horizontally as usual; the canvas is turned after each quarter is completed, until they are all done. Small adjustments in stitch size will be needed along the mitering lines, but these are easily seen as work progresses.

The top of the round stool shown in the center of photograph 20 shows how to use this method on shapes that are not rectangular.

The square canvas, before it is worked, is marked off as usual with basting threads bisecting the corners and running across the canvas. A round design—in this case, a rose —is placed in the center. The background stitches are then worked within the basting lines, quarter by quarter, to the desired circumference. (Note how the size of the Gobelin Stitches in this background is reduced or increased to fit along the basting lines.) Stitch adjustments are extended down to shape the outer edges as well.

Photograph 1 on page ii shows a handsome pillow with mitered strippings in varying colors and stitches surrounding the central motif.

Cording

Cording makes a decorative and professional edging for pillows and chair cushions and all sorts of other objects large and small. Whenever you seam together two pieces—as in the book covers (photograph 43, page 297) or eyeglass cases (photograph 37, page 289) or the pillows (photograph 46, page 303)—a cording will add a finishing touch.

Cording may be bulky or fine, depending on the size of the object and the style. There are several kinds of cordings. Twisted cord is just that: strands of your yarn (or other thread) twisted into a thick cord (as shown on the large book cover in photograph 43,

page 297). Finger cord is made by looping strands of yarn together (as shown in the lower handbag in photograph 14, page 246). Fabric cord is really a tube of fabric filled with a piece of string to give it the desired thickness (as shown in the pillows in photograph 21, page 256). All of these cordings can be bought ready-made, but you can easily make them yourself.

Twisted Cord

Twisted cord can be made of Persian wool, rug wool, rug cotton, or even of embroidery floss and silk. It can be made to any desired thickness by increasing the number of strands used—even fine threads can be made into a heavy cord. Figuring the length of thread required varies a little with each type of cord. For Persian wool, rug wool or cotton, gather about half the number of threads desired for thickness, then measure them six times the required finished length. (Remember to keep wool slack when measuring; don't pull it taut.) Knot all of the loose ends together at one end in a firm overhand knot to make a continuous circle.

The diagrams show a cord being twisted with the aid of a hook. (If two people are working, eliminate the hook, and let each person hold one end and twist with a pencil as shown at the right side of DIAGRAM A. Both people must twist in the *same* direction. The most important thing is to remember to keep the twisting thread pulled taut, no matter what.)

DIAGRAM A

DIAGRAM A shows one end of the circle looped over a hook while, at the other end, an inserted pencil begins to twist the cord clockwise. Hold the cord loosely between the thumb and forefinger of one hand, while turning the pencil with the other. In a short time, you will feel a small bump right next to the pencil (as in DIAGRAM B). This means that enough twisting has been done. Left-handers can reverse the direction of twist.

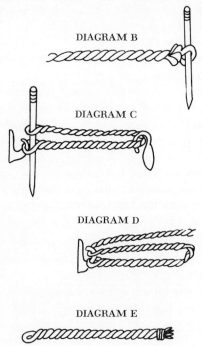

DIAGRAM B

DIAGRAM C

DIAGRAM D

DIAGRAM E

Keeping the yarn taut, bring the two ends together and slip the pencil through both end loops. (The second loop may take a bit of separating with the point of the pencil, as illustrated at the left on DIAGRAM C.) A very long cord would require a second pair of hands at this stage.

Keeping the yarn taut, attach a weight of some sort at the exact center as shown at the right on DIAGRAM C. This doesn't have to be very heavy—just enough to keep the fold in the proper place. (I often use my embroidery scissors, slipping one half of the handle through the fold and squeezing the handle to a shut position.) Whatever you use must be easy to remove. Now, with the pencil in hand, let the weighted end of the cord hang down and it will automatically twist

into a nice firm cord. If the cord is long, you may have to hang it on something high, perhaps a nail on the wall, or stand on a chair while you hold it. The weight will hold it firmly enough so it will twist regularly and smoothly.

A three-fold cord will give an even more luxurious appearance. Again keeping the cord taut, fold into threes before allowing it to fall free and twist on itself. DIAGRAM D shows how to fold the cord back over the hook before letting it hang for the final twisting.

This may sound complicated but making twisted cord is surprisingly simple.

The raw end of your cording should be tightly secured by winding it around with a single self thread, or even with sewing thread of the same color. Insert the needle completely through the cord a couple of times and anchor it off as shown in DIAGRAM E.

Finger Cord

This technique is also called "Finger Crochet." For practice, it is probably easiest to use heavy string or rug yarn. Finger cord can be made in one or two colors, and for clarity, we have diagrammed it with one white and one shaded cord. Work is done from the bottom up.

First knot the two strands together as shown in DIAGRAM F. Then loop one of the strands over the left forefinger while holding the knot with thumb and second finger, as shown in DIAGRAM G. Next, insert the free forefinger into the loop, pick up the other color (shaded in DIAGRAM H) and pull it through the first loop. Transfer this new loop to the left forefinger (holding the knot with thumb and second finger as before). Meanwhile, the right hand tightens up the first loop, as shown in DIAGRAM I. Continue making these loops, alternating hands, working up until the desired length is reached. A partially finished cord is shown in DIAGRAM J. When the final loop has been made, pull the thread completely through. The end of the cord can be trimmed and bound off in the same way as twisted cord.

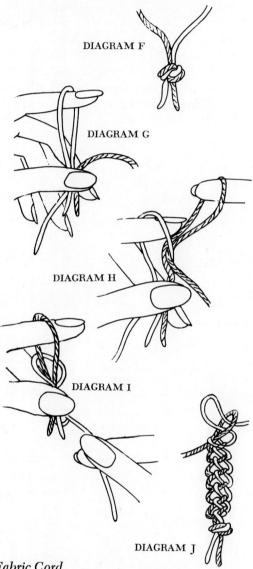

DIAGRAM F

DIAGRAM G

DIAGRAM H

DIAGRAM I

DIAGRAM J

Fabric Cord

Fabric cord makes an attractive edging for all sorts of items, and especially for pillows when you want the cording to match the backing exactly.

The first step is to make a continuous bias strip out of the material left after the backing has been cut. (For pillows, the bias strip should be about two inches wide; for smaller items which need finer cording, the bias strip will be narrower.)

To cut a bias strip, fold over the fabric as shown in DIAGRAM K, so the crosswise edge lies parallel with the long edge. The fold line will be a true bias—a 45-degree angle. Cut along fold. To join bias strips, always seam along the straight grain of the fabric. Press seams open.

If you don't have very much material, you can still make a long bias strip: fold the fabric and cut along the diagonal fold line. Rule off as many strips as you will need (use a white or colored chalk for this). Cut on the last marking. Seam the ends—right sides together—along the straight grain with one end extending the width of one strip beyond the edge, as shown in DIAGRAM L. Note seam pressed open. Start cutting at the extension, and continue cutting around and around (carefully keeping to your strip markings) until you reach the end.

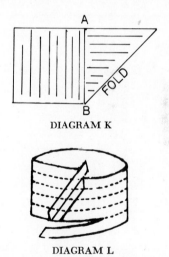

DIAGRAM K

DIAGRAM L

Lengths will vary depending on the project, but you will need about five feet of cording for a 14-inch-square pillow. Note: when measuring, always allow a couple of extra inches for going around corners and for tucking in at the end.

Lay the cord in the center of the bias strip, fold the strip over it and machine-

22 This little pin cushion is done on #14 mono canvas using a full strand of Persian yarn. The center diamond is done in No. 146 Mound Stitch, the corners in No. 36 Continental Stitch. Note the tassels with decorative heads (described on pages 258 and 259).

21 The fishbone pillow is worked on #12 mono canvas using a full strand of Persian yarn. The design is done in No. 36 Continental Stitch; the background is No. 17 Brick Stitch. The watermelon pillow is done on #14 mono canvas using a full strand of Persian yarn. The stitch is No. 10 Bargello.

stitch, using the zipper foot, as close to the cord as possible, as shown on DIAGRAM M. DIAGRAM M also shows the cord anchored at the start by stitching across it.

DIAGRAM M

Tassels

These make effective decorative accents for all sorts of things—not only pillows and cushions, but small items like the pincushion (in photograph 22, page 257) as well. These particular tassels have been further embellished with a pretty heading made of No. 20 Detached Buttonhole Stitch. (Directions for the tassel heading are on page 259.)

Tassels can be made of any kind of thread or yarn, thick or thin. But whatever you use, the finished tassel should not be skimpy. You'll probably find that a good tassel takes more thread or yarn than you think.

First cut a cardboard gauge to the desired length of the tassel. Starting at one end, wind round and round (as shown in DIAGRAM A) and back and forth in layers. With yarn and other stretchy threads, wind firmly but do not pull tight, or it will snap back shorter when released.

Thread your needle as shown in DIAGRAM B, with the loop extended. Cut the wound threads along one edge of the cardboard. Gather up the threads as shown in DIAGRAM C, by passing the loop around the middle and drawing the thread through it. Tie tightly and let the tied ends be included in the bundle.

Thread a needle again in the same way, this time passing the loop around the head of the tassel and pulling it tight, as shown in DIAGRAM D. The head of the tassel can be padded at this point, by making a little ball of the same yarn or thread and holding

it together with a dab of white glue. This is inserted just before pulling the loop tight. DIAGRAM D also shows the needle then being passed up through the head of the tassel. The emerging ends are then knotted tightly and left uncut to be used to attach the tassel.

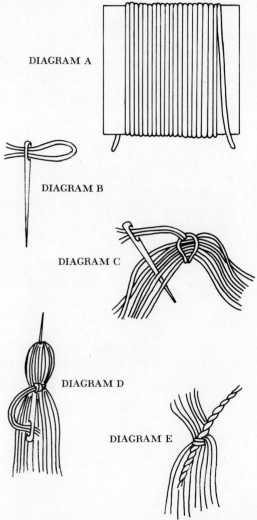

DIAGRAM A

DIAGRAM B

DIAGRAM C

DIAGRAM D

DIAGRAM E

If the tassel is to be attached to a cord (to hang from a belt or any other object), insert the cord into the middle of the bundle and catch it in when first gathering the threads together, as shown in DIAGRAM E. The cord is further secured when the head of the tassel is tied.

Detached Buttonhole Stitch

DIAGRAM A shows a tassel head being decorated with No. 20 Detached Buttonhole Stitch. This is very effective, particularly if done in a contrasting color, as in photograph 22, page 257.

DIAGRAM A

Secure the working yarn by bringing it up through the head of the tassel with a knot to hold it inside. The first two or three stitches may be worked into the yarn of the head. As you work down, increase occasionally by putting two stitches into one loop, until you reach the widest part of the head. After that, decrease by skipping a loop occasionally until the base of the head is reached. Anchor off working thread in the middle of the tassel where it will not be seen.

Turk's Head Knot

This makes a very elegant tassel head. It can be made of fabric cording, or of braid, or some fairly firm yarn (possibly a rug yarn matching your woolen tassel).

DIAGRAMS B through G show how to form the Turk's Head Knot. It will be easiest to keep it laid out on a flat surface until the final tightening. Unless a very heavy cord is used you will probably have to make two weavings. To do this, follow the arrows on DIAGRAM F.

When the looping is completed (as in DIAGRAM G) take the long hanging ends (or cord) of your finished tassel and pass them through the center, at point A. Ease the looping into position around the tassel head. Working one section at a time, from one direction *only*, work each loop as you go until the entire knot has been tightened. Slip top of tassel inside the knot and do final tightening at this time by the same method. When it is firmly in place, cut one end of the knot, put on a dab of white glue and tuck it inside the knot. Then carry the other end once around the head, cut it, put on a dab of white glue and tuck it under beside the first end. The completed tassel is shown in DIAGRAM H.

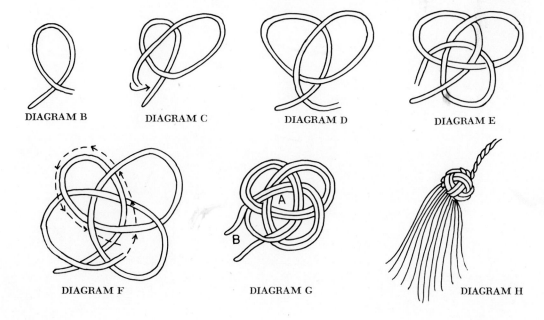

DIAGRAM B   DIAGRAM C   DIAGRAM D   DIAGRAM E

DIAGRAM F   DIAGRAM G   DIAGRAM H

Pompoms

Pompoms, like tassels, are a nice finishing touch for the corners or edges of pillows and other objects.

Pompoms can be made of any fluffy thread or yarn, and, like tassels, they should not be skimpy.

Start by drawing two circles on cardboard, and two smaller circles inside the larger. Then cut around the outside circle and cut out the round centers, as shown in DIAGRAM A. If you don't have a compass, use a glass or cup, or even a coin for the outline, depending on the size pompom you want.

Put the two cardboard circles together and lace around and around them in layers, as shown in DIAGRAM B, until you think the pompom will be thick enough.

When lacing is finished, use a small pointed scissors and snip all the threads around the outside edge, as shown in DIAGRAM C.

When the entire edge has been cut, take a long strand of your thread (or cord, or whatever you're using to attach the pompom) and slip it between the two cardboard circles. Pull tightly and knot firmly, as shown in DIAGRAM D.

Tear (or carefully cut) the cardboard circles and remove them. DIAGRAM E shows the finished pompom.

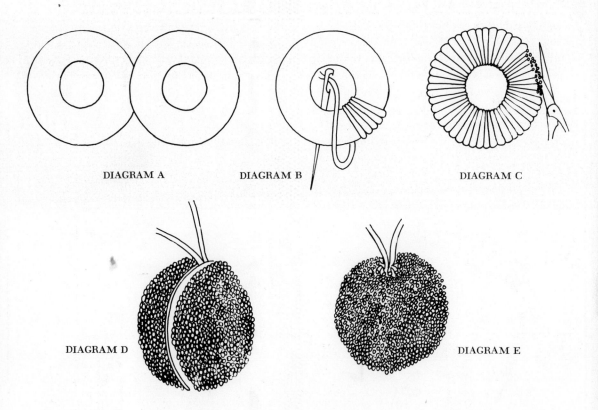

DIAGRAM A   DIAGRAM B   DIAGRAM C

DIAGRAM D   DIAGRAM E

23 The hat band is done on #14 mono canvas using a full strand of Persian yarn. The golf motifs and lettering are done in No. 36 Continental Stitch against a background of No. 17 Brick Stitch.

The key chain tag is done on #18 mono canvas using two threads of Persian yarn. It is worked entirely in No. 36 Continental Stitch.

The watchband is done on #24 mono canvas using crewel yarn. It is worked in No. 10 Bargello Stitch in a scallop pattern.

The fireplace flue tag is done on #14 mono canvas using a full strand of Persian yarn and is worked entirely in No. 36 Continental Stitch.

The ponytail barrette is done on a plastic mesh with a full strand of Persian yarn. It is worked in No. 122 Hungarian Stitch with No. 47 Cross Stitch edging.

The fly swatter is done on #14 mono canvas using a full strand of Persian yarn and metallic thread. It is worked entirely in No. 36 Continental Stitch.

Finishing and Mounting Needlepoint Projects

This part really gives me great pleasure because it will enable the needleworker to complete all the objects that have been so lovingly stitched, instead of sending them out for professional mounting at fair expense.

Everyone knows how costly it is to have a piece of needlepoint corded, backed and zippered and made into a pillow; or upholstered onto a chair; or mounted around a lamp base, or onto a handbag frame. In this section I want to show you how easily you can do-it-yourself—no matter what the project.

Here are all the how-to's, starting with the blocking that almost all needlework needs, and going on to finishing and mounting techniques for every kind of item you are likely to make, whether it be flat or cylindrical, pillow or box shape—or just about any shape.

And this, to me, is the beauty of this book: that it will enable all of you needleworkers—whether new or old hands at it—to create and execute your own projects from start to finish.

Blocking

Once the needlework is completed, before you can finish and mount any project, the first step is blocking. This is often needed because the pull and tension of the stitching draw the canvas out of shape. Some stitches distort the canvas more than others, but in all cases proper blocking will restore the original shape on which your design is centered.

The most important equipment needed for home blocking is a flat surface, which is rigid yet soft enough to put pins or tacks into. A pine board or drawing board is ideal, and wallboard is also very successful. Wallboard is inexpensive, but it comes in large sizes (four by eight feet, usually) and your lumber dealer will have to cut it down for you. Plywood is not recommended, as the surface is too hard to put pins into. I cover my board with heavy aluminum foil; this prevents the board from getting soaked, thus speeding up the drying time.

If you then cover your blocking board with checked gingham (with one-inch squares), stretching it tightly and lining it up with the edges of the board, you will have true horizontal and vertical lines to follow in blocking.

Now for your needlepoint piece. You should have one-and-a-half to two inches of unworked canvas around your design. For blocking you need a sturdy edge to hold the pins at pressure. (Masking tape is not really strong enough.) It is advisable to fold one-inch bias tape all around the outside edge, and machine-stitch it down.

If it has been badly soiled in working, you can wash it with a soap made especially for wool and rinse it carefully—but the less handling the better.

You are now ready to begin blocking.

If the shape of your piece is other than rectangular, you have already made a correct outline of it on brown paper (as described on page 13) *before* you started work on it.

The first step in blocking is to place your original brown paper outline on the blocking board. Then place your needlepoint on it. If you want a flat surface, place the canvas right side down; if you want to emphasize texture, place it right side up. In any case trim away loose yarn ends that might cause bumps.

Now the canvas is ready to moisten. Wet evenly but do not saturate the entire piece with water at room temperature. Remember that the water must penetrate both wool and canvas to enable the weave to be forced back to its original shape.

Now start with your push pins (rustproof!). *All* pins will be placed into the reinforcing bias tape (not into the worked canvas). The pins seem to hold better if they are inserted at a slightly outward slant.

The first two pins should be placed at opposite corners that have been pulled askew by the work. Really stretch when applying the second pin, and a large fold will pop up across the canvas. This will disappear as you continue pinning. (If a piece is badly distorted, you may need canvas pliers or an extra pair of hands to grip the stretched canvas until pins are inserted.)

Next place pins at the centers of top and bottom sides (lining up guidelines on canvas and paper), pulling each in the direction it needs to go. Starting at the center and working out, continue placing pins at regular intervals, about one inch or more apart, always pulling the canvas into correct position. When top and bottom edges are in place, do the same with left and right sides, placing pins opposite each other, starting from the centers and working out, until all outer edges are in place, lined up with your brown paper drawing or with the straight guidelines on your blocking board.

Allow the wool and the canvas to dry thoroughly. If the work is thick, it may take several days or longer. If you can, put the entire board out of doors (in shade, in a protected area like a porch), as even a slight breeze will speed up drying. You can lift a corner and check the underside; if not entirely dry, pin back at the same tension.

Never remove the piece from the board until bone dry, or you'll have to do the whole process over again. If the canvas is really distorted, you may have to block several times before the piece is straight.

When canvas and wool are dry, it is sometimes a good idea to coat the underside with glue to help it retain its shape. If the piece is going to have wear and doesn't cover well in back, or if it's worked with a stitch that distorts and is liable to pop back, or if you used cotton or synthetic threads that also tend to pop back, then use glue. If your work was blocked face down, leave it pinned to the board; if blocked face up, unpin it, reverse and pin down again to precise shape. Now you're ready to apply the glue.

Rabbit skin glue is the oldest and still the best material for pieces that have been badly distorted and thus need stronger holding. Mix according to directions on the can, and brush on a thin coating.

White glues such as Sobo can be diluted with water and applied in the same way. And avoid liquid rubber products, as they cause the wool to deteriorate in time.

Spray starch can also be used for this purpose. This should be sprayed on in several light coats rather than one heavy coat.

Spraying

As a last step, I recommend spraying the right side of your work with a protective silicone coating. The coating will be invisible, but it will cause spilled water and other liquids to bead up instead of penetrating, and the colors will also resist soiling. Read directions carefully, and always spray in several light coats, allowing each to dry before applying the next. Be careful not to soak the piece, or it may cause a painted or inked canvas design to run.

Now, blocked and protected, your needlepoint project is ready to finish and mount.

Pictures in Frames

Many needlework designs lend themselves to being framed and hung on the wall as you would a painting.

Work must always be blocked before framing, so the work and canvas threads run on the straight and are not distorted—this holds true for all shapes, oval and round as well as square.

A needlepoint piece can be mounted on almost anything you have that's firm enough to withstand drawing the canvas tightly around it, so it won't slip about in the frame. Good heavy cardboard, called backing board, is inexpensive and can be purchased at most art supply and stationery stores. If you have some Masonite on hand, this is good and sturdy as well as lightweight. Plywood makes a piece very heavy for hanging, but it can be used as mounting board for small pieces.

When you cut your mounting board to size, you must also allow for the thickness of the canvas work—a heavy canvas and yarn will make a bulkier fold-over, and thus require a smaller size board, than a fine canvas. Measure carefully, and cut your board a bit within the boundaries of the worked area, so you'll have a row of worked canvas covering all side edges when the canvas is wrapped around it.

The first step, before you can start backing your canvas, is to reinforce the canvas edges to hold the lacing. Bias tape makes a good firm foundation for this. If you haven't applied tape at the start, stitch it to all four sides. Or you may prefer to turn under the raw edges and glue them down. Trim the edges if necessary. Then apply white glue, making sure every canvas thread is well covered. Turn the edges under one-quarter or one-half inch, pressing tightly between the fingers until they hold. Do this to all four edges and allow to dry thoroughly.

The next step is to miter the corners, as shown at top left in photograph 24. This simply means cutting a triangle off each corner to eliminate bulk when folded over the backing.

Center the mounting board on the back of the canvas, holding it temporarily with masking tape, to see where your cut should be made. Be sure to leave enough canvas at the corner point so it will not unravel when stitched into place. One-quarter to one-half inch will do nicely, depending on the thickness of the canvas. After cutting, apply a little white glue along the cuts and allow to dry before handling.

Now you're ready for the mounting. Center your mounting board very accurately on back of your design. Fold back the side edges of the canvas and hold them in place with masking tape (as shown top right in photograph 24). You may have to adjust several times before it is exactly centered.

Now the mitered corners are sewn together, using a tapestry needle and strong buttonhole or carpet thread. Fold the narrow edge right down over the corner, then fold the sides over it. Start by passing the needle through both of these side-folds at the outer corner and drawing them up snugly. Then whip the edges together (as shown top right in photograph 24), anchoring off the thread at the inner edge. To keep work even, do the opposite corner next.

When all four corners are mitered, the canvas is then laced across the backing, horizontally and vertically, as shown in the center of the photograph. Use carpet thread or a strong parcel string, depending on the size and weight of the canvas. For a fairly small piece (under 12 inches), begin at one end and work across. For larger pieces, start in the middle of each side and work out.

Thread the needle, but do not detach the thread from the spool or ball. Remove the temporary masking tape. Insert the needle through the bias binding (or glued edge) and carry the thread clear across to the opposite edge. Always pass the needle through the tape from outside to underneath, and lace, zigzagging back and forth, pulling a little extra thread from the spool each time you insert the needle. When you reach the far side, anchor the thread securely with a firm knot.

Now ease the thread back toward the beginning, pulling each crossing thread very tightly. When you reach the original starting point, cut the thread off its spool, rethread the needle and anchor the thread firmly at this point.

The center of the photograph shows lacing completed across the length and beginning across the width. When both sides are laced the piece will be firmly mounted and ready for framing.

If you are having a frame made, measurements should be taken now, after mounting.

If you're using a ready-made frame, measure it to the mounted piece so it wedges right into place. If necessary, hold it in place by tacking one or two tiny headless nails into the sides of the frame in back so they extend over the mounted piece to keep it from slipping out.

Putting some kind of backing on the frame will not only look neat but will keep out the dust. Brown wrapping paper is best for this.

The easiest and quickest way to attach the paper is to use masking tape. It lasts quite well, but masking tape won't hold forever and it may have to be redone at some later point.

Start by cutting your brown paper backing one-half inch smaller than the outside measurements of the frame. Place the masking tape along the top and bottom edges of the paper, leaving a half-inch overhang of

the tape. Place very carefully along the back of the frame so the masking tape comes right up to the outer edges, top and bottom. Press firmly into place.

Now carefully place masking tape across the two sides of the frame, right to the edge, and press firmly into place over both frame and backing paper.

When the tape is secure, lay the framed piece face down and sprinkle water over the brown paper backing, making sure it is thoroughly moist but not soaking. As the paper dries, it will shrink to form a tight covering. The completed backing is shown at lower left in photograph 24.

Another method is to glue the backing paper, which will last indefinitely, unless the paper gets torn. Measure and cut the backing paper to exact size, just slightly within the outer edges of the frame.

Use regular waterproof household glue and spread it along all edges of the brown paper. Place one glued edge of the paper along the frame, and, with the fingertips, work it out from the center toward each corner. Do this, working along opposite sides, until the paper is glued smoothly along all four sides.

Allow to dry thoroughly. Then moisten the brown paper as for the masking tape method and allow to dry.

At this point you attach the hardware needed for hanging. A completed glued backing is shown at lower right in photograph 24.

Two framed needlepoint pieces are seen in photograph 26, page 270. The upper one is a small motif with an oval matting set over it before framing. In the lower piece, the needlepointing is unmatted, and shows clear to the frame.

Coasters and Pincushions

Needlepointed coasters are very useful as well as pretty. They are absorbent, do not stick to the glass, and if they become soiled they can be washed. Monogrammed coasters make a most attractive and welcome gift and they don't take long to work. Designs inspired by slices of fruit are nice for cooling summer drinks; even samplers of flat stitches make up well. Photograph 27, page 271, shows a variety of decorative coasters to give an idea of design possibilities.

Coasters can be made in any size or shape. As with all items done on canvas, squared or angled pieces are much easier to mount and finish than circular ones.

DIAGRAM A shows the measurements (finished size) for the popular hexagonal shape. When making this or any other shape, lay out your design on a larger square canvas so you'll have good square edges for the blocking.

When planning your coaster, allow for an extra two rows of Tent Stitch around the edges, into which the backing will be secured, unless you are going to use No. 161 Plaited Edge (Rug Binding) Stitch instead.

When the needlework is finished, it should be blocked. After blocking, apply several coats of a silicone spray to protect the coaster from moisture.

After blocking and spraying, trim off the excess canvas, leaving one-quarter or one-half inch of unworked canvas around the design. At this point, go all around the raw edges with a bit of white glue to keep them from raveling.

Almost any type of tightly woven, washable fabric is suitable for backing coasters, cotton being the most durable and practical. (Felt is not recommended as it can't be washed.)

Use the trimmed coaster as a pattern to cut out the backing. DIAGRAM B shows the backing with seam allowances turned back and pressed into place. Note that the corners have been clipped to lie flat. DIAGRAM C shows the backing for a square coaster.

Now fold under the excess canvas around the coaster in the same way and if you like, after folding it under, you can edge the canvas with No. 161 Plaited Edge (Rug Binding) Stitch—in which case you will not need the extra rows of Tent Stitch. In either case, you are now ready to attach the backing to the canvas.

Match the two pieces, wrong sides together. Thread a needle with mercerized sewing cotton in a matching shade, and whip the edges together as shown in DIAGRAM D.

DIAGRAM A ← 3⅞" →

|← 1½" →|

DIAGRAM B

DIAGRAM C

DIAGRAM D

Keep your stitches very small and even. You should pick up only a thread or two of the backing, while the needle should go in between each embroidery stitch and each canvas thread or intersection all around the canvas. The sewing cotton will sink down between your stitches and disappear.

If you like, you can slip-stitch a fine cording around it after backing, to give a finished appearance.

Plastic Coasters

Photograph 25 shows the new plastic hexagonal coasters and other shapes now on the market. These are precut to size, and no turn-under is needed. Backing makes them look a little neater, but it really isn't needed. If you don't use a backing, work your design right up to the border. Then work all around the edge using heavy yarn and No. 47 Cross Stitch.

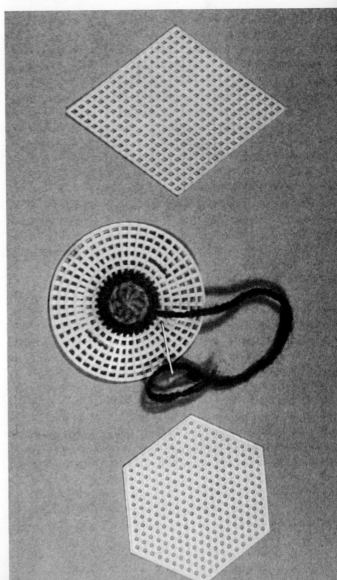

25

26 The top picture is worked on evenweave linen, using
all six Tent Stitches for shading. The bottom picture

27/ Each of these coasters is done on #14 mono canvas using a full strand of Persian yarn. Coasters in the lefthand row are all done in No. 11 Basketweave Stitch. Coasters in the middle row are worked, top to bottom, in No. 124 Hungarian Stitch, No. 140 Milanese Stitch, No. 25 Byzantine Stitch, and No. 183 Scotch Stitch. The bridge set coasters in the righthand row are worked, top to bottom, in No. 11 Basketweave Stitch against a No. 17 Brick Stitch background; the second and third coasters are entirely No. 11 Basketweave; the last is in No. 122 Hungarian Stitch against a No. 11 Basketweave background. Making needlepoint coasters is explained on page 268.

Pincushions

The same technique for canvas coasters is used for making pincushions, with this exception: in the final step, when joining your canvas and backing, leave one-and-a-half or two inches open, and stuff before finishing.

Steel wool is the best material for stuffing, since it will keep needles sharp. After stuffing, finish overcasting the edges. Fine cording can then be slip-stitched around it if you like.

Photograph 22, page 257, shows a charming pincushion worked in a simple geometric black and white pattern, using No. 146 Mound Stitch for extra depth in the center. The color scheme is followed in the little black tassels with their decorative white heads.

Belts, Straps and Other Flat Objects

Needlepoint belts make very attractive, distinctive accessories. They can be lined or unlined, and fastened in a number of ways. In laying out a design, remember that only a small part will be seen at one time, and a motif will be seen to best advantage at center back. Photograph 3, page x, shows a variety of designs for belts.

Depending on the design, you may use fine or heavy canvas, even rug canvas if you like. If done on rug canvas the outside of the work will be bulky, but it is the inside measurement that counts, for this is what must fit close to your waist.

While fastenings are normally finished at the end, they must be considered in your planning, since they will influence the cut and layout at the start. For example, a belt that is to fit snugly and be attached with hooks and eyes (as in DIAGRAM A) must be measured more exactly than those with adjustable ties (as in DIAGRAM B). If you intend to have a buckle closing, its size—and the belt allowance for attaching it—must be included in your measurements. You must decide in advance whether the buckle will be attached to the canvas itself (as in DIAGRAM C) or to an extension of the lining (as in DIAGRAM D). You will have to work an eyelet for the buckle prong in the lining or needlework. Belt holes can be made in No. 1 Algerian Eye Stitch, or you can have metal grommets applied at your needlework store. For belt loops, carry a few threads across the width of the finished belt and work a Buttonhole Stitch over the threads.

Still another simple closing is with short strips of Velcro attached to the upper and under sides of the finished belt (as in DIAGRAM E). Or you may use a loop of thin tubular elastic and run it through the turned-back ends (as in DIAGRAM F). Note that the elastic joining is hidden in one fold-back. This is good for a hatband. (I also stitch one-inch lengths of Velcro to hat and hatband at center front and back and at both sides to hold the hatband down in place.)

You will find many other fastening ideas—just be sure to include all measurements for them before you start.

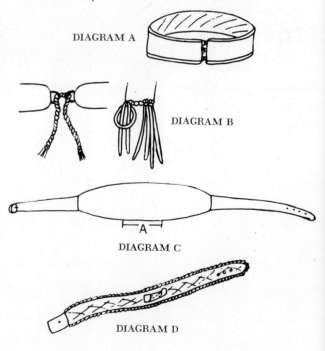

DIAGRAM A

DIAGRAM B

DIAGRAM C

DIAGRAM D

28

Unlined Belts

These can be made very simply as shown in photograph **28**. The edges of the canvas are folded over and basted together, matching up intersections exactly, as shown at the right in the photograph. The more fold-over, the stiffer the finished belt. For a wider belt, or one less stiff, edge the canvas with white glue and use a narrower fold-over (as in DIAGRAM G).

The belt is then worked in a stitch like No. 11 Basketweave which covers the underside of the canvas well. Leave a double row of canvas unworked at the edges.

If the belt needs blocking, do this *before* the edging stitch. Hold the belt down on the blocking board with push pins or T-pins through the holes at the edges of the canvas. Moisten and allow to dry as usual.

As shown at the left in the photograph, the edge is then finished with No. 161 Plaited Edge Stitch, or with a Cross Stitch worked in both directions.

Photograph 23, page 261, shows an unlined hatband with a golf motif made in the same way as an unlined belt.

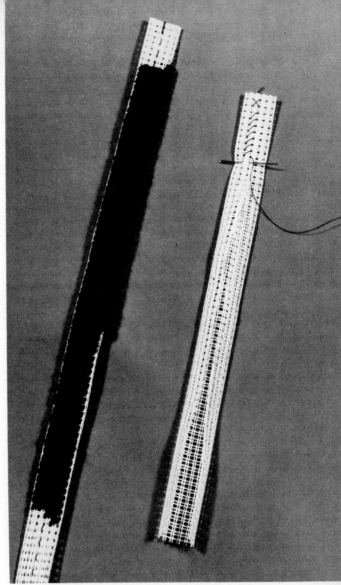

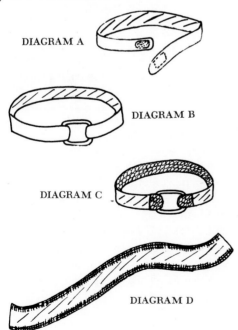

DIAGRAM A

DIAGRAM B

DIAGRAM C

DIAGRAM D

Lined Belts

Outline your belt on a larger oblong of canvas, and reinforce the outer canvas edges with tape in the usual way. After working the needlepoint, block the whole canvas.

After blocking, trim excess canvas to leave an edge of one-quarter or one-half inch all around. Put white glue along the edges and allow to dry. Then turn the edges under.

For the lining: grosgrain or other firm ribbon with a woven edge is best for this purpose. It is slip-stitched to the under edges of the belt. Just remember to allow for any extra fold-over or extension if needed for the belt fastening.

Watch Straps

These can be made in the same way as belts, but very fine mesh canvas would have to be used. The lining would have to be extended to make a loop at each side of the watch, and flexible enough to crush in a bit when the pin is inserted through the loop to hold it. Cotton twill is best for this. The lining would also be extended to loop over the buckle, as for the belt in DIAGRAM D. Photograph 23, page 261, shows a multicolor scallop pattern watch strap.

Luggage Rack Straps

The same method is used for these larger straps. We most often see three narrow straps on luggage racks, each one-and-one-half to two inches wide, but two six-inch straps may be used, as shown in photograph 13, page 243. These give more scope for design, and are just as strong.

Luggage straps are usually attached under the rod of the rack, and it is best to allow an extension of the lining fabric for this, rather than to try to tack through the heavy canvas.

DIAGRAM H gives dimensions for an 18-inch strap, with an additional four inches at each end for the lining extension. Finish and line as for any of the belts described above. Fold back the lining extension at each end, and slip-stitch around the three open edges, as shown at the left in DIAGRAM H. The strap is now ready to be attached to the luggage rack.

Cummerbund

DIAGRAM C shows the general proportion and shape for a needlepoint cummerbund. If made for a man, only the oval front panel need be needlepointed. The side straps may be made of almost any fabric; taffeta or other heavy silk is generally used. If made for a woman, it would be needlepointed all around.

DIAGRAM I gives measurements for the oval front panel for a man with a 34- to 40-inch waist. (The difference is made up in the side straps.) When the front panel is worked and blocked, trim the excess canvas, leaving a half-inch edging all around. Touch the cut edges with white glue and let dry. Then fold edges under, and slip-stitch the lining to it. The lined side straps are inserted in openings left for them before the front lining is completely stitched down.

Or the unlined side straps may be attached to the unlined front oval, and the whole used as a pattern for cutting the lining. The lining would then be machine-stitched to the cummerbund, right sides together, around all sides, leaving an opening in the middle. The whole piece is turned right side out through the opening, then the opening is folded under and slip-stitched into place.

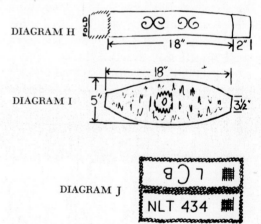

Luggage or Key Tag

This is quick and easy to make up for yourself or as a gift. DIAGRAM J shows a car key tag embroidered with initials and license number. To get in all the lettering, this was worked on #18 canvas, but the size of both canvas and tag may vary at will. Both sides of this tag are needlepointed. The canvas squares at the right are not worked until the very end. They must be in exactly the same place on both sides.

When needlework is done and trimmed,

go along the raw edges with white glue. The two sides are folded over and whipped together all around. Note the double line of stitching at the fold line to give a simple border on both sides.

Finally the unworked canvas square is then worked through both layers with No. 1 Algerian Eye Stitch—this is pulled in very tight to form a small hole in the center of the stitch. A small key chain is then pulled through. (Key chains can be purchased in variety and hardware stores.)

The tag may also be worked on a single side, unlined, if carefully done in No. 11 Basketweave Stitch. Or a single side may be worked, blocked, trimmed and glued. The edging stitch is worked all around, and it is then backed with grosgrain ribbon. The Algerian Eye Stitch is then worked through the canvas and lining at the end.

Many other small objects may be made in the same way. One unusual item is the fireplace flue tag shown in photograph 23 , page 261, which indicates that the flue is open or shut. For this, the entire canvas is worked, and a loop for hanging is made and inserted between the sides before stitching them together. A completed key tag with chain is shown at left in this photograph.

Ties, Collars and Cuffs, Vests and Boleros

A needlepoint tie makes a very handsome gift for a man—and one he will enjoy wearing. Tie patterns are usually found in dress pattern books, but these are too long and heavy to do on canvas. It's much better to take a man's favorite tie and measure the width he likes best.

DIAGRAM A gives measurements for an average-width tie—four inches wide across the base, with a three-inch-wide "knot." The outline pattern can be laid diagonally across the canvas, as shown in photograph 29 , so the points lie on the straight. Note that straight lines of needlepoint stitches form diagonal stripes on the finished tie.

29

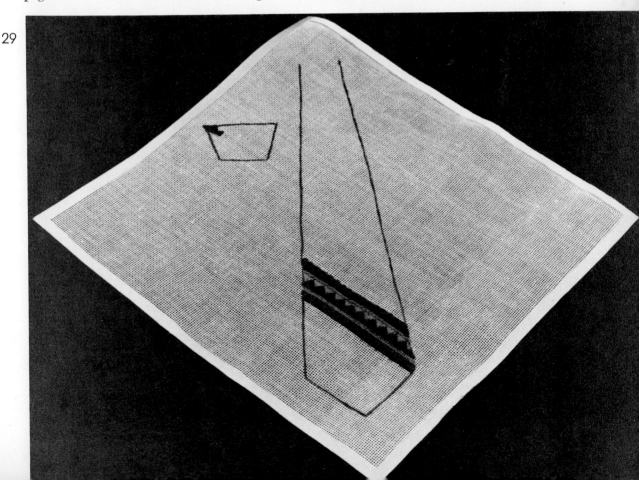

Photograph 30 shows the tie laid on the straight of the canvas—in this case, one of the patterned canvases now available (as described on page 7). The tie is worked in the canvas design in any combination of colors you choose.

After the tie and knot are completely worked and blocked, trim the excess canvas, leaving half an inch allowance all around. Miter the points (as described on page 266) and touch the cut edges with white glue. Allow to dry before handling further.

Cut out a lining for both pieces from the same pattern, adding one-half inch as seam allowance all around.

Now place the tie bottom and lining right sides together and machine-stitch all around three sides, leaving the top side open, as shown at left in DIAGRAM A. Stitch with the canvas side up, using the zipper-foot so you can come up close to the needleworked edge. Do the same with the knot, as shown at the right in DIAGRAM A, stitching around three sides, leaving the bottom open.

Turn both sides right side out. Now pin the lining back out of the way and machine-stitch the needleworked edges, right sides together, as shown in DIAGRAM B. Finally, fold under the lining seam allowance of the knot and slip-stitch in place, as shown in DIAGRAM C.

Place the tie face down on a towel and lightly steam-press edges and seams.

To attach the neckband, use one-inch grosgrain ribbon to hold the tie in place and also to give the knot a slight bulge so it will appear to be tied. Cut a two-inch piece of grosgrain and fold under a quarter-inch seam allowance on both ends. Slip-stitch into place (seam allowance underneath) at the bottom of the knot. DIAGRAM D shows this done.

DIAGRAM D also shows the neckband in place. To make the neckband, measure the neck size desired and add two inches for seam allowance. Fold back one-quarter to one-half inch at the ends and stitch an inch of one-inch Velcro to the ends. DIAGRAM D also shows the neckband sewn into place over the top of the knot. Fold the ribbon to locate the center. Pull the sides of the knot around so it measures one and five-eighths inches across the top and stitch onto the neckband.

Photograph 31, page 278, shows two handsome ties completed.

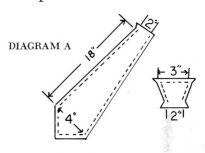

DIAGRAM A

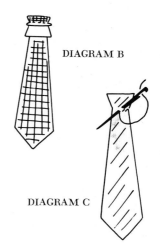

DIAGRAM B

DIAGRAM C

DIAGRAM D

31 The tie shown at the left is done on #14 mono canvas using crewel yarn. The pattern is laid out on the bias, so the lines of stitches form diagonal stripes. Stitches used are No. 36 Continental, No. 116 Herringbone, No. 176 Satin (in two directions), and No. 19 Button-hole, all adjusted to form a solid edge at the sides. The tie shown at the right is done on #8 woven pattern canvas using two threads of Persian yarn. It is done entirely in No. 11 Basketweave Stitch. The collar and cuff set shown in the center is done on #14 mono canvas using a full strand of Persian yarn. The background is done entirely in No. 11 Basketweave Stitch, with scattered, textured stitches done in No. 176 Satin, No. 158 Plait, and No. 51 Cross.

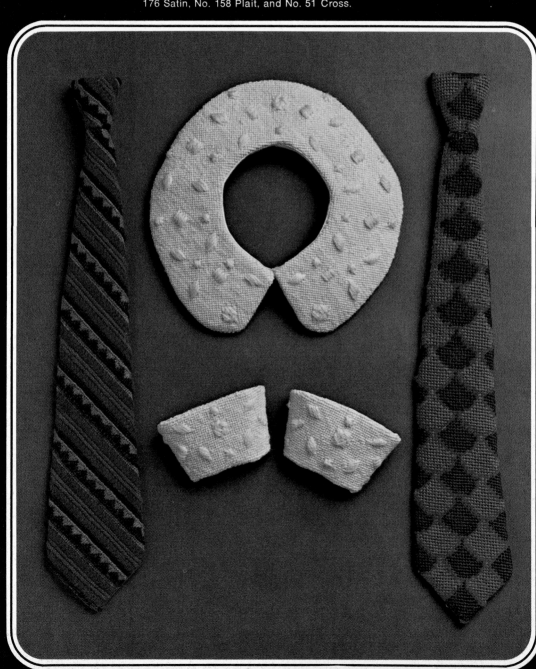

32 This man's vest, done on #24 mono canvas using crewel yarn, is worked in No. 36 Continental Stitch.

33

Collar and Cuff Set

A white collar like the one pictured in photograph 31 is an elegant addition to a simple dark dress. This collar is three inches wide, and is taken from a round-neck dress pattern. For the correct inner neck size, use a dress pattern that fits you; the width can be any size you like.

In this case, it is texture rather than design that gives the collar interest. The textured stitches are No. 176 Satin Stitch going in various directions, with an occasional No. 158 Crossed Plait Stitch (at points and center back) and some No. 51 Double Cross Stitch scattered around. In this photograph, all the textured spots have been worked, and the background is being filled in with No. 11 Basketweave Stitch. (Note how the textured effect becomes less strong once the background is filled in—this is true for all textured effects.)

Cuffs would be done the same way, using a suitable dress cuff pattern.

When needlework is completed, collar and cuffs are blocked and excess canvas is trimmed away, leaving one-half inch edging all around. Touch the cut edges with white glue to prevent raveling. Silicone spray is especially needed for collars and cuffs to help them resist soiling.

Cut collar and cuff linings, using the blocked pieces with their seam allowance as pattern. Place needlepoint collar and its lining with right sides together, and machine-stitch around outer edges, as shown in DIAGRAM E. Work with the canvas side up, using a zipper-foot, and stitch as close to the needlepoint as you can. Trim seam to one-quarter inch and clip the seam allowance every inch or less. Turn inside out.

Place collar face down on a towel and steam-press the *stitched edges only* to give them a finished look.

Use a one-and-a-half-inch bias strip cut from the lining material (or a commercial bias binding) and bind the inner neck edge as shown in DIAGRAM F.

DIAGRAM G shows a cuff lined and finished in the same way. The collar and cuffs are now ready to attach to any dress by basting along the bias tape.

Photograph 31, page 278, shows the completed collar and cuff set.

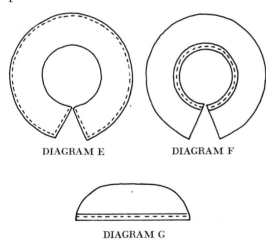

DIAGRAM E   DIAGRAM F

DIAGRAM G

Vests and Boleros

Needlepoint vests make very handsome accessories for a man or woman. Photograph 32, page 279, shows an extremely beautiful man's vest—done by a man—that is practically a museum piece in its fineness.

The main thing to keep in mind about a vest is that canvas work can become quite heavy, so it's generally only the front that

you'll be covering; otherwise, the garment can be too heavy to wear.

You can buy a commercial pattern for a whole vest, and lay out the vest front on your canvas to give the outline. Leave an extra allowance for pulling-in of stitches. Check after blocking, and add extra stitches if needed, usually at underarm or shoulder where they won't show. When needleworking is done and blocked, the canvas is trimmed down to one-half inch seam allowance all around. (Remember to touch the cut canvas edges with white glue to prevent raveling and allow to dry.)

Linings are cut to pattern for all pieces, and the vest is lined and stitched together according to pattern directions.

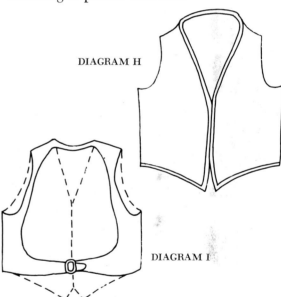

DIAGRAM H

DIAGRAM I

DIAGRAM H shows the general shape of a man's vest with a nice idea for finishing; note the small border running all around the front edges—bottom, sides, and right around the neck. The back neck part should be considered in your design layout at the start.

DIAGRAM I shows another type of man's vest pattern, with a sort of harness and buckle arrangement in back. This is much cooler for summer. Here too the neck back must be considered in your design.

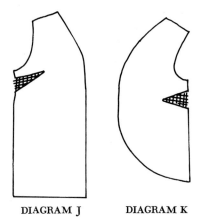

DIAGRAM J   DIAGRAM K

DIAGRAMS J and K show the front shapes for a lady's vest and a bolero. Patterns for both can be bought commercially. Note that the bust dart is not needleworked. The needlepointing is completed, blocked and trimmed as for the man's vest. Then the unworked canvas darts are sewn into place, using the zipper-foot on your machine. Make sure the design lines match when the dart is sewn. For a woman, the vest or bolero back can be of any decorative fabric. Velvet, velveteen, wool and brocade can all be used to handsome effect. The garment is lined and stitched together as in pattern directions.

Another way to make a vest is to cut a paper outline to fit the front of a ready-made vest, and use this for your canvas layout. The completed needleworked vest fronts would be blocked and trimmed as usual, and raw edges touched with white glue. When dry, edges would be turned back and stitched into place on top of the vest, using a whipping stitch around all the edges.

Making buttonholes in canvas is risky at best, and is not recommended. For the *fastening* on any vest, Velcro makes the most satisfactory front closing. This is attached to the lining before it is sewn into the vest. Lay a strip of Velcro along the seam line at the left front just below the slant, and stitch into place. Then lay the other half of the Velcro on top of the right front of the canvas in exactly the same position. Stitch this into place. Then insert lining as directed. Buttons can then be sewn onto the top side for looks. Buttons can also be covered with needlepoint. Button forms are sold at notions counters. Use their pattern as a cutting guide for your canvas. Use very fine canvas and leave one-eighth inch unworked around the outer edge. Saturate the edge with white glue, and put a dab on the wrong side in the center. Dry well. Then see that your design is centered in the form, and snap in the under side. Use a Tent Stitch, or a Spider Web Stitch, or No. 158 Crossed Plait Stitch for an interesting raised texture. Do these small size, surrounded with a couple of rows of a Tent Stitch.

Needlepoint edging can be effective around a lady's vest or bolero, or a short jacket. Lay out your edging strip on the canvas carefully to size, leaving an extra allowance for pulling-in of stitches. If it goes around a corner, the edging would have to be mitered. In this case, leave the mitered portion of the canvas unworked, as shown in DIAGRAM L. When the needlework is completed, the corner would be mitered by stitching the unworked canvas together. You may want to edge it with No. 161 Plaited Edge Stitch. Do this before mounting onto the edge of the garment.

DIAGRAM L

Director's Chair

The actual needlework for a director's chair is very simple, as it is just two rectangles. There is wide scope for design—you can do anything from a family crest on fairly fine canvas to varied modern stitches on rug canvas.

The one important factor I have discovered from the makers of these chairs is that needleworked canvas, no matter how finely woven, tends to stretch with use. For this reason, they advise doing the needlework separately and applying it to the back and seat canvas of your chair.

Use the back and seat as patterns for size of your canvas. When laying out the

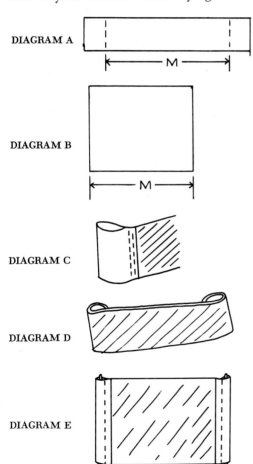

DIAGRAM A

DIAGRAM B

DIAGRAM C

DIAGRAM D

DIAGRAM E

canvas area for the back, allow an extra few inches to go around the fold at each end. This looks much nicer than having it stop at the edge. DIAGRAM A shows the middle section, M, where the design will go; the areas beyond it are the foldover allowance.

The needlework for the seat must be fitted exactly. It must not go beyond the edge, or the chair arms will not fold down properly. DIAGRAM B shows the seat pattern with no extra fold-over.

When measuring, remember to allow at least one-quarter inch in the width and one-half to one inch in the length for the pulling-in of the stitches.

When the needlework is complete, block as usual. After blocking, you may have to add an extra row of stitches to top and bottom edges if needed to make up width. Trim to a one-half-inch edge and touch with white glue to prevent raveling.

There are two ways of mounting that I've found successful. One is to fold under the unworked edges and whip into place along the edges with a strong carpet thread. Whip in between the needlepoint stitches, so it doesn't show.

Another method is to turn under raw edges and spread the entire piece, including folded edges, with white glue. Put it down flat and hold in place with a weight until entirely dry. This makes a tight bond, and is very successful for all but very damp places, such as a porch or poolside.

DIAGRAM C shows the chair back, with the needlepoint area (shaded) going right up to the stitching. DIAGRAM D shows the wraparound effect of the needlepoint when the chair back is in place.

DIAGRAM E shows the needlepoint area (shaded) mounted onto the canvas.

Photograph 2, page viii shows a needlepointed seat and back completed, and mounted on a director's chair. This was done in an unusual stitch: No. 119 Six-Step Herringbone.

34 This needlepointed mirror frame is worked on #7 penelope canvas using DMC heavy yarn. It is done in No. 146 Mound Stitch surrounded by No. 36 Continental Stitch. The centers of the Mound Stitch have been lightly padded to enhance the raised effect. Mirror and picture frames done in needlepoint are explained on page 285.

Mirror and Picture Frames

Mirror frames have been made from needle-point for hundreds of years. Now we are needlepointing frames for photographs as well, although the frame design should be more restrained so as not to detract from the picture.

DIAGRAM A shows the general layout on your canvas: 1, the central area, will hold the mirror; 2 is the area for the needlepoint frame; 3 is the excess canvas needed for mounting. The fit is very important here, especially around the inner measurements of 2, since your frame must lie snugly around the central area. As needlepointing pulls in the canvas, be sure to allow an extra half inch in each direction when measuring. While you can always add an extra row or two of stitches if needed after blocking, this can also throw your design off center.

The next step is to work the needlepoint frame completely. Block the canvas as usual. DIAGRAM B shows it after blocking, with the unworked center left undisturbed. The excess outer canvas will be needed for mounting.

At this point you must decide whether to place your mirror or photograph on top of the unworked canvas, or to remove the center section.

Easiest by far is to mount the entire canvas piece on a firm backing board (as described on page 265). The mirror or picture is then glued right over the unworked section of canvas. The picture will of course be mounted, and it may have a small plain frame around it. If the mirror is mounted on a wooden frame, this can be screwed on from the back, right through the mounting board.

The outer edges of the canvas will then be mitered, folded back, and laced over the backing board as described on page 266. This looks best if the inner frame is matched with a frame on the outer edge of the canvas.

You can also mount the needleworked frame only, though this is a fussy job. Make sure all edges are completely straight after blocking, then cut out the center unworked canvas, leaving about an inch around the frame, as shown in DIAGRAM C. Then clip in each of the corners as close as possible and touch the clipped threads with a dab of white glue to keep them from raveling.

Have your mounting board ready, cut to size, and now fold back all canvas edges over the board and glue them into place. (See pages 265 to 267 for working tips for this.) Make sure all edges of the board are covered with stitching so no unworked canvas shows.

Mount your mirror or photo on another board of the same outside dimension. Use epoxy glue on the back of the needlepoint board and press it into place on top of the backing board. Leave flat, with weights on all sides, until completely dry.

Photograph 34, page 284, shows one version of a completed needlepointed frame.

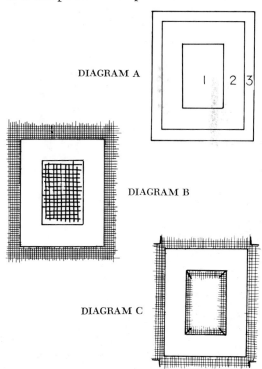

DIAGRAM A

DIAGRAM B

DIAGRAM C

Chair Seats and Footstools

There are as many sizes and shapes of chair seats and footstools as there are designs, so you will have to work to your own exact measurements. Here are the principles.

The easiest kind are those called slip seats—as the name implies, the padded seat slips out of the chair frame, and it can be re-covered and slipped back again. DIAGRAM A shows an irregularly shaped slip seat for a chair. DIAGRAM B shows a rectangular slip seat for a stool.

When measuring, you must allow for the depth. The dotted lines in DIAGRAMS A and B indicate where you measure. The needle-worked portion of the canvas must extend far enough down the sides so no unworked canvas shows above the frame. Remember to allow an extra half inch in both directions for pulling-in of the canvas when worked.

When the needlework is finished and blocked, and trimmed if necessary, it is ready for mounting onto the slip seat.

Center your design on the slip seat; then fold back the canvas sides and hold in place temporarily with strips of masking tape while you check to make sure your needle-point design is perfectly centered.

Now tack into place with small upholstery tacks. Start by tacking the centers of opposite sides into place, stretching so the needlework is taut. Then work the opposite sides out to the ends. Work the other pair of sides in the same way.

Measure a piece of tightly woven cotton, fold back and press a seam allowance; tack this into place in the same way, to cover the raw canvas edges, as shown in DIAGRAM C. This is a good place to tuck in a few strands of your various yarn colors just in case you ever need them.

Photograph 36, page288, shows a needle-pointed slip seat for a footstool.

In other chairs, like the one shown in DIAGRAM D, the needlework is upholstered directly onto the frame. This requires extremely careful measurement. If your chair also needs rebuilding, have this done first by a professional unless you are experienced.

Front corners and the back curves are not needlepointed. The design is laid out on the canvas as shown in DIAGRAM E.

Note that the central design is placed slightly forward of the true center because it will show to best advantage this way.

It's best to pin and cut muslin to exact size and use this to cut your paper pattern. Remember to allow an extra half inch in both

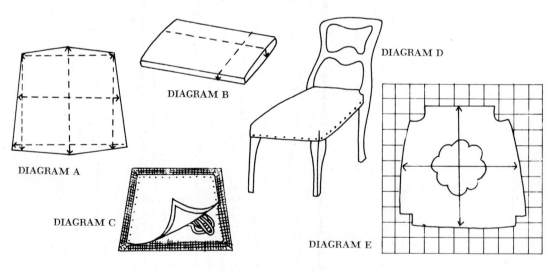

DIAGRAM A

DIAGRAM B

DIAGRAM C

DIAGRAM D

DIAGRAM E

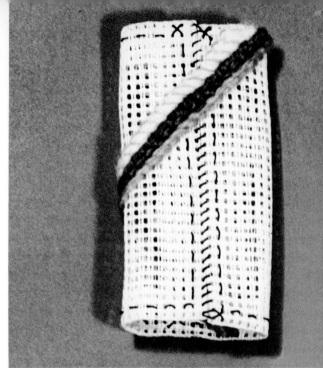

directions for pulling-in of the canvas when stitches are worked.

When the needlework is finished, block and spray the canvas, leaving an edging of one to two inches. At front corners, trim the unworked canvas. Either whipstitch or work No. 38 Vertical Continental Stitch on the last thread of each side. Center the design on the seat, fold back the edging, and tack into place as shown in DIAGRAM D; tack centers of opposite sides as for the slip seats. At front corners, miter the unworked canvas so the needlepointed edges fold together and no unworked canvas shows. At the back corners, the canvas edge will have to be snipped in a few places and folded under. The fold will be hidden down against the frame as the corners are tacked down.

Eyeglass and Other Soft Cases

Soft cases can be made to hold any number of small objects: eyeglasses, pocket tissue packs, rain bonnets, sewing scissors, and many more. By enlarging your design and canvas and using the same techniques, you can make larger soft cases: shoulder bags, tennis racket and golf club covers, even Christmas stockings.

Eyeglass Cases

One good working method for eyeglass cases is to work in the *round*, as shown in photograph 35. Here, as you can see, the canvas for an eyeglass case has been measured and the center seam and all outer seam allowances basted under; now work is proceeding round and round until all canvas is needlepointed.

As frame sizes on glasses vary so much nowadays, you'll have to measure your glasses carefully. Measure around them with the arms folded back, and allow a very little extra so they can slip in and out of the case easily.

DIAGRAM A shows cutting measurements for an average-size pair of glasses. DIAGRAM B shows the center seam turned in, ready for basting. DIAGRAM C shows the finished case (note that the joining seam is in the middle of one side).

The bottom edges are joined with a row of No. 161 Plaited Edge Stitch, which is also used to finish off the edges around the top.

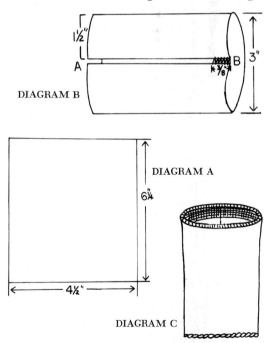

DIAGRAM B

DIAGRAM A

DIAGRAM C

36 This footstool is done on #12 mono canvas using a full strand of Persian yarn. The background is worked in No. 17 Brick Stitch. The leaves are in No. 36 Continental Stitch, shading from light to dark. The flower at the left has a center of No. 34 Chain Stitch, surrounded by No. 179 Scotch Stitch. The middle flower has a center of No. 191 Spider Web with No. 30 Chain Stitch around it, and petals of long and short No. 19 Buttonhole Stitch. The flower at the right has a No. 207 Turkey Stitch center and petals of No. 75 Cross Stitch.

37 The eyeglass case at the top is done on #5 rug canvas with Persian yarn. The background is worked in No. 104 French Stitch with No. 172 Rococco Stitch accents. The French Stitch is worked in diagonal rows in both directions. The case is lined with fabric. The second case, done on #10 mono canvas with Persian yarn, is a sampler with 11 different stitches.

The scissors case, done on #18 mono canvas with crewel yarn, is worked on both sides in No. 36 Continental Stitch. The case is edged with twisted cording attached to the scissors handle. The rain cap holder is done on #10 penelope canvas using Persian yarn. It is worked with No. 147 Oblique Stitch and, at top and bottom, No. 161 Plaited Edge Stitch.

The case need not be lined, although if you wish, you can cut a lining of a *firm* cotton to the same pattern, seam down the side and along the bottom and fold under the top seam allowance. Slip it into the case after working the top edging, and slip-stitch into place.

The same sort of eyeglass case can also be worked *flat*. DIAGRAM D shows dimensions for one side. Cut out two separate pieces for the front and back. When needleworking is completed and blocked, trim excess canvas, leaving one-quarter inch all around. Glue the raw edges so they won't ravel, and fold under. When dry, join all around the edges with No. 161 Plaited Edge Stitch, as shown in DIAGRAM E. Or you can machine-stitch the two pieces, right sides together, leaving the top open. Use a zipper-foot so you come close to the needlework. If you like, you can also insert a fine cording (as described on page 253). Then clip the seams and turn inside out. In both cases, work a continuous border of Plaited Edge Stitch all around the open top.

A variation on the flat construction is to cut both sides in one piece and fold them together, with the fold coming either at the bottom or at one side. Working and finishing are the same as for the flat method. It's preferable to line these (as above), since the glued edges are not covered by needlepointing. DIAGRAM F shows a variation in the curved top. Note that the side is left open about half an inch below the top, which makes it easier to get at the glasses.

DIAGRAM G shows another folded eyeglass case. DIAGRAM H shows the outline pattern. For average-size eyeglasses the overall measurements remain the same (six and a quarter inches by three inches at widest points). For oversize glasses, measurements would have to be taken to fit.

After needleworking is completed and blocked, the canvas would be trimmed to one-quarter inch and edged with white glue.

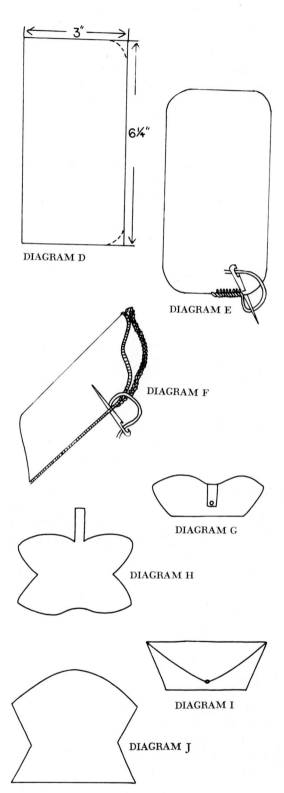

DIAGRAM D

DIAGRAM E

DIAGRAM F

DIAGRAM G

DIAGRAM H

DIAGRAM I

DIAGRAM J

Then as the next step, a lining, cut to the same pattern, would be inserted, and sides and open top edges finished off with No. 19 Buttonhole or No. 161 Plaited Edge (Rug Binding) Stitch, as before. For the other types of cases, a gripper or regular snaps are inserted at the closing before the lining is inserted.

DIAGRAM I shows still another folded case. DIAGRAM J shows the outline pattern. This would be made like the above, except for fastening. Here you would use a loop and small button, unless you preferred a gripper or regular snaps.

Other Small Cases

A charming gift is a small case for embroidery scissors, as shown in DIAGRAM K. DIAGRAM L shows the outline pattern with dimensions for small scissors about three and a half or four inches in length.

This would be made just like the folded eyeglass cases above. Or you can make a simple flat scissors case as shown in photograph 37, page 289. Use a cording trim; run it through the scissors so they are permanently attached to the case. Photograph 37 also shows eyeglass cases (flat method) and a rain bonnet case (round method).

Christmas Stockings

The same flat construction as for eyeglass cases can be used to make a Christmas stocking—something that will really become an heirloom.

DIAGRAM M shows suggested outline and dimensions. Note that the heel section is left quite wide—the canvas isn't elastic, and you'll need the inside width to stuff the toe with little presents.

Good backing fabrics are red corduroy, velvet or red flannel. (Felt is not recommended, as it is easily torn and it would be hard to repair). When seaming, you can insert a cording or a thin strip of red felt later trimmed with pinking shears.

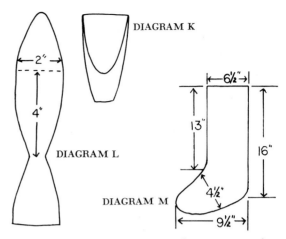

Remember to add a fabric loop on top of the stocking for hanging. A completed Christmas stocking is shown in photograph 42, page 296.

Tennis Racket Covers

Covers for tennis rackets and golf clubs can be made in the same way as the smaller soft and flat cases. They are useful and decorative and make excellent gifts.

The important thing to remember with tennis racket covers is that they should be lined with waterproof fabric, or backed with rabbit skin glue to protect the strings.

Racket sizes vary, so you'll have to measure yours to make a well-fitting pattern. When measuring, trace the outline of the racket for size, then add one and a half or two inches around outer edges to allow for the depth of the racket. Use this pattern for your canvas outline. Most presses are too large for this, but there's a new French press, compact and reasonably priced, that can fit inside the cover. For this, take measurements with the press on.

When needleworking is done, block as usual, and trim away the excess canvas to half an inch all around. Touch with white glue to keep from raveling.

The backing for the cover, when finished, should be the same size as the needlepointed front. However, the backing is cut in two sections to allow for insertion of a zipper, adding an extra inch at each side along the center seam. Follow the instructions on page 307 for inserting a zipper into a pillow backing—this is done the same way, although here the zipper only needs to run from the widest part of the cover to the bottom. Or you can use Velcro, which is more popular. In this case, press your seam edges in one direction, and stitch Velcro to both sides, concealing the raw edges under the Velcro.

The needlepointed front and the backing are then joined in the same way as the eyeglass cases, above. A waterproof plastic lining is cut to the same pattern, seamed and slipped into the outer cover. Open lining edges in center back are turned under and hemmed down along the edges of the zipper or Velcro.

Lower edges are turned in and slipstitched together.

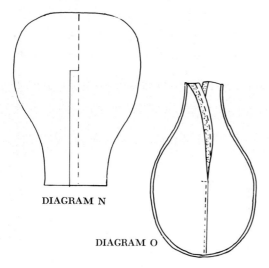

DIAGRAM N

DIAGRAM O

DIAGRAM N shows the back of a completed tennis racket cover with a zipper closing. DIAGRAM O shows a cover with a Velcro closing. DIAGRAM O also shows fabric cording inserted in the outer seams. Make cording out of the backing fabric as directed on page 255, and insert it as directed on page 308.

Photograph 42, page 296, shows a completed racket cover.

Golf Club Covers

These are not only quick and easy to make, they are also a gift to delight the golf enthusiast. The design may be your initials on one side, and the number of the club on the other. You can indicate the club number with horizontal or diagonal stripes, or with a flag with the number on it, or just with a handsome number. (A selection of initials and numbers is charted on pages 312 and 313)

DIAGRAM P shows the outline for your needlepointing for an average wood. DIAGRAM Q shows the outline for a putter. (Putters vary in measurements, so check yours and adjust for size.) You will need two pieces for each cover.

After both pieces are worked and blocked, brush the backs with rabbit skin glue. Trim excess canvas to one-quarter inch, clip on curves and tip cut edges with white glue.

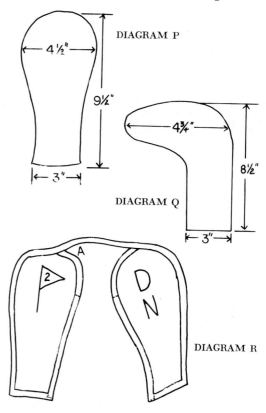

DIAGRAM P

DIAGRAM Q

DIAGRAM R

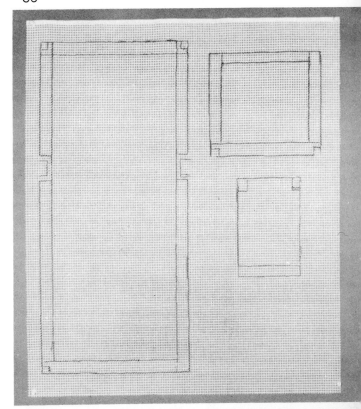

Starting at the top of one of the pieces, bind the outer edges with double seam binding. The synthetic knits are most successful for this, and they come in a full range of colors. You will need about 60 inches of tape to go around both pieces of your cover. When you reach the top of the first piece, shown at A in DIAGRAM R, leave about two inches of free tape, then start at the top of the other piece and tape around that. Now take a seven-inch length of Velcro and cut it in half lengthwise. Stitch a narrow Velcro strip up the inside edges of both pieces, so they will match when pressed together. Fold the seam binding back over the raw edges and pin into place on the other side of each piece; then machine-stitch around them completely.

Place the two right sides together (keeping excess tape in between them) and overcast the outside edges together with good strong carpet thread. Don't stitch the Velcro section, of course.

Turn covers right side out, and take a few stitches at the base of the loop of tape to hold both pieces together.

Shoulder Bag

Using many of the same soft construction principles, you can make a shoulder bag in any size that suits you. The bag pictured is made in a good basic measurement: 10 inches wide by eight inches high and two inches deep.

Photograph 38 shows the canvas layout for such a bag, and for two outside pockets—a larger one for the front of the bag, and an eyeglass case for the back.

Photograph 39 shows the areas to be covered by the front pocket and eyeglass case needlepointed on the bag, and the construction of the outer pieces themselves. As you see, the tops are folded under and stitching is done through both layers. They are then bound off with No. 161 Plaited Edge Stitch. They should now be blocked, if needed.

40

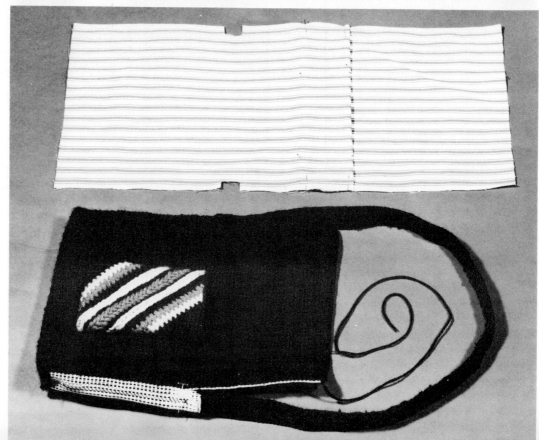

41

Photograph 40 shows the front pocket and eyeglass case basted into position on the canvas. The pocket is given a little extra depth by taking a little extra tuck at the bottom corners. Needlepointing is then completed around them, as the photograph also shows. Note that the bottom and flap edges of the bag are folded under, and stitching is worked through both layers (as shown at the bottom of photograph 40). The sides are left straight out, and needlepointing is done only to the inside pattern line, as shown at lower left in the same photograph. When needlepointing is done, the whole piece is blocked and trimmed to the outer pattern line. Touch cut edges with white glue.

Photograph 41 shows the construction of the shoulder strap (more fully described on page 273).

Now the pouch is ready to complete. The unworked outer side edges are folded together and basted as shown in photograph 41. Close the bottom opening at the base of each side by working a row of Plaited Edge Stitch. The completed shoulder strap is then basted to the top. The bag is now turned upside down and needlepointing is completed through all layers. A line of Plaited Edge Stitch is run around the outer edges of the bag flap.

A lining is cut to the same pattern, sewn together and stitched into place. An inner lining pocket may be added, if you like.

Photograph 42, on page 296, shows two versions of this bag, one a rich chocolate brown, the other in summery colors of blue, green and white, made of No. 104 French Stitch worked in diagonal rows.

Book Covers

Needlepoint book covers are easy to construct, and make decorative accents out of such mundane things as your telephone book or TV guide book. They are nice for small address and memo books, and for check-books, too; these make especially nice gifts for men and women. For the smaller items, a fine canvas is suggested.

Use your imagination for the design, which can be anything from the most modern to a traditional family crest.

DIAGRAM A shows the basic pattern outline. Remember to include the thickness of the spine (shown at 1) in your measurements. Make the height (as shown at 2) one-quarter inch higher than your book, so the binding can slip into the side pockets.

The simplest book cover has no lining. Complete all your needlepointing, except for a row of canvas at the edges. Block your work and give it a coat or two of silicone spray. Trim the edges and touch them with white glue.

You'll now need two side flaps, as shown in DIAGRAM B. These side pieces can be made of a sturdy material, folded double at the inner edge.

Baste the side flaps to the ends, right sides together, and machine-stitch all around the outer edges, using the zipper-foot. Keep the canvas side up, and leave two unworked rows of canvas inside the stitching line. Then turn inside out. DIAGRAM B also shows the edges finished with No. 161 Plaited Edge Stitch worked all around in the unfinished rows of canvas.

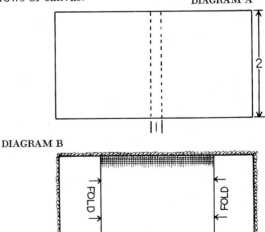

DIAGRAM A

DIAGRAM B

42 The shoulder bags at upper left and lower right (putting them together is explained on page 293) are done on #5 mono canvas using two full strands of Persian yarn. The top bag is worked in rows of No. 104 French Stitch; the other bag has a No. 11 Basketweave Stitch background with the eyeglass pocket worked in rows of No. 11 Basketweave Stitch, No. 144 Mosaic Stitch, No. 31 Chain Stitch, and No. 102 Fly Stitch.

The Christmas Stocking (described on page 291) is done on #12 mono canvas using a full strand of Persian yarn. The lettering is No. 36 Continental Stitch with No. 17 Brick Stitch for background. The green stripe is No. 30 Chain Stitch; the red stripe is groups of No. 106 Gobelin Stitch with No. 36 Continental Stitch in between. Santa's face is done in No. 36 Continental Stitch. Short No. 207 Turkey Stitches

make eyebrows and moustache, and long uncut Turkey Stitches make the beard. Santa's cap is No. 30 Chain Stitch (directions are changed to give a foldover effect), with cut Turkey Stitches making the fur border and pompom. The white section around the tree is done in No. 118 Herringbone, while the tree is made of groups of No. 102 Fly Stitch (with metal thread decorations in No. 188, 189, 190 and 191 Spider Web Stitches), various Cross Stitches, and No. 18 Bullion Knot. The toe is done in No. 30 Chain Stitch worked to give a knitted effect.

The tennis racket cover (see page 291) is done on #12 mono canvas using a full strand of Persian yarn. The pattern has been laid on the bias, which gives a textured effect to the No. 25 Byzantine Stitch background. The ribbon design is composed of No. 111 and No. 112 Gobelin Stitches.

43 The large book cover is done on #12 mono canvas using a full strand of Persian yarn; the No. 10 Bargello pattern is edged with twisted cord (described on page 253). The small checkbook and tissue box cover are also done on #12 mono canvas with a full strand of Persian yarn; the checkbook is worked in No. 179 Scotch Stitch (Gingham Pattern), and the tissue box cover in No. 11 Basketweave Stitch.

The doorstop is done on #14 mono canvas using a full strand of Persian yarn. The squirrel's body is done in No. 11 Basketweave Stitch with mixed thread shading (as described on page 40). The tail, No. 207 Turkey Stitch, is also shaded. The branch is done in No. 147 Oblique Stitch, and the background, leaves and acorns are done in No. 11 Basketweave Stitch.

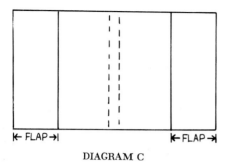

DIAGRAM C

If you prefer a lining for the book cover, this can have the end pockets folded into it, as shown in DIAGRAM C.

Baste the lining to the canvas, right sides together, and machine-stitch around the edges, leaving two unworked rows of canvas inside the stitching line. Leave a few inches unstitched at the bottom so you can turn it inside out; then slip-stitch the open edges together. Finish the unworked canvas rows with a border of Plaited Edge Stitch, as above.

Photograph 43, page 297, shows (standing) a notebook or magazine cover, and (at right foreground) a charming red and white gingham pattern cover for a checkbook.

Boxes and Box Shapes

Whether covering a box, or a brick to make a doorstop, the needlework is simple. The main problem is in the construction, which must be studied before the design is laid out.

If the design is worked down the sides, this too will have to be allowed for in the joining so the design matches up.

The brick itself should be padded with cotton batting, thick wool or felt, glued into place. This will keep it from chipping.

Brick Doorstop

DIAGRAM A shows the pattern outline for covering a brick. The top of the brick is indicated by the dotted lines. The four side extensions will be folded and joined together

after needlepointing and blocking are complete, thus forming a box shape.

The main thing to remember is that your side pieces should not be measured by tape measure, but by *counting the canvas threads down,* so no matter how you join them, they will match up.

When needlepointing and blocking are complete, trim the canvas to leave one-quarter-inch edging all around. Touch with white glue to keep from fraying.

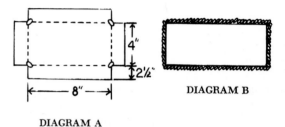

DIAGRAM A

DIAGRAM B

Turn inside out and baste the corners together, matching canvas holes. Check for size and take in a bit more seam if needed. If you prefer to machine-stitch the corners, work from the top down, and stitch as close to the needlepointing as possible. At this point it's a good idea to take a small diagonal stitch across each corner, as shown in DIAGRAM A. Then touch the seam with a bit of white glue so it will hold.

Or, after basting, you can turn back to the right side and join the corners with No. 161 Plaited Edge (Rug Binding) Stitch, working from the corners down to the bottom. The edge stitching can then run all around the bottom to make a nice finish, as shown in DIAGRAM B.

Insert the brick into the cover. The cover may be laced on (as described on page 266). Cut a rectangle of felt the size of the brick or a trifle smaller and glue it onto the base.

The brick doorstop cover shown in photograph 43, page 297, is ornamented with a squirrel whose fluffy tail is made of No. 207 Turkey Stitch. Bricks covered with needlepoint also make great bookends.

Hassocks

A boxed hassock, or pillow, would be made exactly as the doorstop.

For this you will need a filler, and you can buy inexpensive foam rubber fillers in many sizes at most needlework and department stores.

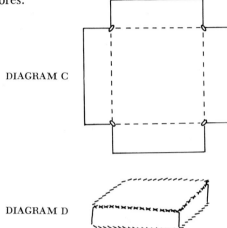

DIAGRAM C

DIAGRAM D

Measure the outline of your canvas design to the size desired, as shown in DIAGRAM C. Work exactly as for the brick doorstop cover.

DIAGRAM D shows the finished hassock with the decorative No. 161 Plaited Edge Stitch run around the top edges of the square as well as the bottom. The base may be made of matching fabric and finished off so it has a zipper, as directed on page 307.

Tissue Box Cover

Photograph **44** shows a cover for a facial tissue box in work. Needlepointing has been finished and blocked; now an unworked strip of canvas is slit, the edges turned back and worked around with No. 161 Plaited Edge (Rug Binding) Stitch.

The piece will be finished in the same way as the brick doorstop cover—except that here you won't have to worry about the base, as the cover just slips over the box.

Note that tissue box sizes vary considerably, so you must measure the kind you use.

44

Other Boxes

You can buy plain wooden boxes with lids at most craft and hobby stores. They come in many sizes, and when covered with needlepoint, make excellent containers for jewelry, cigarettes, recipes, and so forth.

For covering boxes with lids, the procedure is the same as above; you are simply making two boxes instead of one. As Diagram E shows, you're really just making two covers—one for the base, the other for the lid. The top is constructed like a doorstop; the base is a continuous strip, which has to be considered in the design.

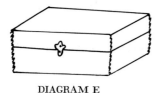

DIAGRAM E

The only special considerations are the hinges and latch. If the hinges are mounted inside the box, the needlepointing is completed as for a doorstop and glued onto the edges of the box. If outside, you can allow unworked canvas for this area, then cut and glue it back underneath before gluing the needlework close up around the hinge. Work one more row than you think you need, so no bare canvas will show.

If the box has a decorative lock, as shown in Diagram E, you can remove the lock until all needlework is completed and glued onto the edges of the box. It's a good idea to leave the canvas unworked as much as possible just under the lock. Then remount the lock to its original position. You can glue a piece of felt to cover the bottom.

Typewriter Covers

Though a typewriter cover is close to a box shape, its sloping top requires a number of different measurements, and it's put together in a different—and unusual—way.

The general principle is seen in the side view, in Diagram A. As the profile shows, the entire center is cut in one piece, including back, sloping top and front. Side panels are first worked along the edges with No. 19 Buttonhole Stitch. Then No. 161 Plaited Edge Stitch is worked between the canvas and the loops of the Buttonhole Stitch. For best results, place the same number of Buttonhole Stitches per inch as there are canvas intersections.

The important thing here is to take your typewriter's measurements exactly (or measure the lid, if it has one). Then test for size by marking on brown wrapping paper and cutting out before applying to your canvas.

You will need two layout patterns—one for the long center panel and another for the two sides.

As Diagram B shows, the center panel of this typewriter has five changes in shape, which means five different measurements— the back, the top, the first slope, another slope, and a narrow front. Diagram B shows the layout pattern for the long center panel with each of these measurements included. The layout for the side will match these, as shown in Diagram A.

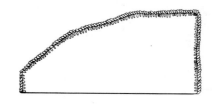

DIAGRAM A

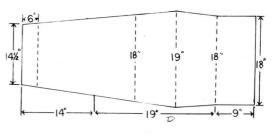

DIAGRAM B

When laying out your design, remember that the back and sides will seldom be seen, so concentrate your design on the top and front slope. You may needlepoint your side panels, but they look equally well in a matching sailcloth or other heavy fabric.

After blocking and spraying, the excess canvas is trimmed to an inch all around. Touch with white glue to prevent raveling.

After the sides are attached to the top (as described above), the cover can be lined if you wish. Cut out your three pieces, machine-stitch them together and press. Then slip-stitch to the cover all around the bottom edge. Whether lined or unlined, a row of No. 161 Plaited Edge Stitch can be worked all around the bottom for a decorative finishing touch.

Lamps and Other Cylindrical Shapes

Any number of cylindrical items can be successfully covered with needlepoint. These include lamp bases, wastepaper baskets, pencil or letter holders, piggy banks, and so on.

The one general construction rule is to choose a cylinder with straight (not sloping) sides, so the top and bottom have the same diameter. Your cylinder may be round, oval, or even square-sided.

Remember that your design will be seen only a small part at a time, so choose an all-over pattern, or a design with small motifs which can be appreciated from one angle and won't be lost in the turning. Linear patterns are very good and allow for interesting combinations of stitches. Of course the size of your cylinder will influence the size of your design, which must meet at the seam.

The first step is to take accurate measurements around the circumference. Then measure the height, top to bottom. Add a quarter to a half inch in each direction to allow for pulling-in of the canvas when worked.

Outline the area on your canvas with light pencil, or with a light shade of permanent ink or acrylic paint. Add a seam allowance of one inch top and bottom and two inches at the sides, as shown in DIAGRAM A.

The easiest working method is to cut out the canvas along the seam allowance. Edge the seam allowance top and bottom with white glue. Then fold back and baste into place, making sure the canvas intersections match. Bind the two-inch side allowances with bias or masking tape.

Finish the needlepointing all around, working through the double layers at the upper and lower edges. Leave a double row of canvas unworked at the very edge.

Block carefully, as described for the folded belt on page 273. When dry, give six to eight thin coats of silicone spray.

Check measurements at this point. You may have to add a row or two of needlepointing at the sides, if the diameter is too small, or even pick out a row if it fits too loosely.

When you are certain the measurement is perfect, work a row of No. 161 Plaited Edge Stitch top and bottom, as shown in DIAGRAM B. If you prefer, you can use a decorative braid edging instead. This would be glued on after the cover is in place.

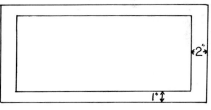

DIAGRAM A

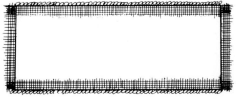

DIAGRAM B

45 The large lamp base is done on #5 rug canvas using cotton rug thread, jute, Swiss straw, and rug wool. Stitches are: No. 36 Continental, No. 51 Cross, No. 175 Roumanian, and No. 93 Fern, with No. 161 Plaited Edge worked on top and bottom edges.

The small lamp base is done on #14 mono canvas using a full strand of Persian yarn. It is worked in No. 176 Satin Stitch (in two directions), No. 175 Roumanian Stitch, and No. 36 Continental Stitch.

The wastebasket is done on #12 mono canvas and the toilet paper cover on #14 mono canvas, both using a full strand of Persian yarn. The design, adapted from a towel pattern, is worked in No. 11 Basketweave Stitch.

46 The pillow at the left is done on #5 rug canvas using shag rug yarn. It is done entirely in No. 169 and No. 170 Rice Stitches reversing the colors at the center. The blue and white pillow at the top is done on #5 rug canvas using rug yarn. The design, which is adapted from an embroidery transfer, is worked in No. 30 Chain Stitch with the background in No. 36 Continental Stitch. The pillow on the right, done on

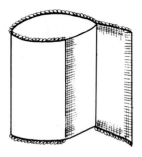

DIAGRAM C

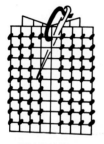

DIAGRAM D

To mount the work, fold back the excess canvas and glue to what will be the upper side of the side-seam joining (at right in DIAGRAM C). Leave the excess canvas flat out on the other side. Brush top and bottom edges, and flat excess canvas, with white glue and press onto your cylinder all around, making sure to smooth it on evenly. Add a bit more glue to the seam, and press the joining together, matching it as closely as possible.

Place it seam down on a clean surface until it is dry.

If you prefer not to glue the seam together you can stitch it by machine or by hand. (Machine-stitching should not be attempted on heavy canvas.)

The best seaming method, if done in Tent Stitch, is shown in DIAGRAM D. Baste the seam allowances together, matching threads, and leaving one intersection unworked. Then work down the seam with No. 38 Vertical Continental Stitch.

Finish off top and bottom edges with the Plaited Edge Stitch after seaming. Then slip the cover over your cylinder. Apply white glue with a dull-bladed knife around under top and bottom edges and press into place.

This method will serve for all sorts of cylindrical objects.

For small *holders for pencils, paper clips or letters,* use small tin cans. Give them a quick coat of matching spray paint before mounting.

For a *piggy bank,* choose a can with a clear plastic lid. Spray the can before mounting, then cut a coin slit in the plastic top.

Your *lamp cylinder* must be heavy enough so it doesn't tip over. Good materials for this purpose are asbestos pipe and stove pipe. Stove pipe can be found at hardware stores. Asbestos pipe is sold at plumbing supply stores, usually in two-foot lengths, and it has to be cut to size with a hacksaw. Whatever cylinder you use, a small hole must be drilled near the bottom for the electric cord. Lamp bases and fixture sockets can be bought separately for these.

Lamp bases of wood or metal, as well as *fixtures* and the *harps* to hold the lampshade, can be bought at hardware and electrical supply stores.

Photograph 45 shows two needlepointed lamp bases fully mounted, as well as an oval wastepaper basket and a small round toilet paper cover (this matches the tissue box pattern shown in photograph 43). All are basically the same except a top is put on the toilet paper cover. I used a plastic sheet for this and joined it on with the Plaited Edge Stitch. The bottom is open.

Handbags with Frames

There are a number of attractive handbag frames now on the market, made with holes on the inner edge for mounting your needlepoint. Many needlework shops carry a variety of frames in stock, or have catalogs from which to choose. So you can make up a handsome needlepoint bag without the expense of professional mounting.

One style is shown in Diagram A. This frame is usually of metal, but there are variations in plastic as well. The little metal loops at the top are for a chain handle that may be bought separately.

For this as well as other frame styles, measurements are always based on the inner edge of the frame—the distance between 1 and 2 in the diagram. And this is the size used to describe the bag. Thus, an eight-inch bag is one that measures eight inches across the inside at the top of the frame; it has nothing to do with overall size of the bag or outer frame and handle.

Another essential measurement is the width from 1 to 3 in Diagram A, going clear down to the hinge and up again. This determines how wide the bag will open, and also how wide the side gusset must be.

With these two measurements in mind, you can plan your needlepointing to include appropriate top measurements for front and back and the width of the side gussets to fit any frame you choose.

The shape of the bag itself may be round or squared off as you like—and it determines the length of the side gussets—so you are really not too limited for styles.

Diagram B shows a Bermuda bag frame—a perennial favorite that can be bought in several sizes. You can also buy the Bermuda frame made up with lining and outside attached. A strip of Velcro is in place across the top, ready for a needlepointed slip cover to be attached to it. Also included is a pattern for your slip cover.

Diagram C shows a typical handbag shape. It can be as deep and wide as you like, keeping it in proportion with the frame. The distance at the top, 1 to 2, should be the same as the top of your frame.

For the side gusset, measure the distance around the outer edge, marked "edge" in Diagram C. This will be the length of your

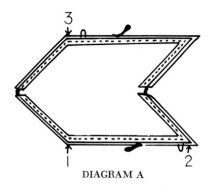

DIAGRAM A

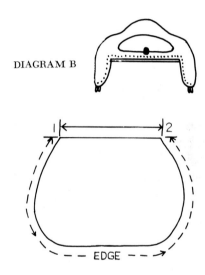

DIAGRAM B

DIAGRAM C

gusset. The gusset width may be two inches or more around the base, widening at both ends to fit the sides of the frame (from 1 to 3 in Diagram A).

When needlepointing has been completed and the entire canvas blocked, excess canvas is trimmed to half an inch around the bag seams and one inch at the top.

The side gusset is then machine-stitched to the front and back of the bag. Use the zipper-foot, and ease the gusset around the curves. You can apply a cording in these seams (as directed on page 255). Or you can make twisted cord or finger cord (as directed on pages 253 and 254) and slip-stitch them on after the bag is completed.

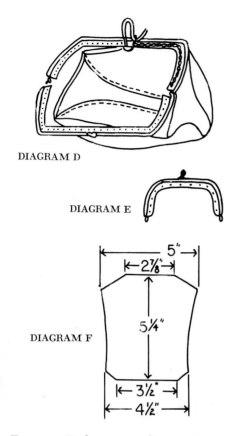

DIAGRAM D

DIAGRAM E

DIAGRAM F

DIAGRAM E shows a small curved handle for the top of a cigarette case, made in the same way. DIAGRAM F gives layout dimensions for the front and back. No gusset is needed for this.

After needlepointing and blocking are completed, trim away excess canvas to one-half inch around all edges. Seam and attach to the frame as directed above.

You can make an eyeglass case with the same small frame by lengthening the cigarette case pattern by one and a half inches or longer, depending on the size of your glasses.

Photograph 14, page 246, shows a selection of Bermuda bags as well as a formal white linen bag with needlepointed motifs done in the waste canvas technique described on page 247. All these handbags were mounted onto their frames in the same way.

Pillows

When you have designed and worked the top of a handsome pillow, it is easy to make it up yourself—sewing on the backing with its zipper opening and applying any decorative accents, such as the cordings, tassels and pompoms described on pages 253 to 260.

The first step is to choose your backing fabric. This should relate to your needlepoint not only in color but in texture as well. Any tightly woven fabric can be used, but I find that velvet, velveteen and corduroy make particularly good, hard-wearing backings easy to match, or contrast, in color. Even suede makes a good backing, but suede cannot be pinned or the holes will show. Therefore it should be marked with chalk and held in place with masking tape before stitching. Various cottons and synthetics can also be used as backing.

You will need half a yard of fabric for a 14- or 16-inch pillow. This will be enough for the backing and for the matching cording as well. For larger pillows, add enough extra

DIAGRAM D shows a needlepoint bag being stitched to the frame. For your needlework, turn back excess canvas all around the top.

Sew onto the frame as shown. Use a curved needle, such as a mattress needle, of a size that will go easily through the holes, and strong carpet or buttonhole thread. Start at the center of the gusset, at the hinge, and attach the needlepointing to the handle with a backstitch, working through the underside of the fold line so no stitches show on top, and making sure no unworked canvas shows.

Cut a lining on the same pattern as the needlepointing (adding seam allowance to all sides). You may add an inner pocket if you like. Stitch together, press and slip into the bag, right side out. Slip-stitch onto the previous stitches around the frame. Glue a piece of decorative braid across the top of the lining to give a finished appearance inside as well as out.

fabric to allow for seams—for an 18-inch pillow, you'll want at least 20 inches of fabric.

Pillow fillings can be made of many materials. The oldest, most luxurious and expensive is down, or down and feathers. This is also the softest, and has to be plumped up to keep its shape. Down-filled pillows come muslin-covered, ready made to place inside your cover, or you can have them made to order. Other fillers are less expensive, but cost should not be the prime factor. Inexpensive foam pads, for instance, do not give much and they will eventually deteriorate. Kapok tends to become lumpy. Dacron, or Dacron and kapok, are generally considered to be non-allergenic. An excellent new filler—called "Pop-in Pillows"—is made of polyester fiber; it is non-inflammable and non-allergenic and comes in a wide range of sizes and shapes.

There is really no end to the needlepoint designs you can apply to pillows. Photograph 4 shows a wide selection, including a bedrest. Still other designs are shown in photographs 21 and 46, on pages 256 and 303.

Knife-Edge Pillows

There is a little trick to making knife-edge pillows look full and straight-sided, avoiding the rabbit-ear effect so often seen. You get a much better looking knife-edge if your four sides are not cut perfectly straight, but curve out just a trifle—no more than a half-inch at the center of each side. The needlework design must, of course, be worked to accommodate this fool-the-eye effect.

When finished, the backing for this pillow style should be the same size as the needlepointed pillow front. However, the backing is cut in two sections as shown in DIAGRAM A, to allow for the insertion of a zipper. Just make sure that the zipper edges are cut on the straight of the fabric. You must therefore allow one extra inch overall in length only. This gives you an extra half-inch seam allowance on the two zipper edges. DIAGRAM B

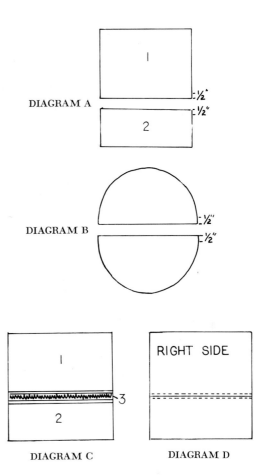

shows the back of a round pillow, cut and ready for the zipper to be inserted.

Insert the zipper as directed on the zipper package. DIAGRAM C shows the inside after the zipper has been inserted; DIAGRAM D shows the finished right side, with a fold of fabric covering the zipper. The backing is now ready to attach to the pillow front.

If you intend to use cording around the edges, make it as directed on pages 253 to 258. Note that if you are using corduroy, it will have an irregular shape somewhat reminiscent of the canvas stitching itself. For fine mesh canvas, pinwale corduroy would be a suitable backing; wide wale corduroy would be used with heavy or rug canvas.

You will need about five feet of cording for a 14-inch-square pillow.

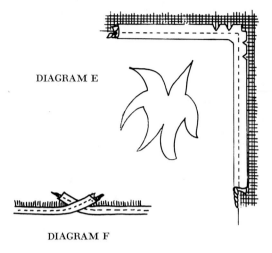

DIAGRAM E

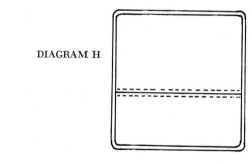

DIAGRAM F

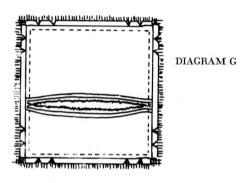

DIAGRAM G

DIAGRAM H

DIAGRAM I

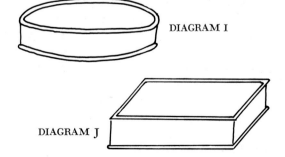

DIAGRAM J

To attach backing to cording, place the cording along the edges on the *right side* of the needlepointed canvas. Baste into place (as shown on DIAGRAM E) so the cording lies toward the center, and the raw edges lie on the outer canvas seam allowance. The stitching line for the cording should lie right on the edge of the completed needlework.

Start laying the cording in the center of one side. Where the ends join, allow to overlap (as shown in DIAGRAM F). When the final stitching has been completed, you can cut away the inner cording from the loose ends so they don't make the backing look lumpy at that point.

Now, *with the zipper open,* baste the fabric backing into place over the needlepointed canvas, right sides together. Machine-stitch all around the outer edges through all three layers—canvas, cording and backing—as shown in DIAGRAM G. Stitch with canvas side up, so you can guide your stitches as closely as possible to the edge of the needle-pointing. Use a zipper-foot for this.

Clip seams along edges and corners. Trim to one-half inch, and if your machine has a zigzag attachment, run a line of zigzagging all around the edges to keep them from raveling. Otherwise add another touch of white glue to the canvas edges.

Turn right side out through the zipper opening. DIAGRAM H shows the back of the finished pillow cover, with its concealed zipper and corded edge.

Boxed Pillows

The construction for a boxed pillow is equally simple—it merely means inserting an extra strip of fabric between front and back to give the pillow extra depth. DIAGRAMS I and J show round and square boxed pillows.

Measure the boxing strip long enough to go completely around your circular or square pillow, adding an extra inch at each end for joining, and a half-inch seam allowance along

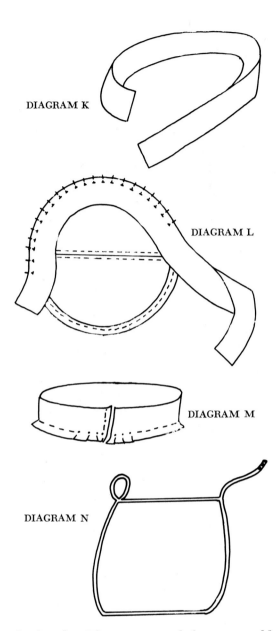

the boxing is pinned into place over the backing, right sides together, as shown in DIAGRAM L.

DIAGRAM M shows the boxing ends joined together; the boxing is then stitched to the backing through all three layers (boxing, cording and backing) just as for the knife-edge pillow.

The other side of the cording is machine-stitched to the front canvas in the same way. Be sure the zipper is open when you do this. Trim seams, clip and finish as for the knife-edge pillow.

Detached Seat Cushions

These are made in the same way as pillows, and may be knife-edge or boxed shape as desired. Measurements of chair size should be taken carefully.

Note that an extra loop of fabric is provided at the back corners to attach the cushion to the chair. These loops are attached at the time you are inserting the cording when sewing the cushion front and backing together, as for the pillows, above. DIAGRAM N shows loops attached to the finished cushion. These are best fastened with Velcro (as shown to the right), or with hooks and eyes, as open ties are hard to keep neat.

Dolls

A needlepoint doll is sure to become a treasured family possession.

You can design the doll yourself, or buy a fabric doll pattern, or use as a pattern one of the fabric dolls that can be bought ready for stuffing. Any of these can be used as pattern pieces for your own needlepointed doll. Pieces would be laid out on your canvas, as shown in photograph 47, which shows a doll of my own design.

Just remember that it's best to use a fairly fine canvas, or it will be very hard to turn the canvas right side out after stitching.

both sides. Thus, a two-inch boxing would be cut three inches wide. DIAGRAM K shows a boxing strip ready to be attached.

If both edges are to be corded, you will need twice the amount of cording as for the knife-edge pillow. You will baste the cording to both front canvas and the fabric backing, as directed for the knife-edge.

After cording is in place, front and back,

Small Dolls

These can be made with just two pieces—front and back. After needlepointing, they are blocked and trimmed to one-half-inch seam allowance all around. Cut edges are touched with white glue to prevent raveling.

Baste right sides together, then machine-stitch all around the outer edges, as close to the worked area as you can get, using a zipper-foot. Leave two inches or so open at the side or bottom for stuffing. Turn right side out, and stuff firmly with cotton batting, polyfil or old, clean nylon stockings. Turn under the edges of the opening and overstitch together in between canvas stitches.

Large Dolls

These can be made like my own doll, shown completed in photograph 2, page viii. The pattern was taken from an old stuffed doll which had been taken apart.

Photograph 47 shows the canvas layout, with pieces outlined in black basting thread. I used No. 11 Basketweave (Tent) Stitch for the body and face, which worked out rather well.

Needlepointing is worked within the basting lines. Then the whole canvas is blocked before the individual pieces are cut out and trimmed to one-half-inch seam allowance. Touch all cut edges with white glue.

Note that small darts in the canvas are left unworked around the head and in the insteps of the leg fronts. Darts are seamed closed after blocking and trimming. For all machine-stitching, use the zipper-foot and seam as close to the needlework as possible. Clip all curved edges before turning right side out.

For the head the main stitch used is the No. 11 Basketweave, but the nostrils and mouth are overstitched—the nostrils with No. 103 French Knots, the mouth with No. 176 Satin Stitch. Add a few straight stitches above the eyes for eyebrows. A row of No. 207 Turkey Stitch is worked for the eyelashes and left uncut.

The hair section at the side front and back is done in varying sizes and slants of Satin Stitch. The slanting should conform to the shape of the head. A middle section of the back, just below the Satin Stitches, is left unworked, later to be filled in with Turkey Stitch. The lower back of the head is worked in Basketweave in the same color as the hair. The bangs are worked in the Turkey Stitch, and the loops are cut after the doll has been sewn together, when the length can be adjusted if needed. Work the bangs before seaming the head sections together; work the long back hair after seaming.

Sew the head darts; then baste the head front and back, right sides together, and machine-stitch all around, leaving an opening at the base of the head for stuffing. Turn right side out and work the long hair in Turkey Stitch just below the Satin Stitch on the back. At the longest part in the center, the loops are probably about ten inches long.

Stuff the head firmly (as for small dolls, above), then fold under the open edges and slip-stitch together.

To assemble the doll's body stitch the two front pieces, right sides together, at center front; then do the same for the two back pieces at center back. At the top of the back, which will be the neck area, a four-inch piece of boning should be sewn inside the center back seam so one and a half or two inches extend above the edge.

Then baste front and back, right sides together, and machine-stitch all around, leaving two inches or so open at the bottom for stuffing. Turn right side out and stuff, then turn in open edges and overcast together.

To join the head to the body follow DIAGRAM A which shows the neck back pinned to the back of the head at hair level (not at the head bottom). Turn the Turkey Stitch loops upside down to keep them out of the way as you do this.

Note that the boning extends up the back of the head to hold it firm and keep it from flopping.

DIAGRAM B shows the body front in place at the lower edge of the head. After pinning, stitch firmly into place, including the boning.

To attach the doll's arms, seam the two pieces of each arm, turn right side out and stuff in the same way as the other pieces. DIAGRAM B shows the arms sewn into place on the body.

For the legs, seam the dart across the front insteps, then attach the soles to the back of the leg, then seam the two pieces of each leg, turn right side out, and stuff as before. DIAGRAM C shows the legs attached to the lower part of the body.

Your finished doll can now be dressed any way you like.

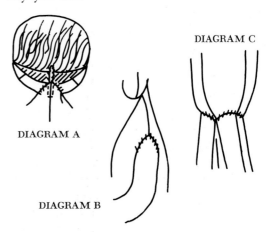

DIAGRAM A

DIAGRAM B

DIAGRAM C

Lettering

Lettering is an integral part of needlepoint work. Many projects, such as samplers and sayings, are composed entirely of lettering. And monogramming, of course, adds an especially personal touch to many needlepointed objects.

In addition, it is nice to sign your work with your own initials—in this case, the letters should be very small so as not to detract from the design. Your signature can be worked in No. 9 Back Stitches between the background Tent Stitches. On backgrounds composed of stitches other than Tent Stitches, you can work your initials in a Tent Stitch in the background color, and they will hardly show at all.

Three lettering charts are shown here. Chart I is a basic style of lettering, with num-

bers as well. Chart II shows more elaborate lettering. Chart III shows a few letters done in Tent Stitch or in a combination of Tent and No. 147 Oblique Stitches. Other letters to complete the alphabet in Chart III would be formed by working to the top and bottom lines, and by making the dividing stitches on the same central level.

To enlarge or diminish a letter's size, add or subtract at both top and bottom to keep the proper proportion. DIAGRAM A shows the letter "A" of Chart II decreased one row top and bottom. Increasing would be done the same way by adding top and bottom and also at each side, as shown in DIAGRAM B.

There are many different lettering styles you can use. Lettering charts are available in needlework stores and are often given in needlework magazines. It's nice to collect the styles you like and have them on hand when you need them.

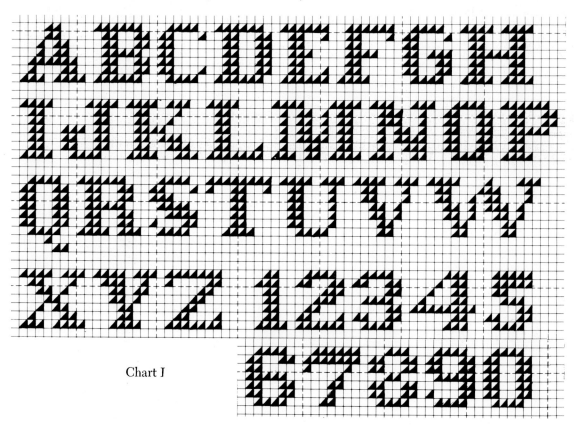

Chart J

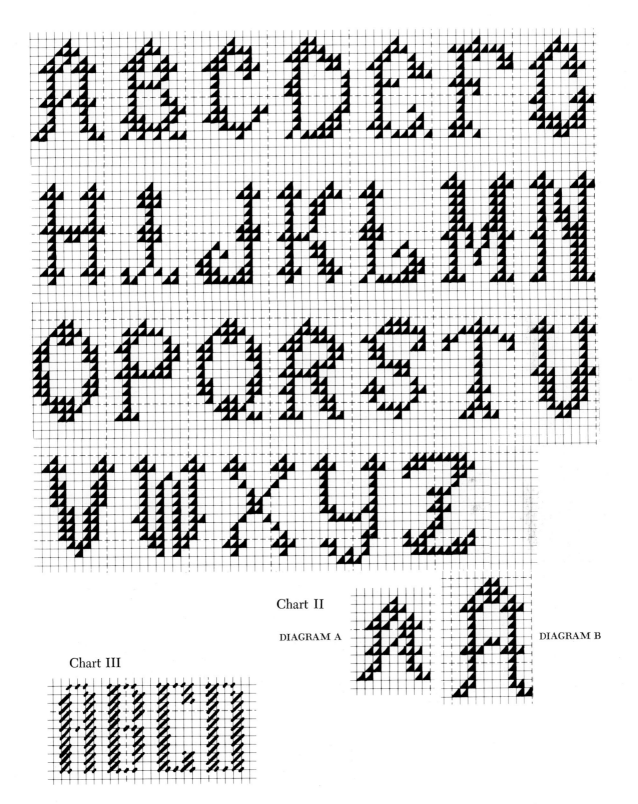

Chart II

DIAGRAM A

DIAGRAM B

Chart III

Appendices

Appendix A: Suggested Uses of Needlepoint Stitches

These groupings are meant to serve merely as guidelines. Many needlepoint stitches can be used in various ways—rows of outline stitches can be used to fill an area, or groups of isolated stitches may make a handsome border. Don't hesitate to experiment and find other uses for your stitches—anything goes so long as it is suited to the project.

BACKGROUND AND AREA FILLING

No. 6. Algerian Eye Filling Stitch
7. Algerian Stitch, Plaited
8. Astrakhan Velvet Stitch
10. Bargello
11. Basketweave Stitch
12. Basketweave Stitch, Reverse
13. Bokhara Couching Stitch
14. Bokhara Couching Stitch, Diagonal
15. Bokhara Couching Stitch, Staggered
16. Brazilian Stitch
17. Brick Stitch
25. Byzantine Stitch
26. Cashmere Stitch No. 1
27. Cashmere Stitch No. 2
28. Cashmere Stitch No. 3
29. Cashmere Stitch, Diagonal
30. Chain Stitch
35. Checker Stitch
36. Continental Stitch
40. Coral Knot Stitch
41. Couching Stitch
45. Cretan Stitch
46. Cretan Stitch, Diagonal
47. Cross Stitch No. 1
48. Cross Stitch No. 2
49. Cross Stitch, Bound
50. Cross Stitch, Diagonal
51. Cross Stitch, Double
52. Cross Stitch, Double, Reversed
53. Cross Stitch, Double Straight

55. Cross Stitch, Half Vertical
56. Cross Stitch, Half, with Laid Thread
57. Cross Stitch, Heavy
58. Cross Stitch, Houndstooth
59. Cross Stitch, Italian
60. Cross Stitch, Long-Armed
64. Cross Stitch, Montenegrin
65. Cross Stitch, Oblong
66. Cross Stitch, Oblong with Back Stitch
67. Cross Stitch, Plaited
68. Cross Stitch, Reinforced
69. Cross Stitch, Reversed
70. Cross Stitch, Staggered
71. Cross Stitch, St. George and St. Andrew
72. Cross Stitch, Tramé
73. Cross Stitch, Triple
74. Cross Stitch, Two-Sided
75. Cross Stitch, Upright
76. Cross Stitch with Bar
77. Cross Stitch, Woven No. 1
78. Cross Stitch, Woven No. 2
79. Cross Stitch, Woven No. 3
80. Cushion Stitch No. 1
81. Cushion Stitch No. 2
82. Darning Stitch
83. Diagonal Stitch
84. Diamond Eyelet Stitch
86. Diaper Pattern Stitch
87. Double Knot Stitch
89. Double Stitch
90. Eastern Stitch
93. Fern Stitch

BORDER AND BROADLINE STITCHES

No. 2. Algerian Eye Stitch No. 2
7. Algerian Stitch, Plaited
11. Basketweave Stitch
17. Brick Stitch
19. Buttonhole Stitch
21. Buttonhole Stitch, Double
26. Cashmere Stitch No. 1
30. Chain Stitch
36. Continental Stitch
38. Continental Stitch, Vertical
45. Cretan Stitch
47. Cross Stitch No. 1
48. Cross Stitch No. 2
49. Cross Stitch, Bound
51. Cross Stitch, Double
54. Cross Stitch, Half
55. Cross Stitch, Half Vertical
56. Cross Stitch, Half, with
    Laid Thread
57. Cross Stitch, Heavy
58. Cross Stitch, Houndstooth
59. Cross Stitch, Italian
60. Cross Stitch, Long-Armed
61. Cross Stitch, Long-Armed
    Reverse
62. Cross Stitch, Long-Armed
    Corner
64. Cross Stitch, Montenegrin
65. Cross Stitch, Oblong
66. Cross Stitch, Oblong with
    Back Stitch
67. Cross Stitch, Plaited
72. Cross Stitch, Tramé
73. Cross Stitch, Triple
74. Cross Stitch, Two-Sided
76. Cross Stitch with Bar
77. Cross Stitch, Woven No. 1
78. Cross Stitch, Woven No. 2
80. Cushion Stitch No. 1
90. Eastern Stitch
93. Fern Stitch
97. Flat Stitch No. 1
98. Flat Stitch No. 2
102. Fly Stitch, Closed
110. Gobelin Stitch, Plaited
111. Gobelin Stitch, Slanting
112. Gobelin Stitch, Straight
113. Gobelin Stitch,
    Straight Tramé
115. Gobelin Stitch, Wide
116. Herringbone Stitch
117. Herringbone Stitch, Double
127. Kalem Stitch

128. Knitting Stitch No. 1
129. Knitting Stitch No. 2
133. Ladder Stitch
136. Leviathan Stitch, Double
139. Loop Stitch
142. Montenegrin Stitch
144. Mosaic Stitch
145. Mosaic Stitch, Crossed
146. Mound Stitch
147. Oblique Stitch
151. Outline Stitch
156. Petit Point
157. Plait Stitch
158. Plait Stitch, Crossed
161. Plaited Edge Stitch
164. Quick Point
166. Ray Stitch
169. Rice Stitch No. 1
170. Rice Stitch No. 2
171. Rice Stitch, Padded
175. Roumanian Stitch
176. Satin Stitch
177. Satin Stitch, Alternating
178. Satin Stitch, Padded
179. Scotch Stitch
180. Scotch Stitch, Alternating
181. Scotch Stitch, Crossed
182. Scotch Stitch, Woven
183. Scotch Stitch with
    Tent Stitch
184. Shell Stitch
186. Sorbello Stitch
187. Soumak Stitch
199. Tent Stitch, Alternating No. 1
200. Tent Stitch, Alternating No. 2
202. Tent Stitch, Reversed
    Alternating
215. Woven Pattern

OUTLINE—NARROW LINE STITCHES

9. Back Stitch
13. Bokhara Couching Stitch
15. Bokhara Couching Stitch,
    Staggered
30. Chain Stitch
31. Chain Stitch, Braided
32. Chain Stitch, Heavy
33. Chain Stitch, Interlaced
34. Chain Stitch, Raised
36. Continental Stitch
37. Continental Stitch, Diagonal
38. Continental Stitch, Vertical
39. Continental Stitch Circle
40. Coral Knot Stitch

ISOLATED STITCHES

SHADING STITCHES

Appendix B: List of Suppliers

American Crewel Studio
P.O. Box 1756
Point Pleasant Beach, New Jersey   08742
> Complete line of needlework fabrics, canvas and threads;
> Bargello charts, transfers, books and custom kits.
> Price list on request.

Embroiderers' Guild of America
120 East 56th Street, Room 228
New York, New York   10022
> Members can receive information about guild branches,
> teachers and suppliers.

DMC Corporation
107 Trumbull Street
Elizabeth, New Jersey   07206
> Will furnish names of local suppliers for DMC threads.

Paternayan Brothers, Inc.
312 East 95th Street
New York, New York   10028
> Distributes imported wool threads and canvas;
> will furnish names of local retail shops.

Joan Toggitt, Ltd.
1170 Broadway
New York, New York   10001
> Imports threads, fabrics and canvas; will furnish names
> of local retailers.

Craft Yarns of Rhode Island, Inc.
603 Mineral Spring Avenue
Pawtucket, Rhode Island   02862
> Carries threads and canvas; will furnish names
> of local retailers.

Sudberry House
Wesley Avenue
Westbrook, Connecticut   06498
> Carries wooden bag handles, footstools, luggage racks
> and serving trays; will furnish names of local retailers.

National Standards Council of American Embroiderers
Corresponding Secretary
739 Orchard Drive
Barrington, Illinois   60010
> Members can receive information about teachers, branches
> and local suppliers.

Index

Stitches marked with an asterisk are recommended to the beginner.

(handwritten: BINDING STITCH p.184 (#161))

Stitches marked with an asterisk are recommended to the beginner.

Stitches marked with an asterisk are recommended to the beginner.

Stitches marked with an asterisk are recommended to the beginner.

Stitches marked with an asterisk are recommended to the beginner.